Studies in Renaissance Literature

Volume 10

JOHN DONNE'S PROFESSIONAL LIVES

In a range of professional positions whose breadth is obscured in standard critical studies, John Donne wrote works considered by his contemporaries to be worthy of interest, collection and annotation. Donne's lifetime also coincided with the period during which the notion of the profession became increasingly significant. This volume makes a strong argument for the importance of Donne's professional writings to our understanding of his oeuvre and of the culture of late sixteenth- and early seventeenth-century England. Studying in depth his remarkable use of a wide range of terms and even whole vocabularies – legal, theological, and medical, among others – it shows how Donne moulded his identity as a professional intellectual with the languages that were at hand. A tightly focussed series of essays by scholars of international reputation and younger experts in the field, *John Donne's Professional Lives* contains new discoveries and fresh interpretations. It offers a revisionist interpretation of Donne's career and makes a polemical case for studying the full range of his writings.

DAVID COLCLOUGH is Lecturer in English at Queen Mary, University of London.

Studies in Renaissance Literature

ISSN 1465–6310

Founding Editor
John T. Shawcross

General Editor
Graham Parry

Editorial Board
Helen E. Wilcox
John N. King
Graham Parry
Paul Stanwood

Studies in Renaissance Literature offers investigations of topics in English literature focussed in the sixteenth and seventeenth centuries; its scope extends from early Tudor writing, including works reflecting medieval concerns, to the Restoration period. Studies exploring the interplay between the literature of the English Renaissance and its cultural history are particularly welcomed.

Proposals or queries should be sent in the first instance to Graham Parry at the address below, or to the publisher; all submissions receive prompt and informed consideration.

Professor Graham Parry, Department of English, University of York, Heslington, York YO1 5DD, UK

JOHN DONNE'S PROFESSIONAL LIVES

Edited by
David Colclough

D. S. BREWER

First published 2003
D. S. Brewer, Cambridge

ISBN 0 85991 775 4

D. S. Brewer is an imprint of Boydell & Brewer Ltd
PO Box 9, Woodbridge, Suffolk IP12 3DF, UK
and of Boydell & Brewer Inc.
PO Box 41026, Rochester, NY 14604–4126, USA
website: www.boydell.co.uk

A catalogue record for this title is available
from the British Library

Library of Congress Cataloging-in-Publication Data
John Donne's professional lives / edited by David Colclough.
    p. cm. – (Studies in Renaissance literature, ISSN 1465–6310 ;
v. 10)
Includes bibliographical references and index.
   ISBN 0–85991–775–4 (acid-free paper)
1. Donne, John, 1572–1631 – Prose.   2. Donne, John,
1572–1631 – Knowledge and learning.   3. Christianity and
literature – England – History – 17th century.   4. Literature and
medicine – England – History – 17th century.   5. Professions –
England – History – 17th century.   6. Law and literature –
History – 17th century.   7. England – Intellectual life – 17th
century.   I. Colclough, David, 1971–II. Series: Studies in Renaissance
literature (Woodbridge, Suffolk, England) ; v. 10.
PR2248 . J648 2003
828'.308 – dc2   2002153107

This publication is printed on acid-free paper

Typeset by Joshua Associates Ltd, Oxford

Printed & bound in Great Britain by
Antony Rowe Ltd, Chippenham, Wiltshire

CONTENTS

Contents

*And if the Authors glorious spirit, which is now in Heaven; can
have the leisure to look down and see me, the poorest, the
meanest of all his friends, in the midst of this this officious
duty, confident I am, that he will not disdain this well-meant
sacrifice in his memory: for, whilst his Conversation made me
and many others happy below, I know his Humility and
Gentleness was then eminent; and, I have heard Divines say,
those Vertues that were but sparks upon Earth, become great
and glorious flames in Heaven.*

Izaak Walton, *The Life of Dr. John Donne*

ACKNOWLEDGEMENTS

I have incurred many debts in editing this volume, and benefited from the generosity of many scholars. It is customary to leave the most important of these till last, but in this case I must state my greatest obligation before any others. Although I am named as the sole editor of this collection, it began as, and remains, a collaborative project. Jeremy Maule and I conceived the idea of a series of essays devoted to the study of John Donne's professional lives after delivering a lecture series together on the subject in the English Faculty of the University of Cambridge in 1998. The plot was hatched, and possible contributors discussed, over a series of meetings often sustained by Jeremy's outstandingly strong coffee and porridge. The first letters of invitation had been sent out at the time of Jeremy's death in November of that year, and the conference that had been planned as a first outing for potential contributions became a memorial to him. Almost all of the authors in this collection were colleagues or students of Jeremy, and the breadth of subjects addressed here is testimony to the astonishing range of his learning and the extent of his generosity to younger colleagues and to peers throughout his too short life. Put bluntly, this volume would not exist without the extraordinary energy, humour, and wisdom of Jeremy Maule, and I have felt his presence – both minatory and encouraging – at my side during the long process of its production.

Many others have been of inestimable assistance. The conference held at Queen Mary, University of London, was part-funded by the Research Committee of the School of English and Drama, and I am grateful to colleagues in the School and a number of graduate students and visitors for support on the day: from Queen Mary, Warren Boutcher, Ana Gonzalez, Andy Gordon, Lisa Jardine and Alex Samson; from elsewhere, Sylvia Adamson, Gavin Alexander, Nicholas Cranfield, Anthony Milton, Joad Raymond and Richard Todd. I would also like to thank Tom Cain and Arnold Hunt, who delivered excellent papers at the conference that did not end up in the collection. Lucinda Platt and Tom Harrison took time out from their own busy schedules to do invaluable behind-the-scenes work.

For encouragement at an early stage, I would like to thank Ian Donaldson, Kenneth Fincham, and Quentin Skinner. For help with hunting down Jeremy Maule's work on Donne, I am very grateful to Guy Newcombe, Richard Serjeantson, and Andrew Zurcher; Anne Barton and Adrian Poole gave me permission to publish it and have been extremely supportive of the project as a whole. Thanks go to Graham Parry, John Shawcross and Helen Wilcox for their interest in this volume, and to Caroline Palmer at Boydell & Brewer – a most accommodating editor. The book was completed during a period of sabbatical leave: I am grateful to the Head of School, Anne Janowitz, and Vice Principal Philip Ogden for ensuring that research continues to be a highly valued part of professional life at Queen Mary. Towards the end of this project I enjoyed conversations about Donne with Randall McLeod at the Folger Shakespeare Library. Finally I would like to thank all of the contributors for their patience and for delivering work of such high quality, and Lucinda Platt, who helped get all this done.

ABBREVIATIONS

Donne's Works

Biathanatos	John Donne, *Biathanatos*, ed. by Ernest W. Sullivan II (Newark: University of Delaware Press, 1984)
Devotions	John Donne, *Devotions upon Emergent Occasions*, ed. by Anthony Raspa (Montreal: McGill–Queen's University Press, 1979)
Essays	John Donne, *Essays in Divinity*, ed. by Evelyn M. Simpson (Oxford: Clarendon Press, 1952)
Ignatius	John Donne, *Ignatius his Conclave*, ed. by T. S. Healy (Oxford: Clarendon Press, 1969)
Letters	John Donne, *Letters to Severall Persons of Honour* (London, 1651)
P-M	John Donne, *Pseudo-Martyr*, ed. by Anthony Raspa (Montreal and Kingston: McGill–Queen's University Press, 1994)
Sermons	*The Sermons of John Donne*, ed. by George R. Potter and Evelyn M. Simpson, 10 vols (Berkeley: University of California Press, 1953–62)

Donne's Life

Bald	R. C. Bald, *John Donne. A Life* (Oxford: Clarendon Press, 1970)
Gosse	Edmund Gosse, *The Life and Letters of John Donne, Dean of St Paul's*, 2 vols (London: Heinemann, 1899)

Journals

ELH	*English Literary History*
ELR	*English Literary Renaissance*
HJ	*The Historical Journal*
HLQ	*Huntington Library Quarterly*
JDJ	*John Donne Journal*
JEGP	*Journal of English and Germanic Philology*
NQ	*Notes & Queries*
PMLA	*Publications of the Modern Language Association*
PQ	*Philological Quarterly*
RES	*Review of English Studies*
SP	*Studies in Philology*

Others

CSPD	*Calendar of State Papers, Domestic*
OED	*Oxford English Dictionary*
PRO	Public Record Office, Kew, London

CONTRIBUTORS

James Cannon currently teaches English at Whitgift School, Croydon. He studied for his M.Phil. and Ph.D. at Pembroke College, Cambridge, where his doctoral thesis was on 'Religious Writing and Controversies over Public Worship c. 1617–1640'.

David Colclough is Lecturer in English at Queen Mary, University of London. He is editing *New Atlantis* for the Oxford Francis Bacon edition, and completing a book on *Freedom of Speech in Early Stuart England*.

David Cunnington is a Lecturer in English at Worcester College, Oxford. He is currently writing a book that looks at forms of intimacy and service in Jacobean epistolary verse.

Louis A. Knafla is Professor of History Emeritus at the University of Calgary, Director of the research group for Socio-Legal Studies, and Editor of *Criminal Justice History: An International Annual*. He has published on early modern English, and Canadian, legal history. His most recent works include edited books on *Policing and War in Europe* (2002), and *Gender, Class, and Sexuality in Criminal Prosecutions* (2001), and an essay on 'Britain's Solomon: King James and the Law' in *Royal Subjects. Essays on the Writings of James VI and I*, ed. Daniel Fischlin and Mark Fortier (2002). He is currently working on a multi-volume edition of court records for early seventeenth-century Kent, and a full biography of Sir Thomas Egerton, Lord Chancellor Ellesmere.

Peter E. McCullough is Fellow and Tutor in English at Lincoln College, Oxford. Author of *Sermons at Court* (Cambridge, 1998), he is presently writing a scholarly biography of Lancelot Andrewes, and editing a new selection of Andrewes' English works (both for Oxford University Press).

Jessica Martin is Fellow in English at Trinity College, Cambridge. She is the author of *Walton's Lives: Conformist Commemorations and the Rise of Biography* (Oxford, 2001). Currently she is working on a biography of the early twentieth-century Egyptologist and theologian Margaret Benson.

Jeremy Maule was, until his death, Fellow of Trinity College, Cambridge, and Newton Trust Lecturer in the English Faculty of the University of Cambridge. He co-edited *The Oxford Book of Classical Verse in Translation* (Oxford, 1995) with Adrian Poole, was the author of articles on John Donne and John Ford, and contributed to the forthcoming Yale edition of the prose works of Andrew Marvell. A formidable manuscript scholar, in 1996 he discovered unknown works by Thomas Traherne in Lambeth Palace Library, and was the founder of Renaissance Texts in Manuscript.

Mary Morrissey studied Paul's Cross preaching for her Ph.D. thesis and is currently preparing a book on the subject. She has also written on preaching styles and genres more generally and on early modern women's religious writing. She is a lecturer in English Literature at Nottingham Trent University.

Stephen Pender (Ph.D., Toronto, 2000) teaches early modern poetry and prose, intellectual history, and literary theory at the University of Windsor, Ontario, Canada. He has published on the history of human exhibition and the history of rhetoric. He is at work on a monograph that explores the ways in which early modern medicine, rhetoric, and moral philosophy treat emotion.

Jeanne Shami is Professor of English at the University of Regina, Saskatchewan, Canada, where she has taught Renaissance literature since 1977. She has published widely on the sermons of John Donne, including a facsimile edition of a sermon containing Donne's holograph corrections which she identified in the British Library in 1992. Her book, *John Donne and Conformity in Crisis*, is forthcoming from Boydell & Brewer.

Alison Shell is a lecturer in the Department of English at Durham University. She is the author of *Catholicism, controversy and the English literary imagination, 1558–1660* (1999) and is completing a study of Tudor and Stuart Catholicism and oral culture.

Johann P. Sommerville is Professor of History at the University of Wisconsin, Madison. His recent publications include *Royalists and Patriots: Politics and Ideology in England 1603–1640* (Harlow, 1999), and 'Literature and National Identity' in the forthcoming *Cambridge History of Early Modern English Literature* (Cambridge, 2003).

Chapter 1

INTRODUCTION: DONNE'S PROFESSIONAL LIVES

DAVID COLCLOUGH

He was earnest and unwearied in the search of knowledge. . . .
(Izaak Walton)[1]

Spake he all Languages? Knew he all Lawes?
The grounds and use of Physicke; but because
'Twas mercenary wav'd it?
(Walton)[2]

He that would write an Epitaph for thee,
And write it well, must first begin to be
Such as thou wert; for none can truly know
Thy life and worth, but he that hath liv'd so.
He must have wit to spare, and to hurl down,
Enough to keep the Gallants of the Town.
He must have Learning plenty, both the Laws,
Civil and *Common*, to judge any Cause.
Divinity great store above the rest,
Not of the last Edition, but the best.
He must have language, travel, all the Arts,
Judgement to use, or else he wants thy parts.
(Richard Corbet)[3]

---

[1] Izaak Walton, 'The Life of Dr. John Donne', in *The Lives of John Donne, Sir Henry Wotton, Richard Hooker, George Herbert and Robert Sanderson* (Oxford: Oxford University Press, 1927), p. 84.

[2] Walton's elegy in Donne's *Poems* (1633), cited in *John Donne: The Critical Heritage*, vol. 1, ed. by A. J. Smith (London: Routledge & Kegan Paul, 1975), p. 93.

[3] Richard Corbet, 'An Epitaph written by Dr. Corbet, late Bishop of Oxford, on his Friend Dr. Donne', in Walton, pp. 84–5. Cf. the final lines of the elegy by Edward Hyde printed in Donne's *Poems* (1633): 'Hee then must write, that would define thy parts: / *Here lyes the best Divinitie, All the Arts*' (*John Donne: The Critical Heritage*, ed. by Smith, p. 89).

I

D ONNE'S fortunes in the two hundred and seventy years since his death have been almost as varied as they were during his life. The tale of this promising youth's fall from grace into a rash marriage, years in the wilderness and eventual recovery into a firmly establishment position as Dean of St Paul's is neatly mirrored by his critical decline in the late seventeenth century under the pressure of disapproving attitudes to his metrical inventiveness, a century of neglect (and, worse, the rough end of Johnson's pencil), and gradual recovery by, initially, Coleridge and Lamb, culminating in the early-twentieth-century canonisation led by Eliot in his famous 1921 essay 'The Metaphysical Poets'.[4] At the beginning of the twenty-first century Donne the poet remains an establishment figure, central to many Renaissance literature courses at university and with a firm place in the canon. Yet, just as during his life and in his writings Donne adopted a range of personae according to the requirements of decorum and the ends he sought to attain, so critics have moulded a series of Donnes whose shapes have been determined by their agendas, and by more general cultural concerns. It is this range of 'lives' – Donne's various vocations, biographies, and textual presences – that is addressed here. One very striking aspect of the critical treatment of Donne until quite recently has been its concentration on his poetry (and within the poetry, on the *Songs and Sonets*). The sermons have long been admired (although generally approached by non-specialists through extracts, and available in a reliable edition to scholars only since 1961), but the remainder of Donne's voluminous prose works still attract little sustained attention and certainly play a small part, if any, in his popular reputation. In this popular reception, one can discern a tendency to accord the poetry a greater authenticity than the prose – that is, the poems (often, partly under the influence of Walton, ascribed to Donne's youth, despite the near-impossibility of dating many of them) are considered as giving access to the 'true voice' of Donne.[5] Whether this voice is that of the rakish young man-about-town of the *Songs and Sonets* or of the spiritually tortured speaker of the *Holy Sonnets*, it tends to be opposed to the voices we encounter in the prose works, from *Pseudo-Martyr* to the sermons. In its most extreme form, this reading describes a decline from the poet of youth and sex to the grave and ideologically conservative divine: a reversal of Donne's own Augustinian

---

[4] On Donne's critical reception see first of all *John Donne: The Critical Heritage*, ed. by A. J. Smith, 2 vols (London: Routledge, 1975–96). Eliot's changing attitude to Donne can be traced in T. S. Eliot, *The Varieties of Metaphysical Poetry*, ed. by Ronald Schuchard (London: Faber and Faber, 1993).

[5] For a recent example of this tendency in a student introduction, see Stevie Davies, *John Donne* (Plymouth: Northcote House, 1994), p. 1. Walton describes poetry as one of 'the Recreations of [Donne's] youth' at pp. 60–1.

patterning of his life into the contrasting personae of 'Jack Donne' and 'Doctor Donne'.[6]

One of the most influential readings of Donne in recent years has taken the opposite approach to this, seeking, in the words of its title, to treat his 'Life, Mind and Art'.[7] John Carey's popular study addresses the full range of Donne's writings, and while the arguments advanced in his psychobiographical reading have been criticised (a very different Donne emerges from the essays in the present collection), his emphasis on the breadth of Donne's activities is refreshing.[8] However, Carey's desire to 'explore . . . the structure of [Donne's] imagination' is far from the aim of this volume, and his conviction that Donne's attachment to specific doctrines can be seen as 'imaginative choices' is not one that would be shared by its contributors.[9] For them, Donne's writings can be kept out of 'the rubbish tip of history' because they comprise important interventions into contemporary debates of whose importance Donne was convinced. He was also convinced of his own ability to make his interventions effective, through his mastery of the professional vocabularies in which these debates were conducted. Carey does not find Donne the professional author at all attractive. He rightly sees that in composing *Pseudo-Martyr* (1610) Donne was acting as a professional controversialist, but argues that in seeking to curry favour with the king he compromised his beliefs: 'he was using, at best, only half his mind'.[10] The verse letters to female patrons, meanwhile, are praised when they supposedly transcend their occasion ('Twicknam Garden' is singled out because it 'outgrows the situation that gave rise to it')[11] – otherwise they are damned for having 'nothing to do with [Donne's] inner passions and attachments'.[12]

Yet, as this volume argues, there is an alternative to this view – one that eschews both the bifurcation of Donne's career into the roles of rakish poet and grave divine and the search for his artistic mentality. The essays below describe a Donne committed to the work that his professional writings are

---

[6] See, for example, Donne's letter to Sir Robert Ker accompanying a manuscript of *Biathanatos*: 'it is a Book written by *Jack Donne*, and not by *D. Donne*' (*Letters*, p. 22). This is, of course, a narrative supported by Walton, in his declaration that in Donne's ordination 'the *English Church* had gained a second St *Austine*, for, I think, none was so like him before his Conversion: none so like St. *Ambrose* after it: and if his youth had the infirmities of the one, his age had the excellencies of the other; the learning and the holiness of both' (Walton, pp. 47–8; cf. pp. 52–3, where Donne is compared to St Paul).

[7] John Carey, *John Donne: Life, Mind and Art* (London: Faber and Faber, 1981; new edn 1990).

[8] Carey firmly rejects what he calls the temptation 'to assume that the worthwhile element in Donne comprises the poems and a few rousing bits from the sermons, and that the rest of his *oeuvre* can be safely consigned to the rubbish tip of history' (*John Donne*, p. xiii).

[9] Carey, *John Donne*, p. ix.

[10] Carey, *John Donne*, p. 19. For a specific disagreement with Carey on this point, see Johann Sommerville's essay in this volume.

[11] Carey, *John Donne*, p. 65.

[12] Carey, *John Donne*, p. 71, of 'A Letter to the Lady Carey, and Mrs Essex Riche'.

intended to perform in the world. This work goes beyond the search for place or status. Donne certainly sought advancement, and wanted to carve out a career for himself (for many years he hoped ardently that it would be a secular career); he also wanted effectively to use and manipulate the structures of language and knowledge by which the debates he chose to enter proceeded. Donne is celebrated for the remarkable way in which his works use a wide range of terms and even whole vocabularies – legal, theological, and medical, among others. This has usually been seen as the sign of a truly voracious Renaissance literary mind, appropriating useful terms, magpie-like, to its own poetic purposes. But Donne did not just read widely in these fields: at various points in his life he was a hired polemicist, lawyer, diplomat, churchman, and self-taught medic. In a range of professional positions whose breadth is obscured in standard critical studies, he wrote works considered by his contemporaries to be worthy of interest, collection and annotation. The cumulative effect of the essays in this volume is to present a Donne who is most interestingly and engagingly consistent in his search for some kind of institution – an intellectual community – where he can carry out the work of writing and the pursuit of knowledge. But we need to consider what form that search took, and what were Donne's 'professional lives'.

II

In a letter to Sir Henry Goodyer written in September 1608, Donne explained his desire to find a position in the world, to get a job:

> I would fain do something; but that I cannot tell what, is no wonder. For to chuse, is to do: but to be no part of any body, is to be nothing. At most, the great persons, are but great wens, and excrescences; men of wit and delightfull conversation, but as moales for ornament, except they be so incorporated into the body of the world, that they contribute something to the sustentation of the whole. This I made account that I begun early, when I understood the study of our laws: but was diverted by the worst voluptuousness, which is an Hydroptique immoderate desire of humane learning and languages: beautifull ornaments to great fortunes; but mine needed an occupation, and a course which I thought I entred well into, when I submitted my self to such service, as I thought might [have] imployed those poor advantages, which I had. And there I stumbled again: for to this hour I am nothing, or so little, that I am scarce subject and argument for one of mine own letters.[13]

Donne's fear of being nothing, his horror of passing through the world without leaving any trace, exists in an uneasy dialectic with his scepticism about the value of worldly pursuits and institutions. He is especially concerned with the deleterious effect that life at Court may have on

---

[13] *Letters*, pp. 50–1.

individuals' virtue and moral coherence – this is a theme that runs through the *Satires* and it gives rise to his advice to Sir Henry Wotton:

> . . . in the worlds sea, do not like corke sleepe
> Upon the waters face; nor in the deepe
> Sinke like a lead without a line: but as
> Fishes glide, leaving no print where they passe,
> Nor making sound, so, closely thy course goe;
> Let men dispute, whether thou breathe, or no.[14]

The Stoical distrust of worldly pursuits and reputation articulated here is typical of Donne's addresses to his friends (especially in the verse letters to Wotton and Sir Henry Goodyer) and continuous with his suspicion of the twin distractions of the court and the country. Yet it is important to note that Donne warns against 'sinking' into obscurity ('the deepe') as much as superficiality. It is the passivity or inaction associated with these two questionable habitats that exercises him and provokes his censure. Throughout his writings, Donne is highly critical of laziness, excessive humility, torpor: in this verse letter, against 'sleeping' and 'sinking' he pits 'gliding' – active, careful motion that demands interpretation and 'dispute' and resists easy categorisation.[15] For it could not be argued that Donne held back from worldly pursuits in the years before his ordination – rather, he felt as if he *was* held back; his periods of retirement were always against his will.

Donne sought a successful career for many years, until he finally found a place in the Church – if we believe Walton's account, under the repeated injunctions of King James.[16] The skill he used consistently to establish such a career, and the one that gained him most success, was writing. Although the only recognised professional appointment that Donne held was as a priest, as I have said, he wrote from a much wider range of positions, and he did so at a time when the notion of a profession was becoming increasingly significant. Some years ago, in an important work on the clergy as a professional class, Rosemary O'Day wrote that 'the development of the professions in early modern England is of profound importance to the social and economic

---

[14] 'Sir, more then kisses, letters mingle Soules', lines 53–8, in John Donne, *The Satires, Epigrams and Verse Letters*, ed. by W. Milgate (Oxford: Clarendon Press, 1967), p. 72.

[15] On Donne's distaste for excessive humility and its associations (especially in relation to human learning), see especially the *Essays in Divinity*. On his linked scepticism towards history and historians, see Jeremy Maule, 'Donne and the Past', in *Sacred and Profane: Secular and Devotional Interplay in Early Modern British Literature*, ed. by Helen Wilcox, Richard Todd and Alasdair MacDonald (Amsterdam: VU University Press, 1996), pp. 203–21.

[16] Donne himself ascribed his entry into the Church to James's exhortations, and the inscription on his monument (which he probably wrote) states that he 'entered into Holy Orders under the inspiration and incitement of the Holy Spirit and by the advice and exhortation of King James, in the year of his Lord 1614 and of his age 42' ('Instinctu et impulsu Sp. Sancti, monitu et hortatu Regis Jacobi, ordines sacros amplexus Anno sui Jesu MDCXIV. et suae aetatis XLII'). See Bald, p. 534.

historian' – the professions she referred to comprising 'clergy, lawyers, doctors, and the newly emerging teaching and civil service groups'.[17] As these professions all depended on the establishment of increasingly discrete vocabularies and modes of argument, their development should also be seen as of profound importance to the literary historian. The question of what exactly defines a profession in the early modern period has been hotly debated: a long tradition of scholarship would have it that professions properly so-called should be defined as 'qualifying associations', laying greatest emphasis on institutional structure as a key feature.[18] This thesis has generally been followed by those investigating early modern professionalism from the perspective of later developments; the question is framed as one of how contemporary or 'post-industrial' professions came to have their final form. But, as Wilfrid Prest has indicated, this retrospective definition has its pitfalls. It is surely important for historians to ask how, if at all, early modern people themselves defined a profession and to use any such evidence, along with evidence of the organisation of bodies such as the church, law, and medicine, to develop a useful working definition. Even when this is done, definitions may vary in their breadth according to the concerns of the historian. Rosemary O'Day's definition of a 'recognisably professional structure', for example, is fairly restrictive. For her, the necessary features of such a structure are

> hierarchical organisation; emphasis upon service; internal control of recruitment, training and placement; internal enforcement of standards and discipline; stress upon the possession of specific expertise, both practical and theoretical; a developed career structure; and a tremendous *esprit de corps*.[19]

Prest, by contrast, is wary of such precise requirements, recognising that they may exclude occupations considered 'professional' by contemporaries or even those that might usefully be studied within such a definition. He points out that in early modern England 'profession' carried both the broad, vague sense of 'calling, vocation, known employment'[20] and the narrow sense of 'particularly dignified, worthy or . . . high-status occupations', as contrasted with 'mere "mechanical" trades or manual labour'.[21] The latter sense might most often refer to the three traditional 'learned professions' – the church, law and medicine. As a result of this broad possibility of meaning, and in the face of 'the absence of . . . widespread concern about professional status' in this

---

[17] Rosemary O'Day, *The English Clergy: The Emergence and Consolidation of a Profession, 1558–1642* (Leicester: Leicester University Press, 1979), p. 1.

[18] See Wilfrid Prest, 'Introduction', in *The Professions in Early Modern England*, ed. by Prest (London: Croom Helm, 1987), pp. 1–24; p. 2.

[19] Rosemary O'Day, 'The Anatomy of a Profession: the Clergy of the Church of England', in *The Professions in Early Modern England*, ed. by Prest, pp. 25–63; p. 28.

[20] Prest, 'Introduction', p. 12, citing Johnson's definition.

[21] Prest, 'Introduction', p. 12.

period, Prest suggests a 'working convention' that would include 'besides the traditional trinity of church, law and medicine, all other non-mercantile occupations followed by persons claiming gentility'.[22] Literary historians have pursued parallel concerns to these in their study of the rise of the professional author, a study that has usefully reinforced the importance of a broad definition of professionalism. Authors had no formal training, were not members of qualifying bodies, had no rights to speak of over their products, and indeed could be said to fulfil none of O'Day's criteria. None the less, there is a story to be told about the increasing professionalisation of writing. The fact that the move from the dominance of amateur, aristocratic authors often concerned about the public availability of their writing to the increasing importance of the author who seeks to make a living from his or her writing in print does not conform to the model of the 'rise of the professions' does not mean that we should eschew the concept or the term when discussing the literary culture of sixteenth- and seventeenth-century England. Indeed, this culture is the site of important discussions of what should be key terms in any debate about professionalism – 'trade', 'vocation', 'profit', 'hire', 'service' and so on. Following Prest's emphasis on the broad definition of the professions in early modern England, and bearing in mind the implications of work on professional authorship, this volume studies those of Donne's works which were written from a position which could be regarded as that of a profession, and which mobilise the increasingly specialised vocabulary of such a position. In doing so it never loses sight of the other sense of 'profess' to which Prest draws attention, and which was a much more immediate connotation of the word in Donne's lifetime than it is now. In this sense a 'professional' is one who professes faith, or friendship, and this provides another vital way of understanding and describing the speech-acts of Donne's works.[23]

III

From his twentieth year Donne was closely involved in a professional world, and one to whose language he had resort throughout his life – the law. He entered Lincoln's Inn in May 1592, after at least a year's preliminary study at Thavies Inn. It was typical for a young man of his social position to spend some time at an Inn of Court, and we are used to the notion that for many of these young men their attendance had more to do with socialisation than with the pursuit of a legal career. But legal and social historians have shown how incomplete this account is: for many sons of gentry the knowledge of the law gained during their time at the Inns proved essential for the maintenance of their estates, and while this was not the case for Donne, his legal training was certainly important to his life and writings. Although he was never called to

---

[22] Prest, 'Introduction', p. 17.
[23] See *OED*, sub 'profess', senses 3a and 4a.

the bar, and did not practise the law professionally, its language and its modes of thought were crucial to Donne's professional lives, as the late Jeremy Maule shows in the essay which opens this volume.

Donne's legal knowledge was in demand while he was secretary to the Lord Keeper, Sir Thomas Egerton (see Louis Knafla's essay in this volume for an important reconsideration of this relationship); and in 1603–04 he prepared a legal opinion for Sir Robert Cotton on Valdesius' *De dignitate Regum Regnorumque Hispaniae*.[24] His first major published work, *Pseudo-Martyr*, is a highly professional legal exposition and defence of the Oath of Allegiance, and he engages in tangled questions of civil and canon law in several other works, notably *Ignatius his Conclave* and the *Essays in Divinity*. While Dean of St Paul's Donne acted as a Justice of the Peace and as a Judge in the Courts of Delegates and High Commission. The poems too are shot through with his legal learning: the *Satires* and the poems collected as *Songs and Sonets* are not just immersed in the social world of the Inns, but use the words and the distinctions of the law to conduct their business of social comment and love. Later writings, including the *Holy Sonnets*, are equally dependent upon Donne's thorough knowledge of common and canon law.

Walton suggests that it was also during his time at Lincoln's Inn that Donne began 'seriously to survey, and consider the Body of Divinity, as it was then controverted betwixt the *Reformed* and the *Roman Church*' and to undertake a systematic reading and annotation of Cardinal Bellarmine's *Disputationes*; certainly his later work shows that he was well acquainted with the Roman Catholic controversialist's works.[25] After his time at the Inn, Donne's career seemed extremely promising: employed by Egerton, the Lord Keeper, he was close to powerful individuals and his work as a secretary was highly valued. In 1601 he entered Parliament as one of the members for Brackley. But his secret marriage to Ann More in the same year caused his dismissal from Egerton's service at the behest of Sir George More, his father-in-law, and the next fourteen years saw him seeking, always in vain, a variety of positions.[26] However, this period, Donne's 'wilderness years', should not be seen solely, or even primarily, as the time of failure, marginalisation, frustrated ambition, and boredom that critics have often described – taking their lead from Donne's own self-representation. Although heavily dependent on the kindness of friends and family for lodgings, Donne remained active

---

[24] Bald, p. 142. In 1598 Donne acted as a litigant, taking out a bill of complaint against the brother of a boy he had taken into his service, Thomas Danby, the boy having disappeared with items from Donne's wardrobe. See Bald, p. 120.

[25] See Walton, pp. 25–6; Bald, p. 69.

[26] In June 1607 Donne sought to fill a vacant place in the Queen's household; in November 1608 he applied for a secretaryship in Ireland with the help of the king's favourite, Lord Hay, and in February 1609 Chamberlain reported to Carleton that Donne 'seekes to be preferred to be secretarie of Virginia' (*The Letters of John Chamberlain*, ed. by N. E. McClure, 2 vols (Philadelphia: The American Philosophical Society, 1939) I, p. 284) – these were probably only a few of the positions he applied for.

and engaged in the world: in 1605–6 he travelled on the continent with Sir Walter Chute, visiting Paris and probably Venice, where Wotton was by now Ambassador. After his return Donne and his growing family moved from the house at Pyrford which Ann's cousin Francis Wolley had lent them to a cottage in Mitcham. They stayed there for five years, and, as Bald states, at this time Donne was 'nearer to being a professional author than at any other time during his life'.[27]

Donne had, it seems, been engaged for some time in a course of reading in canon and civil law, and in casuistry: the works that he composed during the period 1607–10 are steeped in this learning. Donne is determined at once to display his mastery of a vast number of authorities and to cast a sceptical eye on the very use of authoritative textual testimony. The first substantial work that Donne wrote at this time, *Biathanatos* (composed 1607–8, though work on it may have started at Pyrford), is a perfect example of his ambiguous relationship with human learning. It is a cousin to the more frivolous *Paradoxes* and *Problems* (probably composed at around the same time) in its defence of an apparent paradox;[28] yet it is formidably researched, and its fashionably sceptical attitude can be more properly traced to a probabilistic frame of mind inculcated by the study of cases of conscience that occupied Donne throughout his life.[29] *Biathanatos* is a controversial work, in that while pursuing his paradoxical thesis Donne had engaged polemically with a tradition of thought and with a wide range of past and present thinkers. But, in contrast with the other works of this period, it is a private text.[30] Donne's next work, *Pseudo-Martyr* (1610) is both controversial and emphatically public. It is not only the fact that the work was designed to be printed that announces its hopes for a wider reading public: it is a deliberately public intervention into a current controversy, and – as Johann Sommerville argues in this volume – it announces unambiguously Donne's allegiance to the religious policies of James I, to whom it is dedicated. *Pseudo-Martyr* is as clear an example of professional polemic as one can find in the period, and it does its job extremely well. No matter, perhaps, that the book seems to have

---

[27] Bald, p. 200.

[28] Its subtitle is 'A Declaration of that Paradoxe or Thesis, that Self-homicide is not so naturally Sinne, that it may neuer be otherwise'.

[29] On Donne and casuistry see Meg Lota Brown, *Donne and the Politics of Conscience in Early Modern England* (Leiden: E. J. Brill, 1995) and Jeanne M. Shami, 'Donne's Protestant Casuistry: Cases of Conscience in the *Sermons*', *SP* 80 (1983): 53–66. Walton tells us that found in Donne's study after his death were 'divers . . . cases of Conscience that had concerned his friends, with his observations and solutions of them' (p. 68), and Donne refers to his book of cases of conscience in two of his surviving letters (*Letters*, pp. 200, 226).

[30] *Biathanatos* was printed in 1647, sixteen years after Donne's death, and only two manuscripts survive from his lifetime (see Peter Beal, *In Praise of Scribes: Manuscripts and their Makers in Seventeenth-Century England* (Oxford: Clarendon Press, 1998), chapter 2). The letters Donne wrote to Edward Herbert and Sir Robert Ker accompanying manuscripts of the book reinforce this sense of privacy; see *Letters*, pp. 21 and 22.

received little notice from the other participants in the controversy over the Oath of Allegiance; this may very well be an indicator of its success. Donne himself, like the Jesuit controversialist Robert Persons, had noted the inadequacy of the English contributions to the debate, and silence may well have seemed a more satisfactory response than the derision that greeted the king and his other hired pen, William Barlow, when they entered the ring.[31] *Pseudo-Martyr* advertised Donne's skills as a controversialist, and whether or not he was acting at around this time as an assistant to Thomas Morton (chaplain to the Earl of Rutland and, from 1607, Dean of Gloucester), the important research of Alison Shell in this volume shows that his anti-Catholic work probably extended beyond the learned polemic of that book and the violent satire of *Ignatius his Conclave* (1610) to include collaboration with Sir Edward Hoby.

Donne's self-advertisement as a skilled controversialist was clearly success-ful. It is likely that *Pseudo-Martyr* gained him the honorary M.A. from Oxford that he was awarded in 1610, and Walton tells us that it was at this point that King James first suggested that Donne should enter the church. He was determined, however, to pursue his civil ambitions, and while his search for office remained unfulfilled he used poetry as a way of establishing the place in the world that he desired. Donne's poetic output is generally – and under-standably – categorised as amateur, and his occasional verse often dismissed as empty hyperbole.[32] But the verse letters – especially those to his female patrons – are much better seen as part of an important culture of praise and friendly admonition in client–patron relations, and as self-consciously belated contributions to the humanist tradition of letters of compliment. Panegyric was, from its roots in ancient Greek oratory, closely linked with criticism, and its exercise always raised difficult questions of decorum.[33] David Cunnington's essay in this volume shows how Donne often deftly and sometimes awkwardly negotiated the profession of friendship in letters to Lady Huntingdon and others. Cunnington shows how the perspective and the vocabulary of professionalism can shed light on those of Donne's writings that seem in some ways least professional and that have often seemed resistant to interpretation.

Donne's occasional writing must have occupied much of his time in the

---

[31] See Donne's letter to Goodyer (*Letters*, pp. 160–4) for his criticisms of Barlow.
[32] This tradition of criticism was inaugurated with the negative contemporary reactions to the *Anniversaries* (to which Donne responded with some sensitivity – see *Letters*, pp. 74–5) and persists in Carey's dismissive attitude to the verse letters cited above.
[33] On the admonitory exercise of panegyric in early modern contexts, see especially Erasmus, *The Education of a Christian Prince and Panegyric for Archduke Philip of Austria*, trans. by Neil M. Cheshire, Michael J. Heath and Lisa Jardine, ed. by Lisa Jardine (Cambridge: Cambridge University Press, 1997); David Norbrook, 'Panegyric of the Monarch and Its Social Context under Elizabeth I and James I', unpublished D.Phil. diss., University of Oxford, 1978; Kevin Sharpe, *Criticism and Compliment. The Politics of Literature in the England of Charles I* (Cambridge: Cambridge University Press, 1987).

years 1610–15: as well as the *Anniversaries* (which both signalled and cemented his relationship with Sir Robert Drury – Donne travelled on the Continent with the Drurys in 1612 and lived in a house belonging to Sir Robert until 1621), he wrote an elegy for Prince Henry on his death in 1612, epithalamions for the marriage of Princess Elizabeth to the Elector Palatine and for the marriage of Sir Robert Carr to Frances Howard, and the 'Obsequies to the Lord Harrington', brother of his patron, Lucy, Countess of Bedford. He was also briefly involved in the daily business of politics, being returned as MP for Taunton in the short-lived 'Addled' Parliament of April–June 1614. In the midst of all this activity, his attempts to find employment continued to fail – in 1614 alone he tried to be appointed Ambassador to Venice and made more than one direct approach to the king – and once more he was advised to enter the church. John Donne the younger stated it was at around this time that Donne wrote the *Essays in Divinity*, describing them as 'the voluntary sacrifices of severall hours, when he had many debates betwixt God and himself, whether he were worthy, and competently learned to enter Holy Orders'.[34] There is no evidence, internal or external, to support this dating, although the absence of references to any works published after 1615 suggests that year as a *terminus ad quem*. The *Essays* sometimes read like apprentice-work, but they also display a committed and professional attitude to the task of biblical interpretation, and attempt to map out in some detail the proper relationship between faith and reason. In the process of doing so, they reveal a scepticism towards human knowledge that is typical of Donne's thought.

IV

Donne was ordained on 23 January 1614/15, in St Paul's, and for the last sixteen years of his life was dedicated to his professional life as a clergyman. He marked his entry into a new life with a new seal, exchanging the sheaf of snakes he had previously used for an image of Christ crucified on an anchor. As I have argued here, though, it is a mistake to treat his writing after his ordination as entirely discontinuous with his previous work. Even Walton, wedded as he was to Donne's Augustinian self-description, emphasised that priesthood offered a new outlet for his intellectual energies, rather than a turning away from them:

> And now all his studies which had been occasionally diffused, were all concentrated in Divinity. Now he had a new calling, new thoughts, and a

---

[34] John Donne, *Essays in Divinity*, ed. by Evelyn M. Simpson (Oxford: Clarendon Press, 1952), p. 4. Donne's learning was not neglected in this period: Walton tells us that at this time Donne was studying Greek and Hebrew (Walton, p. 46), and Donne himself mentions in a letter that he was employed 'in the search of the eastern tongues' (Gosse II, 16). He may well have made use of the visits of the scholars Isaac Casaubon and Hugo Grotius in 1613/14.

new employment for his wit and eloquence: Now all his earthly affections were changed into divine love; and all the faculties of his own soul, were ingaged in the Conversion of others.[35]

That facility for persuasion, the eloquence turned to the service of conversion, marks an especially strong continuity with Donne's earlier writing, however much Walton here uses it to draw a line between his two lives. The polemical skill that Donne had exercised in *Pseudo-Martyr*, as well as the text's continual return to the question of the nature of the true church, is a recurrent feature of his sermons, whatever their occasion and their auditory. In the *Essays in Divinity*, Donne maps out his exegetical method, and his attitude to human and scriptural tradition and divine revelation, and this method is followed carefully throughout his engagement in his preaching with doctrinal and ecclesiological debates. Peter McCullough and Jeanne Shami have between them transformed the study of early-modern sermons (those of Donne in particular in the work of Shami) through their insistence upon the need to study each sermon in the context of its delivery, and in this volume, along with Mary Morrissey and James Cannon, they again show how such an approach yields rich interpretive rewards.[36] Donne's moderation and his decorous attempt to negotiate between divisive doctrinal labels (of the kind by which he has so often been categorised) in his profession as 'Christian' is explored in Shami's wide-ranging essay. There she shows that what is at issue for Donne is, often enough, the avoidance of unnecessary conflict, or 'wrangling' – the result of his

> care to balance positions, and to reveal them as extremes, or as unnecessarily contentious, in order to illuminate a place of 'mediocrity' which, for him, distinguishes the Church of England, 'our' Church, from other Reformed institutions and from the Church of Rome.[37]

The three essays that follow show Donne at work in a range of different contexts, deftly adapting his speech to his circumstances. Mary Morrissey's essay demonstrates how carefully Donne tuned his rhetorical skills according to the nature of his auditory; she puts his performances at the open-air pulpit at Paul's Cross in the context of other sermons delivered there and shows that discretion – rather than time-serving, or the awkwardness identified by Chamberlain in 1622 – was his watchword.

---

[35] Walton, p. 48.

[36] See especially Peter E. McCullough, *Sermons at Court: Politics and Religion in Elizabethan and Jacobean Preaching* (Cambridge: Cambridge University Press, 1998); Jeanne Shami, 'Introduction', *John Donne Journal* 11 (1–2) ('1992'; actually 1995): 1–20; and, for a study of an individual sermon, *eadem*, '"The Stars in their Order Fought Against Sisera"': John Donne and the Pulpit Crisis of 1622', *JDJ* 14 (1995): 1–58.

[37] Jeanne Shami, 'Labels, Controversy, and the Language of Inclusion in Donne's Sermons', below, p. 157.

The subject of Peter McCullough's essay is Donne's many appearances in a very different preaching context: the court. Donne preached frequently at court but, as McCullough reminds us, the court was a much more fluid concept than the definite article implies, and Donne's performances there were various and sometimes uncomfortable. Studying in detail Donne's court sermons from his ordination in 1615 (here McCullough importantly re-assigns the first surviving sermon by Donne to the court, not the parish church, at Greenwich) to his death in 1631 shows his religious position shaping and, ultimately, shaped by, the Laudian innovations of the period preceding the Personal Rule of Charles I.

Donne's appointment as Reader in Divinity at Lincoln's Inn in October 1616 brought him back to his old Inn of Court, and it was a position he was proud to hold. Here, as well as at his parish church of St Dunstan's in the West and, later, at St Paul's, he addressed a formidably learned congregation. His sermon at the dedication of the new chapel in 1623 was, as James Cannon points out in this volume, extraordinarily popular both on the occasion of its delivery and in its printed form. Again here we see Donne engaging directly with controversial issues, using the occasion of the dedication to establish a position in the debate on the validity of church ceremony and the nature of church sacrality. This was a debate that polarised opinion (or was used in the creation of polarities), but Donne seeks a form of accommodation that will avoid conflict and serve – appropriately for the building of a new chapel – to edify rather than break up the church and its members.

One of the most striking qualities of Donne's sermons, and one which they share with his Holy Sonnets, is their negotiation of the space and the relations between the individual believer and his or her soul, and the wider community of Christians of which they are part. Just as Donne's profession of his faith and his profession as a preacher are more than lexically intertwined, so he employs expressions of his experiences as an individual Christian to make himself a model of his congregation at the same time as being able authoritatively to speak to them as their minister. This is a crucial part of his oratorical practice, as he puts himself on display in order to move his congregation. Jasper Mayne, in his elegy on Donne, wrote of his rhetorical *actio* that

> Such was thy carriage, and thy gesture such,
> As could divide the heart, and conscience touch.
> Thy motion did confute, and wee might see
> An error vanquished by delivery.[38]

Walton, meanwhile, described the effect of Donne's sermon after his wife's death:

---

[38] Jasper Mayne, 'On Dr Donnes Death', in *Donne's Poetical Works*, ed. by H. J. C. Grierson, 2 vols (Oxford: Clarendon Press, 1912) I, p. 384; lines 61–4.

> And indeed his very looks and words testified him to be truly such a man [one who had 'seen affliction']; and they, with the addition of his sighs and tears, exprest in his Sermon, did so work upon the affections of his hearers, as melted and moulded them into a companionable sadness.[39]

Donne often appeals to his own somatic state in his sermons (as well as showing a fondness for Tertullian's idea of the soul as having bones),[40] and most famously, when he delivered his final sermon, *Deaths Duell*, he seemed to be the subject of his own text. As Walton writes, 'when to the amazement of some beholders he appeared in the Pulpit many of them thought he presented himself not to preach mortification by a living voice: but mortality by a decayed body and a dying face'.[41] It is in the *Devotions Upon Emergent Occasions*, however, that his study of his own body and soul are at their most searching and, medically, their most professional. As Stephen Pender shows in his essay, these records of and meditations on the illness that assailed Donne in the winter of 1623–4 demonstrate a highly sophisticated knowledge of contemporary medical vocabulary and method. While the *Devotions* have long been linked with traditions of meditation, Ignatian and otherwise, Pender redirects our attention to the way in which Donne draws on the professional methods of medicine to pursue the possible meanings, spiritual and physical, of his symptoms. He 'uses analogy, sign inference, and the physiology of the passions to suture his afflicted body to his soul, presenting the "image" of his humiliation as instruction to his audience'.[42] In other words, Donne the professional preacher uses the lexicon of another profession to transform his body into the 'text' that he will divide, explain, and apply in the same way that he might a Scriptural passage.

The most celebrated and enduring transformation of Donne into text by another writer remains Izaak Walton's *Life*, first published as a preface to the 1640 edition of Donne's *LXXX Sermons*. The text that Donne becomes in Walton's biography is, as Jessica Martin points out, very like a Scriptural text, meant to be used to edify and instil virtue in its audience: 'a primary aspect of the clerical biographer's task was to facilitate the translation of words into works by mediating his subject's exemplary virtues via the book into the acts of the reader'.[43] Walton, as I have argued in this introduction, determinedly constructed an image of Donne that emphasised his Pauline conversion and his clerical professionalism. Martin stresses the way in which Walton did this by infusing his *Life* with Donne's own words and style – as she says, 'mediating his "reading" of Donne through Donne's words and self-

---

[39] Walton, p. 52.
[40] See, for example, his description of the dangers of being distracted when praying: *Sermons* VII, 264–5.
[41] Walton, p. 75.
[42] Stephen Pender, 'Essaying the Body: Donne, Affliction, and Medicine', below p. 248.
[43] Jessica Martin, 'Izaak Walton and the "Re-Inanimation"' of Dr Donne', below p. 258.

consciously Donneian language' – and she also shows how much more complicated Walton's treatment of Donne's inconstancy is than is usually allowed.[44]

V

Walton's *Life* of Donne is notorious for its numerous inaccuracies. As Jessica Martin writes in her essay, however, in its tracing and reproduction of its subject's own intellectual and linguistic practices, it employs 'a method not dissimilar from that used to foreground professional aspects of Donne in this volume'.[45] The aspects that he chose to foreground were those appropriate to his purposes in writing a clerical biography; as the essays in this volume show, by contrast Donne's professional lives were in fact far more multiple, and his engagement with a wide range of professional languages more constant. Like so many of his contemporaries, Donne wrote in an astonishingly large number of genres; unlike most of them, he also mastered their vocabularies and methods, and put them to his own, local, ends. By paying proper attention to the numerous brilliant interventions Donne made into professional fields, this volume tries to show how important it is to study the full range of his writings, and to consider them on their own terms. The sections into which the volume is divided produce some revealing juxtapositions: in the first section, 'Law and Letters', we see how Donne's training at the Inns of Court and service to Sir Thomas Egerton is intimately linked with his polemical writing in *Pseudo-Martyr* (and for Sir Edward Hoby), as well as with his delicate negotiations in verse with female patrons. Section Two, 'Professing the Word', shows Donne's careful treatment of convention – the conventions of place, and of language; essays in this section also engage in dialogue with one another and with the depiction of a unequivocally loyalist Donne presented by Sommerville. In the final section, 'Professing the Body: Anatomy and Resurrection', Donne's living (but ailing) body is seen alongside Walton's attempt to 're-inanimate' that body in textual form and Donne's own 'resurrection' of a place animated by the word of God.

The treatment of Donne's professional lives here is not exhaustive – yet more testimony to his remarkable versatility. There is much work to be done, for example, on Donne's work as a diplomat, notably on his journey through Germany and the Low Countries with Viscount Doncaster in 1619–20.[46] As Walton recognised, however winding the paths were that his career took, Donne was always 'earnest and unwearied in the search of knowledge'. However, this earnest search was not a disinterested and disengaged intellectual pursuit. While it is vital to recognise the variety of Donne's

---

[44] Ibid., p. 250.
[45] Ibid., p. 249.
[46] An essay on this subject by Jeremy Maule was in preparation at the time of his death.

professional writings, this volume reveals an even more important consistency. Donne's desire to have an intellectual identity in the world – to be publicly recognised as one who searches for knowledge – knits together all his works. In his letters, and in the works treated here, Donne fashions an identity as someone whose activity is that of the intellect; and it is against this aim that all of his writing is measured. In this way, even the poetry that is most obviously 'amateur' is defined in relation to intellectual activity and thus has its own part to play in the construction of a 'professional Donne'. By so clearly articulating the place of his poetry within the project of professionalism, Donne begins to break down the division between the 'amateur' and the 'professional' to which he and his contemporaries had frequent recourse and upon which literary historians rely, revealing their interdependence. The Donne revealed here is an author with a strong degree of agency – subject, of course, to the pressures and obligations of negotiation in Elizabethan and early Stuart society yet determined to mould his identity as a professional intellectual with the languages that are at hand. Here is no prisoner of discourse: as Carew wrote, 'to the awe of thy imperious wit / Our stubborne language bends'.[47] The exercise of this wit – as secretary, client, controversialist, preacher – was the constant occupation of Donne's professional lives.

---

[47] Thomas Carew, 'An Elegie upon the death of the Deane of Pauls, D^r. Iohn Donne', lines 49–50, in *Donne's Poetical Works*, ed. by Grierson, I, p. 379.

I
Law and Letters

Chapter 2

DONNE AND THE WORDS OF THE LAW

JEREMY MAULE

'YOU'LL tell me,' a fee paying father complains, 'his name shall live, and that now being dead, his works have eternised him, and made him divine. But could this divinity feed him while he lived? Could his name feast him?' His friend agrees: 'All this the law will do.'[1]

Jonson's *Poetaster* starts its first act by dramatising a tension implicit in many of the engagements between English law and English poetry in the 1590s. The Inns of Court, the third eye of the kingdom, that alternative university where surgery, mathematics, divinity, astronomy and rhetoric bulked up an official curriculum of the kingdom's law students, is now famous, and is one of the major strains of English Renaissance verse. It is the milieu for which the angry, witty, self-applauding and markedly masculine tone of a Donne or a Marston is now understood as having been produced. What I shall try to argue in this essay is that this sort of identification has narrowed the way in which Donne's later Elizabethan and early Jacobean poetry has been read, by confining the law which pervades that reading into the wit of a conceit or the tonality of a coterie. It is not wrong to think of the

Editor's note:
This essay was left uncompleted at the time of Jeremy Maule's death in November 1998. Jeremy had delivered it as a seminar paper and had intended to revise it for publication in this volume. I was unable to locate a complete version of the essay in his computer files or papers, but found three fragmentary typescripts, one much fuller than the others but all with significant lacunae. In editing this version of Jeremy's essay I have attempted to intervene as little as possible, restricting myself to the correction of obvious errors, the elimination of one or two passages, the insertion of a short linking passage, and the addition of as many references as I was able to supply – a task which reminded me once more of the extent of his learning. For help in the search for this essay, I am indebted to Anne Barton, Arnold Hunt, Guy Newcombe, Adrian Poole, Richard Serjeantson, Alison Shell and Andrew Zurcher. For allowing me to publish it, I am very grateful to Jeremy's literary executors, Anne Barton and Adrian Poole. Finally, I would like to thank Helen Wilcox for recognising its importance and encouraging me to persist with its publication.
[1] Ben Jonson, *Poetaster* [1601–2], ed. by Tom Cain (Manchester: Manchester University Press, 1995), 1.2.89–92; 97 (p. 88).

poet as an 'Inns of Court' author; but this extends to questions of tone or genre or attitude in much larger and longer lasting engagements on Donne's part, with the *idea* of law and with its language. Donne's intellectual interest in English law has been underestimated, as has (I argue) the degree to which it continued to help structure his thought in his later years as a clergyman.

The familiar picture of the Inns of Court is one that hundreds of undergraduates have been taught to recognise (no longer, for various reasons, can they recognise it in themselves) and this is what it looks like. The Inns of Court men among whom Donne moved were for the most part of gentle or noble family; they liked versing, they liked women, the Privy Council distrusted them, not least for their susceptibilities to the new Catholic mission; they aped the Court, whose skirts they fringed, and hoped to get on at it; they enjoyed and sometimes acted in revels and plays, though professional writers didn't much like the pushy literary elitism of these richer dilettantes; religion and politics were their most attractive debating topics, erotic adventurism and a kind of pop Ovidianism their characteristic poses. Surgery, mathematics, divinity, astronomy and rhetoric helped make up their unofficial curriculum; satires, epigrams, paradoxes, characters and that novel form, the essay, were the pithy genres their literary exhibitionism favoured; Essex the handsome sort of younger politician their spiritual younger-son mentality hoped to cultivate. They were, of course, these bright sparks – all the critics agree on this – insecure. And none (the rest of the argument is predictable, too) brighter, none more insecure, than John Donne. The reasons a picture of this kind has proved attractive are not far to seek. It elides social differences but preserves a conscious elitism, and does so sufficiently for a popular form of narrative, the career romance (Mary McCarthy's *The Group* is the sort of work I have in mind), to be implicit in the description. It combines, in a manner irresistible to academics, academic laziness with a certain worldly swagger; it spices the fashion of 'forward wits' with the real dangers of atheism or Romanism in late Elizabethan England; it dresses the patron-jumping of ambition with the nonchalance of *sprezzatura*. Like all group friendships, it is built on exclusion, and ragged at the edges (the limited publication of manuscript circulation has been claimed as a sort of symbol of this edginess). Like few group friendships, it can lay claim to have seeded a masterpiece (Bacon's *Essays* of 1597). And like almost no other circle or coterie in English literature, what its members were ostensibly *doing* has proved almost completely uninteresting. That Keats or Coleridge studied medicine has been thought of some interest to readers of Romantic poetry; that Donne read law seems to have worried very few students of his verse.

It might, though. Donne's first hermaphrodite is a law student: 'Yee of those fellowships whereof hee's one,' he incites his concelebrants in *Epithalamion made at Lincolnes Inne*, 'Of study and play made strange

Hermaphrodits, / Here shine . . .'.[2] Studying law (or not studying it enough) worried Donne, who confessed to his friend Henry Goodyer that his law studies had given way to 'the worst voluptuousness, which is an Hydroptique immoderate desire of humane learning and languages';[3] and worried him not only as a student (such confessions are, after all, only a form of inverted self-praise), but as the keen-eyed observer of its social praxis, in his Satires of the 1590s. *Satires II, IV* and, more particularly, *V* all address the operations, mechanic gestures and general deficiencies of Elizabethan legal practice. And a specifically legal vocabulary of jointures, divorces, regnal years, of titles and prerogatives, of the distinctions between treasonable intent and overt act, of disputation, conviction, suitors and officers, proves yet another language in which the *Songs and Sonets* transact Donne's love business. Titles like *The Disinherited* and *The Legacie* tell a story which is taken up elsewhere in poems so disparate as *The Dampe, Confined Love* and *An Elegie on Himselfe*. Law terms, too, of a different sort are the times in which Donne's letters chase his London friends. Donne studied law, practised it as the Lord Keeper's secretary, observed its imperfect execution as a satirist and suffered it in person as a husband.[4]

The years of employment, and then of underemployment, tell a story in which Donne remains intensely reluctant to concede that the loss of a job need imply the end of a profession. They discover in him, first, a (very insignificant) legislator; later in the 1600s, his cronies of the Mitre and Mermaid were mostly MPs (and mostly troublesome ones at that) in the first Parliament of James' reign. During the same period, Donne himself contributes legal opinions – like that on Valdesius' *De dignitate Regum Regnorumque Hispaniae* prepared for Sir Robert Cotton in 1603–7.[5] His longest continuous prose work, *Pseudo-Martyr*, expounds and defends a recent Act of Parliament (the Oath of Allegiance), and both that work and *Ignatius His Conclave* frequently bounce knotty points of civil and canon law at his opponents; and his longest poem, to an extent only recently appreciated, revisits and echoes that Parliament's debates.[6] We hear nowadays of Donne's career, so long at the margins of what Marotti somewhat too easily hypostatises as 'the Establishment', and of the sympathetic gestures of hierarchal authority with which Donne at once endorses and arrogates the

[2] John Donne, 'Epithalamion made at Lincolnes Inne', lines 29–31, in *Donne's Poetical Works*, ed. by H. J. C. Grierson, 2 vols (Oxford: Clarendon Press, 1912) I, p. 142.

[3] *Letters*, p. 50.

[4] On informing his father-in-law, Sir George More, of his clandestine marriage to his daughter, Donne was imprisoned in the Fleet. He later launched a suit to test the validity of the marriage, which was confirmed in a judgement given on 27 April 1602. See Bald, pp. 135 and 139. On Donne as Egerton's secretary, see Louis Knafla's essay in this volume.

[5] See Bald, p. 142.

[6] 'The Second Anniversarie' (1612); see Annabel Patterson, 'John Donne, Kingsman?', in *The Mental World of the Jacobean Court*, ed. by Linda Levy Peck (Cambridge: Cambridge University Press, 1991), pp. 251–72; pp. 268–71.

power of a Stuart king. But Donne laid claim to other authorities from other margins: Acacius' *De privilegiis juris civilis* (Frankfurt, 1606), Baldus, Castrensis, Galatinus, Antonio di Rosellis and Vercellus are among the civilians, Talmudists and canonists cited, for example, in the *Essays in Divinity*; and a sustained distinction between common law and prerogative underpins the whole of that work.[7]

Early modern England – it is another cliché, but perhaps less easily visualised than 'The Inns of Court as a Socio-Literary Environment' – was notoriously litigious. Donne was, amongst other things (it is not a difficult idea) a lawyer; he read law, in all its kinds as then understood; he made up case-books and sent one to his friend;[8] he practised law on his own behalf, as late as 1622;[9] he preached law; he ended his life as a judge.[10] It was no accident that his first preferment as a clergyman came as Reader to Lincoln's Inn. John Donne the younger has had a deservedly poor press from Donne scholars, but it would be hard to fault the phrase which he found for this abiding interest in his father's life: 'The Author was obliged in Civill business'.[11]

Donne's neglect of the law as an idle Inns of Court student has been suggested, then; but so too have been the occasional attempts to correct the picture. (Dominic Baker-Smith, for example, insists that Donne's 'intellectual formation was completed outside the divinity school'.)[12] Donne himself demanded intellectual elbow-room: 'freedome and libertie, as in all other indifferent things, so in my studies also, not to betroth or enthral my selfe, to any one science, which should possesse or denominate me'.[13] Law was one such study, one such science, for Donne; and there is still perhaps a case to be made for suggesting that Donne's concern with laws and with their vocabularies (national and international, Scriptural and ecclesiastical) would repay attention it has certainly not yet received.

But it is easy, and perhaps important, to see too why such a project may have been deferred. For one thing, it is no easy matter to understand the law in early modern England: as Swinburne states,

---

[7] See *Essays*; Simpson discusses Donne's sources at pp. 101–8.

[8] See *Letters*, pp. 200; 226.

[9] The case was against Henry Seyliard, who had attempted to take possession of the benefice of Keyston (having been promised it by the Archbishop of Canterbury) before, Donne claimed, he as incumbent had resigned. Donne was attempting to secure the living for John Scott, who had previously been given it shortly after Donne, in 1615. See Bald, pp. 386–8, and Appendix D, pp. 570–1.

[10] See Bald, pp. 414–16 (judge in the Court of Delegates); 416–422 (in the Court of High Commission).

[11] In John Donne the younger's epistle to Sir Henry Vane; *Essays*, p. 3.

[12] Dominic Baker-Smith, 'John Donne's *Critique of True Religion*', in *John Donne: Essays in Celebration*, ed. by A. J. Smith (London: Methuen, 1972), pp. 404–32, at p. 405.

[13] *P-M*, p. 12.

so huge is the multitude of their sundry sorts of bookes; as lectures, councels, tracts, decisions, questions, disputations, repetitions, cautels, clausules, common opinions, singulars, contradictions, concordances, methodes, summes, practickes, tables, repertories and books of other kindes (apparent monuments of their endlesse and inuincible labours).[14]

While the emergence of the modern profession and the Inns of Court milieu have been adequately described, at least, there have been few since Maitland who have tried to hold the whole picture of legal practice, legal theory, prerogative justice, emerging international, canon, criminal, civil, statute and judge-made law together. (Not even Maitland made much progress with Hooker's 'law celestial and heavenly . . . which Angels do clearly behold'.) And still the great triumvirs among early Stuart legal thinkers – Coke, Selden and Hale – each await a standard exposition.[15] In this respect, there seems to be a strong contrast between critics of Elizabethan literature and those of the succeeding century. Spenser's allegory of equity, Shakespeare's imaginative engagement with covenant, are standard fare. And while scholars like Richard Helgerson and Marie Axton have attempted to bring legal categories into the study of the period's fiction or its literary criticism,[16] it is harder to point to similar efforts in the study of seventeenth-century writing.[17]

Patterns of Donne mapped out during his own lifetime may also have something to answer for. Donne's notorious fondness for separating out his life before and after it entered priesthood would be one reason: the quick success of this young devil, old saint trajectory (it had clearly taken well before Donne died, not least with its first author) leaves little room for the excluded middle term on which both careers, with their different successes, were founded. And in the most forceful of the modern accounts, John Carey's, the clarity and attractions of a related, though distinct, binarism can be heard, as Apostasy and Ambition are made to generate the shape of Donne's life.[18] There are difficulties inherent, too, in the powerful later chapters of Carey's study. Psychologies ('fabric[s] . . . of imaginative needs', in Carey's finer phrase) that are cast largely in iconic terms are unlikely to find much room for legal terminology, much less for legal thought. It is easy enough to imagine the law personified in a godly magistrate or a sleepy constable; and more exciting, with Donne in *Satire V*, to visualise it as a digestive system:

[14] Henry Swinburne, *A Briefe Treatise of Testaments and Last Willes* (London, 1590), sig. B.
[15] Though see now Alan Cromartie, *Sir Matthew Hale, 1609–1676: Law, Religion, and Natural Philosophy* (Cambridge: Cambridge University Press, 1995).
[16] See Richard Helgerson, *Forms of Nationhood: the Elizabethan writing of England* (Chicago: University of Chicago Press, 1992), chapter 2, 'Writing the Law', pp. 65–104; Marie Axton, *The Queen's Two Bodies: Drama and the Elizabethan Succession* (London: Royal Historical Society, 1977).
[17] Though see now *Rhetoric and Law in Early Modern Europe*, ed. by Victoria Kahn and Lorna Hutson (New Haven: Yale University Press, 2001).
[18] John Carey, *John Donne: Life, Mind and Art* (London: Faber and Faber, 1981; new edn 1990).

officers
Are the devouring stomacke, and Suiters
The excrements which they voyd

or hear it as a clatter of impotent energies:

They are the mills which grinde you, yet you are
The winde which drives them; and a wastfull warre
Is fought against you, and you fight it.[19]

But the *idea* of law is tougher fare. Still, it is there in Donne – in the 'pecuniary and bloudy Laws' in which he justifies a regime's control of its citizens' personal religion; in the 'ideations' of 'Utopian' republicanism, or Plato's *Laws* and *Republic*, with which he struggled in the earlier years of the seventeenth century; and in his *Divine Poems*, and *Essays in Divinity*, and sermons, as they too continue to grapple and negotiate between the law of God, the law of man.

Some good accounts exist of Donne's engagement with Elizabethan law in his Satires, and *Songs and Sonets*, with their many legal conceits, hardly lack for painful expositors. But there is one poem in which echoes of the poet as lawyer deserve to be heard more acutely (Donne prays in *The Litanie* 'That our eares sicknesse we may cure').[20] It is the last in the second sequence of Donne's *Holy Sonnets*, the set that follows *La Corona* and is sometimes entitled *Divine Meditations*. There are some problems about the sonnet's place in the sequence, on which I shall comment briefly.

But first a text, which I give as it appears in a collection dating from Donne's own lifetime, the 1620s manuscript in Cambridge University Library ('Balam' manuscript; the readings are the same as the 'Puckering' manuscript in all but spelling):[21]

12.

Father, part of his doble Interest
Vnto thy Kingdome, thy Sonne giues to Mee,
His Joynture in ye knotty Trinytye,
He keepes & giues mee his Death's conquest,
This Lambe, whose death, wth lyfe ye world hath blest,
Was from ye worlds beginninge slayne, & hee
Hath made two wills, wch wth ye Legacye
Of his & thy kingdome, doth thy Sonnes invest,

[19] Donne, 'Satire V', lines 17–19; 23–5, in *Donne's Poetical Works*, ed. by Grierson, I, pp. 168, 169.

[20] Donne, 'The Litanie', stanza 25, line 217, in *Donne's Poetical Works*, ed. by Grierson, I, p. 347.

[21] Cambridge Balam Manuscript = Cambridge University Library, MS Add. 5778 ($\Delta4$ in Peter Beal, compiler, *Index of English Literary Manuscripts*, vol. I, 1450–1625. Part I, Andrewes-Donne (London: Mansell, 1980)); Puckering MS = Trinity College, Cambridge MS R.3.12 (James 592) ($\Delta13$ in Beal).

> Yet such are these Lawes, y^t Men argue yet
> Whether a Man those Statutes can fullfill;
> None doth, But All healing Grace and Spiritt
> Revive againe what law & letter kill,
> Thy Lawes abridgment, & thy last Comand
> Is all but loue; oh lett that last Will stande.

Let us approach the twelfth *Holy Sonnet*, then, as it is met in the Group I and II manuscripts and in *1633*.[22] We needn't adopt the easy schematism of Ignatian meditation to observe that 'colloquy' (meditation's final stage) is very much its note; but there are other finalities too in the poem's manner of proceeding. The double 'last' of its last couplet ('last command' (line 13), 'last Will' (line 14)) adds its own emphasis – an emphasis necessary, perhaps, in a sequence which had already opened on a finishing note ('As due by many titles I resigne / My selfe to Thee').[23] Here at Donne's last end, other links with the first sonnet can be heard – both have an unusual density of legal vocabulary, both move through a rather dry, resumptive opening to more impassioned address. And for all the pejorative force with which Patrides urges a non-sequential reading ('lest one is *tempted* to detect an underlying design'),[24] it is hard not to sense with Gardner or Lewalski some sense of climax in argument, some plateau reached of spiritual recovery.[25]

What that climax might be, though, Donne's critics have been charier in pronouncing. Marotti, it's true, is predictably swift in discovering 'language that suggests the economic benefits of royal patronage';[26] and Wilbur Sanders takes time out to tell the sonnet off for being witty.[27] But outside the glosses of Gardner's edition, with their helpful cross-references to the *Sermons*, and Lewalski's discussion in her *Protestant Poetics* I have found no substantial account of the sonnet. Donne's other editors gloss only odd phrases; and the waves of New Critical explication which continue (as Donne scholars know to their cost) to visit 'Batter my heart' prefer to leave Donne's own climax high and dry.

The difficulty is largely one of register. The sonnet is conspicuously cooler

---

[22] On the relationships between the different groups of manuscripts of Donne's poetry, see Beal, *Index*.

[23] Donne, 'Holy Sonnet I' (II in Grierson), line 1, in *Donne's Poetical Works*, ed. by Grierson, I, p. 322. The numbering of the *Holy Sonnets* adopted here is that of *1633*, followed in John Donne, *The Divine Poems*, ed. by Helen Gardner, 2nd edn (Oxford: Clarendon Press, 1978); Grierson's text is preferred for his editorial readings.

[24] *The Complete English Poems of John Donne*, ed. by C. A. Patrides (London: Dent, 1985), p. 428; italics added.

[25] See Donne, *The Divine Poems*, ed. by Gardner, pp. xxxviii–xliii; Barbara Kiefer Lewalski, *Protestant Poetics and the Seventeenth-Century Religious Lyric* (Princeton: Princeton University Press, 1979), pp. 273 and (on sequence in the *Holy Sonnets*) 264–5.

[26] Arthur F. Marotti, *John Donne, Coterie Poet* (Madison: University of Wisconsin Press, 1986), p. 255.

[27] Wilbur Sanders, *John Donne's Poetry* (Cambridge: Cambridge University Press, 1971), p. 120.

than its predecessors, with their notorious and arresting dramas of question and aggression. Four of the twelve sonnets start with questions ('If poysonous mineralls . . .' (*V*), 'Why are wee by all creatures waited on?' (*VIII*), 'What if this present were the worlds last night?' (*IX*), 'Wilt thou love God, as he thee!' (*XI*)); four, memorably, open with commands: 'Spit in my face' (*VII*), 'Batter my heart' (*X*), 'Death be not proud' (*VI*) and 'At the round earths imagin'd corners, blow' (*IV*). Even the first three sonnets, which lack such a syntax, are urgent with other features of rhetorical heightening; performatives ('I resigne' (*I*, 1 and cf. *II*, 1)); apostrophe ('Oh my blacke Soule!' (*II*, 1 and cf. *I*, 2)); and spatial or temporal deictics ('This is my playes last scene, here heavens appoint' (*III*, 1–4 and cf. *II*, 1)). *Sonnet XII*, precise and expository by contrast, abandons Donne's solemn geography of human limits and cares not for any of these things.

Yet, as Lewalski admirably sees, carefulness is very much part of its point. But for what? 'The final sonnet', she explains,

> takes up the issue of how the regenerate christian should serve God, how he should exhibit that 'new obedience' to God's will that was understood to be the effect of regeneration and adoption . . . [and] confronts the knotty issue of how to lay claim to his inheritance.[28]

These are a lot of 'how's for a poem without any itself; we might notice, too, how the 'knotty' that Donne reserves for the doctrinal conundrum of the Trinity has shifted in Lewalski's account to the issue that her own climax of Pauline concern now requires. Yet her sense that Paul's analysis of the Christian's peculiar predicament, between the letter of the Old and spirit of the New Covenant, lies at the centre of the sonnet's concerns, can hardly be faulted. What gets lost, I think, in her account (as also in Gardner's glosses) are the terms that lend Donne's paradigms of personal salvation (and surely they *are* Pauline) their own personal note – and, I think, their wit.

Quoting the first quatrain of *Holy Sonnet XII*, in his study of Donne and rhetoric, Thomas O. Sloane commented that 'Donne never stopped sounding like a lawyer', and that 'finding such [legalistic] terms in Donne's writing requires no effort'.[29] Neither statement is quite true – Donne would be a poorer poet if they were – but Sloane's corrective is surely a helpful exaggeration. For the last *Holy Sonnet* is above all else neither Ignatian meditation nor Pauline epistle, but quite simply a legal pleading. Like all such pleadings, it explains the facts (more than once, as lawyers are prone to: ll. 1–2, 3–4), and argues one side of the case that can be developed from them. It develops a history (ll. 5–8), identifies an issue (ll. 9–10), admits a major difficulty (11), sees a way round it (11–12), cites textual precedents (13–14)

[28] Lewalski, *Protestant Poetics*, p. 273.
[29] Thomas O. Sloane, *Donne, Milton, and the End of Humanist Rhetoric* (Berkeley: University of California Press, 1985), p. 149.

and ends (14) at advocate's full throttle. At each stage Donne uses terms and develops distinctions familiar to the early modern lawyer. Nor is he (the point bears emphasis) unusual in so doing – one might compare the (buried) legal language in the alternative stanzas of Herbert's *Praise (II)* for a similar example of intensified legal utterance.

The 'doble interest' of line 1 Gardner glosses, perhaps a shade strongly, as a 'twofold claim'. As *OED* says, on *interest*, 'there is much that is obscure in the history of this word': one curious feature is that its figurative uses (by Tyndale, for example, or in the Countess of Pembroke's *Psalms*) appear to precede its literal. Here, we should understand the primary seventeenth-century sense: a legal concern in, a right or title to, something, especially land. The present tenses ('giues', line 2; 'keepes & giues', line 4) are standard for explication in pleading; and the subject-verb-object inversions fronting 'part' (line 1) and 'joynture' (line 3) are another commonplace of legal oratory, evidently designed to assist focalisation. The stress on 'mee' in the defective third foot of the fourth line may well have a similar effect.

This pleading does contain some paradoxes, however. Though we often expound the intentions of a testator in language that suggests he is still alive ('thy Son giues', line 2), he is not usually a beneficiary under his own will ('his Joynture . . . He keepes', lines 3–4). And 'conquest' (line 4), in the legal sense of 'acquisition of real property otherwise than by inheritance', is by definition something you acquire while you are alive, not dead.[30] These are paradoxes which fit better than most G. K. Chesterton's definition; they are truths standing on their head waiting to be recognised. For of course, they are paradoxes with a solution: Christ is not dead, though He has died. As God, he is testator; as man, purchaser (like 'Testament', 'purchase' is a word made to hang off the end of the sonnet, a serious pun visible to the eye of faith); and as Second Person of the Trinity, co-holder of a joint-tenancy of an unimaginably complicated kind.

Donne's sonnet, it's clear, glances at most of these problems. And if it is witty, its wit consists less, perhaps, in the slow application of such issues to heavenly inheritance (these are Donne's sonnets, not Griffin's *Fidessa*, after all)[31] than in the implicit suggestion that God has made a characteristically complicated job of His testamentary dispositions. Like Mosca praising Voltore for his lawyer's ability 'to make knots, and undoe them',[32] Donne seems rather to admire the Trinity for achieving an intrication it will need all its own skills to untangle. His sonnet, not disinterestedly, offers its own version of legal aid.

So I am making two sorts of point here. One is that we often fail to recognise the terms (not because they are pidgin, like Coscus' 'remitter' and

---

[30] See *OED*, *sub* 'conquest'.
[31] Barthlomew Griffin, *Fidessa, more chaste than kind* (London, 1596).
[32] Ben Jonson, *Volpone, or the Foxe*, 1.3.57, in *Volpone and Other Plays*, ed. by Lorna Hutson (Harmondsworth: Penguin, 1998), p. 231.

'affidavits' but because many of them aren't or aren't only).[33] And secondly that, as Lévi-Strauss observed of animals, some are 'bonnes à penser', good to think with. So too with laws and Donne: he thinks best with the laws of property. It would be banal and reductive to claim that in Donne's poetry he thought *as* a lawyer, any more than Miss Ramsay's discoveries in the decades after Grierson's edition made it plausible to claim that Donne thought as a scholastic theologian.[34] But both skills are necessary for a reader of Donne, as Corbet saw in his elegy of 1632. To interpret Donne's poetry or praise his parts, we

> . . . must have learning plenty; both the Lawes,
> Civill, and Common, to judge any cause;
> Divinity great store, above the rest;
> Not of the last Edition, but the best.[35]

Donne was a lawyer and a divine, but neither exclusively. In the Preface to *Pseudo-Martyr*, he superficially resisted the claims of any one discipline, insisting that his studies should communicate with each other: communicate, not exchange.[36] At exactly the same time, in May–June 1609 in a letter to Sir Henry Goodyer, he records his disgust at William Barlow's fiery apology for James's *Apology, An Answer to a Catholic Englishman*.[37] Both law and theology, rather, were disciplines in which an acute mind trained itself, and in which the sophistications of a technical vocabulary enabled a poet to keep some intellectual, and hence social, distance from other Christians, other citizens. Both too were disciplines that combined dialectic practice in controversies with the attractions of an absolute authority. Law and theology are, as the still fashionable term has it, discourses: discourses in which prayer or plea are intimately bound up, are knotty, intricate, with judgement.

Donne frequently reverted to the plaintiff / judge relationship found in *Holy Sonnet XII*. It was not unusual for him to do so: redemption and testament, after all, are legal ideas implicit in Christianity. But where most expositors of covenant theology after the Reformation stayed within the bounds of Pauline metaphor, dwelling (as does *Holy Sonnet XI*, for example) on a vision of the saved Christian as *adopted*, as *co-heir* with Christ of God (Romans 8:17) before progressing through the complex patterns of assurance, justification and sanctification, Donne lingers, half-possessingly, on the *process* of legacy. The whole of *Holy Sonnet XII* is a serious, exploratory

---

[33] Donne, 'Satire II', lines 55, 57, in *Donne's Poetical Works*, ed. by Grierson, I, p. 152.

[34] See Mary Paton Ramsay, *Les doctrines médiévales chez Donne, le poète métaphysicien de l'Angleterre (1573–1631)* (Oxford: Oxford University Press, 1917).

[35] Richard Corbet, 'On Doctor *Donne*, by Dr C. B. of O.', lines 7–10, in *Donne's Poetical Works*, ed. by Grierson, I, p. 374.

[36] John Donne, 'A Preface to the Priestes, and Jesuits, and to their Disciples in this Kingdome', in *P-M*, pp. 10–28, esp. p. 12.

[37] See *Letters*, pp. 160–4.

pun on the word 'Testament' – an exploration dramatised by Donne's affective enthusiasm for repugnancy. But the terms of that repugnancy in this sonnet have been much simplified, and as a result partly misunderstood. No commentator, of course, is ever reluctant to tease oppositions out of Donne, and the sonnet's modern editors have been understandably quick to gloss once again the old battle of Old and New Testament, Law and Gospel, letter and spirit: 'The law was given Moses, but grace and truth came by Jesus Christ' (John 1:17); 'The letter killeth, but the spirit giveth life' (2 Corinthians 3:6). These are certainly what Donne alludes to, yet perhaps the case is less simple, its issue less assured; 'men argue yet'.

Thomas Wilson, in his *Art of Rhetorique*, laid out the rules to be followed for arguments of this kind, when 'laws seem to have a certain repugnancy, whereof among many riseth much contention':

1. The inferior law must give place to the superior
2. The law general must yield to the special
3. Man's law, to Gods law
4. An old law, to a new law.[38]

Where, then, we may ask, is Donne's problem? He understands the terms (ll. 1–4) of Christ's bequest, its date (ll. 5–6) and the identity of its legatees (ll. 7–8). The trouble lies in meeting the conditions (ll. 9–10) of the legacy, and it is these that men dispute (as they might dispute what part faith or works should play in determining men's eligibility to qualify for Christ's bequest). They shouldn't: no-one qualifies (line 11). Or so Donne seems to say, until his own qualification ('but' + subjunctive (lines 11–12), in the sense 'unless') reformulates the claim: it is only as a gratuitous contingency that the plea for the bequest can be heard again ('revived'), and by implication the award allowed. But here too another subtlety is developed: hard conditions, or conditions almost impossible, do suspend the effect of the disposition. Donne doesn't presume that far; though the 'not' is more confident than the formulation of the first sonnet ('. . . thou lov'st mankind well, yet will not chuse me'),[39] the last does not end, as Lewalski appears to claim, in any certainty of election, any assurance.[40] Donne's morphology of conversion is incomplete, and he is still pleading as the sonnet sequence ends. Is the legator an enemy to the testator?

This position is more remarkable than has perhaps appeared. For what is it to continue to enact a plaintiff's part, at the very point when one has just said that only death inheres in 'law and letter'? Here it is worth remembering

---

[38] Thomas Wilson, *The Art of Rhetoric (1560)*, ed. by Peter E. Medine (University Park, Pennsylvania: The Pennsylvania State University Press, 1994), p. 129.

[39] Donne, 'Holy Sonnet I' (II in Grierson), line 13, in *Donne's Poetical Works*, ed. by Grierson, I, p. 322.

[40] See Lewalski, *Protestant Poetics*, p. 273.

Luther's comment at just this stage of the same argument ('O antissimum argumentum!' he apostrophises, 'Humana longissime memoranda'). It is here (and it is surely some sort of argument in support of sequence) that Donne's use of the law abandons the inert intelligence of an extended conceit for a moment of compacted difficulty and philosophic grandeur. Of course we tend nowadays to exaggerate as artificial the wit of seventeenth-century poets who use land-law to get into Heaven (and indeed such complaints fall oddly from American critics, who are better equipped than British to respond to the edgy, superlitigious qualities of early modern inheritance practices). But when Donne, in *The Litanie*, says that the Virgin Mary 'made / One claime for innocence, and disseiz'd sinne',[41] or when Herbert's *Redemption* sends its tenant off to the manor for a new lease, these are not novel terms. (If you don't happen to know them all, Herbert instructs his country parson in *A Priest to the Temple*, then you can get them up from a digest of the statutes, 'as also by discourse with men of that profession'.)[42] The power behind such apparent conceits rests on a better understanding of property than that now held – property conceived not just as an object, a thing, but as a relationship to that object. For the same reason, it is not a play on legal terms alone (though the pun on 'revive', as earlier on 'conquest', is witty enough to float over the heads of editors) that marks Donne's feeling intelligence, but his strong passion for expressing the juncture (Donne would have said 'jointure') of opposites in terms which insist on retaining their conjoining as visible, as knotty.

This is why Donne chooses to remain lawyerly to the last, for at the last his pleading is there not to claim Heaven as an assured object, an achieved goal, but to express, in the face of all difficulties, his sense of a continuing relationship towards his God. No man, he knows, 'those Statutes can fullfill'. But one man has: Christ came 'not to destroy, but to fulfil' the Law (Matthew 5:17), and it is the nature of that fulfilment that Donne's close explores. It is God whom he addresses – a God no longer in three-personed separation ('Father . . . Sonne . . . Spiritt' (ll. 1, 2, 11); 'his & thy kingdome' (line 8)), but now mysteriously conjoint. Donne's 'thy' enacts this: 'Thy Lawes abridgment, & thy last command' determinedly elides the persons of the Trinity – as in *The Litanie*, they now appear 'distinguish'd undistinct'.[43] (It is no accident that this is the first time in *Holy Sonnets* that the Trinity becomes *theologically* interesting to Donne.)

In another sense, too, a spiritual distance is felt from the sonnet's opening bequest. For between giving ('Thy Sonne giues') and claiming, especially where a will is concerned, stands the whole interpretative process of the law.

[41] Donne, 'The Litanie', stanza 5, lines 39–40, in *Donne's Poetical Works*, ed. by Grierson, I, p. 339.

[42] George Herbert, 'A Priest to the Temple', in *George Herbert and Henry Vaughan*, ed. by Louis L. Martz (Oxford: Oxford University Press, 1986), p. 219.

[43] Donne, 'The Litanie', stanza 4, line 32, in *Donne's Poetical Works*, ed. by Grierson, I, p. 339.

What has looked like a specific provision 'to mee' (Cowell: '*Legacie* [he contrasts it with the larger *Haereditas*] is a particular thing giuen by last will and testament')[44] slides into a larger formula ('doth thy Sonnes invest'), in whose interpretation all disputes are bound ('None doth') to fail. Merit sinks, and Donne's claim to Christ's bequest cannot be made out: only grace revives it. We still speak now of 'resuscitating' a claim, and maybe hear some crank of returning breath in the embedded metaphor. Stuart lawyers too, it is clear, still sensed the Lazarus in their term 'reviving':

> *Reviving*, is a word metaphorically applied to rents and actions and signifieth a renewing of them, after they be extinguished: no less than if a man, or other liuing creature should be dead, and restored to life.

And with that restoration, that revival, a new understanding of law returns too. Milton, in the most legalistic of all his poems, *Upon the Circumcision*, sees the baby's drops of blood as the sputtered sealing wax of a new covenant; but for all the violence of his imagery, his contrast is drawn *against* the Law and not within it: 'O more exceeding love or law more just? / Just law indeed, but more exceeding love!'.[45] What Milton separates, Donne compounds:

> Thy Lawes abridgment, & thy last Comand
> Is all but loue; oh lett that last Will stande.

'In bolting out the true meaning of a law', says Wilson, 'we must use to search out the nature of the same by defining some one word.'[46] 'Abridgement', I think, is the word in question. It has been generally taken (as all Donne's editors take it) to mean 'epitome', and glossed from the *Sermons*: 'where the Jews had all abridged in *decem verba* . . . the Christian hath all abridged in *duo verba*, into two words, *love God, love thy neighbour*.'[47]

Donne certainly enjoyed imagining God abridging Himself. The conceit returns as a fine climax in a sermon of 1622, in which Donne explores the familiar idea of the world as a library, God its sole Author:

> All other authors we distinguish by *tomes*, by *parts*, by *volumes*; but who knowes the volumes of this Author; how many volumes of Spheares involve one another, how many tomes of Gods creatures there are? Hast thou not room, hast thou not money, hast thou understanding, hast thou not leasure, for great volumes, for the *bookes of heaven*, (for the *Mathematiques*) nor for the books of *Courts*, (the *Politiques*) take but the *Georgiques*, the consideration of the *Earth*, a farme, a garden, nay seven foot of earth, a grave, and that will be book enough.

---

44 John Cowell, *The Interpreter: or Booke Containing the Signification of Words* (Cambridge: John Legate, 1607), *sub* 'Legacie', sig. Rr4r.

45 John Milton, 'Upon the Circumcision', lines 15–16, in *Complete Shorter Poems*, ed. by John Carey, 2nd edn (Harlow: Longman, 1997), p. 172.

46 Wilson, *Art of Rhetoric*, p. 128.

47 See Gardner in Donne, *Divine Poems*, p. 74 n.; *Sermons* IX, 150.

Goe lower; every *worme* in the grave, every *weed* upon the grave, is an abridgement of all.[48]

So here in the sonnet, the notion of abridgement as a compaction, a miniature, an epitome – God's laws *in parvo* – has seemed attractive to interpreters. It has a history that long precedes Donne, in fact. This notion that Christ's last command, what Hooker calls 'the one principall command-ment of love' (John 13:34: 'love one another'), capitulates the whole of the law first receives its expression in Cyprian, who after Tertullian and Augustine was Donne's favourite among the Fathers: 'Surely this commandment containeth the law and the prophets, and in this one word is the *abridgement* of all volumes of Scripture.'

Renaissance poets and theologians would have relished this old idea the more for their modern sense of what was involved in abridging laws in this way. 'John Selden liveth on his own', his friend Ben Jonson told Drummond of Hawthornden, 'and is the law-book of the judges of England.'[49] The compliment was a modern one: abridgements, one-volume works that organised law accessibly because alphabetically, briefly overtook the longer, chronologically organised series of Year Books in the years that Donne studied the law. It was also a weighty one: the standard English law-epitome, *La graunde abridgement collecte et escrie par le Iudge tresreuerend Syr Robert Brooke Chiualier, nadgairs chiefe Iustice del common banke* (1576), weighed in at 1,620 grammes. But Christ, the arch-epitomist, boiled down all that. In the words of another sonnet of Divine Meditation, Alabaster's *Christus Recapi-tulatio Omnium*, He had 'writ a brief', sum[med a] digest', 'drawn an inventory'.[50] The Heavenly Book, it turned out, was as simple as a one-letter word:

> O happy school whose master is the book,
> Which book is only text, which text unwrit
> Doth read itself, and they that on it look
> Do read by being read, nor do they flit
> From word to word: for all is but one letter,
> Which still is learnt, but never learnt the better.[51]

Donne's abridgement has seemed as simple; it is 'all but love'. Whatever that means: two editors, Patrides and Martz, see that this might be a problem, and

---

[48] *Sermons* IV, 167.

[49] Ben Jonson, 'Conversations with William Drummond of Hawthornden', line 530, in *Ben Jonson*, ed. by Ian Donaldson (Oxford: Oxford University Press, 1985), p. 608.

[50] William Alabaster, 'Christus Recapitulatio Omnium', lines 5, 4, in *The Sonnets of William Alabaster*, ed. by G. M. Story and Helen Gardner (Oxford: Oxford University Press, 1959), p. 32.

[51] Alabaster, 'New Jerusalem' sonnet 3 (no. 43), lines 9–14, in *The Sonnets*, ed. by Story and Gardner, p. 24.

gloss explicitly 'nothing but' (Martz adds, '*but* in the sense of *only*': though it is hard then to see what he wants 'all' to mean').[52] Both at least see it as a problem; most editors (as they so often do with Renaissance monosyllables) leave the text, like Alabaster's, to read itself. The evidence, though, is harder, and points in the opposite direction. It runs from Bastard in 1598, for whom 'All but resembleth God, all but his glasse, / All but the picture of his majestie', through society, 'all but rude' in Marvell's garden,[53] to the hyperaesthetic qualifications of Gilbert's *Patience*:

> COLONEL: I'm afraid we're not quite right.
> ANGELA: Not supremely, perhaps, but oh, so all-but!
> Saphir, are they not quite too all-but?

'All-but' means the same in all three examples: almost, well-nigh, very nearly entirely, everything short of (*OED, sub* 'all', a.8); not, then (quite), 'nothing but'. This is more than a quibble: Donne's sense needs more, and needs it for a heavenly inheritance.

Again, a better relevance emerges, the phrase fits more easily, where we understand another sense of the word, one more narrowly legal. This type of clash between general and special meanings was one that early modern lawyers often discussed; the preface to Sir Edward Coke's seventh volume of *Reports*, for example, identifies explicitly the problem of 'ambiguity' in 'lawyers dialect' likely to arise from 'palpable mistakings in the verie words of art'.[54] 'Abridgement' is one such word, and for an elucidation, we need look no further than that 'Booke containing the Signification of Words; Wherein is set forth the meaning of all, or the most part of such Words and Termes, as are mentioned in the Lawe Writers, or Statutes', John Cowell's *The Interpreter*. Cowell interprets as follows:

> *Abridge* . . . in our generall language signifieth as much as to make shorter in words, holding still the whole substance. But in the common lawe it seemeth . . . to be more particularly used for making a declaration or count shorter by subtracting or seuering some of the substance therein comprised. So that here (*abridger*) is not (*contrahere*) but rather *subtrahere*.[55]

This sense of 'abridgement' is not uncommon, legally speaking: all the standard law-guides (Brooke's *Abridgement*, Rastell's *Les termes de la ley* and Baker's *Manual of Law French*) all sustain the contrast, which is also heard (though like Donne's, hardly explained) in the 'also' of Cotgrave's 1611 *Dictionarie of the French and English Tongves*:

[52] See Donne, *The Complete English Poems*, ed. by Patrides, p. 445n.; *The Anchor Anthology of Seventeenth-Century Verse*, ed. Louis L. Martz, 2 vols (New York: Doubleday, 1969), p. 87n.

[53] Andrew Marvell, 'The Garden', line 15, in *The Complete English Poems*, ed. by Elizabeth Story Donno (Harmondsworth: Penguin, 1972), p. 100.

[54] Sir Edward Coke, *La Sept Part des Reports Sr Edw. Coke* (London, 1608), sig. avir.

[55] Cowell, *The Interpreter, sub* 'Abridge', sig. A3r.

Abbregement: m. a shortening, abridging, epitomising, abbreuiating; also, an abridgement.[56]

Donne's God, in Cowell's term then, *subtracts* 'all but love' from his 'lawes': He severs his severity.

This has been a long, and in all probability a rather tedious explication of a sonnet. What is a man whose salvation is still in agonised doubt doing fussing around with this witty business about wills? This, I think, is the answer. First of all, because God does: or rather, because St Paul says he does. Donne's sonnet shares one thing with Paul's Epistle to the Galatians: both hinge crucially around that invisible pun on the word 'testament'.[57]

Perhaps a more striking reason, though, is the extent to which it reveals the way in which English common law, even though Donne no longer practised it in 1609–10, cuts right across the general civilian terms of the Continental theologians and participates in debates on ownership and possession very present in those years. Coke's report on Calvin's Case, for example and the debate about the Scottish post-nati and their property rights, wander directly into issues of conquest in Scottish law. Just as the Virgin Mary is to make a dissension, as reoccupying claim of lawful ejection, on the estate of Eden, so the godly in the succeeding stanza of *The Litanie* acquire their residency visas for Heaven confirmed by the Heavenly Croydon: angels, we learn, are 'Native in heavns faire Palaces, / Where we shall be but denizen'd by thee' (like the Dutch in seventeenth-century Norwich).[58] Our conception of early modern heaven, perhaps, needs rethinking through the readings on uses, wills, testaments and jointures, and needs to be redescribed in more subtle and flexible terminology than as a version of the patriarchial Establishment. That this is not an idle claim, is shown, I think, by the fact that this sort of interpretation – the slow bringing of specifically legal exegesis to bear on poetry – was a skill that developed at just about the time Donne was studying at Oxford. Alberico Gentili, the Protestant Italian professor of civil law at Oxford (though he spent most of the time picking up money for opinions

---

[56] Sir Robert Brooke, *La Graunde Abridgement* (London, 1576), sigs. Aiir–Aiiv; John Rastell, *Les termes de la ley: or, Certaine difficult and obscure Words and Termes of the Common Lawes of the Realme expounded* (London, 1629), sigs. A5–A5v; J. H. Baker, *Manual of Law French* (Aldershot: Avebury, 1979), p. 43; Randle Cotgrave, *A Dictionarie of the French and English Tongues* (London, 1611), sig. Biir.

[57] *Editor's note:* This part of the argument should be developed further, but there is a lacuna in the typescript, and I have been unable to reconstruct it. It is perhaps worth quoting some of the remaining text: '"Testament" is a term fundamental to reformation exegesis and to the development of covenant theology. Paul, with an eclectic appeal to his text, the Greek Old Testament, has been talking about God's various promises to Israel in terms of covenant [. . .] This is an issue Donne at once opens and to some degree avoids. 'Let all healing grace *revive* what law and letter kill' leaves a position open to the general Augustinian view (confirmed at Trent); its distance from the language of imputation seems to me quite audible. So by attending to the legal metaphor, we may be able to get some purchase on Donne's credo.'

[58] Donne, 'The Litanie', stanza 6, lines 48–9, in *Donne's Poetical Works*, ed. by Grierson, I, p. 340.

down in London), is perhaps the best example. The *Lectiones virgilianae variae liber* (1603) recounts for his son, Robert (aged 11), their discussion of Virgil from a legal point of view over the last four years. Finally, there is some justification, I think, for feeling that Donne, like Virgil, might in any event be a specially hard case. And this would require us, I guess, to say that we thought Donne not just 'intelligent', or 'learned' or 'various' or wide-ranging' but difficult. For it is certainly true that readers do not always stay to explore what Donne's words mean. Indeed, one needs to be the sort of reader Nietzsche claimed he wanted even to begin the task:

> I admit that you need one thing above all in order to practise the requisite *art* of reading, a thing which nowadays people have been so good at forgetting – and so it will be for some time before my writings are 'readable' – , you almost need to be a cow for this one thing and certainly *not* a 'modern man': it is *rumination*. . . .[59]

All Donne's contemporaries knew he was difficult, but nowadays this difficulty is more often explored as an insecure, nervously aggressive social attitude on Donne's part than as a problem susceptible to philology. The contrast should be an unreal one: words are the first things that give poems tone. It is easy, of course, to hear Donne's tone, and generally speaking only outcrops of mistaken decency on the part of editors (as when Dame Helen Gardner decides that Donne didn't really *want* to write a lesbian love-letter)[60] occasionally get in the way of it. It is even easy, after a while, to hear what we might call 'Inns of Court attitude' in, say, Marston or Donne – as easy, almost, as it is to hear a similar self-proclamatory, rebel effect in the music of the black Los Angeles band Niggaz With Attitude. This tone, this attitude, is in one sense of the word, difficult: the sense would be one not far distant from that of 'a difficult child' today. Difficulties of this sort are not always unpopular, and pleading (for *loquendum ut vulgus sentiendum ut docti*) Donne elides. The most eloquent of sinners pleads in fustian.

To worry that Donne's words are difficult is not quite the truism it sounds: Donne's elegists dwell on his words, in a way that the early tributes to Shakespeare or Fletcher or Jonson never did. 'Did'st thou dispense,' asks Carew in the greatest of the elegies, 'Through all our language, both the words and sense?'[61] Another, Jasper Mayne, praising the gesture and carriage, the

[59] Friedrich Nietzsche, *On the Genealogy of Morality*, ed. by Keith Ansell-Pearson, trans. Carol Diethe (Cambridge: Cambridge University Press, 1994), p. 10.

[60] See John Donne, *The Elegies and The Songs and Sonnets*, ed. by Helen Gardner (Oxford: Clarendon Press, 1965), p. xlvi: 'in spite of its appearance in the first edition of Donne's poems and its inclusion in the manuscripts of Group II, ['Sappho to Philaenis'] is too uncharacteristic of Donne in theme, treatment, and style to be accepted as unquestionably his.'

[61] Thomas Carew, 'An Elegie upon the death of the Deane of Pauls, D'. Iohn Donne', lines 9–10, in *Donne's Poetical Works*, ed. by Grierson, I, p. 378.

'speaking action' of Donne's preaching, as one that 'could divide the heart, and conscience touch', praised it the more for the way that this delivery was subordinated to the sense.[62] Words, he says simply, were at the heart of Donne's 'deepe Divinity'; such was their charm, their mystery, their penetration that 'eare was all our sense'.[63] (Sir Lucius Cary has the same idea: 'None was so marble, but whil'st him he heares, / His Soule so long dwelt only in his eares').[64] And Mayne goes on to contrast this depth and power of the word in Donne with the rant of puritan cushion-bangers:

> Not like our Sonnes of Zeale, who to reforme
> Their hearers, fiercely at the pulpit storme,
> And beate the cushion into worse estate,
> Then if they did conclude it reprobate,
> Who can out pray the glasse, then lay about
> Till all Predestination be runne out.
> And from the point such tedious uses draw,
> Their repetitions would make Gospell, Law.[65]

What Mayne complains of is, in a profounder sense, Donne's achievement in *Holy Sonnet XII*: he makes Gospel, Law. He does so not in the angry denunciations of the Puritan lecturer, but by pleading as eloquently as he can the impossible claims of humanity before a divine judge.

---

[62] Jasper Mayne, 'On D^r. Donnes death', lines 59, 62, in *Donne's Poetical Works*, ed. by Grierson, I, p. 384.

[63] Mayne, 'On D^r. Donnes death', lines 53, 56, pp. 383, 384.

[64] Lucius Cary, 'An Elegie on D^r. Donne', lines 29–30, in *Donne's Poetical Works*, ed. by Grierson, I, p. 381.

[65] Mayne, 'On D^r. Donnes death', lines 65–72, p. 384.

Chapter 3

MR SECRETARY DONNE: THE YEARS WITH SIR THOMAS EGERTON

LOUIS A. KNAFLA

THE basic work on Donne's career as Secretary to Sir Thomas Egerton, Lord Keeper, and his relations with the Egerton family, remains R. C. Bald's *John Donne. A Life*. This essay will advance Bald's work, and the rich scholarship that has succeeded it, with a detailed examination of the culture and working of the environment of York House, the extended Egerton family and its coterie, and the legal and political cultures and structures of the age. It will use Pierre Bourdieu's concept of *habitus* to locate and explore the mental and physical world into which John Donne stepped in the autumn of 1597. The sources used are not only the customary letters to, from, and about Donne that abound in the printed literature; they also include the records of the Chancery, the More papers at the Folger and the Ellesmere papers at the Huntington libraries, and manuscripts at the Bodleian and the British Library. These sources can be used incisively within the contexts above to understand Donne's working relationships in 1597–1602 and later years.

Firstly, the essay will provide a more complete understanding of Donne as Egerton's secretary within the ambit of Lincoln's Inn society and the reform programme of the new Lord Keeper. Secondly, it will explore Donne's professional relationship with Egerton as Baron Ellesmere, Lord Chancellor, from 1603 to 1617, which will include critical political choices that scholars of Donne have not yet fully addressed within the political history of the era. Finally, it will attempt to place Donne, the professional man, more clearly within the legal and political culture of church and state in the Jacobean age.

It has been argued, more recently, that Donne's professional life was shaped by his experiences with the Catholic nobility, and that such associations explain his entry into the Egerton circle. The evidence, however, does not support this revisionist interpretation.[1] A close knowledge of the Egerton

---

[1] Dennis Flynn, *John Donne and the Ancient Catholic Nobility* (Bloomington: Indiana University Press, 1995).

family and its religious and political circles suggests that Donne's professional life was determined more by a Protestant tradition of private and public service than a Catholic one. Given the rich and detailed work on Donne, a historian ventures into his career through a minefield of literary studies. This essay has been informed, but not determined, by that literature. It strives, on the whole, not to revisit Donne the poet or prose writer, but Donne the man as he attempted to work through the labyrinth of Jacobean law and politics in search of a career that would bring wealth and status. This essay is prepared from research on the history of Sir Thomas Egerton, and the Egerton family, patronage, the Inns of Court, and the central common law and equity courts of late Elizabethan and Jacobean England. It will attempt to place the Donne–Egerton professional and personal relationship, and Donne, the professional man, into a more realistic framework within the legal, political, and religious institutions and culture of that era.

The proposition that our knowledge and understanding of John Donne can be enriched by a closer and more detailed examination of the legal and political culture in which he lived and worked stems from Jeremy Maule's work on 'Donne and the Words of the Law'. Just as Maule argues that 'Donne's intellectual interest in English law has been underestimated', as well as 'the degree to which it continued to help structure his thought in his later years as a clergyman',[2] I will argue that his work and associations in the household of the Lord Keeper contributed to shape his political and religious choices and may have proved instrumental in the attitudes and positions that coalesced in his last years as Dean of St Paul's.

FAMILY AND BACKGROUND: EARLY YEARS TO 1591

Some of Donne's family background is important to this essay.[3] His mother Elizabeth, a devout Catholic, was the youngest daughter of John Heywood of Coventry, writer, and Joan, daughter of John Rastell, writer and printer. Rastell was the husband of Elizabeth, daughter of Sir John More, Justice of the King's Bench, and a sister of Sir Thomas More. More's family remained Catholic for more than two centuries. Of their descendants, four men and four women of Donne's contemporaries were of Roman Catholic orders.[4] His grandfather John Heywood fled to Louvain with his wife in 1564 and spent his last years there with his brother-in-law William Rastell, Justice of the Queen's Bench, who had fled to Louvain for refuge. William's brother Thomas, a former monk, was executed in 1574 for saying mass in a house in Cow's Lane near Donne's. William's brother Richard, a Catholic of Lincoln's Inn who was a prothonotary of the Queen's Bench, died in 1570,

---

[2] Jeremy Maule, 'Donne and the Words of the Law', Chapter One above.
[3] Uncontroverted facts have been taken from Bald.
[4] Bald, pp. 21–6.

and his widow married William Parry, a double agent and MP who was executed for treason in 1584. Richard's second son John, a devout Catholic, was a friend of the Donne family.

Two of Donne's uncles, Ellis and Jasper, became Jesuits. Jasper became vice-prefect of the English Jesuit mission in summer 1581, after Edmund Campion was imprisoned and Robert Persons fled. He was captured and imprisoned in the Clink in December 1583, and tried with five other priests for treason in the Queen's Bench in February 1583/4 and found guilty. Jasper was in the Tower of London for a year, receiving visits from his mother and perhaps from Donne himself. He was reported in November 1582 to have converted 228 people in Staffordshire to Catholicism in three months.[5] Exiled to France with nineteen other priests in January 1584/5, he died at Naples in 1598. All had been devotees of Sir Thomas More. Two of More's grandchildren, Dorothy and Margaret, became nuns of Louvain.

The elder John Donne, born c.1535, came from a Catholic family in a strongly Catholic London parish. He completed his apprenticeship in ironmongering in 1557, leasing a house in Bread Street owned by the Ironmonger's Company. He married Elizabeth Heywood in spring 1563. Rising in the Company's ranks, he bought property in Oxford near Hart Hall, in a Catholic neighbourhood, where his married sister lived and where he sent his two sons. He prospered as the business manager of the widow of Thomas Lewin, one of the most important ironmongers of the age and a prominent Catholic.[6] Donne's father died in January 1576, leaving his wealth valued at £3500–£4000 to his widow, children, and charities.[7] The surviving children were Elizabeth (d. 1577), Anne (d. 1616), John, Henry, Mary (d. 1581), and Katherine (d. 1581), all born in Bread Street. In June, Elizabeth remarried John Syminges, a wealthy landed Oxford doctor of physic, past-president of the Royal College of Physicians, and widower with three children. He too was a staunch Catholic who was never investigated because of his position at court as a doctor for noble Catholic families and foreign dignitaries.[8] They lived within the parish of Trinity the Less, a Catholic enclave, until moving to St Bartholomew the Less, where her sister had lived, in autumn 1583.[9]

Donne's sister Anne married Avery Copley of Batley, Yorks, a barrister of Lincoln's Inn, aged thirty, in late 1585 at Syminges' house in Bartholomew Close. Copley, a Catholic, was called to the bar in 1583 and signed the Oath of Association in 1584.[10] Living beyond his means before and after marriage, he

---

[5] PRO, State Papers Domestic [SP], Elizabeth I, 155/96.

[6] Gosse I, pp. 10–11.

[7] PRO, PCC 56 Pyckering, proved 8 February 1576.

[8] Baird W. Whitlock, 'John Syminges, A Poet's Step-Father', *NQ* 200 (1954): 421–4.

[9] Baird D. Whitlock, 'The Heredity and Childhood of John Donne', *NQ*, new ser. 6:7 (1959): 257–62, and 6:9 (1959): 348–53.

[10] *The Egerton Papers*, ed. by John Payne Collier, The Camden Society (London, 1840), pp. 108–11.

ran through Anne's dowry of £500 in addition to her mother's loan of £600.[11] He died in January 1590/1, heavily in debt, leaving Anne with a small child. She moved in with her mother. A Chancery suit brought against her and her mother by Copley's father and elder brother defeated them.[12] Elizabeth lost at least £1000 through these suits. In the meantime, Syminges had died intestate in July 1588. Elizabeth administered the estate, and moved across the Thames to St Saviour's, Southwark, known as 'Little Rome', where she was presented and fined for recusancy on 28 September 1589.[13] Her third marriage was to Richard Rainsford, a gentleman of Southwark, a heavily Catholic area, in late 1590.[14] Syminges had placed £400 from his lands and tenements in trust for her before his death, but the documentation was not completed. Elizabeth and Richard sued for it in the Court of Requests, but lost, thereby precluding her from executing all the terms of his will.[15]

Donne, born between 24 January and 19 June 1572, was educated in French and Latin by a Catholic tutor, and, with his brother Henry, matriculated to Hart Hall, Oxford, on 23 October 1584. Hart Hall produced some notable Catholics. In Oxford he met Wykehamists Henry Wotton, John Owen, John Hoskyns, and John Davies of Hereford, plus Richard Baker, Hugh Holland, and Richard Martin. Donne distinguished himself. But as he would have had to subscribe to the Thirty-Nine Articles and take the Oath of Supremacy in his fourth year, he left after three.[16] He probably went to Cambridge for the cultural and intellectual life. An avid and voracious reader, he became skilled in formal logic and rhetoric, and studied Hebrew, canon law, and medicine.

We have no information on Donne from 1589 to spring 1591. Perhaps he travelled abroad as other young men of that age. He could have been in the expedition against Lisbon in 1589 with Drake and Norreys.[17] He could also have visited his ailing uncle Jasper in Naples. When Donne wrote to his mother upon Anne's death in 1616, he spoke of her love and raising him: 'you, from whom I had that education, which must make my fortune'.[18] He attributed no role to his two step-fathers, but befriended Anne's second husband William Lyly, gentleman of Southwark and a Protestant member of a Catholic family.

[11] Copley v. Copley and Rainsford, PRO, C2, Elizabeth I (November 1591), C10/41.
[12] Ibid.; the commission is in C33/86/126v.
[13] Baird W. Whitlock, 'The Family of John Donne, 1588–91', *NQ* 205 (383).
[14] Baird W. Whitlock, 'The Family of John Donne, 1588–91', *NQ* new ser. 8:10 (1960): 282–3, 348–53.
[15] Alfred Rainsford, 'Abstracts from Rainsford Documents in the Public Record Office', *NQ* 150 (1926): 345–9.
[16] Bald, pp. 42–6.
[17] R. C. Bald, 'Three Metaphysical Epigrams', *PQ* 16 (1937): 402–5.
[18] *A Collection of Letters, made by Sr Tobie Mathews K^t*, ed. by John Donne (London, 1660), p. 325.

EARLY CONNECTIONS: THE LEGAL QUARTER OF LONDON, 1591–4

Donne spent a year at Thavies Inn from May 1591, and entered Lincoln's Inn on 6 May 1592. The Catholic families of More, Roper, Stubbes, Rastell and Heywood had belonged to the society. He met Christopher Brooke, his lifelong friend, Brooke's younger brother Samuel and cousin John, Rowland and Thomas Woodward, and Thomas Egerton Jr who entered in the same year. While his satires refer to him going to court and out into the wider metropolis, the considerable legal knowledge that he demonstrated later in life must have been acquired at Lincoln's Inn. Life at the inns was well known for advancing learning with social skills. Nicholas Hilliard, whom he esteemed, painted a miniature of him in 1591, and stamped him as a connoisseur. His clothes were considered of a fashionable cut.

The first two years there were of plague. The dining hall was closed for half of each year. He was appointed Master of the Revels on 6 February 1592/3, when the season was over, and did not keep the Easter vacation, staying in London. His verse letters refer to empty theatres and hell in the streets, and on 19 June he received part of his inheritance of £232 16s 8d at the Guildhall. He stayed for the Easter 1594 vacation, spent the summer in London, and returned for the autumn vacation where he was chosen steward of Christmas but declined, paying the fine of 26s 8d. He appeared no more in the records.

While in Holborn, Donne's mother appointed tutors in mathematics and the 'Liberal Sciences', as well as 'Principles of the *Romish church*': works of theology, philosophy, politics, chroniclers and poets.[19] Donne confirmed this in 'Satyre I' when he referred to studying in the small chamber that he shared with Christopher Brooke who became a practicing lawyer. A Catholic, with Catholic tutors, he was barred from participation in public life; bestowed with intellectual curiosity, he would have questioned his religion. These were the years of the third Jesuit mission led by Henry Garnet and the poet Robert Southwell. They both arrived in 1586 and, in November 1591, were confronted with proclamations to search for and arrest them. Southwell's *Humble Supplication to her Majestie* was written to defend English Catholics and their missionary priests who were loyal to Queen Elizabeth, and Donne probably was at a meeting with him in late December to discuss the laws and restrictions on Catholics, as he related later in *Pseudo-Martyr*.[20] Southwell's martyrdom was repeated two years later by that of William Harrington.

Henry, Donne's brother, died in 1593. In May a young Yorkshire priest, William Harrington, was arrested in his chambers, and both were sent to the

---

[19] Izaak Walton, 'The Life of Dr John Donne', in *The Lives of John Donne, Sir Henry Wotton, Richard Hooker, George Herbert and Robert Sanderson* (Oxford: Oxford University Press, 1927), p. 24.

[20] John Donne, *Pseudo-Martyr* (London, 1610), p. 46.

Clink. Moved to Newgate for trial, Henry died of the plague there within a few days, and Harrington was tried, convicted, and executed on 18 February 1594.[21] Donne and his sister split Henry's inheritance on 11 April 1594: £149 5s each. Altogether, he received about £750.[22] Anne's husband, Lyly, in his early forties, was fluent in French and Italian. Secretary to Sir Edward Stafford, ambassador to Paris in 1583, he reported on English Catholics and the French civil war, returning at the end of 1590.[23]

Donne made a distinction between Jesuits and Catholics and, like Harrington and Southwell, was not of Robert Persons' persuasion to uphold papal supremacy and work for a Catholic succession.[24] As he noted later, these proactive activities and his studies caused him to renounce the Roman church. Those who tried to determine his understanding (his tutors) retarded his fortune, bred scandal, and endangered his 'spirituall reputation'.[25] According to Walton,[26] Donne systematically studied the works of Cardinal Bellarmine,[27] and took his annotated copies to Antony Rudd, Dean of Gloucester. Rudd was appointed by the Privy Council to discuss religious doctrine with young recusant converts in 1592–4. Donne's conversion, therefore, may have occurred in 1594.

A strong cynicism of religion was revealed in Donne's second 'Satyre II', and knowledge of Bellarmine was expressed later in his sermons. This was the period in which he composed elegies and love lyrics, demonstrating his disregard for conventional attitudes. Richard Baker later wrote of Donne in these years as 'a great visiter of Ladies, a great frequenter of playes, a great writer of conceited Verses'.[28] He enjoyed drama, and later his friend Sir William Cornwallis would write of the idle time they spent 'at the playes'.[29] He also wrote poems dedicated to his group of friends. Donne gave Rowland Woodward a copy of his *Pseudo-Martyr*, and according to a verse epistle of Thomas Woodward, who imitated Donne's manner, his was the dominant voice. The verse epistles, with their keen observation and savage wit, carried over to his elegies. According to Ben Jonson, they were all written by age twenty-five (1597).[30] Thus the first two satires, most of the elegies, verse letters, and some songs and sonnets, were written at Lincoln's Inn. Unlike

[21] Father John Morris, 'The Martyrdom of William Harrington', *The Month*, 20 (1874): 411–23.
[22] Baird W. Whitlock, 'The Orphanage Accounts of John Donne, Ironmonger', *Guildhall Miscellany* 4 (February 1955): 22–9.
[23] Whitlock, 'Family of Donne': 380–6.
[24] Robert Persons, *A Conference about the Next Succession* (London, 1594).
[25] Donne, *Pseudo-Martyr*, Preface.
[26] Walton, *Lives*, pp. 25–6.
[27] Robert Francis Bellarmine, Cardinal, *Disputationes de controversiis Christinae Fiedei, adversus huius temporis haereticos*, 3 vols (Ingolstadt, 1586–93).
[28] Sir Richard Baker, *Chronicles* (London, 1643), Part II, p. 156.
[29] Bodleian Library, Tanner MS 306, fol. 237.
[30] *Ben Jonson*, ed. by C. H. Herford and Percy and Evelyn Simpson, 11 vols (Oxford: Clarendon Press, 1925–52) I, p. 135.

Brooke, he put off what he might do, and became contemptuous of 'men which chuse / Law practise for meere gaine'.[31]

YEARS OF SEARCH AND TRAVEL, 1595–7

Elizabeth Donne and her third husband Richard Rainsford had left England for Antwerp by 10 September 1595. An Exchequer inquisition of 1598, to investigate the possessions of fugitive Catholics, inquired of a statute staple of £2000 granted by Charles Somerset to John Syminges and passed to Rainsford by his marriage to Syminges' widow.[32] It had been forfeited to the Queen because Rainsford went beyond the seas without her approval.[33] He probably met Thomas Egerton Jr's younger brother John when he matriculated to Lincoln's Inn in March 1595. Neither one of the young Egerton men prepared for a career in law, but John was the more studious, attaining a BA degree from Brasenose College, the college of his father, in 1594.[34]

Donne, tiring of his legal studies, awoke to the adventures of 1596. Preparations were made for a major expedition against Spain, the fleet under Lord Howard of Effingham and the army under the Earl of Essex. Donne's friend Henry Wotton was one of Essex's secretaries, and Donne joined as a gentleman volunteer with hopes of booty and gallantry. The fleet sailed from Plymouth for Cadiz on 6 June, and straggled back with its booty in August. Returning to the Inn where he wrote verse, he volunteered again for the Azores expedition that resulted in an attack on the Spanish fleet at Ferrol in 1597. When Essex took the town of Villa Franca, Thomas Egerton was among those knighted. Like Donne, the Lord Keeper's heir was imbued with Essex, and took leave from his newly appointed post of deputy-baron of the Exchequer of Chester to volunteer for Essex's expedition. The fleet returned in late October. Once the shine was off the life of a gentleman volunteer, Donne, turning twenty-five, had to face the world of reality.

In the early to mid 1590s, Donne wrote his 'Paradoxes' within the context of life at the inns of court. At the time, he was 'desirous to hide them'.[35] He would not have wanted to show his new employer numbers four and six: 'That Nature is our worst Guide', and 'That the guifts of the body are better than those of the mind or of Fortune'.[36] But the Lord Keeper would have agreed with Donne's occasional discussions of the law and its weaknesses, especially the growing minority view that customary usage makes law binding, and

---

[31] Bald, pp. 74–9, at p. 79.

[32] PRO, E 178/1383.

[33] PRO, Privy Seal Docquet Book, Index 6744. It was remitted by James I on 26 May 1606.

[34] *Brasenose College Register, 1509–1909* (Oxford, 1909) I, p. 75.

[35] Evelyn M. Simpson, *A Study of the Prose Works of John Donne*, 2nd edition (Oxford: Clarendon Press, 1948), p. 317.

[36] John Donne, *Paradoxes and Problems*, edited by Helen Peters (Oxford: Clarendon Press, 1980), pp. 6–9 and 11–14, respectively. All references to these works are from this edition.

makes law good law (VIII.37–8). He also would have shared Donne's mindset on 'discord': that law is waged from doubts caused by discord (IX.21–4); that there is a struggle in life between peace and unity, and discord and war (IX.5–13); and that in the present age men who harbour discord outnumber those who harbour concord, and are increasing hourly (IX.28–31).

SECRETARY TO THE LORD KEEPER, 1597–1602

It will be useful to sketch the household into which John Donne entered in November 1597. Employed as one of the Lord Keeper's three working secretaries, his duties would have included scheduling, meeting and greeting guests, legal research, and drafting memoranda for the wide range of the Lord Keeper's public, rather than private, businesses. Household and family finance accounts, estate management and stewardship, and handling the large number of estate agents and agrarian and commercial interests were the main domains of secretaries Henry Jones and John Panton. Donne joined this inner circle. He would have become fully aware of the Lord Keeper's personal tastes and dislikes, his cultural, religious, and political ideas, and his associates, friends, and contacts. The space between them would also have been quite clearly drawn. Egerton was a workaholic, a man who demanded complete loyalty, devotion to detail and accuracy in work, and who did not suffer fools. For those who lived with him, he wore his views on his sleeve, and expected them to be acknowledged and appreciated. To obtain a full under-standing of Donne's work as secretary, and some insight into his mindset in these years, it is necessary to explore life at York House, and the cultural and intellectual space in which he worked.

The Religious Culture

There is no evidence to suggest that the Lord Keeper would accept into his service a young Catholic. Egerton's whole professional career from that of a legal officer of the crown as Solicitor-General 1581–92 to Attorney-General 1592–4, an MP in the 1580s, Master of the Rolls 1594–6, and Lord Keeper and privy councillor from 1596, was based on wreaking havoc upon Catholics. He was born into a Catholic family in 1540, tutored by Catholics at Hart Hall and Brasenose College 1556–9, and entered Furnivall's and Lincoln's Inn as a Catholic in 1560 and 1561, respectively. After two suspensions from Lincoln's Inn for his faith, he officially converted in 1572 in the wake of the Northern Rebellion of 1568–9, the excommunication of Queen Elizabeth in 1570, the Ridolfi plot of 1571, and the Bartholomew's Day Massacre of 1572. Making a public renunciation of the Old Faith, he was certified as an Anglican by the Bishop of London.[37] Called to the bar in 1572, he was later cited in 1577 for

---

[37] *The Records of the Honourable Society of Lincoln's Inn: The Black Books*, ed. by W. P. Baildon and James Douglas Walker, 5 vols (London: Lincoln's Inn, 1897–1968) I, 371–2.

refusing to attend divine service. He appeared and made a full reconciliation.[38] The key figure seems to have been Laurence Chaderton, appointed Bishop of Chester that year (the year of his step-father Anthony Grosvenor's death), who, with Henry Stanley, Earl of Derby, and Robert Dudley, Earl of Leicester, had taken an early interest in his career.[39]

Egerton's final conversion in 1577 was sincere. His two step-brothers, Richard and Robert Ravens, were converted by Chaderton shortly afterwards, and both became devout Anglican ministers.[40] Egerton later acquired a copy of Calvin's *Sermons*, translated by Arthur Golding and dedicated to Leicester, which he annotated, and noted works and items of Calvinist theology in the fly leaves of his legal texts and commonplace books.[41] He also made drafts of how a reformed Calvinist church would operate within the traditional institutions of England's church and state.[42] He maintained friendship with his two older Catholic colleagues of Lincoln's Inn, Francis Thynne and Ferdinando Pulton, whom he continued to patronize for their research and publications.[43] He also remained close to his step-mother, Mary Ravenscroft, a devout Catholic to her death in 1594, for whom he obtained leniency in the exercise of the recusancy laws.[44]

The new convert became the major prosecutor of Catholics accused of treason in the 1580s and 1590s. He played a full-time role in the investigations of William Vaux, Baron Harrowden, Sir Thomas Tresham, Robert Catesby and Edmund Campion, Henry Percy, Earl of Northumberland, William Davison, Anthony Babington and Mary, Queen of Scots, Philip Howard, Earl of Arundel, Lord John Perrot, and Dr Roderigo Lopez.[45] In addition, he was involved in investigating Catholics with whom Donne was acquainted in the 1590s: Henry Garnet, William Harrington, John Heywood, Richard Rainsford, and Robert Southwell.[46] Moreover, he appointed household servants and family relations to hunt out and investigate Catholic recusants in Cheshire and the Welsh borderlands, 1583–94.[47] If Donne was interested,

---

[38] *Miscellany XII*, Catholic Record Society, vol. 22 (London, 1921), p. 101; British Library [BL], Lansdowne MS 109, f. 11.

[39] Louis A. Knafla, 'The "Country" Chancellor: The Patronage of Sir Thomas Egerton, Baron Ellesmere', in *Patronage in Late Renaissance England*, ed. by French R. Fogle and Louis A. Knafla (Los Angeles: William Andrews Clark Library, 1983), pp. 38–9.

[40] W. E. B. Whittaker, 'Ravenscrofts of Bretton and Broadlane in Hawarden', unpublished paper, Flintshire Record Office, Flint.

[41] *Sermons of Maister John Calvin*, trans. by Arthur Golding (London, 1580); Henry E. Huntington Library [HEH], Rare Book [RB] 98692; and the study of the marginalia in his law books: Louis A. Knafla, 'The Law Studies of an Elizabethan Student', *HLQ* 32 (1969): 221–40.

[42] HEH, Ellesmere MS 470.

[43] Ellesmere MSS 1203, 1963–4, 2979, 26/A/6, 34/B/11–12.

[44] SP, Elizabeth I, 12/164/183, and Ellesmere MS 415.

[45] Louis A. Knafla, *Law and Politics in Jacobean England* (Cambridge, 1977), pp. 15–21.

[46] *State Trials*, ed. by William Cobbett and T. B. Howell (London, 1809) I, *passim*.

[47] The men were Ralph Egerton, Richard Grosvenor, Richard Harding, Sir John Holcroft,

he had ready access to the Lord Keeper's files and lists of papists on watch, including one on English 'fugitives' in Louvain in 1576 that included Jasper Heywood.[48]

The new Attorney-General of 1592 can be considered one of the architects of the anti-Catholic movement in late Elizabethan England. Arraigning Campion for encompassing the deprivation of the Queen and raising an insurrection as his first order of business, Egerton had him racked and manacled to the extent that he could not hold up his arms in court to plead, and was kept in irons until his execution.[49] Donne warned of John Hammond, one of Campion's interrogators, in 'Satyre V' (84–7). Campion was a friend of William Harrington, Henry Donne's roommate who was executed in 1594. John Donne's friend Southwell was left hanging in manacles for hours at a time, ten times, in 1592, noting the zeal of Richard Younge.[50] Thomas Bell, the seminary priest, was hung upside down in manacles for three days in 1592, finally succumbing and informing on the recusants and priests of Lancashire.[51] Egerton, after becoming Attorney-General, organized the future system for the detection and examination of Catholics in 1593,[52] and encouraged torture when evidence was not forthcoming.[53] Dr Roderigo Lopez, the Queen's physician, who was implicated in a Catholic plot against her in 1594, was so terrified of being handed over to the Attorney-General that he invented incriminating facts to escape being racked and manacled.[54] It made no difference to the Crown whether the trial was before a special commission, the Star Chamber, or Queen's Bench.[55]

Richard Younge, one of Egerton's trusted servants and commissioned investigators, is found in the records of the Privy Council to have more warrants to torture felons, priests, and recusants than any other official in the 1590s.[56] A JP and Customer of the Port of London, he acquired his techniques

Roger Puleston, Roger and Thomas Wilbraham, and Richard Younge. For their work, see Roger B. Manning, 'The Making of a Protestant Aristocracy: The Ecclesiastical Commissioners of the Diocese of Chester, 1550–98', *Bulletin of the Institute of Historical Research* 49 (1976): 60–79.

[48] Collier, *Egerton Papers*, p. 65. See also Ellesmere MSS 2031–2084.

[49] *State Trials* I, pp. 1070–1.

[50] *Unpublished Documents relating to the English Martyrs, 1584–1603*, ed. by J. H. Pollen, Catholic Record Society (London, 1908) V, pp. 212, 329–30.

[51] *Lives of the English Martyrs*, ed. by E. H. Burton and J. H. Pollen, Catholic Record Society, 1st series (London, 1914) II, p. 570; and SP, Elizabeth I, 12/243/51, 71.

[52] Lansdowne MS 72, fols. 125–9; BL, Harleian MS 6996, fol. 19; SP, Elizabeth I, 12/257/1, 12/232/45; PRO, Exchequer Miscellaneous, Elizabeth I, 159/406.

[53] Harleian MS 6996, fol. 50; SP, Elizabeth I, 12/230/57, 12/243/1.

[54] SP, Elizabeth I, 12/247/97; PRO (King's Bench Plea Rolls), KB 8/52/10.

[55] Anthony Babington and his co-conspirators of 1586, as well as Lord John Perrot in 1592, were racked before being tried at King's Bench: KB 8/48/24 and KB 8/50/1, respectively. This was noted by Robert Persons in his later published *The Jesuits Memorial for the Intended Reformation of England under their First Popish Prince* (London, 1690), p. 249.

[56] James Heath, *Torture and English Law. An Administrative and Legal History from the*

for examining thieves on the Thames waterfront, often in his own house.[57] According to Southwell, he had 'complete license to torture' at the London bridewell.[58] According to John Gerard, he was the chief policeman of heretical and treasonous activities in the London metropolis.[59] His colleague Robert Beale, a clerk of the Privy Council and one of Egerton's later Chancery officials, was accused by Archbishop John Whitgift of using torture in the courts of the County Palatine of Chester that the Lord Keeper presided over.[60]

Younge was said to have caused many deaths by his interrogations. On one occasion a casket was left on his doorstep with the corpse of a victim.[61] As the Lord Keeper penned on a bill of information at York House on 14 February 1599/1600, perhaps with Donne at his side, Catholic recusants were 'natural vipers, ready to eat out the belly of your mother'.[62]

The Legal Culture

The Lord Keeper had been a devoted student at Lincoln's Inn. Matriculating in the autumn of 1561, he was one of those students who dedicated his years to the academic study of all law, common and civil. Once he made peace with God and State, he became the Inn's steward in 1578, Bencher and Reader in 1579, Governor in 1580, double Reader in 1585, and Treasurer in 1587.[63] He went on to prefer the young men of more than thirty families connected by blood, work, or locale for admission.[64] The lawyers who worked for Egerton in his affairs, and on his investigatory royal commissions, were Lincoln's Inn men well known to Donne. Thirty-seven of them, excluding Donne, had been at Lincoln's Inn in the period of 1580–1605.[65] Fifteen of them alone, in addition to eight of their elder relations, were with Donne at the funeral ceremony of Sir Thomas Egerton Jr at Chester Cathedral on 26 September 1599.[66]

Plantagenets to the Stuarts (London: Greenwood, 1982), printed in the Appendix, pp. 214–21. See also Ellesmere MSS 2118–2130.

[57] Heath, *Torture*, p. 138.

[58] *Unpublished Documents* V, p. 128, letter to Aquaviva in January 1590.

[59] John Gerard, *The Autobiography of an Elizabethan*, trans. by Philip Caraman (London: Longmans, Green and Co., 1951), p. 68.

[60] John Strype, *The life and acts of the Most Reverend Father in God, John Whitgift D. D.*, 3 vols (Oxford: Clarendon Press) I, 401–2.

[61] Ellesmere MS 2101, 2103, 2107, 2110, 2114.

[62] Folger Shakespeare Library [FSL], MS X.d.351, fol. 14v.

[63] *The Black Books* I, 404–15, 423, 429, 432, 440, 460–1.

[64] *The Records of the Honourable Society of Lincoln's Inn. Admissions* (London, 1896) I, 74–125.

[65] Ralph and William Brereton, Ranulph Crewe, Robert Davies, John Dutton, John and Thomas Egerton Jr, Thomas Foster, Richard and Thomas Grosvenor, Thomas Hanmer, George and John Hope, Edward Hughes, John Jeffreys, Henry Jones, Thomas and Urian Leigh, William Marbury, Arthur, Henry and George Mainwaring, John, Roger and Thomas Mostyn, John Panton, John Parkinson, Edward and Roger Puleston, George, Ralph, Thomas and William Ravenscroft, John Thelwall, and Richard, Ralph and Roger Wilbraham.

[66] Harleian MS 2129, fol. 67, printed by Bald, pp. 105–6.

Donne would have been well aware of Egerton's power of legal patronage. Lincoln's Inn men were receiving offices where the Lord Keeper had influence: in the Council of the Marches of Wales, the Palatine Courts of Chester, Chancery, Star Chamber, and in the departments of state.[67] He may have drafted many of the letters that are extant in the secretarial hand penned by Egerton's secretaries.[68] Donne wrote poems for family occasions, and wrote a prose account of the entertainments for Queen Elizabeth at York House in 1601 that Sir John Davies, the predecessor poet-lawyer at Egerton's household, had undoubtedly helped prepare.[69] Like Donne, Davies compiled recommendations for law reform, and his project in these years was a law reform program for Ireland.[70] Davies was disbarred in 1597 'forever' for brandishing a dagger and sword and making threats at dinner in Middle Temple hall. When the benchers refused to reinstate him, Egerton wrote them a testy letter, one that Donne may have drafted. Beginning with 'I doe somewhat marvell' why they did not reinstate him, 'I put you in mind to take some consideration, and expect some present satisfaction from you on this behalf.'[71] The benchers recanted, restoring Davies without ceremony.[72] Thus the young secretary would have seen how influence in the right hands could be exercised.

The York House of Donne's years was a centre of patronage, and it remained so for Egerton; so too were the households of his two aristocratic successors, the second and third earls of Bridgewater.[73] The Lord Keeper had been a voracious reader of classics, history, and philosophy at Oxford, and of religion, politics and science afterwards. He was also an avid book collector, and in these years was building the early stages of the Bridgewater Library that included works of geography, history, law, medicine, philosophy, science, and theology.[74] With a rapidly growing library, young Donne must have enjoyed being party to its acquisitions and development. Donne accompanied him on his frequent trips to the West Country, complete with travelling library.[75] He went with John Egerton on a commission from the Lord Keeper to visit the hospital of St John the Baptist, Chester, on 18 February 1600/1, with other

---

[67] Robert Ashley, 'In the Praise of Honor' (n.d.), Ellesmere MS 1117, fols. 2–3; and Tobias Shaw, 'Explicatio quaestionis controversae de abrogatione legum Mosis judicialium' (London, 1605), FSL MS V.a.6, fols. 2–3.

[68] Ellesmere MSS 48, 1401; Lansdowne MSS 157, 165; PRO, Patent MSS Ind. 17314–5.

[69] John Nichols, *The Progresses and Public Processions of Queen Elizabeth* (London, 1823) III, 581–6.

[70] Ellesmere MSS 76, 2522–23, 15076.

[71] HEH, Hastings MS 2522 (York House, 30 June 1601).

[72] J. Bruce Williamson, *The History of the Temple* (London: J. Murray, 1924), pp. 213–16.

[73] Louis A. Knafla, 'John Egerton, First Earl of Bridgewater (1579–1649)', and 'John Egerton, Second Earl of Bridgewater (1623–1686)', in the *New Dictionary of National Biography* (forthcoming).

[74] Knafla, ' "Country" Chancellor', pp. 57–62.

[75] HEH, display case, Gallery.

Egerton relatives and friends.[76] He also accompanied the Lord Keeper on trips to Pyrford. Egerton looked forward to escaping the teeming crowds and pollution of London, and his two favourite short-term getaways were Hounslow Heath and Pyrford. As he penned from More's residence, 'this barren place yieldeth me spare diet, good air, and convenient exercise'.[77] He longed for the rustic, spartan life, which encouraged his longer escapes to Dodleston cottage where he had been raised, and, after 1603, to Ellesmere lake and park.[78] It was at Dodleston that he met often with his converter, Laurence Chaderton, 'by your Lord's little table in your gallery', to plan preaching lectureships and an agenda for a Calvinist church and state.[79]

What must have weighed heavily on Donne, however, was the proactive religiosity of York House. These were the years, 1596–1602, when the new Lord Keeper was making his mark upon church and state. York House was becoming a conduit for writers and preachers against Rome. Egerton was subventing books and pamphlets against Rome, patronizing their authors, and promoting zealous Calvinist preachers into church livings across his counties. Donne, as his personal secretary, must have been in the middle of the stream, facilitating young authors and graduates with their journeys and drafting the correspondence of their patronage. According to John Dove, who Donne may have heard preach in London and at Paul's Cross, and/or read drafts of his dedicatory sermons at York House, the Lord Keeper was promoting hundreds of graduates (an exaggeration), well learned with preaching skills, to benefices across the country.[80] He may have met Thomas Bell, like himself, a former Catholic who could have been a Heywood. Bell, from Lancashire, had studied at Douay and Rome, and returned to Lancashire in 1581 as a Catholic priest. Arrested by one of Egerton's agents in 1592, after he recanted he spent the rest of his life writing anti-Catholic polemics. Seeing the Roman church as one that sponsored murder, war, corruption, wanton fornication, pride, and vanity, he saw the present age as the last chapter in the history of the rise and fall of Anti-Christ. Bell dedicated *The Survey of Popery* to Egerton in 1596,[81] with a work on usury. In his survey, Bell wrote scathingly of Jasper Heywood, accusing him of being a priest who lived like a baron. Bell's sponsorship was followed, in 1598–1602, by Edward Bulkeley, John Downame, John Golbourne, John

---

[76] Inner Temple [IT], MS 538, f. 29v (18 February 1601).
[77] *Calendar of the Manuscripts of the Most Honourable Marquess of Salisbury*, Historical Manuscripts Commission [HMC], Parts 6–21 (London, 1895–1970) IX, 1911 (dated 1599).
[78] Ellesmere MSS 503, 510.
[79] Ellesmere MS 75, fol. 1v. For the larger context, see John Morrill, *Cheshire, 1630–1660: County Government and Society during the English Revolution* (Oxford: Oxford University Press, 1974), pp. 17–19.
[80] John Dove, *A Sermon Preached at Paules Crosse* (London, 1597), HEH RB, item 212143, sigs. A3–A4. Dove lived in the household for a few years, where he wrote other sermons.
[81] HEH, RB 227009.

Lloyd, Gabriel Powell, Ralph Ravens, Hugh Roberts, Matthew Sutcliffe, and Andrew Willet.[82]

George Downame, son of William Downame, Bishop of Chester in Egerton's early years who may have helped his admission to Oxford, was a prebend of Chester who frequently visited Egerton at York House. A strong Calvinist, he was writing his first book in 1600–2, *A Treatise Concerning Anti-Christ*, dedicated to Egerton, that was published in 1603. Egerton introduced him to the royal court, and later he became chaplain to James I and Bishop of Derry. Reminiscing in a book dedicated to Egerton, he spoke of these years as ones when the Lord Keeper became a 'true evangelical' who would use the law to ferret out and punish those unbelievers who sought to overthrow 'the true faith'.[83] According to William Barlow, Egerton would only appoint to benefices 'masters of assemblies who can drive in the nail'.[84] Donne would see these appointments as the Lord Keeper entered them into his 'book', a carefully kept register at York House of all the appointments he made to ecclesiastical benefices from 1596, averaging eight folios a year.[85] It was used as a notebook for patents drawn for the Privy Seal. Egerton also began the practice of requiring a bond, which he devised, that guaranteed a minimum number of sermons to be preached yearly.[86] One of the writers he patronized, Matthew Sutcliffe, wrote a three-volume work against Robert Bellarmine that was presented to him in 1600, and further works against papists and Robert Parsons in 1603 and 1606,[87] as well as founding Chelsea College in 1608 as a spiritual garrison of the Protestant crusade.[88] Many of its directors were former beneficiaries of the Lord Keeper's assistance.

Life at York House

There was always a close connection between the Lord Keeper, man of London, and country gentleman who rode his estates. The reform of abuses in the courts and departments of state was accompanied by the reform of abuses in the church. Thus, in the years 1597–1600, Egerton also patronized a number of writers on the abuses of simony, pluralities, non-residency, and the need for learned ministers: Richard Brett, Francis Meres, John Norden, Gabriel Powell, Hugh Roberts, and John Shaw.[89] Brett, Powell, and Shaw all used the phrase of forging 'the New Jerusalem'. Egerton appointed to

[82] Knafla, '"Country" Chancellor', Appendix, items 18, 43, 57–8, 84, 98, 100, 103, 113–14, 127.
[83] George Downame, *A Funerall Sermon Preached at Watton in Hertfordshire* (London, 1607), HEH, RB 60836, fol. 35.
[84] 'The Rehearsall Sermon Anno Domini 1605', Ellesmere MS 1172, fol. 27.
[85] Bodleian Library, Tanner MS 179.
[86] Ibid., for example, fols. 1, 19, 32, 36, 61.
[87] *De Vera Christi Ecclesia Adversus Robertum Bellarminum* (London, 1600), and the printed dedicatory works *De Missa Papistica* (London, 1603), and *The Subversion of Robert Parsons His Confused and Worthlesse Worke* (London, 1606).
[88] Matthew Sutcliffe; see Knafla, '"Country" Chancellor', Appendix, items 113–15.
[89] Knafla, '"Country" Chancellor', Appendix, items 14, 89, 98, 103, 106.

benefices in his country parishes men whose religious vision he shared, such as Robert Hill in Denbighshire, John Rawlinson in Cheshire, Thomas Adams in Buckinghamshire, Andrew Willet in Hertfordshire, and John Dove, Roger Fenton, and Thomas Sorocold in London.

'Mr. John Done Secretary' is how personal correspondents addressed him in his tenure at York House.[90] Donne applied for the post through the Lord Keeper's son Thomas upon his return to London in early November 1597: 'I had a desire to be your Lordship's servant.'[91] York House was a rambling old mansion. Egerton, a widower with three children, had just married Lady Elizabeth Wolley in early October. She was the daughter of Sir William More and one of the Queen's favourite maids of honour. Egerton's daughter Mary had married Francis Leigh of Cheshire in July. Thomas Jr had a wife and three daughters, and John was still at Lincoln's Inn. Wolley's son Francis was betrothed to Mary, eldest daughter of Sir William Hawtrey, who had died leaving her as heiress. She joined her mother-in-law Elizabeth at York House, who became her guardian, and guardian to Ann More, Sir George's daughter who was being brought up by Lady Egerton while her own son, Francis (born 1583), was being brought up by her brother Sir George More of Loseley.

Egerton's staff included servant ushers Thomas Marbury and Arthur Mainwaring, who also served as conveyancers and trustees. Lady Wolley's sister had married Mainwaring's cousin Sir George, and later John Davies of Hereford addressed a poem to Arthur, who served Egerton for his lifetime. Henry Jones and John Panton managed his private business, and Panton had been at Lincoln's Inn with Donne. George Carew and Gregory Downhall were senior secretaries who oversaw the household officials and Egerton's work on the Privy Council in high matters of state. Carew was also a master in Chancery, and was on a diplomatic mission to Poland in 1598. Donne may well have tried to model his career after Carew's at this time. A graduate of the Middle Temple, Carew then studied civil law to rise in the ranks of the Chancery to Master in December 1599, a clerk of the Privy Council, and lucrative offices in Requests, and Wards and Liveries, during Donne's tenure at York House. A student of several languages, he too had been employed on various diplomatic missions, combining the careers of lawyer and diplomat.[92] Carew was working on the reorganization of the Chancery Masters and their work when Donne joined York House, and Donne may have begun his work on the reform of lawyers and court fees under his tutelage. Downhall had a BA at Cambridge or Oxford, and was a teacher at Christ's School, Gloucester,

---

[90] Verses sent by Sir William Cornwallis, printed in *The Poems of John Donne*, ed. by H. J. C. Grierson, 2 vols (Oxford: Clarendon Press, 1912) II, 171–2.

[91] *The Loseley Manuscripts and Other Rare Documents*, edited by Alfred John Kempe (London, 1836), p. 341.

[92] W. J. Jones, *The Elizabethan Court of Chancery* (Oxford: Clarendon Press, 1967), pp. 106–8, 111–17.

before becoming Egerton's secretary. He also became a Master in Chancery, and served Egerton until his death.

John King, Egerton's chaplain until 1600, became chaplain to Queen Elizabeth and King James, Dean of Christ Church, and Bishop of London. Called by Sir Edward Coke the 'King of Preachers', he was a Calvinist writer who lit up the pulpit.[93] Nathaniel Harris, Egerton's second chaplain, had arranged for two private family marriages without banns or license, including Egerton's to Lady Alice Derby that defied the Queen. John Fenton became chaplain in 1602, was awarded a number of London benefices and wrote five theological tracts dedicated to the Lord Keeper.[94] Later, John Williams, a popular preacher who studied civil law and equity, was appointed by Egerton as his chaplain in 1612. He rose quickly in the church after the Chancellor's death, becoming Dean of Salisbury in 1619, Dean of Westminster in 1620, and Bishop of Lincoln and Lord Keeper in 1621 – the first ecclesiastical chancellor since the reign of Queen Mary. He wrote in his memoirs that he owed his career to the Lord Keeper.[95]

That Donne knew most of these men and others who Egerton patronized, including most of those who worked for and with the Lord Keeper, can be seen in a few of his writings after he left York House. In the 'Problems', his discussion of why the Devil reserved Jesuits for the present time suggested that it was not only to end the disputations of the old 'schoolmen', but also to test us by defeating a plague worse than the ten described in the Scriptures. Helen Peters suggests that this discussion was summarized from Willet's *Hexapla in Exodum* (1608).[96] Donne may have read it when he composed this, because the work was dedicated to the former Lord Keeper and now Lord Chancellor, and his wife Lady Derby, as was his earlier work.[97] In *The Courtier's Library*, he parodied in one of his longest titles the prolific Mathew Sutcliffe.

According to Walton, Egerton always treated Donne 'with much courtesie, appointing him a place at his own Table, to which he esteemed his Company and Discourse to be a great Ornament'.[98] The last phrase is facetious because the Lord Keeper kept no ornaments! Thus Donne acquired an intimacy with his family, as well as with his friends and state business. He met Sir Francis Bacon there, who had been promoted to Solicitor-General and to the reversion of the clerk of the Star Chamber with Egerton's help. Bacon, like Donne, would work on Egerton's project of reforming lawyers' and court fees.[99]

---

[93] See Ellesmere MSS 32, 44, 49; and the dedicatory volumes in Knafla, ' "Country" Chancellor', Appendix, items 78–79.

[94] Knafla, ' "Country" Chancellor', Appendix, items 46–50.

[95] Lansdowne MS 985, fol. 81.

[96] Donne, *Paradoxes and Problems*, pp. 127–28.

[97] HEH, RB 23542, and *Tetrastylon Papismi* (London, 1599), HEH, RB 79739.

[98] Bald, p. 98.

[99] *The Letters and Life of Francis Bacon including All His Occasional Works*, edited by James Spedding, vols I–VII (London, 1857–74) II, 57–67.

Donne's major job was to investigate fees charged by the officers of the Chancery, Privy Council, and Star Chamber. This must have appealed to him. Writing earlier in his 'Satyres', he attacked the dishonest and pretentious lawyer Coscus (II), and parodied the lawyer who was a 'bore' (IV), a shifty hanger-on in a world of giant statute books that arraigned sedition and rebellion with penalties that ran amuck (IV.8–9).[100] He was stronger in 'Satyre V' where he displayed a shocked concern with the immoral exactions by lawyers and officials of all courts, central and local. He exhorted Egerton to forge ahead in initiating law reform. Suitors are 'worse than dust, or wormes meat' (20–1), 'the mills which grind you' (23) and 'adulterate lawe' (26). 'Know and weed out this enormous sinne' (34), because the 'Powre of the Courts below Flow from the first maine head' (45–6). He had probably seen and heard of the Lord Keeper's attacks on corrupt JPs, lawyers and officials.[101] Writing in the early days of his appointment, he harangued a royal court that was corrupt, vicious, and dishonest; a place where 'vice doth here habitually dwell'.[102]

The young secretary did not hesitate to go to law himself in these years. Donne sued his servant boy Tom Danby in Chancery for the theft of clothes of over £13 on 10 May 1598. His bill was against Christopher Danby, and it was drawn and signed by Christopher Brooke. Donne pleaded the oral agreement with Mr Danby, and itemized goods at £30 10s, in a short and brief bill that the Lord Keeper was promoting to keep down court costs.[103] The suit was in Chancery because the witnesses were now dead.[104] The bill was uncontested, and Donne was awarded judgment on 29 May.[105]

Donne must have spent some time conveying messages in and out of York House. His verse letter to Wotton of '20 July 1598 at Court' speaks of 'Here's no more newes, then vertue.'[106] With Lord Burghley dying and the Earl of Essex in disgrace, he writes with contempt that all royal courts 'enlarge theyre owne wills' and produce 'envie' and 'other humane weaknesses'.[107] Some of Donne's friends had accompanied Essex on his ill-fated invasion, and Donne wrote often to Wotton. When Thomas Jr was wounded and died in Dublin Castle on 23 August 1599, following again in the Earl's martial footsteps, Donne had a prominent place at the funeral ceremony in Chester Cathedral, bearing the sword, and at the dinner in the

---

[100] References to the 'Satyres' here and below are from *The Poems of John Donne*, ed. by Grierson, vol. I.

[101] *Les Reportes del Cases in Camera Stellata 1593 to 1609. From the Original MS of John Hawarde*, ed. by William Pailey Baildon (privately printed, 1894), pp. 161–2, 186–7, 263–5, 299–300.

[102] John Donne to Sir Henry Wotton (20 July 1598), in Grierson, pp. 187–8, at p. 187.

[103] Knafla, *Law and Politics*, pp. 156–8, 162–3.

[104] Donne v. Danby, PRO, C3, Elizabeth I, 266/93.

[105] PRO, Chancery Decrees and Orders, C33/94, Elizabeth I, fol. 812v.

[106] E. K. Chambers, *The Elizabethan Stage*, 4 vols (Oxford: Clarendon Press, 1923) IV, 111.

[107] Simpson, *Prose Works*, p. 308 (letter to Wotton, 1600).

bishop's palace.[108] The Essex affair occurred during the funeral period, bringing Egerton to London, and the Earl was a prisoner in York House by the time Donne returned there. Donne's letters in this period show disillusionment with the fall of Essex.[109] Gleaning 'the vice of great men', 'Courtier' is 'that reprobate name'.[110]

Lady Elizabeth Egerton was in ill health in autumn 1599, and died on 20 January 1599/1600. It brought Egerton great grief, as they had developed a fine relationship. Her estate at Pyrford, which Egerton enjoyed as a country home, went to her son Francis, who had just graduated from Oxford. He went to live there with his wife and his niece, Ann More, who left London and the court for the quiet life at her father's house. According to Bald, the Donne–More attraction began at York House.[111] There is some evidence, however, to suggest that they met at Dodleston when Sir George More brought Ann with him to the funeral in September 1599, and stayed at Dodleston while Egerton hurried back to London on Privy Council orders for the brewing Essex affair.[112] We do know from the Burley manuscripts that John and Ann had a torrid love affair in the hot summer of 1600.[113] His letter of that autumn related their passionate love-making under the hot sun at York House without a chaperone. His second letter, written I think in the following spring, notes More's suspicion of their relationship and his removal of Anne to Loseley. The third letter, written I think in late summer 1601, admits knowledge of More's opposition to their relationship. Donne declares that he is willing to hold to their private contract of marriage, forsaking career for love, and leaves the final decision in her hands.[114]

The Royal Court and Politics

York House was thrust further into the limelight of court politics and culture with the advent of Alice, Countess of Derby. The Lord Keeper's marriage to Lady Derby took place in October 1600. She was twenty years younger, wilful, and hot-tempered. The household exploded in size with her entry. She brought forty servants, and raised the annual household expenses by £650 p. a. John Egerton was betrothed in secret to her second daughter Frances in October 1600, and married secretly in early 1600/1. Alice's third daughter Elizabeth was married to Henry, Lord Hastings, aged fifteen, on 15 January 1600/1, but she lived with her mother until 1604. Donne became

---

[108] Harleian MS 2129, fol. 67.

[109] Simpson, *Prose Works*, pp. 308–10 (1600).

[110] Ibid., p. 310 (letter to Wotton, 1600).

[111] Bald, *John Donne*, p. 109.

[112] See FSL, MSS L.b. 526–34, 538; and *Bulletin du Bibliophile* 2 (1972): 197–9.

[113] Ilona Bell, '"Under Ye Rage of a Hott Sonn & Yr Eyes": John Donne's Love Letters to Ann More', in *The Eagle and the Dove. Reassessing John Donne*, ed. by Claude J. Summers and Ted-Larry Pebworth (Columbia: University of Missouri Press, 1986), pp. 25–52.

[114] Simpson, *Prose Works*, pp. 304–5, 302–3, 300–1, for the three letters, printed respectively.

good friends with the two younger daughters, and remained so for the rest of his life.[115]

Essex was set free in late August 1600, moved to the country, and returned to London in November to protest at Queen Elizabeth's refusal of 30 October to regrant his farm of sweet wines, his only major source of revenue. This refusal caused him to gather an opposition and lead a revolt at Essex House on 17 February 1601/2, when he imprisoned the Lord Keeper and Chief Justice who went there to parlay for the Queen. Donne probably helped Egerton to examine witnesses and prepare for the trials of the rebels. He saw men whom he knew well, such as Essex's secretary Henry Cuffe, perish on the scaffold.[116] Perhaps he also witnessed his friend recanting his confession on the scaffold to the wild derision of the crowd.[117] Afterwards, he acquired a copy of the *Declaration of the Practices and Treasons committed by Robert late Earle of Essex* (1601) that Bacon drew up, revised by the Privy Council and the Queen. Donne wrote on the title page, in translation from 2 Samuel 16:10, 'Let him curse even because the lord hath bidden him.'[118] This might refer 'with bitter irony' to Bacon's vehement denunciation of his former patron.[119] As he wrote in his two imaginary book titles in *The Courtier's Library*: '27. The Brazen Head of Francis Bacon: concerning Robert the First, King of England'; and '28. The Lawyer's Onion; or, the Art of Lamenting in Courts of Law, by the same'.[120]

In July 1601 Donne was issued a patent for a lease of two parts of the manor of Uphall in Carleton, Lincolnshire, parcel of John Heywood, recusant, for twenty years at a rental of £40 with a fine of 20s.[121] Under the Act of 1587, two-thirds of the lands were forfeit to the crown by a recusancy commission of 3 April 1601, and that was leased to Donne undoubtedly because of his official position. As Bald states, this enabled him to be called 'esquire'.[122] It was common for such possessions to revert to a relative, and the possession ended when Heywood and his wife died. Their eldest son had no recusancy conviction.[123]

Parliament was called on 27 October 1601, and sat until its dissolution on

---

[115] Louis A. Knafla, 'Alice Spencer, Countess of Derby (1559–1637)', *New Dictionary of National Biography*.

[116] Donne owned a copy of *The Differences of the Ages of Mans Life*: Geoffrey Keynes, *A Bibliography of John Donne*, 3rd edition (Cambridge: Cambridge University Press, 1958), pp. 212–13.

[117] SP, Elizabeth I, 12/279/25.

[118] Cambridge University Library, accession 7.60.26.

[119] Bald, p. 113.

[120] *The Courtier's Library, or, Catalogus Librorum Aulicorum*, ed. by Evelyn M. Simpson and trans. by P. Simpson (London: Nonesuch, 1930), p. 51.

[121] PRO, C66/1566, no. 37.

[122] Bald, p. 116. For references to the annual recusant rolls where the terms are entered, see p. 117, n.1.

[123] PRO, E368/521.

19 December. Donne, MP, was not noted for sitting on any committees, or making any speeches. He was obviously engaged in work with Egerton. He sat for Brackley, Northants, which had come under Egerton's patronage through the manor and borough passing from the Earl of Derby to Frances. The Commons, however, would include his inns' friends: William Hakewill and Richard Martin, Dr Julius Caesar and Francis Bacon, John Davies and Toby Mathew, Edward Montague, cousin of Lucy countess of Bedford, John Egerton, Sir George More and his son Robert, Edward Herbert, Francis Wolley and his sons-in-law Thomas Grymes and Nicholas Throckmorton, and Robert Cotton and Sir Maurice Berkeley.[124]

Donne's friends in these years at York House included Sir Henry Goodyer, Robert Cotton, and Sir William Cornwallis. The latter wrote to him as secretary, inviting him for idle evenings 'If then for change, of howers you seem careles / Agree with me to loose them at the playes'.[125] Goodyer (?) wrote another one that spoke of loving friends, with much warmth:

> often I have toulde thee I love thee and a⟨s⟩ often hath my Conscience related thy deserts; our love is now o⟨f⟩ some Continuance, so that to goe still in that long worne Livery (I love thee) would show me to harde a master to soe worthie a Servan⟨t⟩. Noe let Courtiers have Love still in their mouthes, and none in their hartes.[126]

Donne also became friends with the Herbert family. Magdalen lived in Oxford, from spring 1599 to summer 1600, with her eldest son, the ward of Sir George More. Francis Wolley was in residence there until December 1599. Donne wrote Magdalen the elegy 'Autumnal Beauty' on her body and mind when she was aged about thirty-one, he twenty-seven. Their amity was consolidated when she oversaw her younger son William in Oxford 1607–8.[127] Henry Wotton was his closest friend. He preserved many of Donne's letters with some of his own replies. The subject matter highlights their closeness, Donne's fear of publishing his 'Paradoxes', and his utter contempt for the court. His motto, inscribed in his books, was '*Per Rachel ho servito, e non per Lea.*'[128] It means that he serves the contemplative life, not the active one. It was part of his Senecan stoicism, a trait that he shared with the Lord Keeper. Donne and Wotton constantly expressed themselves in such terms.

The years at York House brought Donne into the ways of the court, friendships with men seeking careers in the state, and over-confidence in his success. Modern writers have noted Francis Osborn's comment in *Advice to a Son* (1656):

---

[124] Taken from the list in Bald, pp. 114–15.
[125] Tanner MS 306, printed by Grierson, II, 171–2.
[126] W. G. Zeeveld, 'A Tudor Defense of Richard III', *Proceedings of the Modern Language Association* 55 (1940): 946–57.
[127] H. W. Garrod, 'Donne and Mrs. Herbert', *RES* 21 (1945): 161–73.
[128] Bald, p. 122.

It is not safe for a *Secretary* to mend the copy his Master hath set him, unless own'd as from his former inspirations; Least he should grow jealous, that you valued your conceptions before his; who measures his sufficiency by the length of his Employment, not the breadth of his naturall Parts: This made the Lord Chauncelor *Egerton* the willinger to exchange incomparable Dr. D. for the lesse sufficient, though in this more modest, Mr. *T.B.*[129]

Osborn, however, had no knowledge of the Thomas Bond who succeeded Donne as secretary. A competent lawyer, he made measured critiques of corruption in the House of Commons from 1601, and played an important role in investigating plots against state and church in the reign of James I.

Donne's secretaryship seems to have brought an end to his literary writing. His two active writing periods were 1592–7, as a young single man at the inns of court in Holborn, and 1607–14 when he was out of preferment. The author of the elegies and the satires was quite different from the author of *Pseudo-Martyr* and *Essays in Divinity*. The former were personal and informal, the latter academic and professional. The exception was 'The Progress of the Soul' (or 'Metempsychosis'), written as the Lord Keeper's secretary and dated August 1601.[130] His letters, however, write of exchanging 'witty trifles' in prose and verse with clever young men.[131]

MORE, EGERTON, AND THE FATAL MARRIAGE, 1600–2

Anne came to town with her father Sir George More at the opening of parliament in October 1601. Donne and Ann met in secret several times, knowing they could not convince her father, who was actively seeking a marriage partner for her, of a relationship. Thus, desperately in love, they were secretly married. The ceremony was performed by Samuel Brooke, recently ordained, and Christopher Brooke gave away the bride. Three other persons were there as witnesses. The date, however, is controversial. The older version accepted Donne's account of 'three weeks before Christmas'.[132] A newer version, based on a more precise rendering of a later ecclesiastical commission judgment, places it in late January 1601/2.[133] In any event, Anne returned to Loseley after parliament's dissolution. Donne moved out of York House to the house of Mr Haines, next to the Savoy, due to the congestion at

---

[129] L. I. Bredvold, 'Sir Thomas Egerton and Donne', *Times Literary Supplement* (13 March 1924).

[130] John Donne, *The Elegies and the Songs and Sonnets*, ed. by Helen Gardner (Oxford: Clarendon Press, 1965), pp. lviii–lix.

[131] Simpson, *Prose Works*, p. 316 (letter to Wotton, 1600).

[132] Bald, pp. 128–9.

[133] Edward Le Comte, 'Jack Donne. From Rake to Husband', in *Just So Much Honor*, edited by Peter Amadeus Fiore (University Park PA: Pennsylvania State University Press, 1972), pp. 9–32, the judgment printed at pp. 17–18. I find this interpretation the better one of the original court judgment, regardless of the need to legitimize a possible pregnancy.

York House caused by Essex's imprisonment and the Lady Derby's retinue. The Savoy, originally a hospital, was rented out to fashionable people. As a 'liberty' on the Thames in central London, it was the site of frequent clandestine marriages.

George More was born in 1553, achieved an Oxford BA, entered the Inner Temple in 1574, took service with the Earl of Leicester and travelled with Sir Philip Sidney. Knighted in 1597, he inherited Loseley Park in 1600, and was active in local affairs. A parliamentarian, he served on government commissions and kept a large household including a devout chaplain, Mr Holney. Friend of Sir Thomas Bodley, he contributed generously to his new library, as did Egerton. Widely read, humourless and orthodox, he was generous and passionate to a fault. He was also suspicious of Donne's intellectual abilities. More and his wife had nine children, and only one of four boys lived to give him grandchildren.[134]

Egerton had married his second and third wives without banns, but they were mature widows. He was involved in the archbishop's dispensation of 8 February 1599/1600 for a marriage without banns of Thomas Coningsby, his clerk of the Petty Bag, and Frances Haughton. They were married in the house of his servant Henry Jones, in St Martin-in-the-Fields, by Nathaniel Harris. The witnesses were John Egerton, his sister and brother-in-law Mary and Francis Leigh, and his cousin William Ravenscroft.[135] Donne would have been privy to these activities, as well as to the case of Walter Aston, ward of Sir Edward Coke, and Anne Barnes, whose clandestine marriage was dissolved on 12 March 1599/1600. The papers were collected by Egerton, who may have been appointed to the commission. In this case the interest of the Lord Keeper would have been on the other side. Aston was a wealthy heir, worth £10,000 p. a.,[136] and the marriage broke the royal prerogative of wardship and looked like the appropriation of a fortune. The witnesses were sent to the Clink, and Barnes to the Fleet, for a year.[137]

The relationship between John Donne and Ann More was discovered in a web of duplicity that Donne himself narrated in his highly abbreviated and truncated poem, 'The Curse'.[138] Written in late 1599 (or early 1600), Ilona Bell has done a masterful job of deciphering its contents. The poem features Edward Neville, the Catholic double agent who exposes their love affair to George More, and seeks confirmation of Ann's love, More's approval, and Egerton's continued patronage. Bell argues that Arthur Mainwaring, Egerton's household treasurer, told a 'Davies' in the household, possibly the poet

---

[134] Louis A. Knafla, 'More, Sir George (1553–1632)', *New Dictionary of National Biography*.

[135] Lambeth Palace Library, Whitgift's Register, Part 3, fol. 113.

[136] Bald, pp. 132–3.

[137] Ellesmere MS 5920.

[138] Ilona Bell, '"If it be a shee": The Riddle of Donne's "Curse"', in *John Donne's 'Desire of More.' The Subject of Anne More Donne in His Poetry*, ed. by M. Thomas Hester (Newark: University of Delaware Press, 1996), pp. 106–39.

John Davies of Hereford, who told his friend Edward Neville, who told George More. It is more likely that the original discovery (Davies) was by Robert Davies of Gwysaney,[139] Egerton's agent for his northern Welsh properties who would have had charge of Dodleston where John and Ann may have first met, and related the liaison to Mainwaring.

Donne used Henry Percy, Earl of Northumberland, for his messenger to George, and wrote his account of the secret marriage from his sick-bed on 2 February 1601/2.[140] Percy was an active friend of Essex until his fall, anti-Cecil, a noted patron of science and the arts (including the poet George Chapman), and on friendly terms with George More. Donne said that they were married three weeks before Christmas. His view was that if More allowed his passion to get the best of him, and 'incense my lord', then he would destroy them. He implored him to accept the vows made by the daughter he raised, and give them happiness.[141] His foreboding was soon realized. More saw the marriage as a straight violation of canon law, and went directly to Egerton. Donne was sent immediately to the Fleet, and the Brookes to the Marshalsea. More wanted Donne's dismissal and a trial before the High Commission, a court normally reserved for the highest religious offences against Crown and Church. Egerton counseled More to wait, and settle down. Donne's Catholic background, earlier loves, and debts, weighed against his character, and at last Egerton consented to More's strong demand for his dismissal.

The new resident of the Fleet wrote to More on 11 February. Still ill, he remained reasoned and penitential. He has heard, he wrote, that More sees him as contemptuous and spiteful, but will rest on the opinions of those who have observed him. While More may not seek Donne's total destruction, he is near the abyss. More's action wounds and 'violences' his daughter. More replied that the matter was now in Egerton's hands, not acknowledging that it was he alone who had precipitated his dismissal and arrest. Donne wrote Egerton the next day, humble and submissive, praying for release from prison. Since More will no longer act on his behalf, he prays the Lord Keeper and his wife to be merciful and remember his honest work for them.[142] Egerton was touched by the letter, and released him. Donne wrote again to More and Egerton from his chamber on 13 February. He asked More to help reconcile him with Egerton, and for permission to write to Ann. Apologizing for false rumours that he deceived other gentlewomen before Ann, he begs him to intercede with the Lord Keeper, and allow him to restore his career so that he can be a credit to his wife. For Egerton, he simply asked to be

---

[139] Knafla, *Law and Politics*, pp. 10, 12.
[140] *Loseley Manuscripts*, pp. 328–9.
[141] *Loseley Manuscripts*, p. 330.
[142] *Loseley Manuscripts*, pp. 331–2, 332–3, respectively. See also the different and more pressing draft of the 12 February letter to Egerton in Simpson, *Prose Works*, p. 318.

pardoned.[143] Meanwhile, the Brookes were still in prison, with Sir Christopher's practice waiting for him at the York assizes.

More had initiated proceedings before the High Commission to have the marriage annulled soon after hearing of it. He did this on his own, without the Lord Keeper's counsel. Donne first heard news of the excommunication proceedings and imprisonment of witnesses on 23 February. Christopher Brooke wrote to Egerton from the Marshalsea on the 25th with his submission to the court, and his confession. Reiterating his full submission to all charges against him, and the pain of sureties in £1100, he begs to be released for his mother's sake as well as for his clients.[144] The witnesses were released soon after the end of term. On that day, Mitigation Day, 25 February, the sentences were reduced and the parties pardoned.[145] Donne's letter to More of 1 March mentions their previous meeting after the decree, where he assumes that he made a good impression. He is candid, writing that the storm has shaken him to the roots of his lord's favour where he was once well planted. Only More can remedy this with his patron. Donne cannot go abroad because of Ann (who was pregnant), nor gain preferment with his disgrace at his lord's house. He also seeks permission again to write to Ann, reminding More that God's pardon is never denied.[146] The questionable husband, however, was not leaving his affairs in the hands of others. The next day he initiated a suit in the Court of Audience of Canterbury to certify his marriage at canon law.

Donne also wrote to Egerton on 1 March, noting his pardon by the commissioners in More's suit. Facing the problem of his father-in-law, he states that More says he is now removed from the cause and disgrace, and if he could he would sue for Donne's restoration. The anger, Donne assumes, is now with Egerton. Reviewing the work he did as secretary, with the 'sweetness' and 'security' of the freedom and independence of the house, and the love of his son, he could seek preferment nowhere else.[147] He began his work, and his love, in York House, and it is too late to change course. To seek preferment with anyone else would be madness. His disgrace would be seen as involving greater faults than this one. Affliction, misery, and destruction are everywhere he is, apart from York House. According to Walton, Egerton replied, 'though he was unfeignedly sorry for what he had done, yet it was inconsistent with his place and credit, to discharge and readmit servants at the request of passionate petitioners'.[148] Donne, after hearing this answer, and receiving George's permission to write Anne, wrote the lines: 'John Donne, Anne Donne, Un-done', a witticism that originated in

---

[143] *Loseley Manuscripts*, pp. 334–5, 336, respectively.
[144] *Loseley Manuscripts*, pp. 337–8.
[145] *Loseley Manuscripts*, p. 341.
[146] *Loseley Manuscripts*, pp. 339–40.
[147] *Loseley Manuscripts*, pp. 341–3.
[148] Quoted in Bald, pp. 138–9.

Manningham's diary entry at an earlier date, suggesting that everyone already knew his fate.[149]

The discharged secretary's repeated references for reinstatement because of his close relationship to Egerton's deceased heir was not, however, very useful. Before his death, Thomas Jr had written several letters to his father confessing his extravagant living and extensive debts, letters which the Lord Keeper withheld from his widow. Donne, the fashionable London 'connoisseur', may now have been seen in an altogether different light as one of those friends who drew the Lord Keeper's son down the path of conspicuous consumption and a dissolute life.[150] Egerton himself had written recently that 'a countryman would esteem and have more use for a whetstone than a diamond'.[151]

Donne's suit to test the validity of his marriage was heard by Dr Richard Swale in the Court of Audience of Canterbury. The decree of 27 April reads that in January 1601/2, Donne and Ann were free from all marital contracts or obligations, and thus their marriage was good in law. More, then, had to surrender Ann to her husband, which he did with bad grace and no financial support. Donne's costs were over £40, his patrimony exhausted, and he was in debt without income. The Lord Keeper, however, ordered the payment of Ann's legacy of £100 left by her aunt.[152] The receipt was dated 6 July 1602, with the funds from Lady Egerton, delivered by John Panton to her niece Ann, signed for by Donne.[153] Donne had no hope of reinstatement at York House once More had secured his dismissal and imprisonment, and prosecution before the High Commission, the high court for causes célèbres. More, single-handedly, had disgraced Donne in public life. None the less, there is evidence that Egerton later visited him in that 'barren place' at Pyrford after More had moved to Loseley House.

LIFE AFTER YORK HOUSE: THE QUEST FOR LIVELIHOOD,
1602–15

Francis Wolley, Ann's cousin, offered John and Ann a place in his home at Pyrford, eight miles northeast of Guildford and near Loseley, where they spent their early years. Donne probably helped with accounts and estate management, and made an intensive study of civil and canon law. He had a copy of Diego de Valdes' book on French and Spanish quarrels over precedence given to him by Robert Cotton for his opinion.[154] Donne's

---

[149] *The Diary of John Manningham of the Middle Temple, 1602–1603*, edited by Robert Parker Sorlien (Hanover, NH: University Press of New England, 1976), p. 150.

[150] Ellesmere MSS 55–7, 59, 63, 77.

[151] Hawarde, *Les Reportes*, p. 43.

[152] FSL, Loseley MS 2013/31.

[153] Bald, pp. 140–1, and plate VIIIa.

[154] BL, Cotton MSS, Cleopatra F. VII: *De dignitate regum regnorum Hispaniae et honoratiori loco eis, seu eorum legatis, a conciliis ac Romana sede jure debito* (1602).

daughter Constance was born in early 1603, and son John in spring 1604. Meanwhile, most of his friends were being elevated at the accession of James I in spring and summer 1603. James' first progress began at Wolley's on 10 August, and the next two days were at More's.[155] It has been suggested, appropriately, that there is where Donne met King James and told his story.

Donne had an active correspondence with Toby Mathew in 1603–4.[156] Mathew had entered Gray's Inn in 1599. A close friend of Bacon, he kept Donne in touch with court and city affairs, parliament, and the debate on Anglo-Scots Union. Donne also wrote letters to Wotton, who returned to England in late 1603. His letters from Pyrford in 1604 suggest an inner contentment from marriage with a new sense of religion,[157] and he wrote some of his famous songs and sonnets there. His third child George was born in May 1605, followed by Francis in January 1606/7. Donne went abroad as Sir Walter Chute's travelling companion from spring 1605 to spring 1606, going to Paris, Venice, and perhaps Spain. He returned to Pyrford, but by the end of the year he had moved his family to Mitcham, closer to London.

In these early years after his secretaryship to the Lord Keeper, Donne composed his *Catalogus Librarum Aulicorum*, 'The Courtier's Library'.[158] Modelled after Rabelais' mock catalogue of books in the library of Saint-Victor, Donne kept these jests private, perhaps for the amusement of the literary circles at the Mermaid or Mitre taverns in the years 1603–8. They include diatribes of two legal figures associated with Egerton – Sir John Davies and Francis Bacon, but none of the other lawyers who were associated with the Lord Keeper. He had fun with Dr Mathew Sutcliffe, probably his three-volume 'Refutation of all the errors, past, present and future, not only in Theology but in the other branches of knowledge, and the technical Arts, of all men dead, living, and as yet unborn; put together in a single night after supper' (XXXII). But he did not mimic any of the preachers patronized by Egerton. He raked Dr William Barlow for his sycophantic defence of Essex and obscene Paul's Cross sermon on the Sunday after his execution (XXXI). Barlow was a bitter opponent of Persons, and his *An Answer to a Catholike Englishman* (1609) was scathed by Donne in a long letter to Henry Good-yer.[159] Barlow had dedicated a manuscript copy of a sermon to Egerton in 1605,[160] but Donne would not have had knowledge of Barlow's later patronage by Egerton.

---

[155] John Nichols, *The Progresses, Processions, and Magnificent Festivities, of King James the First* (London: J. B. Nichols, 1828) I, pp. 250–1.

[156] *Tobie Mathews Collection*, pp. 272–90.

[157] Logan Pearsall Smith, *The Life and Letters of Sir Henry Wotton* (Oxford: Clarendon Press, 1907), vol. I.

[158] Donne, *The Courtier's Library.*

[159] *Letters*, pp. 160–3.

[160] 'The Rehearsall Sermon Anno Domini 1605', Ellesmere MS 1172, and the dedicatory letter at fol. 2.

More surprising, perhaps, is that Donne chose to highlight the examiner Richard Topcliffe (II), who died in 1604, and the informer Thomas Phelips (IX). He must have deliberately ignored Younge and Beale, who had been the Lord Keeper's Crown agents in ferreting out Catholic priests and recusants, as well as his personal business agents. Younge, especially, would have been a superb candidate for an author of contemptuous figures. This decision suggests a conscious attempt by Donne to keep open the doors to future employment, and not to burn any more bridges than he had already. He could be more open with Sir John Davies (XVI), whom he had already seen advanced, with the Lord Keeper's patronage, to Solicitor-General of Ireland in 1603, and whose major works were dedicated to Egerton in the later years of 1607 to 1615.[161]

A life that returned to writing included prose work, especially his privately-written 'Problems'. Composed after Donne's exit from Egerton's household in 1603–10, they reveal several reflective thoughts that might have been nurtured at York House. This would begin with his first problem on courtiers: that men's destinies made at court can climb no higher (I.3–6), that familiarity with greatness breeds contempt of all greatness (I.6–8), and that vice prospers best there, putting off fear and knowledge of God (I.13–15). It would continue with his comments on those sycophants who took the yoke of sovereignty (the unbridled vision of the royal prerogative) and made laws to tie them to it faster (X.10–13). And it would encompass the vision of a new age that required new men in government who had not yet drawn much water to their mill so that they could grind others more easily (XIV.20–1), and who would then attack the institution of reversions that allowed offices to be bought and sold (XIV.26–31).

The 'Problems' would also include his dilemma concerning friends who encouraged him to turn to the church: 'Why doe young Laymen so much study divinity?' While those who seek preferment neglect it (VI.1–A2), opportunities opened up after Lutherans broke down their doors and Calvinists picked their locks (VI.3–5). This would not include those Puritans of a 'Zealous Imagination' who thought of themselves as kings to reign forever (XV.11–14). As Helen Peters has observed, he was well aware of the new age of theological discourse and preaching in the 1590s.[162] It is interesting to note that his 'Problems' included bastardy, where he argued that men of illegitimate birth, robbed of their legitimacy and familial succession, had wits and abilities well suited to nature's (law's) pattern to succeed (IX.8–10, 17–22). Or perhaps, in defence of legitimacy, they abound at court where fortunes are made and sold (IX.35–7). He may well have had the career of his former employer, who was born a bastard, in mind when he wrote this.

The Donnes lived at Mitcham until 1611, John maintaining a room in the

---

[161] HEH, Appendix, items 34–7.
[162] Donne, *Paradoxes and Problems*, pp. 101–2.

Strand. He wrote to Goodyer on 13 June 1607 to ask William Fowler, the Queen's secretary, for a household position that had become open, and was refused. Then, in November 1608, he applied for a secretaryship in Ireland through the great 'dandy' Lord James Hay. That was also refused. After watching the rapid promotions of Sir John Davies, he must have recognized the lifeless promises that came from corrupt favourites of the King. Writing to Goodyer, he lamented such compliments and promises that turned ineffective. He told Hay, begging, that Egerton and More had been satisfied and would support him.[163] Obviously the key figure who held the Great Seal did not. In February 1609, he was also refused the secretaryship of Virginia. This must have hurt him with Bacon, Roe, and Christopher Brooke on the Council.[164] His affairs were not helped by his choice of spokesmen after 1602. Northumberland was in the Tower of London for fifteen years for complicity in the Gunpowder Plot, and Toby Mathew, who converted to Catholicism at Florence in 1606, was imprisoned in the Fleet at his return in 1607 and exiled in April 1608. Donne had failed to recognize the significance of what he had observed and worked on at York House.

In 1606–7, Thomas Morton composed his *Apologia Catholica*, which won him royal approval and appointment to the Deanery of Gloucester on 22 June 1607. Donne could have met him at Cambridge, or through John King. Morton called for Donne the next day, offering him his benefice of Long Marston, just outside York, as recompense for his past failures to attain the advancement that he deserved. But Donne declined because of his 'conscience' (read, past problems).[165] Donne had been in Morton's employment since 1605, collecting arguments against Catholics for the Church of England. His past employer, meanwhile, was still on the chase, managing the trials of Catholic conspirators in the Main and Bye plots against James' succession in 1603,[166] and commissions to seek out and examine recusants, Jesuits and seminary priests from 1604 to 1608.[167] Perhaps the office was not sufficient, or perhaps he still held an unattainable view of his prospects in affairs of state.

Donne's copy of his *Pseudo-Martyr*, sent to Egerton with a holograph dedication in 1610, was sold at a Sotheby's auction.[168] Written for the King, the work pulled together his ideas on the relationship between Catholics and Jesuits, or Catholicism and the papacy. Sympathizing with the dilemma of Catholic laymen who supported the ecclesiastical hierarchy and the King, he outlined how he had to 'blot out' elements of the Roman Catholic church and

---

[163] *Tobie Mathews Collection*, pp. 81–2, 146, 145, 330–1, respectively.
[164] *The Letters of John Chamberlain*, edited by N. E. McClure, 2 vols (Philadephia: American Philosophical Society, 1939) I, 284.
[165] Bald, citing Walton, pp. 202–7.
[166] HMC, *Ashburnham*, MS 86.
[167] For example, SP, James I, 8/148, 187, 448.
[168] *Sotheby Catalogue* (London, 1951), copy with the Curator of Manuscripts, HEH.

digest 'the whole body of Divinity'.[169] A youthful follower perhaps of Campion, the death of his brother Henry, and the possible complicity of William Harrington, were still strong in his mind. He paid a debt to Egerton in his dedication when he wrote of 'those poor sparks of understanding or judgement which are still in me, were derived and kindled from you, and owe themselves to you.'[170] This suggests that he had been an integral part of a household, including several ex-Catholics, dedicated to a reformed, Episcopal Protestant church.

In the political world that opened up with the death of the Earl of Salisbury in 1610, Donne moved towards the cultural and social life of the capital city that had been so much a part of his younger years. After a brief sojourn on the Continent with Sir Robert Drury 1611–12, the Donnes moved to Drury Lane, where they lived from 1612 to 1621. It was a street inhabited by lawyers, courtiers, and government officials. His sons were now sent to the best London schools, and from here he hoped to launch his civic career. His past, however, which he never fully renounced, caught up with him again. His step-father Richard Rainsford was imprisoned in Newgate in February 1611/2, and convicted for failing to take the Oath of Allegiance. Later released, he was re-indicted in August 1613 and re-imprisoned.

Donne seemed destined to become a member of the Mitre Tavern group and its literary connections in the years 1611–14. George Chapman, Samuel Daniel, John Davies of Hereford, and Ben Jonson were in the centre of the Sidney–Spenser–Pembroke circles, writers who satirized the evils of society as they saw them: adultery, prostitution, fraud, corruption, and greed.[171] Ben Jonson, Donne's friend and admirer, attacked each of these vices in one or other of his works. These writers and dramatists were patronized to influence contemporary society through their works. Poetry, prose, revels, masques, and plays became increasingly political, with authors and patrons meeting at inns and taverns 'to break bread.'[172] The Mitre Tavern became the social hub of the anti-Spanish faction in these years. On a September evening in 1611, a group of them travelled to Oxford with several MPs to dine in the hall of Brasenose College, the alma mater of the new Vice-Chancellor of Oxford, Lord Ellesmere.[173] It is not easy to understand why Donne was not among them. His eyes and feet were taking him in another direction.

His more radical friends who had caught the wave of Protestant politics and the New Jerusalem, Sir Edward Herbert, Martin, Brooke, Chute,

---

[169] *P-M*, p. 13.
[170] *Sotheby Catalogue*, p. 16.
[171] See Alexander Leggatt, *Citizen Comedy in the Age of Shakespeare* (Toronto: University of Toronto Press, 1973), and Margot Heinemann, *Puritanism and Theatre: Thomas Middleton and Opposition Drama under the Early Stuarts* (Cambridge: Cambridge University Press, 1980).
[172] Knafla, '"Country" Chancellor', pp. 72–3.
[173] SP, James I, 66/2.

Hoskyns, and Hakewill, brought him several offers of seats in the House of Commons, and he took that of Taunton in the Parliament of 1614. He was on a joint committee for the grievance of impositions, and several others, but there is no notice of any participation or work. At the dissolution, Chute and Hoskins were imprisoned for their speeches. It seems that Donne was still unwilling to commit himself to the political high road of his friends, for which he had been tutored at York House. Seeking preferment in the corrupt world of James' favourites, he saw his civic future in the brittle hands of Hay and the King's alleged lover, the Scot Sir Robert Carr, Viscount Rochester and Earl of Somerset.

Donne first wrote to Carr for preferment in July 1614, requesting an ambassadorship to Venice,[174] and begging Hay for the same.[175] He even approached Egerton. Writing Goodyer, he said that Egerton 'gave me so noble and so ready a dispatch; accompanied with so fatherly advise, and remorse for my fortunes, that I am now, like an Alchymist, delighted with discoveries by the way'.[176] One can read the words 'dispatch' and 'fatherly advice' in two ways. The Lord Keeper was a virtual co-chair of the anti-Spanish faction of George Abbot, Archbishop of Canterbury, Sir Julius Caesar, Sir Robert Naunton, William Herbert, Earl of Pembroke, Sir Edward Coke, Fulke Greville, Lord Brooke, and Sir Ralph Winwood. It was working to fill the void left by Salisbury's death and dislodge Carr and the Howards, ridding the kingdom of these 'sychopants' and 'caterpillars' of the realm.[177]

The absolutist Donne, usually seen later in his sermons,[178] was visible in his choices in court politics after 1611. He entered the service of Rochester, and considered writing a treatise defending the nullity of the young Essex's marriage with the Countess, Frances Howard.[179] While that, to his credit, was never written, he did leave to posterity a verse epithalamium for the wedding of Lady Frances and the Earl on 26 December 1613, detailing the merrymaking at Whitehall's Banqueting House: 'The tables groan, as though this feast / Would as the flood, destroy all fowl and beast, . . . They tread the air, and fall not where they rose'.[180] He then wrote that after they went to bed, she would perform, virgin though she was:

---

[174] *Tobie Mathews Collection*, p. 315.
[175] *Tobie Mathews Collection*, p. 335.
[176] *Letters*, p. 172.
[177] Knafla, *Law and Politics*, pp. 93–104.
[178] Debora Kuller Shuger, *Habits of Thought in the English Renaissance* (Berkeley and Los Angeles: University of California Press, 1990), pp. 159–217.
[179] Anne Somerset, *Unnatural Murder. Poison at the Court of James I* (London: Weidenfeld & Nicholson, 1997), p. 140.
[180] John Donne, *Complete Poetry and Selected Prose*, ed. by John Hayward (London: Nonesuch, 1962), p. 113; and John Donne, *The Epithalamions Anniversaries and Epicedes*, ed. by W. Milgate (Oxford: Clarendon Press, 1978), pp. 10–19.

Thy self must to him a new banquet grow
And you must entertain
And do all this day's dances o'er again.
. . .
Therefore at first she modestly might start,
But must forthwith surrender every part
As freely as each to each before, gave either eye or heart.[181]

Donne would have been aware of Somerset's predicament by 1615, when his former employer refused to accept the King's plea for a general pardon to his favourite, absolving him of all criminal offences past and present. Ellesmere also held up renewal of all Somerset's patents of monopoly, thereby stemming his lucrative income. He had the Earl and his Lady Frances Howard imprisoned for the poisoning of Sir Thomas Overbury in September 1615, while Richard Weston and Richard Turner were tried as their agents, found guilty, and executed. He also presided over the trial of the Earl and his Lady in May 1616, while deathly ill. Convicted, they were pardoned from the death penalty but imprisoned in the Tower for five years. Catholic sympathizers bathed in corruption and arbitrary government had no place in the Chancellor's kingdom.[182]

Having taken the wrong road, the force of events had now convinced Donne that the church was his only avenue to a profession. He wrote along these lines to George More on 3 December 1614, after Somerset said that the patent for his post would not be moved without him.[183] Financial difficulties were now becoming acute. He also wrote Goodyer on 20 December that, in a process served against him, Egerton was incensed because some refused to appear,[184] and a large part of Toby Mathew's estate was concealed. Desperate for his debts, Lady Bedford agreed to pay them if he would take to the church; in the end, she only gave him £30. He also was assembling a collection of his poetry to dedicate to Somerset.

DR JOHN DONNE AND LINCOLN'S INN, 1615–21

Donne was ordained on 23 January 1614/5 by John King, former chaplain to the Lord Keeper who had advanced him, and later called by Donne 'a companion to me in my first studies'.[185] He received a DD from Cambridge University in April 1615, and was Reader in Divinity at Lincoln's Inn from October 1616 to February 1621/2. His first two benefices were Keyston, Huntingdonshire, obtained from the King on 16 January 1615/6 at £20 p. a.,

---

[181] Hayward, *Poetry and Prose*, p. 114.
[182] Ellesmere MSS 444, 1435, 1437–8, 2943–5, 2947–8.
[183] Gosse II, 60–1.
[184] *Letters*, p. 195.
[185] Gosse II, 139.

and Sevenoaks, obtained from the Lord Keeper on 7 July at £13 13s 4d.[186] His sureties were Christopher Brooke and his neighbour Walter Bailey. These were duly recorded in Egerton's book. His third post was Reader in Divinity for Lincoln's Inn on 24 October 1616 at £60 p. a.[187] He had chambers, a chaplain, and gave about 50 sermons a year. Meanwhile, at home, Ann died on 15 August 1617. Of her twelve child-births, two were stillborn, and three predeceased her. Now the religious expressions in his sermons became more intense.

The new Reader guided the religious life of the Inn, including conformity, which he had to certify, and preached against lazy and uneducated ministers. He also grasped for a bishopric whenever one came due. Aspirations apart, it appears that Donne was now on the same course that he had begun in 1597: he was becoming part of the reform of spiritual life that he had witnessed in his years at York House. His friends now were said to be Archbishop George Abbot, Henry Hobart, Chief Justice of the Common Pleas, and Sir Julius Caesar, all political allies of his former and now deceased employer. Eventually he was even made an honorary member of the Virginia Company in May 1622, joining his old friends. He continued to live at Drury Lane until he became Dean of St Paul's on 19 November 1621, when he moved into the deanery where he lived until his death there on 31 March 1631. In some of his sermons, Donne spoke as a reformer against non-residence, pluralities and simony, and became an honorary bencher of the Inn upon resignation as its preacher on 11 February 1621/2,[188] relinquishing his chamber on 23 November 1624. He left some verses with Caesar, who lived in the parish of St Dunstan-in-the-West where Donne was vicar in 1624 and often preached. There were many lawyers, judges, printers, and stationers there who would have reminded him of the legal culture of Lincoln's Inn and York House that had occupied his life from 1592 to 1602.

Inhabiting the church, and blessed with a legal background, Donne was called into service where his talents could be utilized. He sat on several ecclesiastical commissions for appeals and in the Court of Delegates thirteen times, sitting variously with bishops, judges, Chancery masters and civilians. He also sat on three cases in the High Commission, and a few arbitrations. Thus he came to sit with most of the judges and civilians who he would have met and discoursed with throughout his career.[189] He also continued to read classical satire. His satire idolizes 'a census of such estatelesss or pretentious urbanites' as broking lawyers, merchant ventures, slimy courtiers, corrupt officials, and foolish suitors who pursue and satisfy personal ambitions.[190]

---

[186] Tanner MS 179, 'Beneficia sive Ecclesiae promotiones concessae per Thomam Egerton'.

[187] *Black Books* II, 187.

[188] *Black Books* II, 230.

[189] Based on the SP, and PRO C66, C193, and Court of Delegates: Bald, pp. 414–24.

[190] Lawrence Manley, *Literature and Culture in Early Modern London* (Cambridge: Cambridge University Press, 1995), pp. 382–9, at p. 382.

Thus his strutting lawyer Coscus, upwardly mobile and active in counterfeiting. This erosion of moral potential uproots souls, consumes them and sweeps them away. In this regard, not even his appointment to Egerton accommodated his vision of the realities of power. This corrosive corruption at the centre of the social order leads office-holders to 'surprised disillusionment'.[191]

FAMILY FEUDS AND THE SPOILS OF AFFECTION

Donne's association with the Egerton family did not end with the Lord Keeper's death in 1617. Just after Egerton's death, the widow and daughters of Thomas Jr began a series of law suits in Chancery against Egerton's successor, Sir John Egerton, the new Earl of Bridgewater. Lady Egerton laid claim to properties under the terms of her marriage settlement, which had been invalidated when her husband died before his father.[192] Her children Mary, wife of Sir Thomas Leigh, and Vere, wife of William Booth, joined with their husbands in a suit to recover profits of a wardship, whose lease was inherited by Bridgewater, which they alleged was held in trust for them by the Lord Keeper.[193] Sir Thomas and Lady Mary also sued Bridgewater for the parsonage of Gresford in Denbighshire. The Queen's lessees, Ellis Wynn and Thomas Middleton, London merchant, assigned their rights in the lease to Thomas Jr on 23 December 1598, who had assigned his rights, before going to Ireland on 10 March 1599, to John Panton and Richard Cartwright, who with the reversionary lessees assigned their interests to the Lord Keeper.[194] The transactions were arranged by Thomas Ravenscroft and Thomas Jr. The Leighs argued that the transactions were for Thomas Jr, and that his lessees and the Lord Keeper were trustees for Thomas and his heirs. Bridgewater held that his brother was in debt, could not have bought them, and that the trustees acted for his father.

There were twenty-eight witnesses, including Donne. The main question for Donne, witness for Bridgewater, was whether there was a falling out between Panton and Thomas Jr before he went to Ireland. Donne replied on 17 June, answering 'no', but that Bridgewater had a 'hard opinion' of Panton. The case was argued before Bacon in Michaelmas term 1618. Briefs were to be drawn on both sides,[195] and Bacon appointed John King, Bishop of London, and Sir Henry Mountague, Chief Justice of the King's Bench, to mediate.[196] The plaintiff's petition was dismissed in an absolute decree on 19 April 1619.[197]

[191] Manley, *Literature and Culture*, p. 402.
[192] PRO C24/451; Ellesmere MS 624–631.
[193] PRO C2, James I, L16/38; Ellesmere MS 7930.
[194] PRO C24/448, Part 1; C33/135, fols. 284v, 843r; Ellesmere MSS 1837–61.
[195] Ellesmere MS 1855–6.
[196] PRO C33/135 (Chancery Orders and Decrees, Book A, 1618–19), fol. 284v.
[197] C33/135, fol. 843r.

The Lincoln's Inn men who deposed were largely from the household of the late Lord Keeper.[198] It is quite clear from the documents that widow Lady Egerton sued in despair, and that the facts were on the side of the new Earl of Bridgewater. The household was firm and tight on the facts, and intentions, of the old Lord Keeper. Service and devotion would not be split asunder. Shortly afterwards, Bridgewater's wife Frances presented the Earl with a beautifully bound copy of Donne's *Paradoxes and Problems* on gilt-edged vellum paper.[199] While the copy was full of errors, it was made from the original in Donne's hands.[200] A similar manuscript volume of Donne's poems was given to the Earl by his wife which included several poems written for family members, including one on the Countess.[201]

Donne presented Bridgewater with a copy of his Lent sermon at court, after the opening of Convocation, on 10 March 1626.[202] He also preached at the wedding of Lady Mary Egerton, Bridgewater's daughter, to Lord Herbert of Cherbury, on 19 November 1627,[203] and signed the indenture to the marriage contract. Donne, after his flirtation with Scottish and royal favourites in mid-life, had come to see, perhaps, the virtues of a world where honesty, hard work, and godliness were not to be ignored, even by those who believed in contemplation. Later, in revising his Gunpowder Plot sermon of 1622 for publication, he wrote clearly on how important it was for the King's officers to take their responsibilities with earnest commitment, even if it meant criticizing his favourites. The King has discretion in the exercise of his prerogative, but he needs guidance for which his chief officers are responsible.[204] These words would have been appreciated by his former employer, Lord Keeper Egerton.

---

[198] Their names – Thomas and Urian Leigh, Thomas Foster (admitted 1574), John Jeffries (1587), William Phillips (1586), George Hope (1595), John Parkinson (1604), William Johnson (1621), and William Ravenscroft (1580), plus Ellis Wynn, clerk of the Petty Bag and a son of the original lessee, and Valentine Sanders, a Six Clerk and Egerton family friend for twenty years – are in the list printed by Bald, pp. 332–7.

[199] Ellesmere MS 6893. That Frances presented it to her husband is indicated by her initials, and Bridgewater's signature on the front flyleaf is the customary way he signed books he possessed.

[200] See Donne, *Paradoxes and Problems*, pp. lxiv–lxvi, lxxviii–lxxix; and Evelyn M. Simpson, 'More Manuscripts of Donne's *Paradoxes and Problems*', *RES* 10:40 (October 1934): 412.

[201] Ellesmere MS 6893, undated.

[202] Keynes, *Bibliography*, p. 116.

[203] *Sermons* VIII, 3.

[204] *John Donne's 1622 Gunpowder Plot Sermon. A Parallel-Text Edition*, ed. by Jeanne Shami (Pittsburg: Duquesne University Press, 1996), pp. 33–4. This is also how James I saw it: Louis A. Knafla, 'Britain's Solomon: King James and the Law', in *Royal Subjects. Essays on the Writings of James VI and I*, ed. by Daniel Fischlin and Mark Fortier (Detroit: Wayne State University Press, 2000), pp. 235–64.

CONCLUSION

As Maule has observed, there are many 'margins' in the life of John Donne. His era has not been easily visualized on the ground, in its *habitus*, whether it is in the business of law, politics, or religion. Language, events, and linkages are not easy to discern in a world of post-modernist thought. But there is a rich historical record that can be accessed, re-read, and reinterpreted. There is probably also more to be discovered once we know what we are looking for. As more frames of the picture are taken from different angles, directions, sources, and contexts, the better chance we have to recreate the life of Donne as it may have been lived in the London of the late sixteenth and early seventeenth centuries. As he may have read in Francis Thynne's dedicatory letter to the Lord Keeper for Christmas 1600 (a noted scholar of history and literature, and London resident), 'in those younger years, when Lincoln's Inn society did link us all in one chain of amity', an individual is the sum of many parts.[205]

---

[205] 'Emblemes and Epigrames' (20 December 1600), Ellesmere MS 34/B/2, fol. 3.

Chapter 4

JOHN DONNE THE CONTROVERSIALIST: THE POET AS POLITICAL THINKER

JOHANN P. SOMMERVILLE

JOHN DONNE was a clergyman by profession, and he had taken a deep interest in the writings of divines long before his ordination in 1615. In 1610 he published *Pseudo-Martyr*, a weighty contribution to the debate on church–state relations between James I's supporters and papalists, and obviously the fruit of long labours. The book was dedicated to the king, and won Donne royal patronage. In his later writings, too, Donne continued to contribute to religious controversy, and to disputes on kingly and papal power. Like such other scholarly members of the higher Jacobean clergy as Lancelot Andrewes, John Buckeridge, and Thomas Morton, Donne wrote on a wide range of theological matters, and on questions of political theory. His writings on these subjects were far more extensive than his poetry. On its own, that proves little. Poets need to earn a living, and in doing so they sometimes have to write things other than poetry – things that often tell us rather little about them. Philip Larkin, for example, was a librarian, and the author of *The Brynmor Jones Annual Library Reports*, but it would be difficult to show that these shed all that much light on his poetry, or on his attitudes to much beyond the University of Hull. Donne's prose writings, by contrast, are extremely revealing of his thinking on a wide variety of fundamental issues. Indeed, as we shall see, it is arguable that Donne himself considered such works as *Pseudo-Martyr* his most lasting monuments.

Donne wrote a great deal on political theory, and on church–state relations. But historians of political thought have virtually nothing to say about him. In recent years, however, literary scholars have done some remarkable work on his religious and political ideas, employing close textual analysis, and psychoanalytical techniques, to reappraise his thinking. Donne used to be thought of as an establishment figure, who took much the same line as James I himself on religious and political questions. Recent literary critics have cast doubt on that notion, and presented us with an altogether more ambivalent and subversive Donne. Some – like Jeanne Shami – have adopted a nuanced position, arguing that the poet did indeed broadly agree with the king on major questions, but that in many sermons he discreetly criticized particular royal policies.[1] Others more crudely claim that Donne's apparent agreement with the king on basic principles was ironical, and that he in fact held opinions which were radically opposed to James' monarchical absolutism, and tended rather to republicanism. The present chapter is about this second set of views, and more generally about Donne's political thinking and its historical contexts. It draws in particular on his prose works, and especially on the *Pseudo-Martyr* of 1610 – arguably the most neglected of his writings. We tend to think of Donne as first and foremost a poet, but it is worth reminding ourselves that he wrote far more in prose than in verse, and that he came to regard poetry as a rather undignified form of expression. Indeed, he does not seem to have bothered to keep copies of his poems, and when he thought he was going to be forced to publish them in 1614, he commented wryly that it was harder to track them down than it had been to write them in the first place.[2] A couple of years earlier, he described in a letter to his friend Sir Henry Goodyer recent debates on church government in France, asserting that 'I look upon nothing so intentively as these things'.[3] His nice sense of irony might have appreciated that modern scholars devote so much time to writings he thought were ephemeral, and so little to those he took seriously.

At first glance, the old thesis that Donne saw eye to eye with the king on key issues has much to commend it. He was appointed to the deanery of St Paul's – one of the best livings in the English church – by James, and his *Pseudo-Martyr* was dedicated to the king. Purportedly, at least, it defended James' ideas about religion and royal power against Catholic attack. In 1605 a group of Catholic gentlemen attempted to blow up the king and parliament in the famous Gunpowder Plot. The following year, James approved an act of parliament which instituted a new oath of allegiance. The oath was intended

[1] See, for example, Jeanne Shami, 'Donne on Discretion', *ELH* 47 (1980): 47–66; *eadem*, 'Kings and Desperate Men: John Donne Preaches at Court', *JDJ* 6:1 (1987): 9–23.

[2] John Donne, *Letters to Severall Persons of Honour*, ed. Charles Edmund Merrill, Jr (New York: Sturgis & Walton, 1910), pp. 89–90: Donne remarked (in a letter to Sir Henry Goodyer probably written around May 1609) that he had embarked upon 'a graver course, then of a Poet, into which (that I may also keep my dignity) I would not seem to relapse'. Writing to George Gerrard on 4 April 1612, Donne said: 'Of my Anniversaries, the fault that I acknowledge in my self, is to have descended to print any thing in verse, which though it have excuse even in our times, by men who professe, and practise much gravitie, yet I confesse I wonder how I declined to it, and do not pardon my self' (ibid., p. 206; see also p. 219 for a very similar statement in another version of this letter). Writing to Goodyer on 20 December 1614, Donne said that 'I am brought to a necessity of printing my Poems, and addressing them to my L. Chamberlain. This I mean to do forthwith; not for much publique view, but at mine own cost, a few Copies. I apprehend some incongruities in the resolution; and I know what I shall suffer from many interpretations . . . By this occasion I am made a Rhapsoder of mine own rags, and that cost me more diligence to seek them, then it did to make them' (p. 170).

[3] Ibid., p. 114.

for use against Catholics. Many Catholics, including such major figures as the Spanish Jesuit Francisco Suárez and the Italian Cardinal Robert Bellarmine – perhaps most famous nowadays for his central role in the silencing of Galileo – asserted that the pope had the authority to depose Christian monarchs who opposed Catholicism. They claimed that to deny this deposing power was to err grievously, and perhaps to fall into heresy. Pope Pius V had deposed Elizabeth I. In Catholic theory, a deposed ruler had no legitimate authority, and could be violently removed by anyone. The Gunpowder Plotters had attempted to use violence to get rid of James and parliament, and they retaliated by making a law which said that Catholics could be given an oath of allegiance renouncing the deposing power. Catholics who twice refused the oath could be imprisoned indefinitely and forfeit all their goods. In 1606 Pope Paul V forbade Catholics to take the oath, and Bellarmine soon argued against it. James then defended it in a book entitled *Triplici nodo, triplex cuneus, or an Apologie for the Oath of Allegiance* (1608), and once more in an expanded version of the same work, which came out in 1609 with a lengthy *Premonition* to other Christian rulers, warning them of the dangers of papalist principles. In January 1610, Donne travelled to Royston to present James with a freshly printed copy of his *Pseudo-Martyr*.[4] The dedication to the king asserted that the oath secured the sovereign and his subjects, and declared that therefore 'it is reason, wee defend it'. Donne insisted that his own defence of the oath was largely indebted to James' books.[5] The influence of the king is also patent in Donne's anti-Jesuit satire of 1611, *Ignatius his Conclave*.[6] In 1622, James issued 'Directions to preachers', greatly restricting what clergymen could say in the pulpit, especially on political matters. He called upon Donne to justify the 'Directions' in a sermon at Paul's Cross. The sermon so pleased James that he requested its publication. It was the first of Donne's sermons to appear in print.[7] All of this might suggest that the king and the poet shared similar views on important political and religious questions. But a number of critics challenge any such claim. Some argue that Donne did not straightforwardly endorse the Protestant religious establishment of Jacobean England. He was, they contend, a Catholic by birth and upbringing, and his apostasy from Catholicism centrally affected his outlook, leaving him perpetually worried 'about fidelity and falseness'. Though 'he forsook the Roman Church', this case goes, 'he never, in a sense, escaped its grasp'.[8] Others claim that he was deeply ambivalent about the political views of James. They detect in his writings signs that he sympathized with the king's political opponents, and that he diverged from the divine right theory of kingship (which James

[4] Bald, p. 221.
[5] *P-M*, p. 3.
[6] *Ignatius*, pp. xxvi, 102–3, 116, 124, 126–7, 132–3, 148.
[7] Bald, pp. 433–5.
[8] John Carey, *John Donne. Life, Mind and Art*, new edition (London: Faber and Faber, 1990), pp. 23, 21.

endorsed) on crucial points. In place of Donne the confident defender of the
king and the established church, modern critics offer us Donne the subversive, guilt-ridden, semi-Catholic. What follows suggests that the historical
evidence supports the old rather than the new interpretation. The first section
briefly surveys what critics say to show that Donne was an apostate from
Catholicism, and that his betrayal of his faith scarred him for life, leaving its
mark on most of his literary productions. The second section describes the
arguments of those who claim that Donne was not an advocate of royal
absolutism but an oppositionist, or at least no more than a lukewarm
supporter of the king's policies. The third section turns to Donne's texts
and contexts, examines his attitude to royal power, and responds to modern
interpretations which portray him as a subversive. The fourth and final
section discusses the contexts of *Pseudo-Martyr* in more detail. It locates
Donne's thinking on church–state relations close to the king's, arguing that
the general case which he developed in *Pseudo-Martyr* was much like that
found in other defences of the oath. But whereas some of James' supporters in
that controversy were concerned mainly to refute the false tenets of the
papists, Donne's objective was to persuade Catholics to accept the oath by
using arguments derived largely from Catholic sources. Much reading had led
him to abandon Catholicism, but he remained sympathetic to his former co-
religionists, and in *Pseudo-Martyr* he employed his learning to undeceive
them from ill-grounded principles liable to lead them to false martyrdom –
martyrdom in the interests of the pope and the Jesuits, perhaps, but not of the
faith or the truth.

I

John Carey strikingly begins his well-known study of Donne by affirming that
'The first thing to remember about Donne is that he was a Catholic; the
second, that he betrayed his Faith'.[9] Carey calls his first chapter 'Apostasy' and
his second 'The Art of Apostasy'. He argues that Donne's 'betrayal of
Catholicism' deeply marked his love poetry, fuelling his fear 'that nowhere
"Lives a woman true, and faire"'. Having betrayed others, he was forever
worried that he would be betrayed.[10] His Catholic background , says Carey,
influenced him in other ways. In his later years Donne was to attack Jesuits,
notably in *Ignatius his Conclave*. Two of his uncles – his mother's brothers –
were Jesuits, and one of them served on the mission to England when Donne
was a boy. When her brother was captured and imprisoned, Donne's mother
visited him and carried letters from him to another Jesuit.[11] Carey contends
that the English Jesuits were men of 'unswerving probity', and argues that this

---

[9] Carey, *John Donne. Life, Mind and Art*, new edition (London: Faber and Faber, 1990), p. 1.
[10] Ibid., p. 23.
[11] Bald, pp. 44–5.

was why they were so hated. He says nothing about the historical context which might make anti-Jesuit feeling more defensible, or at least comprehensible. Wicked people, his account implies, enjoy being unpleasant to good people. But he adds a special reason why Donne in particular so disliked the Jesuits. The poet, he says, 'let loose his rancour against the Jesuits with a pertinacity that seems to reflect a personal grudge', and he suggests that he had a grudge against the hold which Jesuits – 'these stern, devoted men' – had over 'his mother's love and allegiance'.[12] On Carey's psychoanalytical account, Donne harboured an Oedipal resentment against Jesuits for decades after the English government released his uncle and sent him abroad. He also claims that Donne's betrayal of the Catholic cause lay behind his long-term preoccupation with martyrdom. If he had remained loyal to the faith, he might have suffered martyrdom himself. Having betrayed it, he 'could not help comparing the agonies of the English Catholics with his own relative ease', and as 'if to quiet a lingering guilt . . . about his escape from persecution' he argued that 'less valiant types of endurance' could be 'as meritorious as martyrdom', declaring that all 'martyrdom is not "a Smithfield Martyrdome"'.[13] Carey does not inform us what a 'Smithfield Martyrdome' was, but his account strongly implies that it was the obscene and unjustified execution of stern and devoted Catholics by Protestant bigots in the reign of Elizabeth.

One problem with the idea that Donne was wracked by guilt for betraying his co-religionists, and for failing to share their martyrdom, is that in *Pseudo-Martyr* he argued at length that many Catholics who got themselves killed for their beliefs were false, and not true martyrs – pseudomartyrs. The Jesuits, he said, were especially prone 'to beget or cherish this corrupt desire of false-Martyrdome'.[14] He asserted that people who were executed after refusing the oath of allegiance did not count as genuine martyrs. Anyone who died in defence of the papal deposing power was a pseudo-martyr. The Catholic church, he said, was itself split on the nature of papal authority. This was perfectly correct, for Gallicans and conciliarists strongly dissented from Bellarmine's views on this question, and Archpriest George Blackwell – the head of the Catholic secular priests in England – himself at first accepted the oath of allegiance, though under pressure from Bellarmine he later for a while reversed his stance.[15] To die for one contested theory about the pope's power was evidently not to die for a principle that all Catholics endorsed. But Catholics acknowledged that 'he only is a Martyr, whom all the Church esteemes to be so'.[16] You could not, therefore, become a martyr by getting

---

[12] Carey, *John Donne*, p. 7.

[13] Ibid., p. 35.

[14] *P-M*, p. 101 (title to chapter 4); cf. pp. 110, 120.

[15] A discussion of Blackwell's shifting position is in J. P Sommerville, 'Jacobean Political Thought and the Controversy over the Oath of Allegiance' (unpublished Ph.D. diss., University of Cambridge, 1981), pp. 28–30, 34, 36–7, 46–50.

[16] *P-M*, p. 172.

yourself executed for some doctrine that, say, Jesuits accepted, but other Catholics rejected. According to Donne, taking the oath of allegiance was perfectly compatible with the law and good morals. But anyone who 'refuses to defend his life by a lawfull acte . . . destroyes himselfe'. No man, he declared, 'by lawe of nature may deliver himselfe into a danger which he might avoide'.[17] But Catholics were delivering themselves into danger by disobeying the laws of England, especially if they refused the oath of allegiance. This looks very much as though he is saying that Catholics are acting against the law of nature. Carey acknowledges the point, but claims that Donne was being dishonest here. Dishonest because not long earlier, in his manuscript *Biathanatos* he had precisely defended endangering yourself, and, indeed, committing suicide. Moreover, says Carey, in *Biathanatos* he had adopted a 'considerably more sceptical' view of the law of nature. Indeed, he informs us, Donne had argued that 'nature is simply a word people use to embrace everything which happens in the world; so it's absurd to suggest that anything which has actually happened can be contrary to the Law of Nature'.[18] So, when Donne in *Pseudo-Martyr* claimed that Catholics might break the law of nature by seeking martyrdom, he was dishonestly disguising his real views about the law of nature. His motive in writing *Pseudo-Martyr*, argues Carey, was to win advancement by currying favour with the king. He therefore filled the book up with a 'medley of superstition and assertion' which 'tallied . . . conveniently with James's theory of the divine right of kings', but which in no way represented his real views. When he wrote it, Carey tells us, Donne 'was using, at best, only half his mind'.[19]

Like Carey, Anthony Raspa stresses the importance of Catholicism to Donne. So too does Dennis Flynn. Raspa says that 'the worst sore of Donne's private life' was 'his apostasy from Roman Catholicism', and asserts that as late as 1610 – when he published *Pseudo-Martyr* – Donne was known (to the few people who knew him at all) almost exclusively as a relative of important Catholics, including Thomas More's sister.[20] Raspa does not dismiss *Pseudo-Martyr* quite so readily as Carey. But like Carey, he does not take its arguments at face value. He notes the 'scurrilousness' of some of Donne's comments about Catholic beliefs, and the 'bitter precision' with which he demolished popish legends. A simple-minded critic might take such things as signs that Donne enjoyed poking fun at ludicrous Catholic tales, but to Raspa they suggest 'the anguish of an individual who has still not succeeded in reassuring himself' of the truth of what he is saying. The very vigour of Donne's attack on popery leaves Raspa with an 'impression of . . . over-

[17] *P-M*, p. 155. The thought of Donne and others on the law of nature is discussed in Johann P. Sommerville, *Thomas Hobbes: Political Ideas in Historical Context* (London: Macmillan, 1992), pp. 43–5, 69.

[18] Carey, *John Donne*, p. 19.

[19] Ibid.

[20] Raspa's introduction to *P-M*, pp. xxxviii–ix.

eagerness to prove that he is convinced against Rome'.[21] Flynn emphasizes the links between Donne's forebears and noble Catholic families.[22] He claims that Donne's sympathies remained Catholic for many years, and detects a great deal of irony in the apparently anti-Catholic *Pseudo-Martyr*. Like Carey, he connects the book with *Biathanatos*. The latter work argues that suicide can be justifiable in some circumstances. Flynn affirms that if 'death over the Oath is not martyrdom but suicide, as the government's apologists claimed, then a book on the lawfulness of suicide provides a cynical argument for refusing the Oath anyway'.[23] On the surface, then, *Pseudo-Martyr* seems to agree with James's anti-Catholic and divine right views. But in fact it is deeply subversive of them. Some literary critics write as though contemporaries of Donne such as King James had less than half a mind, and that the poet could therefore easily hoodwink them by concealing meanings which only modern scholars, armed with psychoanalytical insights, have been able to perceive. Flynn avoids this kind of position. He claims that 'the established views of Donne's deep respect for the King at this period of his life should be reassessed', but notes that this raises the problem of how he was able to gain approval for the publication of the book. The answer, he asserts, is that it contained an attack on Chief Justice Sir Edward Coke, whose common law theories of the constitution James greatly disliked.[24]

Not everyone has been persuaded by the Catholic interpretation of Flynn and others. In the opinion of David Norbrook, Donne's sympathies lay with puritans rather than Catholics. But like Flynn, Norbrook perceives important differences between the poet's politics and the king's. The next section surveys his claims and those of Annabel Patterson, who similarly argues that Donne was no kingsman.

II

Norbrook notes that ever since Walton published his life of Donne in 1640, the poet has conventionally been seen as 'quintessentially a monarchist'. He bemoans such 'pessimism' about Donne, and does his best to counter it, while cautiously insisting that he does not want to argue that he 'was a full-fledged oppositional figure'.[25] Nevertheless, he asserts that Donne wrote 'mordantly

---

[21] Ibid., pp. xl–xli.
[22] Dennis Flynn, *John Donne and the Ancient Catholic Nobility* (Bloomington: Indiana University Press, 1995).
[23] Dennis Flynn, 'Irony in Donne's *Biathanatos* and *Pseudo-Martyr*', *Recusant History* 12 (1973): 49–69, at 55.
[24] Ibid., pp. 69, 66–7.
[25] David Norbrook, 'The Monarchy of Wit and the Republic of Letters: Donne's Politics', in *Soliciting Interpretation. Literary Theory and Seventeenth-Century English Poetry*, ed. by Elizabeth D. Harvey and Katharine Eisaman Maus (Chicago: University of Chicago Press, 1990), pp. 3–36, at 4–5. A fine rebuttal of the claim that Donne was (at least at times) an oppositional figure is in Richard Strier, 'Donne and the politics of devotion', in *Religion,*

antimonarchical poetry' in the 1590s, and argues that it was not until later that he moved closer to absolutism or monarchism. While Carey views *Pseudo-Martyr* as dishonest, and Flynn sees it as subtly critical of James, Norbrook argues that it meant what it said, and that in it Donne 'repudiated his earlier critical stance towards monarchy'. He suggests that Donne's change of political position was linked to a more general 'shift to the right' which occurred 'after the deaths of Cecil and Essex'. Yet he detects signs of oppositionism still later, linking him to Calvinists, and asserting that in 1627 he went 'so far as to declare that he himself wanted to be a puritan'. That same year, he got into trouble for preaching things that the king took to be critical of his policies. True, in 1622 Donne was chosen to preach in defence of James' *Directions to Preachers*. 'But', Norbrook informs us, 'it seems that it was precisely because he was not regarded as a partisan of the conservatives that James regarded him as a suitable person to justify his policies in public.'[26]

Norbrook draws on work by Annabel Patterson to confirm his interpretation.[27] According to Patterson, Donne had friends who 'vehemently adopted an oppositionist stance' in the Addled Parliament of 1614.[28] Sir Robert Phelips was a leading critic of royal policies in a number of early Stuart parliaments, and it was his father Sir Edward (the Master of the Rolls) who found Donne his seat in 1614, 'no doubt through the request of his son'.[29] Patterson detects sympathies for these oppositionists, or at least ambiguities, in a number of Donne's writings. In *Pseudo-Martyr* itself, she claims, democratic elements are uneasily combined with more monarchist ones, and she states that at times the book seems to argue '*with* James rather than for him'.[30] If the king read Donne's 'account of the origins of monarchy carefully', he 'could have scarcely approved' it, and 'might even have seen it as a warning'. For Donne 'advised against the claim that either the papacy or the monarchy draws its authority "Immediately from God"', claiming that not just monarchy, but also other forms of government had 'divine

Literature, and Politics in post-Reformation England, 1540–1688, ed. by Donna B. Hamilton and Richard Strier (Cambridge: Cambridge University Press, 1996), pp. 93–114; at 94 Strier notes the possibility of *principled* loyalty to the established church and state. In 'Essay 6: Impossible Radicalism I: Donne and Freedom of Conscience', in his *Resistant Structures: Particularity, Radicalism, and Renaissance Texts* (Berkeley: University of California Press, 1995), pp. 118–64, Strier argues that at least at some points Donne was a radical advocate of freedom of conscience. But Strier arguably overestimates the radical nature of Donne's claim that even an erring conscience binds; Strier associates this doctrine with Sebastian Castellio, but it is a conventional Catholic principle and may be found in Aquinas, *Summa Theologiae*, 1a2ae, q. 19, art. 5–6; in *Biathanatos*, p. 102, Donne notes that this is Catholic doctrine, citing especially Azorius on it.

[26] Ibid., pp. 8, 16, 17, 24, 23, 22.
[27] Ibid., p. 18.
[28] Annabel Patterson, 'All Donne', in *Soliciting Interpretation*, ed. Harvey and Maus, pp. 37–67.
[29] Annabel Patterson, 'John Donne, Kingsman?', in *The Mental World of the Jacobean Court*, ed by Linda Levy Peck (Cambridge: Cambridge University Press, 1991), pp. 251–72, at 267.
[30] Ibid., p. 262.

sanction'.[31] James, she implies, believed that only monarchy had God's blessing, while other forms were invalid and perhaps even diabolical. Donne, however, held that although 'monarchy was the most perfect form of sovereignty . . . its superiority was only relative'.[32] She finds subversive ideas in his poetry too. For example, the 'Ecclogue' prefixed to his Epithalamion on the Carr–Howard marriage of 1613 uses language to record 'the virtues of James and Carr' which 'treads that slippery line whereby the claim for good is rendered as a denial of the converse imputation'.[33] In other words, by denying that they had vices, he subversively intended to suggest that they really did have them. Again, she sees the reference in *The Sunne Rising* to the king hunting as a 'reflection on James's unpopular obsession'. In the sermon defending the *Directions to Preachers*, Donne argues that kings can pursue an effective foreign policy without going to war, for instance by setting a good example abroad through the moderation of their government at home. Patterson takes this to be an oblique criticism of James for immoderation.[34] She also detects subversion in the *Second Anniversarie*, a poem in which Donne at one point compares various qualities of the dead Elizabeth Drury to royal prerogatives. One prerogative, says Patterson, is very conspicuous by its absence, namely the royal right of levying extra-parliamentary impositions on trade. In 1612, when the poem was published, it 'would have been impossible for Donne's readers . . . not to notice' this omission.[35] Impositions had, of course, elicited vocal criticism in the House of Commons in 1610, and were to do so again in 1614.

To sum up, a number of modern critics contend that Donne used words in devious ways, guilefully conveying meanings that were the opposite of what they seemed on the surface. In this way, he gulled such witless contemporaries as James I, who failed to realize quite how subversive a figure he was. But his writings, though steeped in arcane ancient and medieval learning, were not sufficiently subtle to outwit modern critics. Armed with finely honed psychobiographical tools, they decoded his hidden agenda. To test these views we need to see how they connect to what Donne said.

---

[31] Ibid., pp. 260–1.

[32] Ibid.

[33] Patterson, 'All Donne', p. 52.

[34] John Donne, 'A Sermon upon the XX. Verse of the V. Chapter of the Booke of Iudges. Wherein occasion was justly taken for the Publication of some Reasons, which his Sacred Majestie had been pleased to give, of those Directions for Preachers', in *Sermons* IV, no. 7, pp. 178–209, at 187. Annabel Patterson, *Censorship and Interpretation. The Conditions of Writing and Reading in Early Modern England* (Madison: University of Wisconsin Press, 1984), pp. 94 (hunting), 98–9 (sermon).

[35] Patterson, 'John Donne, Kingsman?', p. 271.

III

In 1558, England was a Catholic country. In theory, the whole population was Catholic, and Queen Mary did her best to ensure that this would be true in practice also, burning some three hundred heretics in a reign of five years. The fires of Smithfield, where the London martyrs suffered, became especially famous. But Mary's half-sister and successor Elizabeth formally broke from the church of Rome and in 1559 introduced a Protestant religious settlement. Elizabeth did not burn Catholics as heretics. But in 1570 the pope excommunicated and deposed her, effectively licensing anyone to assassinate her. A number of leading English Catholics lobbied abroad for military aid to help them restore the faith by force. Eventually, Spain, the greatest Catholic power in Europe, went to war with England, repeatedly sending invasion fleets to conquer the English, oust Elizabeth, and bring back Catholicism. The Queen and her advisors grew increasingly suspicious of Catholics, and over the course of her forty-five year reign, she executed nearly two hundred for treason.

Historians debate exactly when the bulk of the English population became Protestant. We will probably never know the answer. But it seems clear that it was very common indeed for people of Donne's generation to change some of their religious views, moving from a broadly Catholic to a broadly Protestant set of attitudes under the influence of preaching, reading, education, and official pressure. It would be rather odd to describe all of these people as betrayers of the Catholic faith, and odder still to suppose that they were wracked by guilt for having become Protestants. It seems highly likely that the deposition of Elizabeth and the attempts at invasion by Spain helped to persuade many English people to become Protestants. At the age of twenty-four John Donne enlisted in an English expedition to counterattack Spain at Cadiz. In Carey's account of Donne, selfish ambition is portrayed as the motive for the poet's betrayal of his faith. But Carey's version of events is somewhat eccentric in saying virtually nothing about such elementary facts as that the head of the Catholic church licensed the assassination of the head of the English state, that a number of Catholics tried to kill her, and that the leading Catholic power in Europe planned to conquer England. He also neglects to mention that Mary martyred many more people than did Elizabeth. When Donne talked about the Smithfield martyrs, it was, of course, the Protestants who suffered under Mary that he had in mind, and not the Catholics who bulk so large in Carey's interpretation.

We actually know very little about Donne's childhood and early religious convictions. He did, indeed, have Catholic relatives, and in *Pseudo-Martyr* he remarked that he was 'derived from such a stocke and race, as, I beleeve, no family, (which is not of farre larger extent, and greater branches,) hath endured more in their persons and fortunes, for obeying the Teachers of

Romane Doctrine, then it hath done'.[36] Since one of *Pseudo-Martyr*'s main aims was to convince Catholics that they should take the the oath of allegiance, it made sense for Donne to stress his own Catholic antecedents. In *Biathanatos*, he recorded that 'I had my first breeding, and conversation with Men of a suppressed and afflicted Religion, accustomed to the despite of death, and hungry of an imagin'd Martyrdome'.[37] We know his mother had two brothers who were Jesuits and that one was for a while a prisoner in the Tower. The twelve-year old Donne perhaps accompanied his mother in visiting the captive.[38] When Donne was twenty-one, his own younger brother was arrested for harbouring a Catholic priest, and died of plague in prison.[39] We do not know what Donne felt about this. Nor do we know when he became a Protestant, though a date in the early- or mid-1590s is commonly accepted. There is no evidence to support Raspa's idea that as late as 1610 Donne was known largely for his kinship with More and Jesuits – and no one except Donne seems to have mentioned it. The diplomat Beaulieu sent his friend Trumbull a copy of *Pseudo-Martyr* soon after it was published, commenting that it was by 'one Mr. Donne, secretary to my Lord Chancellor', but saying nothing about his kin or religion.[40] When the Jesuit Thomas Fitzherbert responded to *Pseudo-Martyr* in 1613, he said that the book was full of 'impious, blasphemous, and Atheisticall iests against Gods Saints and Servants', quite failing to notice the poet's abiding Catholic sensibilities. He suggested that Donne should stick to 'his old occupation of making Satyres' rather than delve into theology.[41] Another Jesuit, John Floyd, referred in the same year to the way in which one 'I. D.' blasphemously worshipped his mistress's picture in morning and evening devotions. Yet 'I. D.'s fellow-Protestants accused Catholics of idolatry in their honouring of Christ's image. They would never have done so 'were not their witts as dull in divine matters, as they are sharpe in sensual obiects, were they not a kin to the creature of *Dunne* colour, or to that monster whose head is as blockish as his body swinish'.[42] Floyd, too, did not detect Donne's quintessentially Catholic aesthetic, nor connect him to Catholic kin, aristocratic or otherwise.

---

[36] *P-M*, p. 8.

[37] *Biathanatos*, p. 29.

[38] Bald, pp. 44–5; Carey, *John Donne*, pp. 6–7.

[39] Bald, p. 58.

[40] J. Beaulieu to William Trumbull, 31 January 1610, in *H. M. C. Downshire* II (1936), 227.

[41] Thomas Fitzherbert, *A supplement to the discussion of M. D. Barlowes Answere* (1613), pp. 106, 107.

[42] John Floyd, *Purgatories triumph over Hell, maugre the barking of Cerberus* (St Omer, 1613), pp. 17–18. The passage from Floyd, and some other Catholic reactions to Donne, are briefly discussed in Sommerville, 'Jacobean Political Thought and the Controversy over the Oath of Allegiance', p. 69. A fascinating discussion of Donne's possible collaboration with Sir Edward Hoby, which draws on Floyd's remarks, is Alison Shell, 'Donne and Sir Edward Hoby: Evidence for an Unrecorded Collaboration', in this volume.

In *Pseudo-Martyr*, Donne asserted that his conversion to English Protestantism had taken place slowly, and only after he had 'survayed and digested the whole body of Divinity, controverted betweene ours and the Romane Church'.[43] The range of Protestant and especially Catholic writings cited in *Biathanatos* and *Pseudo-Martyr* is staggering, and confirms his claim that he had delved very deeply into the relevant literature. If he became a Protestant only after careful and mature consideration, it is difficult to see how we can properly describe him as betrayer of his faith, who sacrificed religion on the altar of ambition. Yet that is precisely how Carey does describe him. To support his position, he cites a letter from Donne to Goodyer, written eight months or so before the publication of *Pseudo-Martyr*. In *Pseudo-Martyr*, Donne justified the oath of allegiance, but in the letter (says Carey) he claimed that 'there is right on both sides' in the controversy.[44] What the letter actually says is that the oath takes away papal powers, and that it is reasonable for Catholics to stand up for authority claimed by popes, 'so enlightened as they are presumed by them'.[45] In other words, if you begin with the presumption – as 'they' (the Catholics, not Donne) do – that popes are extraordinarily enlightened about everything, including their own powers, then you (but not Donne) will conclude that if a pope says he can depose a king, he can. This reads like the thoughts of someone trying to work out how to refute papalist political ideas on their own terms, and not of someone tempted to endorse the deposing power. In *Pseudo-Martyr*, Donne does in fact try to show that Catholic teachings support taking the oath of allegiance.

Biathanatos argues that suicide can *sometimes* be justified. Donne strongly rejects the idea that it is *always* defensible.[46] He also very vigorously rejects the idea that the law of nature vindicates everything that has actually happened. Carey argues that in *Biathanatos* Donne portrayed the law of nature as nothing more than a description of what people have actually done. So he was being dishonest when in *Pseudo-Martyr* he argued that natural law requires us to take lawful means to defend ourselves. This claim is central to Carey's thesis that *Pseudo-Martyr* is a weak and fraudulent work. It is also utterly without foundation. In *Biathanatos*, Donne declared that '*all the precepts of Naturall Law, result in these, Fly Euill, Seeke Good*. That is, Do according to Reason'.[47] He stressed that what people have actually done is no good guide to the law of nature. If it were, then how could we 'accuse Idolatry, or immolation of Men to be sinnes against Nature?'. In Hispaniola alone 20,000 children a year were sacrificed.[48] Donne did not think this was according to the law of nature. He claimed that that law was equivalent to

---

[43] *P-M*, p. 13.
[44] Carey, *John Donne*, p. 18.
[45] *Letters*, p. 139.
[46] *Biathanatos*, p. 127.
[47] Ibid., p. 46.
[48] Ibid., p. 43.

right reason and held that its dictates were binding moral principles. However, different principles of natural law could in some circumstances conflict with one another. It was, indeed, natural for individuals to preserve themselves. But self-preservation could give place to a higher good. For example, 'rectified Reason' – the law of nature – showed that we should often 'preferre publique, and necessary Persons, by exposing our selves to unevitable destruction'. In other words, natural law tells us to prefer the public good to our private concerns, and the lives of important officials to our own.[49] 'When two naturall Lawes, contrary to one another occurre', said Donne, 'we are bound to that which is *Strictioris Vinculi* [of the stricter bond]', and he argued that we should therefore set greater store by our obligations to God than to our fellows.[50] On Carey's account, of course, it is simply nonsense to suggest that we have any natural obligations, since whatever we in fact do is according to nature, whether it be worshipping God or the devil, or murdering children in Hispaniola. Carey's interpretation seems to apply much more convincingly to the Marquis de Sade than to John Donne. Eccentric results may follow if we confuse the two. Donne's writings are steeped in the philosophy of the ancients and the scholastics. We are liable to miss much of what he said if we dismiss his arguments from these sources as 'a medley of superstition and assertion'.[51] *Biathanatos* was an academic exercise, composed in a tradition of paradoxical writing, and, as Donne remarked, 'upon a misinterpretable subject'. This was why he prevented its publication. The book has, indeed, often been misinterpreted.[52]

In *Biathanatos*, Donne argued that suicide can sometimes be licit if it is in a good cause. In *Pseudo-Martyr*, he claimed that opposing the oath of allegiance was a bad cause, and that those who died after doing so were not true martyrs. There is no incompatibility between these propositions, and no evidence for supposing that one work was sincere and the other a dishonest performance intended to gull a stupid king. In neither book does Donne show the slightest remorse for giving up Catholicism. There is no reason to think that fears of infidelity expressed in Donne's love poetry have anything whatever to do with feelings that he had himself betrayed the faith, for the idea that he ever had any such feelings is purely speculative. It is easy to think of other reasons why he might have feared that beautiful women would be unfaithful to him, and difficult to show that such fears had any connection with his religious biography. Jesuits were very widely disliked in England because they were seen as the leading Catholic advocates of the violent suppression of Protestantism.[53] There is no evidence whatever that Donne disliked them

---

[49] Ibid., p. 47.
[50] Ibid., p. 116.
[51] Carey, *John Donne*, p. 19.
[52] *Letters*, pp. 18–19.
[53] Important discussions of hostility towards Catholics in general and Jesuits in particular include Peter Lake, 'Anti-Popery: the Structure of a Prejudice', in *Conflict in Early Stuart*

because of their hold on his mother's affections. This thesis is pure invention combined with outmoded psychological theory, and an uncharitable critic might style it a medley of superstition and assertion.

Norbrook tells us that Donne wrote mordantly anti-monarchical poems in the 1590s, but does not name them, and they are exceedingly hard to find. If we stretch anti-monarchism to include all criticisms of courtiers, flatterers, and tyrants, we shall find that everyone was an anti-monarchist, including James I, Hobbes, and Bodin. Since James' hunting was not particularly unpopular it is hard to perceive oppositionism in *The Sunne Rising*. The fact that Donne had social links with some people who were critical of royal policy tells us nothing about his political views. The English elite was a small body, and almost every member had multiple social connections with every other member. If we could draw from these connections the conclusion that they all took the same side politically, we could prove that there was no Civil War. But there was one.

The fact that Donne denied that the king or Carr had certain vices cannot (*pace* Patterson) safely be used as evidence that he really thought them guilty of those vices – unless we are willing to turn all his other negatives into positives. For instance, he said there was no family which had suffered more for the faith than his. So did he really mean that all families had suffered more? If all his negatives are really positives, what are his positives? When he is particularly assertive, argues Raspa, we should actually take him to be ambivalent. But why exclude the possibility that he asserted things strongly because he believed them strongly? And are we to conclude that what he stated weakly or hesitantly or ambivalently, he in fact believed sincerely and strongly? Or simply trust the critics, though we do not grasp the rules (if any) that they employ? Suppose Donne had wanted to assert that James' government was moderate, as he seems to in the sermon defending the *Directions to Preachers*. Patterson reads this as a hint that it was immoderate. In Monty Python's *Life of Brian*, Brian denies that he is the Messiah, but is met with the devastating Pattersonian response that 'Only the true Messiah denies his divinity.' Brian asks 'What sort of a chance does *that* give me?'[54] We could ask the same question on Donne's behalf.

Norbrook tells us that Donne said he wanted to be a puritan. But all he actually said was that where puritans were right he wanted to be one, and where Catholics were right he wanted to be one of them too, which adds up to him wanting to be right – and that is not surprising.[55] Norbrook also informs

England: *Studies in Religion and Politics 1603–1642*, ed. by Richard Cust and Ann Hughes (Harlow: Longman, 1989), pp. 72–106; Anthony Milton, *Catholic and Reformed: The Roman and Protestant Churches in English Protestant Thought, 1600–1640* (Cambridge: Cambridge University Press 1995); *Catholicism and Anti-Catholicism in Early Modern English Texts*, ed. by Arthur Marotti (Basingstoke: Macmillan, 1999).

[54] Graham Chapman et al., *Monty Python's The Life of Brian (of Nazareth)* (London: Eyre Methuen, 1979), p. 43.

[55] *Sermons* IX, p. 166.

us that some modern scholars hold Donne to have been a conservative, and that there was a shift to the right after the deaths of Essex and Cecil (in 1601 and 1612). He invites us not to be so pessimistic. People in the early seventeenth century did not distinguish between right and left, or between conservatives and their opponents. There is no evidence that Donne was appointed to defend the *Directions to Preachers* because he was known to be no partisan of the conservatives, as Norbrook claims. It was the absolutism of James I, rather than the constitutionalism of Coke and some members of the Commons, which was innovatory in Donne's lifetime. Why we should see the king as further to the right than his opponents is radically unclear in Norbrook's account. Those opponents were staunch defenders of individual property rights and reduced taxation, while James wanted to subordinate individual rights to the welfare of the community. Many of those opponents were Christian fundamentalists, of rigidly puritanical moral views. Why it is pessimistic to suppose that Donne sided against them is mysterious.

Patterson says that the *Second Anniversarie* was a subversive work, since its list of prerogatives does not include the right of levying impositions. There are a number of problems with this contention. Lists of prerogatives standardly included a great many royal powers which Donne does not here discuss. A simple-minded approach might be to observe that this poem is intended to say nice things about a dead woman (Elizabeth Drury) and that he therefore mentioned those prerogatives which reminded him of flattering things he could say about her, and kept silent on others. But suppose we want to insist (without any evidence) that he really is making profound political points here. In that case, we could argue that he was an extreme radical, since he did not mention the royal prerogative of imprisoning without cause shown. Yet that prerogative was widely acknowledged until the 1620s. So, by saying nothing whatever about it, Donne was expressing his advanced political radicalism. In 1612, a prerogative action which may well have bulked larger in people's minds than impositions was the king's recent dissolution of parliament. It was almost universally recognized that monarchs had the prerogative to call and dissolve parliaments at will. Yet Donne passes over the right in silence. We could argue, in Pattersonian manner, that he was therefore challenging that prerogative, and that he looked forward to the day when parliament would meet without the king's summons. Or, equally, we could argue that by failing to mention parliament at all, Donne was suggesting that the king rule without it. A preferable alternative might be to search for Donne's political ideas in his political writings rather than in poems in praise of dead women.

A lengthy political writing which seemingly endorsed James I's views was *Pseudo-Martyr*. Patterson – one of the few critics who does not dismiss the book in a sentence or two – argues that appearances are deceptive and that if we read the book closely, as James seemingly did not, we will find that it subtly subverts the king's ideas. She grounds this contention on the claim that

Donne, unlike James, believed that although monarchy was 'the most perfect form of sovereignty', other forms (like aristocracy and democracy) were also valid and divinely sanctioned. The problem here is that practically everyone in the early seventeenth century held that all forms of government are from God – after all, St Paul had said that 'the powers that be are ordained of God' (Romans 13:1), and the Venetian Republic (which James fully recognized, and indeed abetted) was manifestly a power that was. In the opening words of his famous *Trew Law of Free Monarchies*, James asserted that monarchy was the 'forme of government' which 'approcheth neerest to perfection' – a strikingly similar claim to Donne's.[56] Neither in the *Trew Law* nor anywhere else did the king suggest that monarchy alone had divine sanction. Patterson detects democratic elements in the account of the origins of government which Donne gives in *Pseudo-Martyr*. But they are absent. Donne said that if a company of savages agreed 'to a civill maner of living', 'Magistracie, & Superioritie, would necessarily, and naturally, and Divinely grow out of this consent.' He spelled out what this meant. Whatever form of government the savages introduced, the power of the sovereign would be from God alone: 'And into what maner and forme soever they had digested and concocted this Magistracie, yet the power it-selfe was *Immediately* from God.'[57] Patterson informs us that Donne 'advised against the claim' that 'monarchy draws its authority "Immediately from God"'.[58] In fact, Donne asserted precisely that claim. *Whatever* form of government the original people chose, including monarchy, their governors would hold power from God alone, not from the people. Some thinkers (Suárez was one) claimed that the original people in any state had been a self-governing democracy, and that later rulers therefore held power from the originally sovereign people on the terms which it had stipulated. Donne's account of the origins of government was calculated to combat this thesis, denying that the first rulers had been accountable to the people rather than to God alone. Patterson's contention that Donne in fact *adopted* a 'theory of original democracy'[59] is unfounded.

Opponents of royal policy under the early Stuarts typically argued that the English constitution was a limited or mixed monarchy, and that the royal prerogative was subordinate to the law. They rejected the notion that in every state there must be one person or assembly which held ultimately sovereign power. The theory that there must be a single, indivisible sovereign in each state was characteristic of the famous French absolutist Jean Bodin, with whose works Donne was certainly familiar (he cited them in *Biathanatos*). In *Pseudo-Martyr*, the poet made it clear that he too endorsed the idea of absolute and indivisible sovereignty. 'God', he declared, 'inanimates every

---

[56] James VI and I, *The Trew Law of Free Monarchies*, in *Political Writings*, ed. by Johann P. Sommerville (Cambridge: Cambridge University Press, 1994), pp. 62–84, at 63.

[57] *P-M*, p. 79.

[58] Patterson, 'John Donne, Kingsman?', p. 261.

[59] Ibid.

State with one power, as every man with one soule.' In a monarchy sovereignty – 'which is a power to do all things availeable to the main endes' – was in the hands of the king. It followed that the power of kings was unlimited. When the original people at first congregated together and decided to live in a monarchy, God granted the king full sovereignty. The people could not limit his power or subject it to conditions, any more than parents could decide to modify a child's soul: 'when therefore people concurre in the desire of such a *King*, they cannot contract, nor limitt his power: no more then parents can condition with God, or preclude or withdraw any facultie from that Soule, which God hath infused into the body, which they prepared, and presented to him'.[60] Critics of royal policy in the early Stuart parliaments standardly insisted that different countries had different constitutions, and that the extent of royal power varied from place to place. But James I argued that all true monarchs had the same sovereign powers, and Donne agreed, repeating the point in the *Devotions*: 'the sovereignty is the same in all states'.[61]

Since the king held sovereign power, he could use his prerogative to override the law if he thought that such a course was necessary. Prerogative, he declared in *Biathanatos*, 'is incomprehensible, and overflowes and transcends all Law'.[62] 'Nature', remarked Donne in his *Essays in divinity*, 'is the Common law by which God governs us', while 'Miracle is his Prerogative . . . And Miracle is not like prerogative in any thing more than in this, that no body can tell what it is.'[63] This was, perhaps, the central tenet of early Stuart absolutist thinking, and it was wholly at odds with the views of the king's parliamentary critics. For they argued that prerogative was defined and measured. The king's prerogative, they said, was simply what the law permitted him to do. The king and his supporters, on the other hand, maintained that good government requires that the prince possess prerogatives to act outside the law if need be. On this crucial question, as on the linked question of unlimited sovereignty, Donne sided definitively with the king. There were differences between Donne and James. Their attitudes to Thomas More diverged profoundly, as Patterson perceptively notes.[64] But on fundamental questions of political thought, there seems to have been little to distinguish them.

IV

On questions of church–state relations, too, Donne took very much the same line as the king. His *Pseudo-Martyr* was a contribution to the debate over the

---

[60] *P-M*, p. 133.
[61] *Devotions*, p. 35.
[62] *Biathanatos*, p. 48.
[63] *Essays*, p. 81.
[64] Patterson, 'John Donne, Kingsman?', p. 258.

Jacobean oath of allegiance, and its arguments are often similar to those of other defenders of the oath, such as Thomas Morton, Lancelot Andrewes, and James I himself. Papalists like Bellarmine argued that the family, the state, and the church were all divinely appointed institutions, and that each corresponded with a basic human aim. The family secured the preservation of people, while the state furthered their temporal ends, and the church promoted their spiritual good. Since spiritual welfare was more important than mere material comfort, the church – which Christ had established to lead us to salvation – was superior to the state, and Christ's vicar – the pope – had authority over kings. This authority, the papalist case proceeded, included the power to employ temporal means in order to gain spiritual ends. If a king fell into heresy and endangered the salvation of his subjects, the pope could depose him. Papal power, they said, came to the pope directly from God, for though the Cardinals elected a particular person to be pope, it was God and not they who conferred authority upon him. Kings, on the other hand, got their powers from the people and not from God alone. If a pope deposed a king, good Christians could use force to oust him. True, in early Christian times the clergy had preached obedience rather than resistance to pagan and heretical emperors. But this was because they lacked the means to overthrow them.

Like other defenders of the oath of allegiance, Donne vigorously rejected Bellarmine's claim that ancient Christians had possessed the right to depose kings, but had refrained from exercising it for reasons of expediency.[65] Like Andrewes, Morton and the rest, too, he rejected the papalist idea that the church is superior to the state, arguing instead that kings and clerics had separate functions and that they were 'sheepe to one another'.[66] In spiritual matters, kings were part of the clergy's flock, while on temporal questions the king was the shepherd. Kings had no power to preach or administer the sacraments, and clerics could never use temporal coercion (unless the king granted them the power to do so). Bellarmine argued that the pope derives his authority from God alone, though the Cardinals elect him. Donne responded that kings likewise get their authority only from God.[67] Human means might determine who is king but royal power came directly to the king from God. John Buckeridge and William Barret used just the same analogy between popes and kings to make precisely the same point. Robert Bolton and Thomas Morton argued very similarly.[68] Barret was a Catholic – of a Gallican, anti-papalist stripe – while Buckeridge – Laud's tutor at Oxford – belonged to the anti-Calvinist wing of the English church, and Bolton and Morton were stern

---

[65] *P-M*, p. 249. Sommerville, 'Jacobean Political Thought and the Controversy over the Oath of Allegiance', pp. 305–6.

[66] *P-M*, pp. 38–9.

[67] Ibid., p. 78.

[68] J. P. Sommerville, *Royalists and Patriots. Politics and Ideology in England 1603–1640* (London: Longman, 1999), p. 25.

Calvinists. All held that rational argument from the basic elements of human nature could tell us about the fundamental principles of politics. In grounding his political ideas on the law of nature, Donne was doing nothing unusual, and nothing which in any sense committed him to a particular theological position, whether Calvinist or Arminian.[69]

In the dedication to the king of *Pseudo-Martyr*, Donne said that armies commonly included volunteers as well as conscripts, and that the army which was fighting in defence of the oath of allegiance was no exception.[70] He himself was a volunteer, since he had not been commissioned to write. One of the conscripts was William Barlow, Bishop of Lincoln, who had replied to the Jesuit Parsons' attack on the king's own book. Though he did not say so in print, Donne took a dim view of Barlow's performance, criticizing him for distorting evidence and for insulting his adversary. The book, he said, had 'given new justice to my ordinary complaint, That the Divines of these times, are become meer Advocates, as though Religion were a temporall inheritance; they plead for it with all sophistications, and illusions and forgeries'.[71] In *Pseudo-Martyr*, Donne similarly inveighed against Catholics for casting 'personall aspersions' upon those who disagreed with them even on small points.[72] He took great delight in exposing the 'blasphemous detorsions, & bold mis-applications' of Scripture which he found in Catholic writings.[73] But his tone towards his opponents was generally polite, and he often used the term Catholics – rather than Roman Catholics, or papists – to describe the members of the Roman church.[74]

While Barlow was concerned simply to rebut Jesuit attacks on James I's ideas, Donne had the further purpose of persuading Catholics to abandon the papal deposing power and take the oath of allegiance. *Pseudo-Martyr* included a lengthy preface addressed to Catholics, in which he exhorted them 'to a just love of your owne safetie, of the peace of your Countrey, of the honour and reputation of your Countreymen, and of the integritie of that, which you call the Catholicke cause'. The country suffered as long as English Catholics acknowledged the papal deposing power, which destabilized and weakened the king's government. The Catholic cause suffered from the apparent equation of Catholicism with treason.[75] In the body of the book, Donne drew almost exclusively on the writings of Catholics, and on sources they recognized as authoritative – Scripture, the Fathers, Canon Law. *Pseudo-Martyr* was not a mere academic exercise, intended to win royal favour, but a

[69] A fuller discussion of the debate on the papal deposing power is in Sommerville, 'Jacobean Political Thought and the Controversy over the Oath of Allegiance', pp. 248–328.
[70] *P-M*, p. 3.
[71] *Letters*, pp. 139–40, 138.
[72] *P-M*, p. 11.
[73] Ibid., p. 81.
[74] Ibid., for example, pp. 164, 165, 167, 168.
[75] Ibid., pp. 28, 27.

genuine attempt to persuade Donne's former co-religionists to abandon the papal deposing power and take the oath of allegiance. The oath included a clause denouncing as heretical the doctrine that excommunicated kings could be murdered by their subjects. Most of the king's supporters in the controversy paid little attention to this passage, but Donne found that the clause worried Catholics with whom he discussed the oath. A central contention of the king's – and Donne's – case on the oath was that it was wholly civil, and did not require the swearer to deny any Catholic doctrine on purely *spiritual* questions. But a number of Catholics felt that this clause *did* intrude on the spiritual realm. 'I have found in some *Catholiques*', said Donne, 'when I have importuned them to instance, in what part of the oath *spirituall* Jurisdiction was oppugned, or what deterr'd them from taking the same, that they insisted upon this, That it belonged onely to the *Pope*, to pronounce a *Doctrine* to be *Hereticall*', and they also claimed that a General Council of the Church had endorsed the papal deposing power. Donne asserted that on every other point, 'great, and reverend persons' had shown that the oath said nothing about the pope's spiritual powers, but he believed he had something new to contribute on the heretical clause, and he spent the concluding pages of his book attempting to remove Catholic scruples on the issue by arguing that it was not the excommunicating but the murdering of kings which the oath condemned as heretical.[76]

Many of his Protestant contemporaries regarded papists as Antichristian idolaters with whom there was little point in conversing. Donne was far more sympathetic to Catholics, believing they were misguided on important points, but that at least some of them might be persuaded to drop their errors and reunite with other Christians.[77] He was particularly sympathetic towards Gallicans. In 1612 Donne was in France with Sir Robert Drury. There, the Syndic of the Sorbonne, Edmond Richer, had recently published an ultra-Gallican work against papal power, and been called in question by the clergy in consequence. Donne had an appointment to meet him, and was keen to prove to him that 'there was no proposition in his Book, which I could not shew in Catholique authors of 300 years'. Richer backed out of the meeting, on the grounds that associating with English people would do him no good, and that the Jesuits were plotting to kill him. In *Pseudo-Martyr*, Donne drew on French and Venetian anti-papalists.[78] He plainly agreed with them in

---

[76] *P-M*, ibid., pp. 255, 254, 266.

[77] No doubt Donne's own Catholic background played a part in the formation of his eirenical and ecumenical approach to Catholicism, though some converts from Catholicism became rabid enemies of the old faith – Richard Sheldon, for instance, and John Gee. A thinker and poet who like Donne had a Catholic background (through his mother), and who adopted tolerant and latitudinarian religious attitudes, was Lucius Cary, Viscount Falkland. Falkland regarded Donne as 'the most wittie, and most eloquent of our Modern Divines': *Sir Lucius Cary, Late Lord Viscount of Falkland, His Discourse of Infallibility, with an Answer to it: And his Lordships Reply* (1651), p. 288.

[78] *P-M*, for example, pp. 15, 171, 176, 188.

rejecting the papal deposing power, but his key argument did not entail the truth of Gallican views on church–state relations. Rather, it centered on the very fact that Catholics disagreed with one another on such matters – with Jesuits taking a different stance from Gallicans, and with even such staunch papalists as Bellarmine and Baronius at loggerheads with each another on details.[79] Since a wide variety of views on the deposing power circulated amongst Catholics, and since none of them was in fact punished as heretical at Rome, it was no part of a Catholic's religious duty to undergo martyrdom in England for a doctrine which was at best doubtful, and certainly not an article of faith: 'it will not constitute a *Martyrdome*, to seale with your bloud any such point heere, as the affirming of the contrary, would not draw you into the fire at Rome'. English people *certainly* had a duty of allegiance to the English government, and it was quite unclear that the pope could ever release them from it. But it was a rule of moral philosophy that we should not 'abstaine from a practique duety, for a speculative doubt'.[80]

Donne's arguments most closely resemble those of a small group of *Catholic* defenders of the Jacobean oath, including William Barret, William Warmington, the Franco-Scot John Barclay, and most of all the Benedictine Thomas Preston (who wrote under the name of Roger Widdrington). All of these writers were influenced by Gallican ideas, and all used Catholic sources to rebut Bellarmine's views on the deposing power. In a series of books published from 1611 onwards, Preston mounted a case in favour of the oath strikingly similar to Donne's.[81] He argued that the deposing power was controverted amongst Catholics, and that as long as the question remained unresolved, it would be wrong to put the power into practice against any king. The pope's claim to be able to depose rulers, he said, is merely a claim, 'which so long as it is disputable, and debated on either side, can never be put in *practise* by any man, what opinion so ever he follow in *speculation*, without doing the *Prince*, who is deposed by the *Pope*, manifest wrong, and if he be a subject, by committing that detestable crime of treason in a most high degree'.[82] For Preston, as for Donne, practical duties trumped speculative doubts. There are many other resemblances between the two writers. For instance, both held a high opinion of Preston's fellow-Benedictine Gregory Sayer – 'A great *Casuist*, and our Countreyman',

[79] Ibid., pp. 188–9, 252.
[80] Ibid., pp. 252–3.
[81] William Barret, *Ius Regis, siue de absoluto & independenti secularium principum dominio & obsequio eis debito* (Basle [really London], 1612); William Warmington, *A Moderate Defence of the Oath of Allegiance* (1612); John Barclay, *Pietas, sive publicae pro Regibus, ac Principibus, et privatae pro Guilielmo Barclaio parente Vindiciae* (Paris, 1612); Thomas Preston (alias Roger Widdrington)'s many works include *Apologia Cardinalis Bellarmini pro Iure Principum* (1611); and *A Cleare, Sincere, and Modest Confutation of the unsound, fraudulent, and intemperate reply of T. F.* (1616).
[82] Preston, *Cleare, Sincere, and Modest Confutation*, sigs. A4v–B1r.

as Donne called him.[83] But it is hard to prove any direct link between Donne and Preston.

As Donne noted, a number of 'great, and reverend persons' had written in defence of the oath.[84] Since he was a relatively junior member of the king's team, it is not surprising that his book attracted less attention than the writings of such more senior figures as Andrewes, Barlow or Morton. Again, *Pseudo-Martyr* was not targetted against any specific Catholic work, so there was no great polemical urgency for Catholics to reply to it. Moreover, Catholics (like Preston) who *supported* the oath had a disincentive to refer to Donne explicitly, since his Protestantism might make him suspect to a Catholic readership. Given these considerations, the book gained quite a favourable reception. The Jesuit Thomas Fitzherbert referrred to it on the titlepage of his own answer to Barlow, and in the text expressed the hope that a fuller reply to *Pseudo-Martyr* would soon be published. Donne himself believed that the Jesuits were preparing one. Soon after *Pseudo-Martyr* came out, John Boys, Dean of Canterbury, referred with praise to Donne's discussion of canon law.[85] When Andrewes' defence of the oath was attacked by the Jesuit Martinus Becanus (or Martin Van der Beek), the cleric Robert Burhill penned the official response, which was published by the King's Printer in 1611. Boasting that the oath had able advocates, he provided a short list of them, with Andrewes first, Barlow in second place, and Donne third.[86] We sometimes think of early modern religious controversies as utterly arid exchanges of jibes and sarcasm. They also had more laudable objectives and consequences, including the removal of corruptions from the texts of Scripture and the writings of the church Fathers. This was a particular preoccupation of Bodley's first Librarian, Thomas James, who published a book on the subject in 1612. In it he praised Donne, and repeatedly drew on *Pseudo-Martyr*.[87]

The professional path on which Donne embarked when he started to study controversial theology led him eventually to fame and honour as Dean of St Paul's. His *Pseudo-Martyr* began the work of establishing his reputation as a divine, as well as winning him the king's patronage. But the purpose of the book was not merely to enhance his wealth and reputation. It also had more altruistic goals. One was to save lives by preventing Catholics from going to

[83] *P-M*, p. 263. Preston drew extensively on Sayer's writings: for example, *Apologia Cardinalis Bellarmini*, pp. 39, 40, 236, 357.

[84] *P-M*, p. 254.

[85] Thomas Fitzherbert, *A Supplement to the Discussion of M. D. Barlowes Answere . . . And By the way is briefly censured M. Iohn Dunnes Booke, intituled Pseudo-Martyr* (St Omer, 1613), p. 107 (hopes for a reply to Donne). Bald, p. 226 (Donne expects a Jesuit reply; Boys).

[86] Robert Burhill, *Pro Tortura Torti* (1611), p. 21: '*Advocati* non erubescendi, Episcopus Eliensis quem tu *Sacellanum* vocas, Episcopus Lincolniensis, *Iohannes Donnus* in Pseudomartyre . . .'.

[87] Thomas James, *A Treatise of the Corruptions of Scripture, Councels, and Fathers, by the Prelats, Pastors, and Pillars of the Church of Rome, for maintenance of Popery and irreligion* (1612), part 3, p. 55; part 4, pp. 6, 9.

death needlessly in the vain hope of martyrdom. Another was to secure the state by discouraging doctrines permitting the use of violence for religious ends. And a third was to clear the path to truth by exposing forgeries, corruptions, and misinterpretations – or medleys of superstition and assertion.

Chapter 5

THE PROFESSION OF FRIENDSHIP IN DONNE'S AMATORY VERSE LETTERS

DAVID CUNNINGTON

D ONNE'S first verse letter to a woman opens on a familiar scene of first beginnings. It is a new image of 'That unripe side of earth' redolent with the oldest story of man and woman through which Donne shapes the dimensions of his desired attachment to Elizabeth, Countess of Huntingdon. In the scenic discovery of a displaced Eden within an anciently preserved new world the letter enacts its attempt to initiate a register for the familiarity it negotiates between poet and countess. What the first lines also initiate is that disarming paradox of scale by which magnitudes become the trivia of compliment, dignity an exaggerated obeisance, and within which Donne can measure the tone of his most sociably practised of forms, those verse letters to aristocratic women, by recourse to the aspect of a primal narrative. An aspect:

> That gives us man up now, like *Adams* time
> Before he ate; mans shape, that would yet bee
> (Knew they not it, and fear'd beasts companie)
> So naked at this day, as though man there
> From Paradise so great a distance were,
> As yet the newes could not arrived bee
> Of *Adams* tasting the forbidden tree.[1]

The scene has a hope for starting anew, at a closeness not compromised by a knowing sexuality, in which man and woman might look on each other with new eyes, hear with innocent ears. But renewal is also reform and the poem is not deaf to the practices of persuasion it inherits, the history of poetic courtesies which are material to its voice. As the uncertainties of an

---

[1] 'To the Countesse of Huntington' [hereafter 'That unripe side . . .'], lines 1, 3–8; John Donne, *The Satires, Epigrams and Verse Letters*, ed. by W. Milgate (Oxford: Clarendon Press, 1967). See pp. 193–4 for discussion of the authorship and date of this letter.

introduction to a new patroness are made consonant with the difficulties of an encounter with received forms of poetic compliment, the letter recognises the condition of its own tropes of flattery in the burdened innocence of those primitive figures, 'Depriv'd of that free state which they were in, / And wanting the reward, yet beare the sinne'.[2] In the sixteen lines that follow this memory of Eden, the search to discover terms for poetic companionship becomes the search for a voice. The letter repudiates those outworn lyric voices it supersedes:

> Yet neither will I vexe your eyes to see
> A sighing Ode, nor crosse-arm'd Elegie
> I come not to call pitty from your heart,
> Like some white-liver'd dotard that would part
> Else from his slipperie soule with a faint groane,
> And faithfully, (without you smil'd) were gone.[3]

Where these lines profess themselves innocent of the deceits of lyric seduction their innocence is such as keeps its social poise, aware of the fashionable demands made on poetry of compliment. Donne sounded the exequies for courtly *amour* again in his letter to Katherine Howard, Countess of Salisbury, where his voice and her beauty are set off from a climate in which:

> the Sunne
> Growne stale, is to so low a value runne,
> That his disshevel'd beames and scatter'd fires
> Serve but for Ladies Periwigs and Tyres
> In lovers Sonnets.[4]

The lesson that the sun of female beauty has set as a vocabulary of praise appeals to Lady Salisbury as a reader able, by appreciation of its parody, to rejuvenate a lexicon that has 'shrunken, and dri'd'. To deliver the poet and the language of praise from the social reputation of the Elizabethan *amator* the verse letters displace the erotic sincerity of their professions, flattering the countesses for their ability to disdain the tropes of tired poetic fashion.[5] Although, at their most laboured, these poems can manage to sound both raw and fatigued – 'The honesties of love with ease I doe, / But am no porter for a tedious woo' – to dismiss their banality as elemental to an attachment that neither desires nor deserves the attention of others risks misunderstanding how, in the fashionably aware erudition they credit to recipients, Donne's letters suggest an image of the female

---

[2] 'That unripe side . . .', lines 9–10.
[3] Ibid., lines 21–5.
[4] 'To the Countesse of Salisbury' [Hereafter 'Faire, great, and good . . .'], lines 3–7.
[5] 'That unripe side . . .', lines 35–6.

courtier which was to become satirically conspicuous in Jacobean literature and court life.[6]

David Norbrook has observed a paradox in which Donne's political ambition 'to become part of a society from which he feels alienated' contends with a desire 'to maintain a critical distance, a standpoint outside the existing social order from which he can criticise it'.[7] This account also describes well a tension felt within the letter to Lady Huntingdon between a satire which seeks to negotiate an idea of companionship detached from the conventions of persuasive sentiment and the writer's imaginative need for a language which embraces the vulnerabilities and 'honesties of love'.[8] If the former purpose threatens to flatten the activity of reading into a coy traffic in satiric commonplaces, a more difficult encounter with the past of literary desire, a struggle with the frustrations it tries to internalise, is audible in the letter's formal awkwardness. In pursuit of a form in which to address the aristocracy it was not to the sonnet structure of his earlier verse epistles that Donne turned, but to the running couplets of his elegies and satires. But those couplets lose their agility as the poem describes its transition from 'cross arm'd elegie' to epistolary counsel:

> As all discoverers whose first assay
> Findes but the place, after, the nearest way:
> So passion is to womans love, about,
> Nay, farther off, than when we first set out.
> It is not love that sueth, or doth contend;
> Love either conquers, or but meets a friend.
> Man's better part consists of purer fire,
> And findes it selfe allow'd, ere it desire.
> Love is wise here, keepes home, gives reason sway,
> And journeys not till it finde summer-way.[9]

This is laboriously put, the narrative continuity of the poem's account of its pioneering course being set against the rhythmic rigidity of syntactic units conspicuously deprived of that facility across the line which characterised Donne's earlier couplets. For if in the satires and elegies the patterns of contrastive stress, and the enjambment which disorients the integrity of the poems' constituent couplets, give the effect of a voice contending against its formal inheritance, in these end-stopped couplets the studied consonance of rhetorical and metrical stress sounds the letter's difficulty in conceiving possibilities for erudite friendship while having only the conceits of erotic

---

[6] Ibid., lines 75–6.
[7] David Norbrook, 'The Monarchy of Wit and the Republic of Letters: Donne's Politics', in *Soliciting Interpretation*, ed. by Elizabeth D. Harvey and Katherine Eisaman Maus (Chicago: University of Chicago Press, 1990), pp. 3–36.
[8] 'That unripe side . . .', line 95.
[9] Ibid., lines 53–62.

lyricism in which to speak that friendship. The struggle for fluency tells in the lines' attempt to conceive of a new form of companionship while working within a vocabulary charged with the motives of Petrarchan desire. In preciously discriminating the qualities of its professed sentiment the semantic contortions imposed on 'love' (passionately 'pure' but regardful of its success, conquering and amicable) with the tentative echo of 1 Corinthians 13:4–6 in the central couplet, indicate the pressure the lines are under to discover a character of companionship for which Elizabethan dedicatory verse was without a voice.

It may be that the extravagance, like the involved stiffness, of the letter conceals a real neediness behind the performance of one. A reader familiar with Erasmian guides for brevity in letters of compliment would have reason to consider specious loquacity an insufficiency of style. But in Donne's verse pleonasm becomes a style of insufficiency, as garrulity unable to disguise the effort of its own performance shows excess to be a measure of want. A want of something like an available elegant, verbal gesture with which a poet might invite himself into familiarity with a patroness, and which could also convince as to the value of that invitation. The awkwardness of the letter to Lady Huntingdon has the double effect of a voice learning the possibilities of a social form and of a deliberate faltering which catches the manner of the suitor overimpressed by the attention of his grand recipient.

Donne did not write at such length to a living woman again and the apparent textual corruption of the letter in its first printed form (that of the 1635 *Poems*) has been taken up by those who have doubted its authenticity. Yet the textual discontinuities (lines 10–11, 20–1) have a way of complementing the letter's stylistic entanglement – the oscillation between ellipsis and prolixity, the abrupt changes of direction (lines 76–7, 94–5) and the pronounced syntactic contortion – so as to indicate the difficulty of the poet's desire to find a style sensitive to the letter's social conduct. The readiness to mock the inherited tradition of love poetry as a body of insensible formalities coheres obliquely with the attempt to invent new tropes of persuasion. For the satire pulls against the cheapening of its heritage, working to restore a credibility to the poetry of compliment. The jolting recourse from ridicule of tropes of enamoured subservience to the brittle exorbitance of 'nice thinne Schoole divinity' conveys a felt need for a language that could supply a social understanding of the familiarity possible between poet and female superior.[10]

Something of the uncertain identity of the attachment that the verse letter negotiates is expressed in Donne's account to Sir Henry Goodyer of how, in the differing claims exerted by differing degrees of friendship, the lesser 'hath many deviations, which are strayings into new loves, (not of other men; for that is proper to true wise friendship, which is not a marring; but of other

---

[10] 'Madame, You have refin'd . . .', line 61.

things)'.[11] Despite straying, Gosse served this letter well with the mis-transcription: 'true wise friendship, which is not a marrying'.[12] Where this turns an aside into a consideration of the comparative closure of two different loves, it draws the letter into reflection on epistolary verse where friendship, if not a marrying, exerts a compromising hold on the terms of participants' honour. Perhaps this slip is useful because the divisive properties of friendship, as conducted in poetry of compliment, are rarely more conspicuous than when they encounter the respectably possessive binds of the marriage contract. Where Jacobean verse epistles to women combine techniques from literary traditions of different repute, their formal coupling can create a hybrid intimacy which inherits the persuasive impetus of erotic petition but justifies its social value by its identity with the friendships of humanist correspondence. In Donne's letters the translation of a convention of friendship, which consists in shared habits of reading, into terms of familiarity between poet and married Lady involves the accommodation of the character and value invested in the idea of literary companionship to the other responsibilities to which each countess was obliged for her honour.

If not expressly a marrying, a transaction not unlike a betrothal rite echoes in the oddly liturgical profession of fidelity that closes Donne's second verse letter to Lady Huntingdon:

> Now that my prophesies are fulfill'd,
> Rather then God should not be honour'd too,
> And all these gifts confess'd, which hee instill'd,
> Your selfe were bound to say that which I doe.[13]

In saying 'I doe', binding herself by and to the words of her profession, the countess commits to a memory that the poet prefers of the devotion promised by his earlier epistle. This request for the countess to recall praise delivered as 'long agoe' as her youth attempts to element the present compliments with a shared past, as if to enable them with an integrity. This, in a way, is an evidence of the difficulty that Barbara Everett identified as a 'problem of sincerity, of purity of motive in love and art'.[14] For, slightly differently to Everett's meaning, Donne's effort to imbue his compliments with a history, to give them the weight of an affection that can develop only over time, registers

---

[11] *Letters*, p. 27.

[12] Gosse I, p. 225. Gosse's transcription may have a kind of fidelity, 'marring in marrying' being idiomatically current when this letter was written. See Morris Palmer Tilley, *A Dictionary of the Proverbs in England in the Sixteenth and Seventeenth Centuries: a Collection of the Proverbs Found in English Literature and the Dictionaries of the Period* (Ann Arbor: University of Michigan Press, 1950), M701.

[13] 'Mans to Gods . . .', lines 61–4.

[14] Barbara Everett, 'Donne: A London Poet', *Proceedings of the British Academy* 58 (1972): 245–73 (264), hears the dilemma exactly: 'It was in fact in the relationship of poet to patroness that the problem of sincerity, or purity of motive in love and art, confronted him in one of its most searching and explicit forms.'

how words carry a value which intention alone cannot give them. Readers once disliked Donne's epistolary flatteries less because they were found incredible than because insincere. But the poem to Lady Huntingdon understands the difficulty of its own sincerity, recognising how words and phrases accumulate significance through the custom of their exchange between individuals. This is why, for example, although 'I love you' can, perhaps, be said with sincerity at any time from a first date to a golden wedding anniversary, it is the value the lovers concerned have learned to place in those words, the previous uses they have been asked to serve and, in a shared life, a memory of the moments at which they have been delivered that gives the words their bearing. Donne may have met Lady Huntingdon, then Lady Elizabeth Stanley, during his service in her father's household or later when she became a ward of York House.[15] But that he needed to seek assurance from Goodyer and remind him, 'though I had a little preparation to her knowledge in the house where I served at first, yet I think she took her characters of me from you' suggests he recognised how his allusion to the countess's 'yonger dayes' affected an intimacy to which it was not entitled.[16] Where the second poem undertakes the preparation of its own character, summoning the past as witness for its present integrity, it apprehends how imposture can become imposition. The capitalised nouns of the final stanzas pronounce to the eye the letter's attempt to solicit trust by availing the poet of the security of clerical office:

> So I, but your Recorder am in this,
> Or mouth, or Speaker of the universe,
> A ministeriall Notary, for 'tis
> Not I, but you and fame, that makes this verse;
>
> I was your Prophet in your yonger dayes,
> And now your Chaplaine, God in you to praise.[17]

The substantial weight of this chain of offices – 'Recorder . . . Or mouth, or Speaker . . . Notary . . . your Prophet . . . your Chaplaine' – where the assonantal succession of possessive pronouns after conjectural conjunctions promotes the effect of resolution to the letter's dedication – needs to be balanced against the evasive grammar of its persuasion. The penultimate full stanza begins in a tense of accomplishment, 'Now that my . . .', only for the following lines to turn parenthetically aside, absenting the personal presence of the writer from the note of his conviction. The line that does conclude the sentence returns to the simple present of 'I doe' only by way of an indirect imperative, an injunction – 'were bound to say' – impersonally distanced

---

[15] See Dennis Flynn, *John Donne and the Ancient Catholic Nobility* (Bloomington: Indiana University Press, 1995), Chapter 6.

[16] *Letters*, pp. 184–5.

[17] 'Man to Gods . . .', lines 65–70.

from a pronominal subject as if the obligation were less the poet's impertinence than a self-imposed duty. Perhaps a woman of Lady Huntingdon's position could be bound not to regard any indecorum, but in the dictional field where praises become precatory words, 'honour' assumes a dependence on both the bonds of correspondence and the countess's fidelity as a reader. The several ways in which the 'ministerial Notary' interposes – as mediator between His and her 'gifts', between the countess and her voice, her 'selfe' and her 'honour' – are also ways in which the correspondence contract exerts a tenure on the terms of the countess's social dignity.

Another work of 1608 with an interest in the habits of companionship to which married couples contract can help to illustrate the liberal and confining quality of Donne's praise. An instruction in the decorum of married life, William Heale's *Apologie for Women* envisages how a husband should be the example of his own propriety: 'for the abbreviarie of a husbands words and actions, is as it were the chamber glasse whereby a wife shoulde addresse herselfe. At his tongue she should learne to speak, by his carriage she should compose her behaviour'.[18] Even as they emphasise a husband's responsibility, these lines make idiomatic contact with the tropes of epistolary counsel, and doing so signal the possibility for a divergence from such suits as Jonson's presentation of his letter to Katherine, Lady Aubigny as a 'glasse' wherein she might 'see / In my character, what your features bee'.[19] An antinomy awaits the wife advised to take her character from the voice of her husband and from her familiar, each of which impose limits on and afford possibilities for the conduct of her virtue. Such 'gifts' as Donne's letter praises are not those acquired by imitation of a husband's prudence but those realised by a reader of judgement, by an address to the poet's own words. This is not to say that Donne's poem feeds the rivalry that Jonson could imply between a poet's and a husband's interest. Nor does it appear that jealous resentments blighted Lady Huntingdon's married life. Yet where it projects a kind of social virtue associated with the countess's ability as a reader, the letter identifies a quality of honour distinct from that manifested by a good wife's attention to her husband. In some respect, even as it consecrates the preceding stanza's praise of the countess's literary 'judgement', the letter's ceremonial ending dramatises an effect of the possessive instincts of amicable compliment.

Perhaps this is not the only image of anticipated union that the later letter remembers. Again it is the possible rivalries between two kinds of attachment that are intimated by the conduct of an Ovidian legacy suppressed within the earlier letter's image of Edenic unity:

[18] William Heale, *An Apologie for Women* (Oxford, 1609), p. 44. Idiomatically and thematically close to Donne's poem, Heale's work is dedicated to a 'Lady MH'. It is attractive, to me at any rate, to see a connection between Walton's confusion about Donne meeting Mrs Herbert in Oxford in 1608 and this dedication.

[19] Ben Jonson, '*Epistle. To Katherine, Lady Aubigny*', lines 23–4, in *Ben Jonson*, ed. by C. H. Herford, Percy and Evelyn Simpson, 12 vols (Oxford: Clarendon Press, 1925–52) vol. 8.

What pretty innocence in those days mov'd!
Man ignorantly walk'd by her he lov'd;
Both sigh'd and enterchang'd a speaking eye,
Both trembled and were sick, both knew not why.[20]

An 'Unripe willingnesse' the poem calls it, the appetite shared in that 'unripe side of earth' by our first parents. And if this is the first man and woman, then this should be the chaste courtship of the first marriage story, with each anticipating desires not yet fully imagined or understood. Yet, within the created innocence of these couplets is another worldly, lyric motif that bewrays an intimacy refined to subvert marital closure. For faintly but suggestively, these lines are claimed by an image of the Ovidian conversation of desire in which lovers 'enterchang'd a speaking eye'. When adulterous desire speaks at urbane Ovidian *cenae* its amatory professions are as silent as the interchange of speaking eyes. The '*amator*' of the *Amores*, first instructs Corinna 'keep your eyes on me, to get the language of my eyes', then accuses her of attracting him, with the reminder: '*non oculi tacuere tui*'.[21] There is an unsettling similarity here between the poem's instructive purpose and the Ovidian tutelage that Donne had twice rehearsed in his *Elegies*. A similarity compounded by a confusion the letter sustains about the kind of intimacy it is describing. The twinned references to Adam and Eve at the opening to each letter to Lady Huntingdon and the emphasis on the 'first' awakening of sexual love seem to intend a conjugal focus. Yet by its parody the letter contracts itself to a lyric tradition of poet and mistress. This distinction discloses an uncertainty about the poet's status. A doubt as to whose, when Adam and Eve walked in 'pretty innocence', the third voice of counsellor and praiser might have been. The verse letter's flattery is shadowed by the memory of that first serpentine voice that slipped between man and wife with an appeal to feminine intellect. This parallel betrays an elision integral to the poem's discretion. For while Donne worries about which language is suited to friendship, the intrusive third voice silently becomes part of the closed symmetry of man and woman. Inasmuch as the created ambiguity of the image of the lovers understands the compromising attachment of the friend to the newly married couple, the letter becomes the legacy of a poetic voice trained in elegies as the third voice given to eluding domestic propriety.

The ingenuity of Donne's elegiac voice is intimate with the character of jealousy; practised in the devices which celebrate poetry's possessiveness towards the female form and conscious of its competition with a husbandly solicitude. The poem 'Jealosie' carries the deceitful arts of its Ovidian source back from Roman high society into the marital house. In a domestic setting

---

[20] 'That unripe side . . .', lines 47–50.
[21] *Amores*, I.iv.17 (I use the loose Loeb translation); II.v.17 ('your eyes, too, girl, were not dumb'). Also see III.iii.13–14 where the speaker appeals to a pledge made with the eyes as some sort of rival vow to marriage.

claimed by emphatically possessive pronouns ('his boord', 'his own bed', 'his house', 'his realme', 'his houshold policies') the poem brings home the power of 'hidden language' to create a 'third place'.[22] Even as the lines narrate the difficulty of finding a safe place for adulterous 'kiss and play', they cheat domestic security within their own literary space. So that, reading an alternative manuscript version of the prospect of an illicit encounter at line thirty, 'We into some third place retyred are', rather than the usually preferred 'Wee play'in another house', suggests less a fantasy about a secret rendezvous, than a promise that it is here in the textual third space of the written missive that the encounter is realised. In the spatial terms of the Southwark landscape with which it concludes, the poem is the liberty it seeks to take.

In another elegy, 'Tutelage', female inconstancy confronts the poet with the promiscuity of his own created voice, available to the coarsening imitation of contemporaries. Yet the poem holds on to the human drama of betrayal. The poet has taught his mistress to read discreetly and so equipped her with a voice for privacies that elude the stricture of the marital home. The words which first liberated her from her virtue, taken up by her voice, deliver 'arrands mutely,'and mutually', not inaudible to their recipient but with 'discreet wariness' for her reputation. This erotic espionage that cheats 'household policies' occupies the lyric memory of those suits to Lady Bedford in which it is considered virtuous 'to spie, / And scape spies' only with the adjunct 'to good ends'.[23] In 'Tutelage' discretion, like the practice of reading, hovers between the silent and the spoken. All the more eloquent for its silence, its 'speechlesse secrecie' anticipates the mute mutuality of 'The mystique language of the eye' in the verse letter to Lady Huntingdon.[24] The suggestion that professions of literary service could themselves resemble a travesty of lyric seduction prepares for what Donne's sermons would confess of the verse letters. For as a preacher Donne did not share his own letters' regard for their dignity. One sermon which links letter writing with illicit sexuality, charges St Jerome's complaint against the epistolary practice of veiling forbidden relationships in terms like 'Friend, and Sister, and cousin' with the warning that it is 'perchance prophetically enough of our times too'.[25] In two further sermons on adultery Donne alleged the falsity of finding infidelity a singularly physical act: 'They mistake the matter much, that thinke all adultery is below

---

[22] John Donne, 'Jealosie', in *The Elegies and the Songs and Sonnets*, ed. by Helen Gardner (Oxford: Clarendon Press, 1965), lines 16–26.

[23] Compare 'Jealosie', lines 30–2, 'This twilight . . .', lines 51–5.

[24] 'Tutelage', line 4.

[25] *Sermons* I, 199. It is interesting to compare how Gosse imagined Donne's place at Twickenham to how Hans von Campenhausen depicts St Jerome 'at the intellectual centre of a circle of aristocratic and wealthy ladies . . . the first example of the spiritual counsellor and confidant, almost in the manner of the later domestic chaplain of noble and aristocratic society' (Hans von Campenhausen, *Fathers of the Latin Church*, trans. by Manfred Hoffman (Stanford: Stanford University Press, 1964), pp. 151–3).

the girdle: A man darts out an adultery with his eye, in a wanton look; and he wraps up adultery with his fingers in a wanton letter.'[26] In a look (a speaking eye) or a letter *that* sin may be committed. The fantasy of 'Jealosie', in which a man, his wife and her lover at 'boord together being satt / With words, nor touch, scarce lookes adulterate', has returned as the admonishment: 'that sinne may have beene committed in a looke, in a letter, in a word, in a wish'.[27]

In the terms of the sixteenth-century guides that taught procedures for letter writing by reference to the parts of rhetorical performance, the lovers of this sermon and of the letter to Lady Huntingdon may be understood to find a private application for the orator's *actio*, untroubled by the writer's sense of physical remoteness from his words. It seems reasonable to put it this way because in letters to his friends Donne often explained how his requests might be better received by reference to the practices of spoken conversation. He assured Goodyer: I 'deliver to you an intire and clear heart; which shall ever when I am with you be in my face and tongue, and when I am from you, in my Letters'.[28] Such comparisons, however, attest to a difference in the demands made by the words of friendship as Goodyer might hear them spoken or encounter them in a letter. A difference Donne considered in terms of the methods of inquiry to which a listener has recourse when attempting to identify his friend's intentions: in 'words of men present, we may examine, controll, and expostulate, and receive satisfaction from the authors; but the other [the writings of those absent] we must beleeve, or discredit; they present no mean'.[29] If already here there is a doubt as to the ability of the written voice, conditioned in the arts of sociable expedience and divested of the physicality of its writer, to dictate the terms of its own sincerity, the letter anticipates the note of 'I wish I could be beeleved' which troubles the necessary excesses of the verse letters written after the publication of the *Anniversaries*.[30] Those letters might, as Donne feared, be thought to have forfeited the language's hope either for 'purity of motive' or fashionable credibility. Yet in this earlier letter to Goodyer it is the detachment of the written page from its writer's presence that is considered the obstacle to faithful, intimate interpretations. It may be, as has been observed, that Donne deliberately excluded physical contingency from his familiar correspondence, but even had he so wished there are effects of physical exertion instinct to the practice of conversation (in the use of the lungs, vocal cords, facial muscles and manual emphasis) which he could not have committed to writing.[31]

[26] *Sermons* III, 318.
[27] 'Jealosie', lines 19–20; *Sermons* IX, 399.
[28] *Letters*, pp. 68–9.
[29] Ibid., p. 107.
[30] Ibid., p. 260.
[31] John Carey, 'John Donne's Newsless Letters', *Essays and Studies* (1981): 45–65. Frank Whigham, 'The Rhetoric of Elizabethan Suitors' Letters', *PMLA* 96 (1981): 864–82, also considers attempts to reconstruct in writing 'strategies' familiar to oral petition.

Where 'face' and 'tongue' serve metonymically for the repertoire of gesture and vocal intonation which assists (induces) a listener to draw the inferences a speaker purposes, they constitute the body of performative features which evade incorporation into the written material of correspondence.[32]

What Donne's letter understood as the disembodiment of its voice, sixteenth-century treatises registered in their curtailment of the rhetorical faculties necessary for consideration in epistolary composition. The difficulties of translating acoustic intention into epistolary style are observed by Italian and Erasmian manuals which, in assimilating their *ars epistolica* to rules for procedure in the practice of oratory, detached the conditions of decorum for *actio* and *pronuntiatio* from the conduct of written eloquence. Donne's quoted letters to Goodyer apprehend this detachment in their negotiation of the distance (between Mitcham and court, or London and Ashby) which was one practical circumstance of their writing. They are a report of absence, both the spatial separation of friends and the analogously perceived absence of the physical voice from the written letter. An effect of this analogy in letters which profess themselves 'seals and testimonies of mutuall affection' is an obligation on the recipient to furnish the letter with a credible sense of its writer's 'tongue' and 'face'. To do so he may not have the benefit of the listener's inquisitorial privilege, but neither is he set adrift, or at liberty, to imbue any character of his liking to the absent correspondent. For the Erasmian manuals which prompted letter writers to a regard of the circumstance of their petitions – the social rank of correspondents, an epistle's function, the occasion of writing – exacted a reciprocal demand of the understanding reader. Obliged to inform the received letter with an idea of the writer's needs and circumstance, the recipient is committed to an interpretative fidelity to the possible intentions of his correspondent.[33] John Carey has described the recipient's task as expressed by a letter to Lady Bridget White. Donne: 'hath it as much to say as you can think; because what degrees of honour, respect, and devotion, you can imagine or beleeve to be in any, this letter tells you, that all those are in me towards you. So that for this letter you are my Secretary.'[34] Carey: 'It adapts itself precisely to its recipient's state of mind, but it does so at the expense of its own identity. The recipient's state of mind will determine its form and content.'[35] This is true to the extent that the understanding exercised by the reader (her 'state of mind') is formed by her acquaintance with the persuasive techniques of previous and similar letters. For her sense of what may be imagined or believed is dependent on her

---

[32] See Terence Cave, *The Cornucopian Text: Problems of Writing in the French Renaissance* (Oxford: Clarendon Press 1979), pp. 55–77, 157–67 for the dense significance of the topics of the heart, tongue and face in humanist theory.

[33] See Erasmus, *Methodus*, ed. by G. B. Winkler (Darmstadt: Wissenschaftliche Buchgesellschaft, 1967), p. 64.

[34] *Letters*, pp. 5–6.

[35] Carey, 'Newsless Letters', p. 51.

experience of the ways form involves with content in other suits to elicit an intended response. It is right to say that the letter expects its reader to construct a presence for its writer, but the reader's liberty to do so is not entirely at the expense of the letter's identity. Rather, the discipline to which her reading is subject effects a mutual compromise between letter and recipient such as realises an ideal of the liberties and bonds of friendship. In this respect, the inability of the suitor to impose the terms of his 'respect and devotion' is also an enabling of the reciprocity in which correspondents can discover conditions of trust.

The knowledge that the qualities of presence achieved in vocal command are qualities resistant to graphic representation troubles Donne's correspondence with the possible misunderstandings by which spoken familiarity becomes written importunity. For where the character of a word is beholden to the tone and circumstance of delivery, the force of the letter's implication depends in part on the interpretative habits of the recipient. For such a reader to make sentences which may seem severe or forward read as considerate or benign, requires him to deliver to the written page a knowledge, not just of epistolary conventions but of the writer's character, his needs, his past. The need for a reader to exercise these kinds of knowledge is felt more keenly in those letters for which 'the strongest friendships may be made of often iterating small officiousness'. It is routine officiousness that assumes so grand a bearing in the promise to Goodyer that 'Letters have truly the same office as oaths', yet the indicative conviction of this outbraves the mixed tone of the preceding qualification: 'In the History or style of friendship, which is best written both in deeds and words, a Letter which is of a mixed nature, and hath something of both, is a mixed Parenthesis.'[36] This aphorism, that charges promises with an obligation to action, tries not to recognise how the reciprocal accountability consigned by oath differs from the liabilities encountered where friendship is itself an issue of style. Whereas oaths secure bonds of trust by committing a private understanding to a language that depends on wider recognition, an effect of intimacy in Donne's letters is formed by an apprehension of the misunderstandings likely to result from their mixed nature of devotion and self-interest. In the friendship of 'small officiousness', reciprocal and self-regarding importunities are a currency that depends on the existence of a shared language. Yet the exclusivity of the friendship created also depends on the possibility that requests might be misunderstood, that correspondence might fail. The letter's vulnerability to misjudgement creates the terms of its exclusivity for those knowingly inside its importunity. A fact registered in Donne's insistence: 'So are letters to some complement, and obligation to others'.[37]

By November 1608 Donne was pursuing Sir Geoffrey Fenton's former

[36] *Letters*, p. 114.
[37] Ibid.

position as secretary in Ireland, a business, he told Goodyer, that gave him need and 'occasion to imploy all my friends'.[38] The letter does not think it an affront to the dignity of friendship to admit a practical motive for its employment, yet a subsequent note of self-reproach issues a shock to the verbal sophistications of 'civil dishonesty' in which compliment is received as an evasion of sincerity. For when Lord James Hay, one of the 'court friends' petitioned, undertook the assistance he had promised, it surprised Donne into registering a new value for the familiar contraries of compliment and obligation, friendship and courtesy: 'he promised so roundly . . . as I suspected him, but performed whatever he undertook . . . so readily and truly, that his complements became obligations, and having spoken like a Courtier, did like a friend'.[39]

Among the many reasons Donne had for gratitude to George Garrard was his friend's care to impute generous intent to what could sound like letters of obligation. He obliged Garrard to persist in this charity: 'I thank you for expressing your love to me, by this diligence, I know you can distinguish between the voices of my love and of my necessity if anything in my letters sounds like an importunity.'[40] In one respect the manner in which love involves with necessity in Donne's letters makes Garrard's distinction appear a tacit misrecognition, another 'civil dishonesty', on which the integrity of friendship depends.[41] For what Donne recognises as a vulnerability to misunderstanding, also testifies to how the letter's voice may be resourcefully double; both because self-interest and benevolence share the same solicitous vocabulary and because the written page sustains tonal ambiguities in a manner different to speech. If it is possible for the silence of the letter to act as an obstacle to friendship for those who misjudge desired effects, it is equally possible that letters which set recipients to distinguish their tone, or which confront them with uncertainty as to the writer's motive (his love or necessity), create the conditions in which those recipients might come to recognise their familiarity with the character of their correspondent. Reading a letter on these terms is an exercise of friendship, recipients being called to contemplate the nature of their own affection in their decisions as to the tone they are willing to credit to the written lines and the knowledge which enables those decisions.[42]

The creative ambiguities, or the doubleness, of Donne's voice are material to the persuasive method of the later verse letters. For as letters in verse, highly conscious of their lyric heritage, they invite their recipients' voices to realise the possibilities of their metrical form, on the understanding that the sense of a line may be decided by the placing of an emphasis. More than seventy years

---

[38] Ibid., p. 145.
[39] Ibid.
[40] Ibid., p. 283.
[41] Ibid., p. 114.
[42] Ibid., p. 11.

ago Empson considered the nature of vocal attention necessary to meet the demands of the *Songs and Sonets* and identified how the reading voice's capacity to manifest shifting stress patterns could ascertain a range of distinct, perhaps contradictory meanings for a line. He remarked an effect of this as a type of ambiguity in which 'alternative versions seem particularly hard to unite into a single vocal effect': 'You may be intended, while reading a line one way, to be conscious that it could be read another; so that if it is to be read aloud it must be read twice; or you may be intended to read it in some way different from the colloquial speech-movement so as to imply both ways at once.'[43] This gives the reading voice something to which to aspire. It is demanding, if non-committal, to imply that performed 'some way different' from English speech-movement, a voicing might decide one sense for a line yet remain resonant with the possibility of other meanings. But these are the demands of verse letters whose tonal contradictions are maintained from the same difficulty that confronts a poet attempting to give an identity to a type of familiarity for which even elite Jacobean society had no easily recognisable place or precedent.

Annabel Patterson has observed that writing within 'restraints imposed by political censorship' Donne developed a 'strategy of self-division'; manifest in the *Satyres* as a dialogic form whereby the poet 'divides himself into two voices'. For Patterson, a voice of frivolous loyalty and of censured but sincere libel.[44] But there is also a sense in which Donne's verse letters to aristocratic women compose these satiric and careerist imperatives into a single voice. The persistence of alternative readings that the voice can no more dispel than compose into a single vocal effect keeps in earshot the uncertain past of the letters' flattery. As they create a voice for friendship out of the abrasive accents of the satires, the verse letters discover an eloquence which could speak for the poet's divisions, and whose ambiguity elicits a doubleness from the recipient receptive to its flattery but conscious of its potential duplicity. Donne could describe his flattery as 'busie praise', a phrase slyly open to the arts of trade, but as Coleridge recognised, it was a tonal versatility that could express the 'idea of degradation & frivolity that Donne himself attached to the character of a professed Poet'.[45]

Hearing of his own supposed ambitions for a career at law, Donne was quick to demure from a reputation of professionalism: 'For my purpose of proceeding in the profession of the Law so far as to a Title, you may be pleased to correct that imagination where you finde it. I ever thought the study of it but my best entertainment and pastime, but I have no ambition, nor design

[43] William Empson, *Seven Types of Ambiguity* 2nd edn repr. (London: Peregrine, 1961), pp. 147–8.

[44] See Annabel Patterson, 'All Donne', in *Soliciting Interpretation*, pp. 37–67.

[45] S. T. Coleridge, *Marginalia*, ed. by George Whalley, 5 vols (London: Routledge, 1984) II, 234–5.

upon the Stile.'[46] A similar anxiety about the nature of poetic professionalism is carried as a manner of 'Stile' by verse letters that sound their affinity with the *Satyres*. Identifying the 'restless activity' of Donne's satires as the industry of professional 'self-advertisement', Carey observes: 'When Donne had managed to attract the interest of his superiors, he quickly dropped satire writing.'[47] This is true to the satires' temper but misleading, perhaps, as to their persistence in Donne's voice. For if Donne put off the guise of the satirist on entering Egerton's service, he didn't put aside the texts or silence the satiric accent in his poetry of praise. Perhaps as late as 1607 he edited *Satyre III* to present to Lady Bedford; the same year, noticeably, in which he began to find the voice of his verse letters to her.[48] 'T'have written . . .' describes the reworking of an earlier reputation as a transformation which keeps in sight a dissident past:

> So whether my hymnes you admit or chuse,
> In me you'have hallowed a Pagan Muse,
> And denizend a stranger, who mistaught
> By blamers of the times they mard, hath sought
> Vertues in corners, which now bravely doe
> Shine in the worlds best part, or all It; You.[49]

'Denizend' because the satiric purpose that survives this transformation is not easily domesticated into the topics of praise. The lines repair to their earlier character in the *Satyres* with a show of reparation for their past resentments. But where the confident iambic lilt of the first closed couplet gives way to repeated enjambment, the disorienting effect on the movement between lines can sound the difference between an accustomed social ease and the wary civilities of the denizen. The first sense unit carried across the line effects a grammatical shift (and in consequence a semantic reversal) which causes the reading voice to check its momentum and adjust the sense it has made of the previous line end. In the tribute to Lady Bedford's redeeming power, 'And denizend a stranger who mistaught', the terminal verb has momentary potential as active and intransitive before being claimed by the following line as an expiatory passive. The doubling of the word's positional ambiguity (apparent syntactic closure opening out into a qualifying retreat) with its lexical ambivalence, retains an unsettling immediacy in the written letter, as the reader is required to modify the metrical sense she has made of the preceding lines. But in shifting the blame to other 'blamers', the letter can itself appear shifty, inasmuch as it obliges the recipient to doubt in her agility at sounding the lines. The created effect is of an inward estrangement, each

[46] *Letters*, pp. 254–5.
[47] John Carey, *John Donne: Life, Mind and Art* (London: Faber and Faber, 1981), p. 49.
[48] Milgate, pp. lix–lx, suggests that Donne had *Satyre III* in mind (or at least in voice) when writing to Goodyer in 1608. (See *Letters*, pp. 26–31.)
[49] 'T'have written . . .', lines 15–20. This itself reworks 'To R. W.', lines 7–8.

line at variance with its predecessor, and each in turn exacting an answering condition of estrangement from a recipient challenged to voice her familiarity with the absent correspondent.

'Madam, You have refined . . .' allows for the estrangement of the recipient from the epistolary voice as a proof of the newly discovered sincerity of its deference. The letter reflects on its own 'flattery': 'Oft from new proofes, and new phrase, new doubts grow, / As strange attire aliens the men wee know.'[50] The simplicity of the rhetorical structure of the first line (a *conduplicatio* of 'new') should not be allowed to decide the stress unequivocally. It is possible to deliver the line with each 'new' subordinated to the stress of the following noun, as if the letter insisted on its novelty only under its breath. Yet, placing a double stress on each noun phrase and on the final verb can realise a monosyllabic innocence in the assurance that the epistolary voice is 'new'. Such doubts as may grow as to the letter's sincerity arise where the 'new phrase' resonates with the accent of the former stranger. Vestiges of an uncertain past live on in the voice of Donne's verse letters, not least because their recipients are understood to retain an ear for the defiance of which the *Satyres* had made their sound an enactment. 'T'have written . . .' allows for Lady Bedford's resistance to its flattery with the commonplace that 'To admit / No knowledge of your worth, is some of it'.[51] The self-knowing worldliness these lines admit (as the indicative factuality of the preceding lines' certainty as to what is 'knowne', 'worth' and 'true' is compromised by that verb of discretion, 'admit') supplies the ambivalence to the following tribute, 'to you, your praises discords bee', where the line manages to respect both an innocence of conduct and a formidable social intelligence.[52] To hear praises as 'discords' requires that aristocratic modesty which is contingent of an acquaintance with suitors' flattery, insofar as it is the countess's reluctance to believe her ears that preserves the continuity between the office of counsellor and satirist. As a secretary Donne knew the responsibility of sentiment to the duties of office: 'No man is a good Counsellor, for all his wisdome, and for all his liberty of speech, except he love the person whom he counsels: If he do not wish him well, as well as tell him his faults, he is rather a Satyrist, and a Calumniator, and seeks to vent his own wisdome, and to exercise his authority, then a good Counsellor.'[53] Though for the verse letter it may be said that no employer is a good reader except that she practise an innocence in her discretion. Defined in the characters of 'virtue', the complexion of feminine discretion becomes a series of mutually qualifying reversals. The 'Perverseness' of self-indifference that sustains itself by an intent watchfulness, is of a kind with the paradox by which too encompassing

---

[50] 'Madame, You have refin'd . . .', lines 65–6.
[51] 'T'have written . . .', lines 29–30.
[52] Ibid., line 31.
[53] *Sermons* IV, 317.

a virtue begets 'unjust suspicion' in the motives of compliment and certain 'wise degrees of vice' enable aristocratic sympathy for a suitor's needy sincerity. Again fragments of Edenic imagery are used in a way that realises and confines the countess's agency as a reader. As 'vertues best paradise' Lady Bedford becomes the inviting garden of her own continence, her judgement in receipt of Donne's 'praises' a subtlety that 'ransoms one sex'. To adapt the terms of the letter to Lady Huntingdon, the craft of the countess's discretion gives a semblance of Eve before she ate; a state in which she might be said to bear the reward yet want the sin. In the pulpit Donne had further recourse to an Edenic paradigm to account for the human ability to construe praises as discords: 'As soon as Adam heard the voice of God, and in an accent of Anger, or as he tuned it in his guilty conscience, to an accent of Anger, . . . for as a malicious man will turne a Sermon to a Satyre, and a Panegyricke to a Libel, so a despairing soule will set Gods comfortablest words, to a sad tune'.[54]

When uncertain as to *his* accent, Donne trusted to the ears of Goodyer and Garrard to detect importunity. His letters to each can have the character of an indirect disclosure, messages awaiting the attention of someone else. In a letter to Goodyer on the history of epistolary conventions, proofs that 'no other kinde of conveyance is better for knowledge or love' prompt the aside: 'either you write not at all for women, or for those of sincerer palates'.[55] Conveyed discreetly, this commonplace (at women's expense) becomes a rare compliment to the one Lady to whom it was worth writing. Dame Helen Gardner identified the divisive force of Donne's flattery as characteristic of a poetry that 'exalts the Lady at the expense of her whole sex'.[56] A judgement that suggests both the socially competitive temper of flattery, intent to dignify its recipient against her contemporaries, and the compromises it exacts from the integrity of her femininity, the wholeness of her sex. A similar considera-tion of how the accomplishment attributed to recipients might have implications for the character of their femininity occupies the verse letters as a concern with the language of praise; most conspicuously, with the terms on which the interpretative judgement of a female aristocrat might be called a virtue. A central difficulty in the characterisation of 'virtue' in Jacobean verse letters to women is the ability of the word to carry a large number of related or not fully worked out meanings, each imbued with the developments of discrepant and changing social attitudes. The pronounced syntactic awk-wardness of the opening quatrains in the 1608 epistle to Lady Huntingdon gives the effect of a poem conducting a study into its own vocabulary of praise – weighing the attributes of 'virtue' as a newly feminine substantive in relation to the history of the word's usage. It is the 'virtue' manifest in the accidents of the countess's femininity that the eighth stanza addresses as it shapes to

---

[54] *Sermons* V, 333–4.
[55] *Letters*, p. 108.
[56] Helen Gardner, 'Notes on Donne's Verse Letters', *Modern Language Review* 41 (1946): 318–21.

believe her new social presence continuous with the decorum of domestic honour:

> Though you a wifes and mothers name retaine,
> 'Tis not as woman, for all are not soe,
> But vertue having made you vertue,'is faine
> T'adhere in these names, her and you to show.[57]

The grammatical reluctance of this, and of preceding stanzas, to achieve lucidity delivers a sense of uncertainty as to the social conduct of this 'virtue' and its cohesion with those qualities of virtue exercised in motherhood or conjugal fidelity. Verbally repetitive, each clause qualified by a dependent successor, the lines turn back and in on themselves, as if their expository technique consisted in the ability to draw a number of mutually incompatible, equally tenable, characters for virtue. Yet, emerging as a series of adjustments, the 'virtue' credited to the countess is less narrowly that of a good wife and mother than the socially adept sophistication sustained by the equivocal tone of the 'prophesies' that 'vertue should your beauty,'and birth outgrow'. For the virtue which 'outgrows' rank and beauty may cease to fit within their compass but it also grows out from them, like fruit from a tree.[58] The dedicatory register that can call a patron's interpretative ability a 'virtue' can mark its relation to the humanist epistolary friendships in which shared habits of reading authenticate themselves as evidences of integrity, just as it can shape itself into the idiom of exclusivity where honour and elegance are terms of each other. As poems with a calculating sense of how much or little their own literary fashionableness is worth, Donne's letters collaborate in the invention of that social milieu being cultivated by an elite and competitive group of women in the early years of the century. They belong, however uneasily, to the Twickenham of Lady Bedford's correspondence, where reports of the countess reading, collecting paintings and laying out gardens for Moor Park convey the aspirations of a world in which intelligence served for a form of social elegance.[59]

In 'This twilight . . .' the discretion which discovers a distance between the public and private confinements of honour is recommended to Lady Bedford as holy and profitable duty. Through God's benefaction of 'a discreet warinesse' will the countess make morality a social performance but preserve the innocence of her conscience from its knowledge of pretence. It is with similar discretion that the verse discovers a consciousness of difference, between 'beeing and seeming':

---

[57] 'Mans to Gods . . .', lines 29–32.
[58] Compare *Letters*, p. 115.
[59] See *The Private Correspondence of Lady Jane Cornwallis 1613–1644*, ed. by Lord Braybrooke (London, 1842), pp. 33–7, 43–53.

> He will make you speake truths, and credibly,
> And make you doubt, that others do not so:
> Hee will provide you keyes, and locks, to spie,
> And scape spies, to good ends, and hee will show
> What you may not acknowledge, what not know.[60]

Lexical cognates suggest semantic deceptions ('acknowledge'/'know'), as words of like purpose qualify each other suspiciously ('truths'/'credibly'). Holding together, but opening up, a distance between words and their implications, the verse enacts the reserve it proposes. Counsel of this nature may be shadowed by the deceits of 'Tutelage', but its ambiguity is closer in type to the improvisations in 'That unripe side of earth' first addressed to Lady Huntingdon. For the primitive shapes formed in that earlier Edenic resemblance and the guidance offered on the arts of discretion lead, in intention, from social vulnerability to a performance of integrity. The proximity of the two poems is that of the naked and the artful, where what is innocently human amounts to what is only ostensible.

If 'Mans to Gods Image . . .' is the poem that Goodyer, though still in service to Lady Bedford, solicited from Donne for Lady Huntington, something of the relations between Twickenham and Ashby may be evident in Donne's response to Goodyer's request. For although he acquiesced, Donne gave reasons why he felt it wiser to give reason sway and refrain.[61] His first reluctance can appear, characteristically, to set a care for his social respectability against another kind of obligation, a poet's duty to the repute of his occupation: 'That that knowledge which she hath of me, was in the beginning of a graver course, then of a Poet, into which (that I may also keep my dignity) I would not seem to relapse. The Spanish proverb informes me, that he is a fool which cannot make one Sonnet, and he is mad which makes two.'[62] Mindful of a responsibility to its dignity, one office Donne's gravity declined was that of the professional poet–counsellor. Yet his socially motivated reticence also carries an expedient sense of how integrity is accomplished in poetry of friendship. Opportunism is complicit with sincerity in the discretion needed to 'keep my dignity':

> The other stronger reason, is my integrity to the other Countesse . . . for her delight (since she descends to them) I had reserved not only all the verses, which I should make, but all the thoughts of womens worthiness . . . I have obeyed you thus far, as to write: but intreat you by your friendship, that by this occasion of versifying, I be not traduced, nor esteemed light in that Tribe, and that house where I have lived.[63]

---

[60] 'This twilight . . .', lines 51–5.
[61] *Letters*, pp. 259–61.
[62] Ibid., pp. 103–4.
[63] Ibid., p. 104.

'Integrity *to* . . .'. It can sound less than sincerely palatable when a noun (meaning 'undivided, whole') takes a preposition that modifies its wholeness into the relative or usefully partial. Donne's care for the uses of integrity can look like another way of applying his pronouncement on 'strayings into new loves' so as to register the value for poetic 'honesties' in the economy of fashionable interest where value is contingent on exclusivity. There is good business sense to Donne's profession of fidelity, but a recognition that to versify for the countess's delight while declining terms of professional service introduced the poet to a different kind of vulnerability. Not, perhaps, the vulnerability of the would-be gentleman in the aristocratic household, but that of the fashionable companion whose value, so long as it lasts, is not to be earned by any amount of scholarly professionalism. In the place the letter to Goodyer finds for the verse epistles – the social world being invented within households like Twickenham and Ashby – the restrictive amatory logic that Donne identified by his reluctance to court Lady Huntingdon alongside Lady Bedford can be an expression both of a poet's unwillingness to consider himself a professional and of a need to keep credit.

The end of the 1608 letter to Goodyer, which seems to have been enclosed in the same envelope as the requested poem for Lady Huntingdon, suggests how Donne could engage his need to be believable with his recipients' aspirations to credibility as astute readers. It sought Goodyer's assurance: 'if these verses be to bad, or too good, over or under her understanding, and not fit; I pray receive them, as a companion and supplement of this Letter to you'.[64] One implication of this is that should Lady Huntingdon not prove a fit recipient, her image in the poem might become lyric currency passed between Goodyer and Donne as a supplement to their friendship. A similar consideration of a possible failure finds its way into the verse letter as a challenge to the countess to justify her status as its recipient:

> If you can thinke these flatteries, they are,
> For then your judgement is below my praise,
> If they were so, oft flatteries worke as farre,
> As Counsels, and as farre th'endeavour raise.[65]

Proof of a sincere palate is here held as the willingness to credit the sincerity of praise. But for the countess not to be flattered does not mean she should entirely believe Donne's tributes. A year earlier Donne had felt his way into familiarity with Mrs. Herbert, censuring casual ambiguities while opening his suspiciously ambivalent verse letter to her judgement: 'I can as ill endure a suspicion and misinterpretable word as a fault. But remember that nothing is flattery which the speaker believes; and of the grossest flattery there is this

---

[64] *Letters*, ibid., pp. 104–5.
[65] 'Man to Gods . . .', lines 49–52.

good use, they tell us what we should be.'[66] The misinterpretable requires in Mrs Herbert a compliant and practised credulity, able to credit the accent of honesty in the currency of friendship but discern its coercive intent. A sophisticated kindness then, to let the letter 'be beleeved'. Yet elsewhere Donne found it decorous to promise disbelief. In what Coleridge considered a 'truly elegant letter', Donne entreated Lady Bedford to send him copies of her poetry, that 'excellent exercise of your wit'. He swore: 'that I will not shew them, and that I will not beleeve them; and nothing should be so used which comes from your brain or heart'.[67] For Coleridge this was an example of 'that dignified Courtesy to Sex and Rank, of that white Flattery, in which the Wit unrealizes the Falsehood'.[68] If to unrealise falsehood is not to dispel its possibility but to implicate a countess's need for sincerity, then it is also the achievement of the Jacobean verse letter to unrealise the reputation of its heritage, its commercial purpose, its professional impersonality. It is an unrealisation that requires the collaboration of recipients whose imagined dignity as readers allows an idea of familiarity across Sex and Rank.

Letters to Garrard and Goodyer show Donne careful to avoid becoming the victim of his patrons' need to demonstrate discretion. It was the imitative and competitive forces of fashion that Donne observed when he implored Goodyer to keep the details of Lady Bedford's fading interest in him from Lady Huntingdon, lest 'the example of this Lady, should work upon that Lady where you are: for though goodnesse be originally in her, and she do good, for the deeds sake, yet, perchance, she may think it a little wisdome, to make such measure of me, as they who know no better do'.[69] Delicately put, but in this worldly aside the elite society of sincerest palates comes across as a contest of shared vanities, anxious not to consort with yesterday's fashion.

In 1614 Donne confided to Garrard, now in service to Lady Salisbury, his apprehension that by publishing the *Anniversaries* and addressing verse letters to too many 'friends' he had bankrupted the sincerity of his voice. He enclosed a verse letter to the countess with the confession:

> I should be loath that in any thing of mine, composed of her, she should not appear much better then some of those of whom I have written. And yet I cannot hope for better expressings then I have given of them. So you see how much I should wrong her, by making her but equall to others. I would I could be beleeved, when I say that all that is written of them, is but prophecy of her.[70]

His desire to 'be beleeved' associates the recipient's confidence in a letter's sincerity with its ability to confer social prestige. Expressings that carry their past with them, wrong the countess's dignity by being unable to credit her

---

[66] Gosse I, p. 165.
[67] *Letters*, p. 67.
[68] Coleridge, p. 236.
[69] *Letters*, p. 220.
[70] Ibid., pp. 259–61.

superiority, by making her 'but equall to others'. To claim past eulogy as but prophecy of the present letter is an act of betrayal that discloses the competitive tension latent in tropes of singular devotion. Donne's tributes to Lady Bedford do not require that she countenance rivals for elegance, yet the comparative register of the epistle to Lady Salisbury works to release a competitive tone back into the earlier dedications. The poem's regeneration of its own capacity to believe in itself is made analogous to a fantasy of Adam's progression towards consciousness. The voice enlists evidence of its former innocencies to counter suspicion of commercial expediency: 'He might have said the best that he could say, / Of those fair creatures, and not be chid for praising yesterday.'[71] The diminution this works on earlier praise consigns Lady Bedford to yesterday, her virtues to that 'old fashion of the court' the poet had earlier mocked with her.

In an attempt to recover credibility for its professions of devotion the letter performs an oblique reversal of the pledge of constancy with which Horace had dedicated his epistolary verse: '*Prima dicte mihi, summa dicende camena*'. This half-promise, half-threat of fidelity issues from the first line of Horace's first epistle, an exemplum of poetic integrity, faithful in intimacy from first words to last. The poem to Lady Salisbury works a return to Donne's own *primitiae*, an opening scene in which the images of devotion had encountered their own distance from Edenic innocence. It defends the dedications of earlier epistles, 'And if things like these have been said by me / Of others; call not that idolatory', with the intimation that it is Lady Salisbury who has realised the fidelity for which the lines had all along been waiting. Not deceived and deceitful idolatry but Adamic innocence had formed those letters: 'For had God made man first, and man had seen / The third days fruit' with sincerity 'He might have said the best that he could say / Of those fair creatures, which were made that day'. The Horatian ideal of sustained devotion is refigured by the conviction that, as virtue had always been their subject, the countess had always been the recipient for whom Donne's letters had only to discover their intention. Rather than being an expedient promiscuity, previous confidences have enabled the letter's present aptitude for the 'honesties of love'. With the effect that at the end of his poetic career, in his final verse letter, Donne can claim to issue his first conscious words of sincerity:

> And as I owe my first soules thankes, that they
> For my last soule did fit and mould my clay,
> So am I debtor unto them, whose worth,
> Enabled me to profit, and take forth
> This new great lesson, thus to study you;
> Which none, not reading others, first, could doe.[72]

---

[71] 'Faire, great and good . . .', lines 45–6.
[72] Ibid., lines 65–70.

By claiming the past as an education of their voice, these lines answer a criticism which Heale was not alone in making of Jacobean poets and husbands alike: 'Many loue not women, because they knowe not how to loue them'; have not the voice in which to conceive that love. Heale's words are again useful here because their Ovidian image of Eve's creation, 'man by a strange kinde of Metamorphosis converted into woman', unites the inwardness of masculine intelligence creating images of its own virtuosity, with the innocence of the voice hearing itself for the first time, and for the first time confident that it might 'knowe' another individual: '[Adam] turning vnto this new perceived himselfe imparted vnto her. Wherefore his first words and morning song, were words of amity, & a song of loue'.[73] From the beginning Donne's verse letters had realised they could not hope for this perception without the awareness of how created novelty suffers under another Ovidian judgement. That of the old *lena* who prepares Corinna for a lifetime of new songs of amity, in which the same old thing will be just the same new thing:

> *Ecce, quid iste tuus praeter nova carmina vates*
> *donat? amatoris milia multa leges.*[74]

---

[73] Heale, pp. 2, 55.

[74] '"Think, what does your fine poet give you besides fresh verses? You will get many thousands of lovers' lines to read"': *Amores* I.viii.57–8.

Chapter 6

DONNE AND SIR EDWARD HOBY: EVIDENCE FOR AN UNRECORDED COLLABORATION

ALISON SHELL

THIS chapter presents and discusses evidence which strongly suggests that Donne was an intellectual associate of the courtier and controversialist Sir Edward Hoby, and may have helped him with some of his writing. Though this particular collaboration is hinted at in a reference which has passed scholars largely by, the idea of Donne as collaborator is not new; it has often been argued that he assisted Thomas Morton, Bishop of Ely, during the part of his working life which preceded his own ordination. Hoby's work, like Morton's, was on religio-polemical topics; but Hoby's authorial stance is less scholarly and more satirical than Morton's, developing by the time of his later works into Menippean satire of a kind which invites broad comparison with Donne's polemical prose, especially *Ignatius his Conclave*. Trying to ascertain Donne's contribution to specific parts of Hoby's œuvre would be a fruitless exercise; this article instead invites one to consider the accusations of ghost-writing and self-interested intellectual patronage levelled at Hoby by his religious opposites, Hoby's response to these accusations, and the nature of the collaboration which may in fact have taken place.

The reference in question comes from a controversial pamphlet by the Jesuit John Floyd, *Purgatories triumph over hell* (1613).[1] It concerns a favourite point of dissension between Catholics and Protestants, the honour which is legitimately due to images without idolatry.

> Wherfore now to satisfie your sensualitie, tell me I beseech you, what you think of that relatiue honour, which one [marginal note: 'I.D.'] of your fellow Tobac-caean writers did use to practise towards the picture of his Mistresse, which he kept in his Chamber, with this prayer vnto it, *Illumina tenebras meas* [marginal

---

[1] The only previous citation of it I have seen is in a footnote to J. P. Sommerville, 'Jacobean Political Thought and the Controversy over the Oath of Allegiance' (unpublished Ph.D. thesis, University of Cambridge, 1981), p. 69. See further Sommerville's essay in this volume, p. 83. I am grateful to David Colclough for this reference.

note: *Lighte[n] my darkenes deare Lady.*] before which he did not omitt to doe morning and evening devotions, prostrate on the ground? was that prayer made to the dumbe Image, and not to his louing Mistres? Did his thoughts adore the dead colours of the picture and not her fresh rosie cheeks which therein he did behold? O glorious cause which by such *Epicureans* is impugned who worship *Bacchus* or *Cupid* in their chambers, yet against us professe themselves graue Cinicks, *Doggish* and Diogenicall writers! They cannot, forsooth, understand the relative honour of Christ his Image, yet before Images of *Venus* they can direct their humble duty and harty affection unto *Queanes*, which is nothing els but their relative honour of foule pictures. Certainely they could never misconster or mislike the pious directing of diuine honour to Christ before his sacred Image, were not their witts as dull in divine matters, as they are sharpe in sensual obiects, were they not a kin to the creature of *Dunne* colour, or to that monster whose head is as blockish as his body swinish.[2] [Marginal note, not italicised: Cui caput est Asini, cetera membra Suis.] If this discourse seem to you sharpe, remember the cause you haue given, who runn rayling at ancient doctrines, and pious practises of the Church, declared in my Treatise, without bringing any sillable of new proofe against them. (pp. 17–18)

Both the marginal initials and the pun, 'the creature of *Dunne* colour', make the allusion to Donne fairly plain; but the description of idolatrous practices clinches the case. The motto, *Illumina tenebras meas*, refers to that of the well-known Lothian Portrait of Donne: *Illumina teneb[ras] nostras domina.* Though unmistakable, the description is inexact: either Floyd is half-remembering Donne's picture of himself as one of his mistress;[3] or, conceivably, Floyd and the Lothian portrait both refer to parodic liturgical activities which Donne used to enact – or wished, at some point in his life, to depict himself enacting – in front of a woman's picture.[4]

[2] Judging from the construction of the sentence, 'that monster . . . swinish' seems not to be an additional insult directed at Donne, though it may be a veiled reference to another of Hoby's alleged fellow writers, or to Hoby himself.

[3] This can be opposed to the pious misquotation of the motto in R[ichard] B[addeley], *The Life of Dr. Thomas Morton* (1669): 'For my selfe have long since seen his Picture in a dear friends Chamber of his in *Lincolnes Inne*, all envelloped with a darkish shadow, his face & feature hardly discernable, with this ejaculation and wish written thereon; *Domine illumina tenebras meas*: which long after was really accomplished, when . . . he took holy Orders' (pp. 101–2). Commenting on this passage, Catherine J. Creswell remarks that 'one may inevitably misread Donne's portraits because they do not open themselves to our perception': 'Giving a Face to an Author: Reading Donne's Portraits and the 1635 Edition', *Texas Studies in Language and Literature* 37:1 (1995): 1–15, quotation at 11.

[4] Donne bequeathed this portrait to Robert Carr: his will is transcribed in Augustus Jessopp, *John Donne sometime Dean of St Pauls* (London: Methuen, 1897), Appendix C. For its reidentification as a likeness of Donne in the twentieth century, see John Bryson, 'Lost Portrait of Donne', *TLS* (13 October 1959). The portrait is described and discussed in Geoffrey Keynes, *A Bibliography of Dr. John Donne*, 4th edn (Oxford: Clarendon Press, 1973), pp. 373–4; Roy Strong, *Tudor and Jacobean Portraits*, 2 vols (London: HMSO, 1969) I, p. 66 (and plate 118), and *The English Icon: Elizabethan and Jacobean Portraiture* (London: Routledge & Kegan Paul/ Paul Mellon Foundation, 1969), pp. 37, 353. See also Kate Gartner Frost, 'The Lothian

The Lothian portrait of John Donne. Reproduced by kind permission of the
Earl of Ancram.

Portrait: A New Description', *JDJ* 13:1/2 (1994): 1–11; 'The Lothian Portrait of John Donne: A
Correction', *NQ*, n.s. 41:4 (1994): 455–6, and 'The Lothian Portrait: A Prologomenon', *JDJ* 15
(1996): 95–121. Portraits of Donne have in general attracted much critical attention. See
Douglas Chambers, 'A Speaking Picture: Some Ways of Proceeding in Literature and the Fine
Arts in the Late 16th and Early 17th Centuries', in *Encounters: Essays on Literature and the Visual
Arts*, ed. John Dixon Hunt (New York and London: Studio Vista, 1971), comments pp. 30–1;
Annabel Patterson, 'Donne in Shadows: Pictures and Politics', *JDJ* 16 (1997): 1–31; W. Milgate,
'Dr. Donne's Art Gallery', *NQ*, 194 (1949): 318–19. Nigel Foxell, *A Sermon in Stone: John
Donne and his Monument in St Paul's Cathedral* (London: Menard Press, 1978) is typical in
commenting on the extreme complexity of Donne's iconographical designs (p. 22). Richard
Wendorf, *The elements of life: biography and portrait-painting in Stuart and Georgian England*
(Oxford: Clarendon Press, 1990), ch. 2, comments on the portraits in relation to early
biographical studies of Donne by Walton and others

The controversial tract in which it occurs is part of a pamphlet war between John Floyd and Sir Edward Hoby. Hoby can best be understood as part of the courtly background within which Donne was seeking to prove himself in the wilderness-years between marriage and ordination, roughly 1606 to 1614.[5] He was a diplomatist and courtier, who gained a fortune through royal letters patent and licences to buy and sell wool, and who frequently entertained James I in his mansion at Bisham in Berkshire.[6] We know, at least, that Donne was acquainted with Hoby enough to joke about his habits. In Donne's satirical mock-catalogue of fashionable books, *The Courtier's Library*, Hoby is given a title all to himself, which translates from the Latin as *Sir Edward Hoby's Afternoon Belchings; or, A Treatise of Univocals, as of the King's Prerogative, and Imaginary Monsters, such as the King's Evil and the French Disease.* The title gives a vivid picture of a liquid luncher who, as Evelyn Simpson suggests in her edition of *The Courtier's Library*, might well have been in the habit of laying down the law to his companions in a dogmatic and 'univocal' manner.[7] Hoby certainly admitted in his tracts that he saw conviviality and controversy as going together.[8]

Hoby engaged in two pamphlet wars, which interlinked with each other: thus, while the question of Donne's possible input into Hoby's writing may well be most relevant in relation to Hoby's later work, all Hoby's controversial writings need in the first instance to be taken together.[9] Hoby first essayed religious controversy in 1609, with *A letter to Mr. T. H[iggons]*, responding to the Catholic convert Theophilus Higgons's tract *The first motive*, published the same year.[10] Higgons replied to Hoby straight away in another pamphlet, *The apology of T[heophilus] Higgons* (1609), but was also taken to task in a pamphlet by Thomas Morton, *A direct answer*, again published in 1609. Morton, at that time Dean of Winchester and subsequently Bishop of

---

[5] The chronology of those years runs roughly as follows: 1606–7, takes lodgings in the Strand, unsuccessfully seeks employment at court; 1606–10, possibly assisting Thomas Morton; 1607, refuses offer of Holy Orders; 1608–9, various unsuccessful secretaryships; 1610, *Pseudo-Martyr* published; 1611, *Ignatius his Conclave* published; November 1611–September 1612, on continent; 1614, unsuccessful attempts to find state employment; January 1615, ordained priest.

[6] For Hoby's life and background, see his entry in *DNB*; comments on the pedigree of the Hoby family in *The Travels and Life of Sir Thomas Hoby Kt*, ed. by Edgar Powell, Camden Miscellany, vol. 10 (London: Royal Historical Society, 1902), p. vi; *The Private Life of an Elizabethan Lady: the Diary of Lady Margaret Hoby, 1599–1605*, ed. by Joanna Moody (Stroud: Sutton, 1998), pp. xxvi, 118, 123, 125, 130, 207, 230.

[7] John Donne, *The Courtier's Library, or Catalogus librorum aulicorum incomparabilium*, ed. by Evelyn M. Simpson and trans. by P. Simpson (London: Nonesuch, 1930), pp. 50–1, 70–1.

[8] See below, pp. 130–1.

[9] A detailed account of the controversies is given by Peter Milward, *Religious Controversies of the Jacobean Age* (London: Scolar, 1978), pp. 162–7.

[10] For Higgons, see *DNB*; Michael C. Questier, *Conversion. Politics and Religion in England, 1588–1625* (Cambridge: Cambridge University Press, 1996), pp. 30, 35–6, 42–7, 57, 60, 62, 71–2, 66–7, 80–1, 86–7 (for his relationship with Hoby, see pp. 42, 60, 80).

The sequence of the exchange between Theophilus Higgons, John Floyd and
Sir Edward Hoby

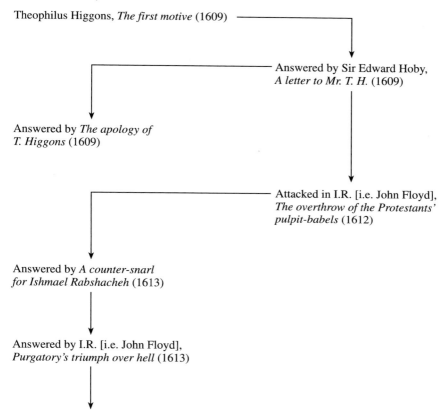

Theophilus Higgons, *The first motive* (1609)

Answered by Sir Edward Hoby,
A letter to Mr. T. H. (1609)

Answered by *The apology of
T. Higgons* (1609)

Attacked in I.R. [i.e. John Floyd],
*The overthrow of the Protestants'
pulpit-babels* (1612)

Answered by *A counter-snarl
for Ishmael Rabshacheh* (1613)

Answered by I.R. [i.e. John Floyd],
Purgatory's triumph over hell (1613)

Answered by 'Nick Groom', *A curry-comb for a cox-comb, or, Purgatory's knell in answer
of a lewd libel lately foricated by Iabal Rachil against Sir Edw. Hoby's Counter-snarl,
entitled Purgatory's triumph over hell: digested in form of a dialogue by Nick-Groom of
the Hoby-Stable Reginoburgi* (1615)

Durham, was a friend of Donne's; some scholars have argued that he and
Donne collaborated on controversial tracts put out under Morton's name,
and though Donne's biographer R. C. Bald is sceptical about the hypothesis,
current consensus seems to be against him.[11] At all events, Donne attended at
some stage to the three-way exchange between Hoby, Higgons and Morton.
As Geoffrey Keynes describes, a volume of tracts from Donne's library

[11] Peter Beal, *In Praise of Scribes: Manuscripts and their Makers in 17th-Century England*
(Oxford: Clarendon Press, 1998), p. 34, n. 13. Bald sets out his argument at pp. 210–12. See
also Thomas Clancy, *Papist Pamphleteers* (Chicago: Loyola University Press, 1964), pp. 213–
14; Evelyn M. Simpson, *A Study of the Prose Works of John Donne*, 2nd ed. (Oxford:
Clarendon Press, 1948), pp. 179–80; and *Ignatius*, pp. 171–3.

contains marked-up copies of *A letter to Mr. T. H.* and *A direct answer.*[12] Though there is no direct evidence of how Donne and Hoby first came across each other, the Morton connection would have been one reason for their meeting up.[13]

The controversial engagement between Hoby and Higgons lasted only a short time. In February 1610, Hoby wrote to Lord Salisbury asking for information of Higgons's whereabouts 'for I doubt not to reclame him home'.[14] Higgons did indeed return to England shortly afterwards, preached a recantation sermon, and remained a staunchly anti-Catholic clergyman thereafter. Francis Bacon, drawing up Higgons's pardon for the eyes of James I, did so on the direct authority of Hoby and was moved to remark on the 'special obligation' that Higgons owed to Hoby.[15] But, despite Higgons's return to Church-of-England orthodoxy, the exchange was revived when John Floyd, the Jesuit who had reconciled Higgons to Catholicism, attacked Hoby's reply to Higgons in his tract *The overthrow of the Protestants pulpit babels* (1612).[16] The point at issue is Hoby's alleged misquotation of points from St Augustine, points which, Floyd claims, were

> ignorantly, and impudently corrupted, not by *Syr Edward* himself (I cannot thinke so dishonourably of men of his calling) but by his *trencher-School-maister*, or some *mercinary Lecturer*, perchance even by M. *Crashaw* himself,

[12] University Library, Cambridge, Bb*.11.42 (bound volume of tracts, items 5 and 6). Identified as belonging to Donne's library in Keynes, Appendix IV where the items in the volume are listed separately and their annotations described (the shelfmark is given as Bb*.11.45).

[13] Morton, like Hoby, is accused by Floyd of utilising research assistants: pursuing the question of Hoby's co-authors in *Purgatories triumph*, Floyd asks Hoby 'Your valiant Writer and Deane D. *Morton*, was he not driven by his adversarie to acknowledge, that he had taken some corrupted testimonies of our Authors, upon the credit of *Io. Stocke*. or *R.C*? Why should that taking authoritys in grosse, be thought a blemish in a Knight, which was esteemed tolerable, yea laudable in a Doctour?' (p. 31). Though the use of 'your' in this passage may simply mean that Morton and Hoby were both Protestants, it may also indicate that they knew each other.

[14] Hoby to Salisbury, 8 February 1609/10 (*CSPD*, LII, no. 55, 586).

[15] 'I have no Warrant for the drawing of this Bill, save that Sr *Edward Hoby*. to whom the party bears special obligation, did by his Letter to me signifie Your Majesties pleasure to this purpose: But because the parties conversion was so notorious, and so generally liked, I have presumed to commend this Bill to Your Majesties Signature.' Quoted from the English summary of the Latin pardon: the full text of both is printed in *The Narrative History of King James, for the First Fourteen Years* (1651), ff. Bb*4b–Cc*1b. Higgons's conversion is mentioned in the Annual Letters of the Venerable English College, Rome, for 1609: see Henry Foley, S.J., *Records of the English Province of the Society of Jesus*, 7 vols (London: Burns & Oates, 1877–83) II (Series II–IV), 185–6.

[16] Floyd was writing under the initials I.R., probably standing for his pseudonym John Rivers. See Hoby, *Letter to Mr. T.H.*, p. 17: 'The small liking you have to the Romish Religion, you sufficientlie manifested, when as being reconciled to that *Synagogue*, by one *Flud* a Priest, you did yet after your returne out of *Yorkeshire*, write a little Pamphlet of *veniall* and *mortall* sinnes, flat against the principles of that profession.' For Higgons's correction of the statement, see *Apology*, pp. 24–5.

who is great in the booke of this credulous Knight, whom they make fly hoodwinke to catch flyes; which hood if I pull from his eyes that he may see how they abuse him, I hope he will take it in good part. (p. 133)

Here Floyd is adapting, and parodying, a phrase from Hoby's *A letter to Mr. T. Higgons*: 'For my owne part, . . . I could neuer perswade my selfe, that the multiplicitie of *Schools*, needlesse *Lecturers*, and trencher *Schoole-masters*, would sort to any better effect' (p. 23).

Catholic mistakes are often Protestant orthodoxies, but the actual charge of error is less important here than the manner in which the charge is levelled. Giving Hoby the opportunity to admit that these mistakes are someone else's appears more generous than it is; by making Hoby look like a gentleman amateur, reliant on research assistants for citations, it belittles Hoby's whole endeavour. An accusation of this kind, though not unparalleled, is not an especially common way for an early modern controversialist to throw doubt upon his opponent, and it needs to be seriously attended to. Floyd may well be taking up a suggestion thrown out by Theophilus Higgons in his *Apology*. Higgons indeed goes even further, accusing Hoby's tract of mendaciousness, then declaring to him 'I am glad, as well for your owne, as my sake, that you have some other Authour, than your self . . . Wherefore, remoove these wrongs from your self unto their proper Authours, that I may behold them in their owne center: then you are free, whoever shal be found guilty in this matter' (p. 27). Yet both Floyd and Higgons are vague at this juncture, Floyd echoing Hoby's phraseology to conceal his lack of substantial evidence.

Certainly, to name names was to lay oneself open to explicit denials from one's opponent. Floyd's one concrete suggestion of an unnamed collaborator, William Crashaw, was one that Hoby was to dismiss contemptuously in his reply, *A counter-snarle for Ishmael Rabschacheh*.[17] Explaining how 'it is unpossible for the pallat of my fancie, to be fitted by any other Cooke than my selfe', he complains: 'hee hath taken wrong course, to wound M. Crashawe (a man with whom I never had the least domestique concourse,) through my sides' (pp. 62–3). Hoby's equation of domestic concourse with literary collaboration is particularly suggestive, in view of his known penchant for

---

[17] Ishmael Rabshacheh = a facetious enlargement of I.R. Ishmael was the son of Abraham and Hagar ('And he shall be a wild man; his hand will be against every man, and every man's hand against him', Genesis 16:12); Rabshacheh was the outspoken messenger from the king of Assyria to Hezekiah ('it may be the Lord the God will hear all the words of Rab-shakeh, whom the king of Assyria his master hath sent to reproach the living God', 2 Kings 19:4). All references are from the King James Bible. 'Cecropidan' (sic) refers to the Cercopes (Ovid, *Metamorphoses* 14) who were punished for lying by being turned into misshapen animals at once like and unlike human beings; 'Lycaonite' refers to Lycaeon, an Arcadian tyrant and scoffer at religion, who served up a cannibal feast to Jupiter in disguise. A copy of *A counter-snarle* in the British Library (class mark 3935.b.27) has the more difficult allusions glossed by hand, by or (more probably) for Lady Elizabeth Berckleye; and George Abbot, archbishop of Canterbury, requested a copy of *Purgatories triumph over hell*: HMC 75, Downshire MSS, IV, *Papers of William Trumbull*, 1613–14 (1940), Abbot to Trumbull, 19 January 1613/14 (p. 291).

entertaining, and Floyd's charge that Hoby and his co-writers formed a smokers' fellowship. Thus, the assertion that Donne is one of Hoby's 'fellow Tobaccaean writers' can be seen to occur in a context where Hoby has already been accused of employing people to help with his controversial endeavours: research assistants at least, at most very like what future generations would call ghost-writers. The phrase is more specific than merely saying that Donne and Hoby are both Protestant controversialists, and seems too to be going beyond a statement that Donne and Hoby are cronies and both writers. One needs to ask, at this point, whether the charge amounts to anything more than unfounded polemical allegation, either arbitrary or – as Hoby asserts in the case of William Crashaw – mistaken.

For an answer, one is obliged to read the gaps; but then, gaps are significant within a genre so adversarial that the least misrepresentation is delightedly seized upon. If there were no connection of this kind between Donne and Hoby, one would expect Hoby to deny it as vehemently as he does collaboration with Crashaw; but even though Hoby animadverts Floyd's accusations in detail, in the next and last pamphlet, this never happens. This pamphlet possesses a title difficult even by the standards of seventeenth-century controversy: *A curry-combe for a coxe-combe, or, Purgatories Knell in answer to a lewd libell lately foricated by Iabal Rachil against Sir Edw. Hobies Counter-snarle, entituled Purgatories triumph over hell: digested in forme of a Dialogue by Nick-Groome of the Hobie-Stable Reginoburgi*.[18] Unlike any of the previous pamphlets in the sequence, *A curry-combe* is written in dialogue-form, the three fictional participants being the Mayor of Queenborough in Kent – the town of which Hoby was then Constable – the minister of Queenborough, and the pseudonymous author cited on the title-page, Nick Groom.[19] Hoby's own name is being played on, with the title assigning him a stable of intellectual hobby-horses. The tract was presented to James I as a new-year's gift at the beginning of 1615, and is probably too the book for which Hoby supplied William Trumbull with a list of errata a month later. His accompanying request, 'Now I shall crave this favour at your handes that you will learne by some how this last booke is taken: and to discover what further intention they have to proceede therein', shows his alertness to the continued possibility of polemical worsting.[20]

[18] Iabal Rachil = another facetious enlargement of I.R.; Reginoburgi = Queenborough (Hoby was made Constable of Queenborough, Kent in 1597).

[19] For the relationship between this pamphlet and Thomas Middleton's play *The Mayor of Queenborough or Hengist, King of Kent*, see two articles by Julia Briggs: 'New Times and Old Stories: Middleton's *Hengist*', in *Literary Appropriations of the Anglo-Saxons from the 13th to the 20th Century*, ed. by Donald Scragg and Carole Weinberg, Cambridge Studies in Anglo-Saxon England, 29 (Cambridge: Cambridge University Press, 2000), pp. 107–21, esp. pp. 115–16; and 'Middleton's Forgotten Tragedy *Hengist, King of Kent*', *RES*, n.s. 41 (1990); 479–95.

[20] 'Sr Edward Hobby presented the king on newyearesday wth his booke against one Floude a papist that had aunswered his writings and used him rudely, and therfore entitles his booke a

In the pamphlet, the anecdote about Donne's blasphemous worship of his mistress is unequivocally described as a fiction:

> The like fable the Licaonite coyneth to disgrace one I. D. whom he describeth to be one of the knights fellow tobaccaean Wrighters; who (saith the Cecropidan) with morning and evening devotions, did prostrate himselfe on the ground to the Picture of his Mistresse, with this praier; Illumina tenebras meas (pp. 24–5)

The Mayor of Queenborough is given this speech, 'Nick Groom' voices an indignant response, 'O notable figment!', and the Minister concurs 'As I am a true man, I cannot imagine that so impious an affection can harbor in any Protestant breast'. One needs, here, to attend to the form which this denial takes. All the characters are denying that Donne ever worshipped his mistress – perhaps all the more truthfully because of Floyd's mis-remembering the nature of the Lothian portrait – but this contrasts with the way in which Hoby's writerly acquaintance with Donne is treated. It is put into the mouth of Hoby's opponent, but it is neither confirmed nor denied by the participants in the dialogue. As discussed above, Hoby was not slow to deny the only other specific charge of co-authorship that was levelled at him. But this pamphlet leaves open the question of Donne's collaboration, even while explicitly, almost gratuitously, reminding readers of it. Hoby does not animadvert all Floyd's remarks, and he could just as easily have said nothing; readers, then and now, are invited to infer that Donne did indeed have a role in Hoby's controversial writing.

Here one needs to look more carefully at the generic mutations of this pamphlet controversy. While all of Hoby's pamphlets indulge in satirical abuse to varying degrees, his two later pamphlets, *A counter-snarle* and *A curry-combe*, explicitly cross the border into Menippean satire: a shift heralded by – among other genre signals – the sardonic picturesqueness of the titles. Menippeanism, strongly associated with the kind of learned abuse where the act of flyting becomes almost more important than the point at issue, is common enough in early modern controversial pamphlets, the most obvious example in this context being Donne's own *Ignatius his Conclave*.[21] However, the dialogue format, a frequent characteristic of Menippeanism, is only employed in *A curry-combe*. Since this is the pamphlet written just after Floyd has named Donne as collaborator, the reader may be meant to interpret the pamphlet's dialogic composition as a second ludic acknowledgement that collaboration is, in fact, taking place.

---

currie-combe for a cox–combe.' (John Chamberlain to John Carleton, 5 January 1614/5: *CSPD*, LXXX, no.1, p. 269). Hoby's letter to Trumbull, dated 1 February 1614/5, is calendared in *HMC Downshire* V, 123.

[21] I discuss the dialogic aspect of Menippean satire in 'Multiple Conversion and the Menippean Self: the Case of Richard Carpenter', in *Catholicism and Anti-Catholicism in Early Modern England*, ed. by Arthur Marotti (Basingstoke: Macmillan, 1999), pp. 154–97. For Donne's use of the genre, see Eugene Korkowski, 'Donne's *Ignatius* and Menippean Satire', *SP* 72 (1975): 419–38.

It would be missing the point to identify Donne – or any other possible collaborator – as Nick Groom, the 'groom from the Hobie-stable' under whose name the pamphlet appears, or with any of the other characters who speak the satire. While the name 'Nick Groom' may have coterie resonances lost to us, it can also be read simply as a brilliant soubriquet, suggesting multiple puns relevant to the work of satirists in general. At this date, the noun 'nick' could mean an incision or indentation, or the exact mark aimed at; it could also be used – with particular relevance to animadversion – for a verbal correspondence or resemblance. As a verb, it could mean 'to nickname', 'to criticise', 'to catch unawares' or 'to hit the mark'.[22] We are perhaps intended to notice the connotations of servitude explicit in 'groom'; as well as denoting someone employed in a stable, the term could also be used for a serving-man in someone's household. Certainly one of Hoby's employees identifiably contributed to *A curry-combe*: the pamphlet has a Latin appendix attacking the Jesuit Henry Fitzsimon's *Britannomachia ministrorum*, written by Anthony Tunstall, Hoby's secretary.[23] But again, the term may imply nothing more than the fictional construct of a loyal, slightly indiscreet servant.

Certainly Hoby himself, not long before in his polemical career, had been indignant at the suggestion that he employed assistants. As mentioned above, he gives particular attention in *A counter-snarle* to refuting I.R.'s suggestion that his pamphlets were ghost-written:

> that I euer suffered my Penne to be guided, or my course ouerruled by any other Pilot than my owne Genius, were he not a meere stranger to my proceedings, hee would neuer be so shamelesse as to auerre. Though it be my error, yet I must needes say, I could neuer endure to let my Clarke passe any Letter, but from my owne mouth: And should the greatest Architect in the Land, giue mee a plot for a building, I am verily perswaded, I should in the end take a cleane contrary course. When I can hardly please my selfe, it will be a matter of more difficultie for others to giue me content. Euery man (as I take it) hath his proper veine: . . . Should 1 have eyther an Adjutor, or Supervisor, in any worke I undertake, I thinke it would proue little better then the confusion of Babell: Wee should sooner fall together by the eares, then bring the Treatise to an end. . . . I can gladly heare what others will say, yet when it comes to the point, I loue to doe what likes my selfe best. (p. 62)

Here, Hoby claims overall intellectual control of his work, and objects to two ideas: that it is possible to guide or overrule him, and that he employs an assistant or 'Adjutor'. We are probably to take this as sincere. However, as Hoby freely admits, this in no sense precludes the kind of collaboration which he characterises as the free exchange of information and opinion between

[22] Summarised from early-seventeenth-century uses in the *OED*. However, its use in the context of farriery, conveniently relevant to a groom, seems to begin only in the eighteenth century.
[23] Milward, *Religious Controversies*, p. 163.

intellectual equals. He sees comparing ideas with other learned men as a crucial part of arriving at a reasoned judgement, and admits that he uses entertaining as a means of bringing this about: 'I cannot well discerne what reason hee hath to debarre mee of that conference at my Board, which their owne Doctors have in their Libraries.' (p. 61) To suggest that Hoby collaborated with other scholars and polemicists, perhaps attached to his household and certainly indebted to him for hospitality, is entirely in keeping with Hoby's own statements. This, of course, still leaves Hoby open to the accusation of extending his entertainment and patronage to hack scholars prepared to help him out:[24] the type of person whom John Floyd calls 'trencher-School-maister' – one who constantly frequents his patron's table – and 'mercinary Lecturer'. Depending on one's point of view, Hoby's learned dining companions and Floyd's mercenary lecturers could be one and the same. This uncertainty of status would be applicable enough to Donne at this liminal stage in his career, or to anyone else on the fringes of court life, hoping for preferment: someone known to be talented but perforce in a deferential position, who had an obvious reason to give powerful individuals access to his scholarly skills.

Whether, despite his protestations, Hoby eventually found that he could allow his dining-companions to take a compositional part in his work must remain an open question. *A counter-snarle* precedes Floyd's mention of Donne in *Purgatories triumph*, where Floyd sees the topic of Hoby's fellow writers as still worth pursuing; and the tacit suggestion of collaboration represented by *A curry-combe* might extend as far in this case as actual co-writing. At any stage, too, Hoby might have been the kind of unconscious plagiarist who borrows from his associates without fully realising it. But though the evidence suggests that Donne and possibly other, unidentified collaborators had some input into some of Hoby's controversial writing, this essay has not been arguing that works previously attributed to Hoby should be transferred to the Donne canon. Scholarly authors seek out checks, balances and opinions from the academy, topical satire lends itself well to anonymity, pseudonymity and collaborative writing, but the fact that these works appeared under Hoby's name is, as Hoby himself appreciated, an admission of overall responsibility. Even the dialogic *A curry-combe* demands to be read simply as what it presents itself as being: representative of ways in which Hoby's coterie thought, but not susceptible to sentence-by-sentence dissection for purposes of attribution.

Lastly, what is one to infer from the phrase 'One of the knights fellow Tobaccaean writers'? 'Tobaccaean' means someone under the influence of tobacco. The properties of tobacco and the ethics of smoking were the subject of constant debate in early Stuart England, not just because of James I's negative opinions on the topic: some writers regarded tobacco as a medicine or a stimulant beneficial to the brain, others as both physically and morally

[24] See *OED* under 'trencher'.

dangerous. Because Hakluyt and other well-known travel writers described tobacco as being smoked by pagan priests in the Americas for purposes of divination, it carried especial implications of religious madness and frenzy for its detractors.[25] The association of tobacco with notions of heresy is ubiquitous at this date. John Deacon accuses recusants of being affected by tobacco, and explains how the chief conspirators in the Gunpowder Plot acted as they did because they were befuddled by heavy smoking.[26] Floyd turns the charge back on Protestants in general, and Donne and Hoby in particular – in Hoby's case, seemingly with some inside knowledge. In *A counter-snarle*, Hoby admits smoking in the past, but crossly repudiates any suggestion that he might still be under the influence. 'I confesse in my time I have not been an enemy to that *Indian* weede, . . .[but] the Informer may put up this jest in his boxe; If he be as free from all his olde vices, and drunken conceites, as I am from this vanity, hee shall not neede any great pennance' (p. 39).

So was Donne himself a smoker? Floyd could simply mean that Donne's brain, like Hoby's, had been stupefied into dark hallucinogenic conceits of the kind that either smoking or heresy might engender. Or conversely, he could be saying more literally that smoking formed part of Donne's and Hoby's social intercourse, affording a stimulus to their heretical notions. At all events, the notion of Donne, Hoby and their dining-companions chain-smoking and brainstorming, stubbing out their opponents as mercilessly as cigarette-butts – for all the world like the proponents of a somewhat later satire boom – is a pleasurable idea, and it may even be true.

---

[25] C. M. MacInnes, *The Early English Tobacco Trade* (London: Kegan Paul, Trench, Trubner, 1926), pp. 28–46, gives a comprehensive account of the arguments surrounding the use of tobacco in Stuart England. See also Janine Hartman, 'Dangerous American Substances in Jacobean England', *Cahiers Élisabéthains* 46 (1994): 1–7. For the association of tobacco with Indian priests, see MacInnes, op. cit., pp. 13, 30; John Deacon, *Tobacco Tortured* (1616), p. 48; Sir John Beaumont, *The Metamorphosis of Tobacco* (1602), sig. B1v.

[26] *Tobacco Tortured*, title-page and pp. 81–2, 174–6. Deacon also equates profiting by the sale of tobacco with making money out of popish wares (p. 184).

II

Professing the Word

Chapter 7

LABELS, CONTROVERSY, AND THE LANGUAGE OF INCLUSION IN DONNE'S SERMONS

JEANNE SHAMI

I N 1625, following the accession of Charles I, the Duke of Buckingham asked William Laud, then Bishop of London, to construct a list of clergymen according to a simple classification: 'o' (for 'orthodox') and 'p' (for 'puritan').[1] This distinction was important to him (and to King Charles, for whom the list was intended) as the old reign of King James modulated into the new one of his son. Under the informal systems of censorship and patronage then operating, it was a way of distinguishing between trustworthy and potentially troublesome divines, presumably for the purpose of preventing the fomentation of sedition, or the circulation of heretical ideas in religion. Although the list does not survive, the need to label and classify early Stuart clergymen, including John Donne, persists. In fact, in Donne studies today, the desire to label Donne has become acute, leading to a dizzying profusion of Donnes and an equally muddled scholarly discourse.[2] I could stop here by announcing that there are still some openings for scholars

---

[1] The Works of the Most Reverend Father in God, William Laud, D.D., ed. by W. Scott and J. Bliss, 7 vols (Oxford: John Henry Parker, 1847–60) III, 159.

[2] The spectrum of criticism on the subject of Donne's religion is described in Jeanne Shami, 'Anti-Catholicism in the Sermons of John Donne', in The English Sermon Revised: Religion, Literature and History 1600–1650, ed. Lori Anne Ferrell and Peter McCullough (Manchester: Manchester University Press, 2000), pp. 137–9. Since the delivery of this paper (7 July 1999) as the keynote address at a one-day conference entitled 'Professional Donne', several important contributions to the subject of labelling Donne's religion have emerged. Achsah Guibbory's essay, in English Literary Renaissance cited below in note 16, Peter McCullough's contribution to this volume, and my own essay ' "Speaking Openly and Speaking First": John Donne, the Synod of Dort, and the Early Stuart Church' (forthcoming in John Donne and the Protestant Reformation, ed. by Mary A. Papazian (Detroit: Wayne State University Press, 2003)) have advanced more detailed and sophisticated discussions than the preliminary observations advanced here. These developments suggest that the question of Donne's 'profession of faith', his articulation in his sermons of the orthodox doctrine of the Church of England as he interprets it, remains central to Donne studies at this time, and still debated.

wishing to label Donne according to his religious 'rhetoric', a word which too often is used to suggest a superficial, or merely verbal, allegiance, or, as Donne says, 'as though *Protestant,* and Papist were two severall callings; and, as you would make one son a Lawyer, another a Merchant, you will make one son a Papist, another a Protestant'.[3] However, for now, it seems worth considering the impact of this desire for definition on the way we read early-modern texts, and the consequences for Donne studies of this way of reading.

In this paper, I propose to examine, first, how Donne used the sensitive, controversial vocabulary of religion in his sermons of the 1620s, and secondly, how recent scholars have interpreted the public religious identity he constructed from this vocabulary. The first part of such a project, understanding how Donne used controversial religious language, is fraught with its own set of difficulties, hinging on the labels, definitions, and classifications by which religious identity was expressed in the early Stuart Church. My work in this section follows upon the groundbreaking scholarship of Anthony Milton, who defines religious identity in the early Stuart period along a religious spectrum, ranging from radical to moderate puritanism at one end, through various versions of largely Calvinist conformity in the centre, to Arminianism and crypto-popery at the other end. If that isn't complicated enough, we also have to remember that much religious controversy, particularly in moments of crisis, was conducted in polarised terms, 'us' vs. 'them', 'o' vs. 'p', with 'us' and 'them' as relative rather than absolute terms.[4] When Buckingham imagined all clergymen as either 'orthodox' or 'puritan', that crude, largely political, way of dividing the group tells us something about his definition of orthodoxy, and about Laud's as well. It also tells us something about our own assumptions. I, for one, find the two terms incommensurate, 'puritan' expressing a more particular set of values than 'orthodox', and 'orthodox' a term that begs the question of the standard against which it is measured.[5] In other words, my sense that 'orthodoxy' was very much a contested site in 1625 makes me uneasy about the application of such a term today. Also, the relative proportions of orthodox to puritan divines are not made clear from Buckingham's request, although, once again, I think that 'orthodox' was a much broader category than 'puritan' and would have included the majority of clergymen. For scholars, these considerations and many others mean that whenever we gauge what a particular term such as 'puritan' or 'orthodox'

---

[3] *Sermons* IV, 263. Future page references are included in parentheses in the text.

[4] Anthony Milton, *Catholic and Reformed: The Roman and Protestant Churches in English Protestant Thought 1600–1640* (Cambridge: Cambridge University Press, 1995), pp. 7–9.

[5] At a conference on 'The Worlds of John Winthrop: England and New England 1588–1649' (Millersville, PA, 17–19 September 1999), Peter Lake and Kenneth Fincham presented papers exploring the complexities of defining the terms 'puritan' and 'conformity' in current historiography. See Kenneth Fincham, 'Clerical Conformity from Whitgift to Laud', in *Conformity and Orthodoxy in the English Church, c.1560–1660,* ed. by Peter Lake and Michael Questier (Woodbridge: Boydell, 2000), pp. 125–58.

means, we have to consider the issue being discussed, historical circumstances, and the rhetorical context of the debate.[6]

The names of sectarian religious controversy which current scholarship uses to identify religious positions were already freighted with their own historical baggage in Donne's time. Consequently, after the Reformation, many churchmen of all stripes claimed to prefer the name of Christian to that of Calvinist, Lutheran, or any other religion named after mere men. Francis Bunny, a puritan, felt the sting of such labelling from the Catholic side, and rejected their use of 'reprochfull names of "Lutherans, Zwinglians, Calvinistes, Bezites", and such like'.[7] Richard Montagu, charged with Arminianism, noted that his opponents were willing to be called Calvinists, but asserted that he did not wish to be accounted 'Arminian, Calvinist, or Lutheran . . . but a Christian'.[8] Called by King James to adhere to a common Reformed faith at the Synod of Dort, Joseph Hall asked what, then, to make of those infamous names of Remonstrant, Counter-Remonstrant, Calvinist and Arminian. In the end, he exhorted his hearers to remember that 'We are Christians, let us also be "of like spirit." We are one body, let us also be of one mind'.[9] Donne states the point clearly, managing to include Catholics among these religions named after men by calling them 'papists':

> If we will goe farther then to be Christians, and those doctrines, which the whole Christian Church hath ever beleeved, . . . if we will call our selves, or endanger, and give occasion to others, to call us from the Names of men, Papists, or Lutherans, or Calvinists, we depart from the true glory and serenity, from the lustre and splendor of this Sunne; . . . Here in the Christian Church, God hath set a tabernacle for the Sunne; And, as in nature, Man hath light enough to discerne the principles of Reason; So in the Christian Church, (considered without subdivisions of Names, and Sects) a Christian hath light enough of all things necessary to salvation. (VII, 310)

Nevertheless, adherence to a specific religious identity mattered for a number of reasons – legal, political, and moral – in the religious climate of the early Stuart period. Under the law, identification as a recusant, or a nonconforming puritan, separatists at the extremes of the spectrum, could mean exclusion, deprivation, fines, imprisonment, and other penalties. Politically, King James sanctioned a specifically anti-Catholic and anti-puritan rhetoric as part of official Church policy, although this rhetoric had to be sensitive to

---

[6] Awareness of the deeply occasional nature of Donne's sermons informs Peter McCullough's essay in this volume.

[7] Francis Bunny, *Truth and Falshood* (London, 1595), sig Cc7v.

[8] Richard Montagu, *Appello Caesarem* (London, 1625), p. 10. Milton, *Catholic and Reformed*, observes that 'Montagu's rejection of "names of division" represented not just a standard distaste for exclusive terminology, but a more radical detachment from the churches to which this terminology was generally applied' (p. 447).

[9] Joseph Hall, *The Works of the Right Reverend Joseph Hall, D. D., Bishop of Exeter and Afterwards of Norwich*, ed. Philip Wynter, 10 vols (Oxford: Clarendon Press, 1863) X, 261.

shifts in public opinion, especially about James's foreign policy.[10] Within this officially sanctioned discourse, 'papist' and 'puritan' (and, later, 'Arminian') were provocative terms, like 'heretic' and 'atheist', almost always polemical rather than descriptive. Everything else in the middle was acceptable. Most important, while orthodoxy carried political and legal benefits, a stable religious identity established the conscience. The multitude of works of casuistry, both Catholic and Reformed, attested not only to a broad, popular concern for outward religious conformity, but also to the desirability of a principled and coherent personal religious identity in early Stuart England.[11] And it is Donne's conscience that is the prize in current scholarly debate.[12]

But the problems of definition and classification that arise from early-modern religious discourse have created difficulties for historians of the period, and this is the second concern of my paper. In the early seventeenth century, we find many examples of controversial labels applied polemically, misapplied, rejected, or contested. However, Buckingham's crude distinction in 1625 between 'o' and 'p' has been amplified today to include Calvinists, puritans, conformists, avant-garde conformists, Laudians, Arminians, anti-Calvinists – groupings which overlap or collapse doctrinal, ecclesiological, and political categories. And yet, the sophistication promised by these categories hardly improves upon the oversimplification of 'o' vs. 'p'. Scholarly assessment of Donne's religion and politics mirrors this broader historical debate on religious labelling, producing a full range of Donnes: Donne of the puritan imagination; Donne the 'Calvinist episcopalian'; Donne the conformist; Donne the avant-garde conformist, and now – inevitably – Donne the Arminian. These Donnes occupy a spectrum from reluctant to enthusiastic conformity to the Church of England, from an emphasis on godly preaching to a preference for sacrament and ritual, from connection with international Protestantism to connection with Rome, from predestinarian theology to a stress on universal grace and good works. The key issue here is how the

---

[10] Kenneth Fincham and Peter Lake, 'The Ecclesiastical Policies of James I and Charles I', in *The Early Stuart Church, 1603–1642*, ed. by Kenneth Fincham (London: Macmillan, 1993), pp. 23–49.

[11] On Donne's casuistical habits of thought see Camille Wells Slights, *The Casuistical Tradition in Shakespeare, Donne, Herbert, and Milton* (Princeton: Princeton University Press, 1981); Meg Lota Brown, *John Donne and the Politics of Conscience in Early Modern England* (Leiden: Brill, 1995); and Jeanne Shami, 'Donne's Protestant Casuistry: Cases of Conscience in the *Sermons*', *SP* 80 (1983): 53–66. On the discourse of conscience in early-modern England and Europe, see *Public Duty and Private Conscience in Seventeenth-Century England*, ed. by John Morrill, Paul Slack, and Daniel Woolf (Oxford: Clarendon Press, 1993); Perez Zagorin, *Ways of Lying: Dissimulation, Persecution, and Conformity in Early Modern Europe* (Cambridge: Harvard University Press, 1990); and *Conscience and Casuistry in Early Modern Europe*, ed. by Edmund Leites (Cambridge: Cambridge University Press, 1988).

[12] See a superb essay by Camille Wells Slights which discusses how people experienced subjectivity in late Elizabethan and early Stuart England in terms of the concept of conscience: 'Notaries, Sponges, and Looking-Glasses: Conscience in Early Modern England', *English Literary Renaissance* 28 (1998): 231–46.

evidence is marshalled. In what follows, then, I would like to articulate, even if I can't resolve, some of the problems of definition that Donne's religion has raised and to suggest alternatives to this 'over-precise' language within the profession.[13]

In another context, I have identified several potentially misleading practices by which religious positions have been established in modern scholarly discourse. These include a practice of selective quotation that I have called 'the politics of quotation'.[14] Such a strategy is bolstered by a practice of creative 'pairing', what I call the 'sounds-like' argument, and by the problematic use of an unexamined biographical narrative (from apostasy to ambition) to establish Donne's network of religious allegiances. The 'politics of quotation' is the most egregious example of misreading, but is not something invented in the twentieth century. The polemical uses of quotation were well-known to Donne's contemporaries.[15] The application to Donne studies has been a concern of mine for some time now, and I have used the phrase to expose the pedigree in modern scholarship of several faulty notions about Donne's theology and politics.

A second, closely-related methodology pairs Donne with other figures by means of brief quotation. This method of pairing sometimes allows brief verbal similarities to modulate into biographical and then full-fledged religious identifications. Even where it doesn't, quotations showing where Donne sounds like puritan preachers Richard Sibbes or Henry Smith have been used to support the claim that Donne's imagination was 'puritan', while pairings with quotations by Laud and Montagu have supported arguments

---

[13] See Peter White, *Predestination, Policy and Polemic: Conflict and Consensus in the English Church from the Reformation to the Civil War* (Cambridge: Cambridge University Press, 1992), pp. 175–202, for a discussion of how, on the instructions of King James, the English delegates to the Synod of Dort aimed to avoid 'over-precise definitions' which might lead to separation from other Reformed churches or irreconcilable differences with the Lutherans. In a separate paper, cited in note 2 above, I examine Donne's appropriation of the discursive style of the Dort debates to his own professional pulpit discourse. That Donne conceived of his role within the Church as a professional one is suggested, I think, by his focus on the authorisation and calling of the minister (particularly in his Jacobean sermons), by his sensitivity to preaching and sacraments as ordinances and institutional means for establishing the true church of God, by his sense of rhetorical decorum and occasion, and, most importantly, by his many comments on the processes by which religious debate ought to be handled.

[14] See Jeanne Shami, 'Donne's Sermons and the Absolutist Politics of Quotation', in *John Donne's Religious Imagination: Essays in Honor of John T. Shawcross*, ed. by Frances Malpezzi and Raymond-Jean Frontain (Conway, AK: University of Central Arkansas Press, 1995), pp. 380–412.

[15] See the discussion of Henry Burton's quarrel with Joseph Hall in Rudolf Kirk, 'A Seventeenth-Century Controversy: Extremism vs. Moderation', *Texas Studies in Language and Literature* 9 (1967): 1–35. Anthony Milton describes this practice in the context of censorship in the early Stuart period. See his 'Licensing, Censorship, and Religious Orthodoxy in Early Stuart England', *The Historical Journal* 41 (1998): 625–51.

for an Arminian Donne.[16] Daniel Doerksen's argument for Donne's puritan imagination stresses Donne's conformity to a 'non-Laudian Church that welcomed those Puritans (a significant number) willing to conform either completely or to an acceptable level as specified by King James'. This is an important observation, as is his claim that Donne shared with the puritans 'their evangelical vision, their concern for a wholehearted and practical Christianity, and their view of preaching as a chief means of propagating the gospel'.[17] Doerksen, in fact, makes it clear that Donne is a conformist, not a puritan; nor is he trying to label Donne by means of such quotations. However, many of the things which Doerksen shows Donne shared with puritans were the professed concerns of a wide range of clergymen, and the tonal similarities which Doerksen cites between Donne, and, say, Richard Sibbes on the joys of heaven prove only that, like all Christians, Donne and Sibbes imagined a heaven that corresponded in some measure to this world. Doerksen's resistance to the older, rigid Anglican–puritan classification, however, complicates the dynamics of give-and-take within the early Stuart church. It also challenges a whole practice of categorisation that has marked Donne scholarship. In fact, recognising Donne's affinities with puritan values can lead to the productive insights noted above, as can studies that show Donne's doctrinal affinities with Arminians, and through them, with Donne's Catholic past. None the less, the following claim for an Arminian Donne based, in part, on a brief, uncontextualised similarity to Laud, demands qualification: 'Donne's expression that Christ is "not so strait" a gate "as that all may not enter", his vision that salvation is "displayed as the Sunne, over all" [VI, 164, 165] anticipates Laud's insistence that "*Salvation* is not shut up into . . . a *narrow Conclave*", and that he [Laud] has "endeavour'd to lay open those *wider-Gates* of the *Catholicke Church*, confined to no *Age, Time, or Place*" [*Relation of the Conference*, sig A4r]'.[18] That these sentiments, expressed in similar terms, mark the sermons of clerics such as Hall or Ussher (not thereby rendering them 'Arminian') shows that comparison on such a basis is insufficient. In a 1623 sermon, for example, Hall said that in churches which share one baptism, differences of administration and ceremonies, even differences of opinion, were 'diversely-coloured feathers of the same dove', while James Ussher delivered a June 1624 sermon on the subject of church unity that merits comparison with Donne's.[19] Nor does the

---

16   See, especially, Daniel Doerksen, 'Saint Paul's Puritan: John Donne's "Puritan" Imagination in the Sermons', in *Donne's Religious Imagination*, ed. by Malpezzi and Frontain, pp. 350–65. While the essay itself does not claim that Donne is a puritan, the label 'puritan' in the title is misleading. I am grateful to Achsah Guibbory for many productive discussions on these issues, and for sharing with me her important paper 'Donne's Religion: Montagu, Arminianism, and Donne's Sermons, 1624–30', *ELR* 31:3 (2001): 412–39.

17   Doerksen, pp. 351, 361.

18   Guibbory, 'Donne's Religion', p. 424.

19   Joseph Hall, 'The Beauty and Unity of the Church', in *Works* V, 282; James Ussher, *A Briefe*

identification of these statements by Laud and Donne distinguish sufficiently between the ambiguity of Donne's claim that Christ is 'not so strait a gate as that all may not enter', and Laud's more overtly politicised claim that he has endeavoured to lay open the wider gates of the Catholic Church – with that statement's emphasis on Laud rather than on Christ. It is important to determine to what extent Hall, Laud, Ussher, and Donne had similar motives in using this inclusive language, but to conclude that all such rhetoric was 'Arminian' is to oversimplify. So, too, does the conclusion that Donne's evangelical zeal was 'puritan'. Kenneth Fincham has shown compelling examples of preaching among bishops occupying every position on the spectrum.[20] For the terms 'Arminian' and 'puritan' to have any meaning in relation to Donne, these larger questions need to be addressed, as do the consequences for interpreting Donne's texts.

To some extent, all quotation and all comparison participates in this interpretative practice, and the habit of noticing linguistic similarities and being sensitive to the language of texts is a defining feature of the best literary scholarship. But as Anthony Milton, Peter Lake, and others have amply shown, what one 'sounds like' has to be gauged much more precisely in terms of context, and larger patterns of emphasis and rhetorical strategy. Rhetorical moderation could be sincere or could serve a tactical function, as Lake's studies of Joseph Hall demonstrate, and it is notoriously difficult to take statements made in the 1620s at today's face value.[21] In many cases the minute *differences* between like-sounding sentences are more important for us than the similarities. The 'sounds-like' argument can alert us to unexpected and fruitful connections, and can suggest important qualifications of received notions, but unless it is accompanied by detailed and comprehensive reading in the period as well as in the authors being compared, its promised insights can be illusory or unattainable. If Donne 'sounds like' Montagu, or Hall, or Sibbes, or Laud, then a scholar can bring a host of assumptions to bear on the voice being heard. Certainly Laud did when he thought Donne 'sounded like'

Declaration of the Universalitie of the Church of Christ, and the Unitie of the Catholicke Faithe professed therein (London, 1624).

[20] See Kenneth Fincham, *Prelate as Pastor: The Episcopate of James I* (Oxford: Clarendon Press, 1990), especially his discussions of bishops who were especially dedicated preachers in their sees: Henry Robinson (Carlisle); Richard Vaughan (Chester, London); George Abbot (London, Canterbury); John King (London); Richard Parry (Gloucester); Arthur Lake (Bath and Wells); Thomas Morton (Chester, Coventry and Lichfield); Gervase Babington (Worcester); Robert Abbot (Salisbury); Tobias Matthew (Archbishop of York); Laud (St David's).

[21] See, especially, the following essays: Peter Lake, 'The Moderate and Irenic Case for Religious War: Joseph Hall's *Via Media* in Context', in *Political Culture and Cultural Politics in Early Modern England*, ed. by Susan Amussen and Mark Kishlansky (Manchester: Manchester University Press, 1995), pp. 55–83; and Peter Lake, 'Joseph Hall, Robert Skinner and the Rhetoric of Moderation at the Early Stuart Court', in *The English Sermon Revised*, ed. by Ferrell and McCullough, pp. 167–85.

Abbot in 1627, and Donne was called before him to justify a sermon that to modern ears seems entirely orthodox in doctrine.[22]

Finally, use of Donne's biography to establish the network of Donne's religious allegiances has proven problematic, because scholars have not agreed on which details to emphasise or ignore, if they challenge at all the biographical narrative (from apostasy to ambition) constructed by R. C. Bald and John Carey.[23] But, the importance of rewriting the narrative of Donne's biography cannot be overestimated. In his own day, Donne was not identified clearly with any particular faction in the Church of England; in fact, his associates included a wide range of people, connected with virtually every named religious party in England. Still, the record has been difficult to interpret for modern scholars. In my own work I have stressed Donne's political and social connections with people along the full spectrum of religious positions in England, and, especially, with continental Protestantism. So, I have emphasised Donne's connections with Archbishop Abbot in 1622 (at a time when Abbot was out of favour); his connections with Lincoln's Inn puritans, including Thomas Gataker; his participation in a cipher or coded correspondence among continental supporters of Protestantism; his possible associations with Paolo Sarpi, the Italian republican; his medal commemorating the Synod of Dort; and his election as Prolocutor to Convocation.[24] Others have stressed his Catholic Baptism, his status as royal chaplain, the presence of a controversial Arminian book in Donne's library,

[22] This sermon has provoked considerable interest among scholars interested in defining Donne's religious position in 1627 because it is one recorded example of Donne's failure to satisfy the authorities. For full discussion of the sermon see Annabel Patterson, *Censorship and Interpretation: The Conditions of Writing and Reading in Early Modern England* (Madison: University of Wisconsin Press, 1984); Jeanne Shami, 'Kings and Desperate Men: John Donne Preaches at Court', *JDJ* 6 (1987): 9–23; Richard Strier, 'Donne and the Politics of Devotion', in *Religion, Literature and Politics in Post-Reformation England, 1540–1688*, ed. by Richard Strier and Donna Hamilton (Cambridge: Cambridge University Press), pp. 93–114; Joshua Scodel, 'John Donne and the Religious Politics of the Mean', in *Donne's Religious Imagination*, ed. by Malpezzi and Frontain, pp. 45–80; Shami, 'Anti-Catholicism', pp. 147–8; Guibbory, 'Donne's Religion', 434–5. McCullough's essay in this volume offers the most persuasive account of the sermon's politics to date. Its discussion of those elements of the sermon that would have been 'most noxious' to Laud's sensibilities, and particularly of the significance of preaching *those* words in *that* chapel (the Chapel Royal) over which Laud exerted influence, marks this sermon as the turning point in Donne's political fortunes at the Caroline court.

[23] Bald; John Carey, *John Donne: Life, Mind, and Art* (London, Faber, 1981). For reappraisals of Donne's biography which call into question these formulations and which reassess Donne's Catholicism see, especially, Dennis Flynn, *John Donne and the Ancient Catholic Nobility* (Bloomington: Indiana University Press, 1995); M. Thomas Hester, ' "This cannot be said": a Preface to the Reader of Donne's Lyrics', *Christianity and Literature* 39 (1990): 365–85.

[24] See especially Jeanne Shami, ' "The Stars in their Order Fought against Sisera": John Donne and the Pulpit Crisis of 1622', *JDJ* 14 (1995): 1–58; Dennis Flynn, 'Donne's Politics, "Desperate Ambition," and Meeting Paolo Sarpi in Venice', *JEGP* 99 (2000): 334–55; Jeffrey Johnson, *The Theology of John Donne* (Cambridge: D. S. Brewer, 1999).

and Donne's participation on the High Commission with Neile and Laud.[25] Even where the record is silent, scholars have also interpreted that silence. I have noted, for example, that Donne was not promoted to the bishopric that his absolutist theology might have predicted, that he was not a participant at the York House Conference of 1626 that debated Arminian theology, and that, while Donne was elected prolocutor of the 1626 Convocation, Richard Montagu was absent from the proceedings altogether.[26] It seems clear that in the future scholars will have to pay much closer attention to these biographical narratives, and continue to develop a methodology for applying such information to Donne's texts.

Faced with the profusion of Donnes that the scholarly practices outlined above have produced, I have adopted as one goal of my work the task of specifying foundational principles that can help to interpret these fragments and these narratives. One such principle, I believe, is Donne's 'discretion', which constitutes the politics, the rhetoric, and, most important, the ethics of his religion.[27] Distinguishable from sycophancy, flattery, hypocrisy and a variety of other attitudes with which it has been associated, discretion is

---

[25] Guibbory, 'Donne's Religion', 437–8. At Laud's trial, the prosecution associated Laud with Montagu on the grounds that Laud had Montagu's books in his study. Laud denied having given his approbation to Montagu's *published* views, adding 'I have Bellarmine in my study [and] therefore I am a Papist, or I have the Alcoran in my study [and] therefore I am a Turk, is as good an argument as . . . I have Bishop Montague's books in my study [and] therefore I am an Arminian' (Laud, *Works* IV, 289–90). Tyacke notes that Laud appears here to acknowledge that Montagu was indeed an Arminian: Nicholas Tyacke, *Anti-Calvinists: The Rise of English Arminianism c.1590–1640* (Oxford: Clarendon Press, 1987), p. 268. W. B. Patterson, *King James VI and I and the Reunion of Christendom* (Cambridge: Cambridge University Press, 1997) distinguishes between Arminianism as focused on liturgical practices (Cosin), episcopal authority (Laud) or theology (Montagu), calling Montagu a 'quasi-Arminian' and accepting Laud's denial of himself as an Arminian (p. 290).

[26] This work on Donne, Montagu, and the Synod of Dort is part of my essay '"Speaking Openly, and Speaking First": Donne, the Synod of Dort, and the Stuart Church', part of which was delivered as a paper at the 'Donne Returns to Loseley' conference, held at Loseley Park in Surrey, 18–20 May 2000. In itself, the claim that Donne's politics are absolutist is unobjectionable, if by 'absolutist' one means an advocate of obedience to the king, whose power derived 'either from a direct divine gift or an irreversible grant from the people', who was 'under a moral obligation to obey the laws of the land', but who, theoretically at least, was 'free to override any of the legal rights of their subjects in case of necessity'. Donne's theoretical support of absolutism is readily demonstrable. However, if by 'absolutism' one means simply a lust for power, and if one cites Donne's comments on *God's* power to support a claim about *Donne's* politics, the situation is altered. Peter Lake, *Anglicans and Puritans? Presbyterianism and English Conformist Thought from Whitgift to Hooker* (London: Allen & Unwin, 1988), p. 7. J. P. Sommerville refutes the revisionist definition of 'absolutism' as the power to 'rule by proclamation' without any obligation to 'consult with their subjects or uphold old constitutional agreements' (*Royalists and Patriots: Politics and Ideology in England 1603–1640*, 2nd ed. (Harlow: Longman, 1999), pp. 228–34).

[27] Jeanne Shami, 'Donne on Discretion', *ELH* 47 (1980), 48–66, 'Politics of Quotation', pp. 390–2, and 'Anti-Catholicism', pp. 140–1. My forthcoming study of Donne's Jacobean sermons is entitled '*Active Discretion': John Donne and Conformity in Crisis in the Late Jacobean Pulpit.*

manifested primarily in Donne's interpretative middle way, in his respect for due process in religious debate, and in his essentially practical divinity formulated by long years of immersion in casuistical habits of thought and discourse. Motivated by this principle of 'discretion', Donne seeks to avoid controversy by creating the climate for constructive religious debate, and the conditions of inclusion.

I would argue further that Donne's rejection of controversial labels distinguishes his sermons throughout his career, from his ordination in 1615 until his death in 1631. An early sermon on the text 'without controversy, great is the mystery of godliness' (III, 206–24) marks out this territory as important to Donne. So does Donne's rejection of 'names' or 'labels'. These fundamentals are supported in the sermons by an emphasis on consensus rather than on what he calls 'singularity', and on due process in discussing controverted points. Of recusants, he says 'we love them at Church [i.e. we don't debate with them there, and we worship with them together]; . . . But we hate them in our Convocations, where wee oppose Canons against their Doctrines, and we hate them in our Consultations, where we make laws to defend us from their malice' (III, 382). In another sermon, Donne censures the Pharisees not for the *substance* but for the *manner* of their disagreement with Christ: 'That which they say of Christ, they say not to Christ himself, but they whisper it to his servants, to his Disciples'. Donne goes on to explain how contention ought to be managed: 'A Legal and Juridical Accusation, is justifiable, maintainable, because it is the proper way for remedy: a private reprehension done with discretion, and moderation, should be acceptable too; but a privy whispering is always Pharisaical. The Devil himself, though he be a Lyon, yet he is a roaring Lyon; a man may hear him: but for a privy Whisperer, we shall onely hear of him' (VII, 151).

For Donne, the key example of moderate and constructive religious debate was the international Synod of Dort in 1618. Making claims for Donne's moderation, however, is also problematic. Almost all scholars who talk about moderation warn us that even apparently moderate or charitable statements of doctrine and attitude were tactical (especially among conformists), designed to cast opponents (especially puritan opponents) as extremists.[28] Guibbory concedes that 'people on both sides of the controversies accused their opponents of lack of charity', but makes the startling claim that 'charity' became 'the particular code word of the Arminians and the Laudians' who charged the puritans with uncharitable zeal.[29] To read the scholarship which

[28] Peter Lake, 'Moderation at the Early Stuart Court'; Lori Anne Ferrell, *Government by Polemic: James I and the Rhetorics of Conformity, 1603–1625* (Stanford: Stanford University Press, 1998).
[29] Guibbory, 'Donne's Religion', 422. Donne has a great deal to say about 'zeal', not all of it negative. See Shami, 'Donne's Protestant Casuistry': 60–1. In this part of the discussion, I argue that, while Donne warns his hearers against inordinate zeal, he is also careful to warn against extremes of discretion. Two examples to which Donne returns here are Abraham,

handles the discourses of moderation is to believe that no one who sounded moderate actually was. In this case in particular we need much more detailed discussion of how the language of moderation was used before we can formulate, with certainty, the rules and codes by which it can be interpreted. But surely, *excluding* puritans, or wanting to appear mainstream, were only two of many possible motives for speaking moderately. And focus on sermons more than on polemical pamphlets suggests that a great many preachers – especially those we define as conformists – were working to interpret and express the religious values of the Church of England by resisting as well as participating in religious controversy. This paper argues that Donne's rhetoric of moderation was tactically *inclusive* rather than *exclusive*, and that his goal was to expand rather than to limit the grounds of conformity to the Church of England.[30] To that end, I argue that Donne sympathised with the goal of 'public tranquility' which the various Protestant churches attempted at Dort, and that he would have seconded George Carleton's attack on Richard Montagu for publishing his provocative anti-Calvinist views.[31] But neither Montagu's 'roaring' nor the Pharisaical 'whispering' of some of his opponents comprehends Donne's goal of 'mutuall consent' through religious debate. For Donne, the damage to religion caused by polemical labelling could be avoided only by establishment of fundamental

who was not zealous enough on behalf of the Sodomites, and Peter, whose advice to Christ to retire from evident danger shows the danger of labelling lack of zeal and retirement from the duties of one's calling 'discretion'. I agree entirely with Carrithers' and Hardy's qualifications of my false distinction between discretion and zeal in the sermon, preferring their emphasis on Donne's 'zealous alertness that tried to avoid the dejection of spirit or uncharitable disputatiousness he associated with Separatism and to avoid the power-mongering tenden-tiousness he associated with spiritual complacency, Pelagianism, and Rome'. See Gale Carrithers and Thomas Hardy, Jr, *Age of Iron: English Renaissance Tropologies of Love and Power* (Baton Rouge: Louisiana State University Press, 1998), pp. 151–2. These authors are following the suggestion of David Norbrook that Donne 'preferred evangelical 'zeal' to the decency that was so much a feature of High Church rhetoric'. See 'The Monarchy of Wit and the Republic of Letters: Donne's Politics', in *Soliciting Interpretation: Literary Theory and Seventeenth-Century English Poetry*, ed. by Elizabeth G. Harvey and Katherine Eisaman Maus (Chicago: University of Chicago Press, 1990), p. 23.

[30] McCullough's argument that Donne's first sermon to Charles offers 'a polemical view of religious controversy even while it professes irenicism' is compelling, but I would stress that Donne's polemical and irenical purposes are not mutually exclusive. Nor would I suggest that his real purpose is 'polemical' but that he conceals this purpose with a veneer of 'irenicism'. Both of us would agree, I think, that Donne's polemic is aimed at those whose own polemical motives are exclusive rather than inclusive. While it seems odd to speak of a rhetorical stance that is both polemical and inclusive, I believe that is what Donne's sermons frequently achieve.

[31] Milton notes that 'when Richard Montagu attacked the Dutch Contra-Remonstrants, Carleton, for all his misgivings and conflicts with them, leapt to their defence, emphasizing that between the Dutch ministers and the Church of England "in the matter of the doctrine there hath been a care of mutuall consent sought, and by his late Maiestie graciously entertained; and for the publicke good the desire thereof may be continued, though this man should be offended"' (*Catholic and Reformed*, p. 422 and n. 61).

principles governing public religious discourse. As he explains in a rhetoric that is reassuringly *immoderate*: 'there is an over-fulnesse of knowledge, which forces a vomit; a vomit of opprobrious and contumelious speeches, a belching and spitting of the name of Heretique and Schismatique, and a losse of charity for matters that are not of faith; and from this vomiting comes emptiness, The more disputing, the lesse believing' (III, 240).[32] Equally, for Donne, the proliferation of books of controversy serves no Christian purpose: 'And yet every *Mart*, wee see more Bookes written by these men against one another, then by them both, for *Christ*' (VI, 246).

Donne's late Jacobean sermons clearly express an emerging and self-conscious awareness of the impact of public discourse on the expression of religious orthodoxy, and the importance of establishing principles governing this discourse. One of the first tasks of each generation of the post-Reformation Church in England was to define its terms and to express itself in relation to competing versions of the 'true' Church. Whereas most Elizabethan and Jacobean divines had defined themselves in large part in opposition to the Church of Rome, the Synod of Dort had ensured that public religious discourse now also took into account the relations between the *Thirty-Nine Articles* and the confessions of the Reformed Churches.[33] To some degree, Donne's professional status as Dean of St Paul's, royal chaplain, and Prolocutor of Convocation in the 1620s was constructed in the larger international context and in opposition to the professional print controver-sialists who had usurped public discussion of the Church of England's doctrine by means of their provocative polemics. Donne's own sense of service implied a public religious identity, not simply a private discourse of conscience. His sermons continually speak of the Church as an institutional necessity: those means and ordinances by which God's scriptural promises are fulfilled.[34] So the notion of Donne as a 'professional' voice is useful insofar as it counters the notion of Donne the apostate, or worse, Donne the church-papist.[35] It is even more useful insofar as it speaks to the dignity rather than

---

[32] This is just one example of Donne's charging all name-callers with lack of charity, rather than focusing only on the lack of charity of zealous puritans. In his sermon on foundations, discussed in my 'Anti-Catholicism in the Sermons of John Donne', Donne contrasts puritan lack of charity with the 'universall *Deluge*' of uncharitableness pouring from Rome (VI, 246).

[33] The significance of the Synod of Dort for the formulation of English doctrinal positions has been discussed by several scholars. See, especially, Milton, *Catholic and Reformed*, pp. 395–426; W. B. Patterson, pp. 260–292; White, pp. 175–202; Johnson, pp. 120–7; Tyacke, pp. 87–105.

[34] See, for example, II, 253, where Donne says that 'the knowledge which is to salvation, is by being in Gods house, in the Houshold of the Faithfull, in the Communion of Saints'. See also I, 29 and IV, 106; Elena Levy-Navarro, ' "Goe forth ye daughters of Sion": Divine Authority, the King, and the Church in Donne's Denmark House Sermon', *JDJ* 17 (1998): 163–73; and Johnson, pp. 33–6, 69–72 and *passim*.

[35] See Shami, 'Politics of Quotation', pp. 401–3; Peter McCullough, 'Preaching to a Court Papist? Donne's Sermon Before Queen Anne, December 1617', *JDJ* 14 (1995): 59–82.

the ambition of Donne's vocation, and its requirement of integrity or correspondence between rhetoric and conscience.[36] Construing Donne's 'conformity' in these terms makes sense of his radical faith in the mediating processes and institutions that had evolved historically in England, and that he used not simply as the unfortunate remnant of religious faith and devotion, but as the authorised means by which salvation was achieved. Donne rejects controversy not because he lacks principles or skill as a controversialist, but because his professional aims and standards differ fundamentally from those of controversialists. At stake for public controversialists may have been a particular view of the Church of England and its doctrine, but at stake for Donne is the application of doctrines necessary for the salvation of his hearers. So when we examine Donne's theological vocabulary, it is important to interpret his discourse as not primarily that of a controversialist but that of a pastor.[37] Though his rhetoric is deeply occasional, it is not useful to think of this vocabulary as careerist, changing with the times, except insofar as the Church of England was itself an institution changing with the times and responding to both Catholic and Reformed impulses and engaging in a process of self-definition and interpretation by no means complete in the 1620s.

Unlike works of controversy, then, Donne's sermons focus on revising the terms of the debate and stressing the interpretative possibilities rather than the absolute meanings of words. His practice of redefining controversial terms so that they lose their current polemical baggage and become available for more inclusive spiritual purposes is a major contribution to the negotiation of doctrinal positions in this period. I have shown how Donne, following James's ecclesiastical policy, uses the terms 'papist' and 'puritan' (and, more often, 'separatist') as rhetorical opposites; how he uses the terms 'Antichrist', 'recusant', and 'idolatry' as metaphors, rather than limiting them to a specifically Catholic, historical signification; and how the terms 'supererogation' and 'transubstantiation', terms of religious debate with Roman Catholics, become renovated terms for Reformed spiritual concepts in the sermons.[38] Antichrist is not limited to the Pope, then, but to 'all *supplanters*, and all seducers, all opposers of the kingdome of Christ, in us' (VI, 150). Recusants are not only Catholics who refuse the worship of the Church of England, but anyone who engages in deliberate separation from Church practices. Idolatry does not refer simply to Roman Catholic superstitions but to all sins: 'As many habituall sins as we embrace, so many Idols we worship' (V, 203). Equally, true 'supererogation' occurs, not when we earn and apply

---

[36] For a detailed, theoretical reading of Donne's vocational self, see Terry G. Sherwood, '"Ego videbo": Donne and the Vocational Self', *JDJ* 16 (1997): 59–113.

[37] On Donne as 'pastor' see Daniel Doerksen, 'Preaching Pastor versus Custodian of Order: Donne, Andrewes, and the Jacobean Church', *PQ* 73 (1994): 417–29; Lori Anne Ferrell, 'Donne and His Master's Voice, 1615–1625', *JDJ* 11 (1992): 59–70.

[38] Shami, 'Anti-Catholicism', pp. 150–2.

merit to the souls in Purgatory, but 'when our good works . . . not only profit *us*, that *do* them, but *others* that *see them* done' (III, 374). And transubstantiation' occurs when 'I have received it [the Sacrament] worthily, [and] it becomes my very soule' (VII, 321).[39]

Even in a series of sermons expressly committed to the polemical handling of matters of controversy between Catholics and Protestants, Donne takes three particular 'errors' and transforms them, demonstrating in the process how the definitions themselves are what is at stake. The three errors are prayer for the dead, purgatory, and indulgences, and Donne distinguishes between faulty (that is, Catholic) and 'justifiable' interpretations of these terms. A 'justifiable' prayer for the dead is not one that advocates for those who have died, but 'for our soules, dead in their sins' when we pray '*O Lord create a new heart in me.*' A 'justifiable' purgatory is not a literal standing house of correction between earth and heaven, but a floor which God fannes to 'make us cleane'. Finally, we have 'justifiable' indulgences when we can interpret God's corrections as marks of his indulgence to us, saying 'Thou hast been indulgent to thy people, O Lord, thou hast been indulgent to us.' This sermon ends with 'our humble thanks, for all Indulgences which God hath given us in our Purgatories, for former deliverances in former crosses, and with humble prayer also, that hee ever afford us such a proportion of his medicinall corrections, as may ever testifie his presence and providence upon us in the way, and bring us in the end, to the Kingdome of his Son Christ Jesus' (VII, 188–9).

In fact, one of Donne's rare topical references in a sermon illustrates precisely this kind of redefinition, both alluding to and standing back from a subject of considerable contention. In April 1626, Donne preached a sermon at a time when Parliamentary leaders were debating the publication of Montagu's works, while religious leaders meeting in Convocation were discussing Bishop Goodman's too-strong assertion of the Real Presence of Christ in the Eucharist. This sermon ends with a call to end controversy in a pointed political statement that announces its professional intentions by its determination to renovate the terms of the debate. The statement is complex for the way in which it chastises controversialists of all descriptions, including Catholics who wrangle about the exact manner of Christ's presence in the Eucharist (a 'piece of bread' or 'a sacramentall box'), and rigid Calvinists who interpret the phrase in its narrowest sense to focus on God's power rather than on human efforts of faith. Donne renovates the term to locate 'real

---

[39] One of Donne's strategies of inclusiveness is to strive for perceptual wholeness, a way of comprehending that modulates from the letter to the spirit by enlarging the literal sense rather than pitting it against the metaphorical. I discuss the ways in which Donne figures interpretative infirmities in 'Squint-Eyed, Left-Handed, Half-Deaf: *Imperfect Senses* and John Donne's Interpretive Middle Way', forthcoming in *Centred on the Word: Literature, Scripture, and the Tudor-Stuart Middle Way*, ed. by Christopher Hodgkins and Daniel Doerksen (Newark, N.J.: University of Delaware Press, 2003).

presence' in an active and 'ascending faith' to mean a process rather than a place, or, more accurately, a place within the believer rather than a physical location. Donne says: 'Drive him [that is, Christ] not away from thee by wrangling and disputing how he is present with thee; unnecessary doubts of his presence may induce fearfull assurances of his absence: The best determination of the Reall presence is to be sure, that thou be really present with him, by an ascending faith: Make sure of thine own Reall presence, and doubt not of his: Thou art not the farther from him, by his being gone thither before thee' (VII, 139–40). The language of this definition moves skillfully and carefully between positions, concluding in an affirmation both of Christ's real presence in believers ('doubt not of his'), a reformed position that goes beyond Catholic literalism, and of degrees of faith, an anti-Calvinist position that stresses the necessity of human efforts, if not their merits.[40]

Clearly, then, Donne's suspicion of the terms in which religious controversy was conducted stems from his own distrust of 'singularity', or extremism, and his preference for what he calls 'mediocrity'. Donne easily exposes failures to achieve 'mediocrity' in contemporary Catholicism, which he defines consistently as a religion of excesses occasioned and defined by its immoderate, absolutist discourse. A favourite example in the sermons is the Roman Catholic fondness for singular names. On several occasions, Donne calls attention to the Minims, and the Nullans, orders of Catholic friars who competed for precedence, ironically, by striving to be named the least. Donne exposes this impulse as 'contentious', 'quarrelsome', and 'vehement', rather than humble, an excess to be rejected by Christians. But 'mediocrity' is difficult to achieve, as the naming of these religious orders within the Catholic Church reveals. 'In one degree you finde embroydered shooes, for Kings to kisse, and in another degree bare feet; we finde an Order of the *Society of Jesus*; and that is very high, for, Society implies community, partnership; And we finde low descents, *Minorits*, men lesse then others, and *Minims*, least of all men; and lower then all them, *Nullans*, men that call themselves, *Nothing*; And truly, this Order, best of all others have answered and justified the name, for, very soone, they came to nothing. Wee finde all extreames amongst them, even in their names, but none denominated from this mediocrity' (VI, 307–8). The Society of Jesus is Donne's prime example of an order that has chosen a name that is too high, and that offends against this principle of

---

[40] In an extended discussion of Donne's 1626 sermon, Robert Whalen concludes that Donne's rhetorical formulation of the doctrine of real presence shows his 'recognition of the Church of England's failure to develop a sacramental theory distinct from that of Rome yet adequately suited to the church establishment's sacramental and sacerdotal orientation. Despite its denial of a purely signifying function for the elements and insistence on the presence of the whole Christ, Calvinist sacramentalism for Donne simply may have not gone far enough in recognizing the incarnational dimension of Holy Communion'. I am grateful to Robert Whalen for allowing me to see unpublished portions of his *The Poetry of Immanence* (Toronto: University of Toronto Press, 2002).

'mediocrity'. In fact, the name 'Christian' is to be preferred before Jesuit, Donne states, because it is more humble. As Donne explains, because 'Jesus is God, and Man in Him; And Christ is Man, and God in Him. So the Name *Iesus* seemes to taste of more Mystery, and more Incomprehensblenesse; And the name of *Christ*, of more Humility, and Appliablenesse' (VII, 309). The Jesuits go too high, the Nullans too low, but 'Christian' is 'a name of Communication, of Accommodation, of Imitation' (VII, 309). Donne frames his criticisms of religious positions almost entirely in terms of such excesses, defining a spectrum that excludes singular extremes of papist and puritan, what Donne calls '*by-religion*[s]' (I, 219) and focuses on the 'mediocrity' of 'our' church.

Breaking down binary oppositions is not an invention of the post-modern age. It is Donne's constant rhetorical intellectual strategy, not only in the sermons but in his earlier poetry and prose, reflecting the inclusivity of his imagination. First of all, Donne works within certain dichotomies that allow him to frame, but not to pinpoint, faulty or distorted attitudes and beliefs. Typically, Donne frames his criticism of singular, separatist impulses within the Church of England in these terms.[41] So, when God leaves the Church to itself, 'devested of the *Spirit* of GOD . . . those imaginary *Churches*, that will receive no light from Antiquitie, nor Primitive formes, GOD leaves to themselves, and they crumble into *Conventicles*; And that *Church*, which will needes be the *Forme* to all *Churches*, God leaves to her selfe, to her owne *Traditions*, and Shee swells into tumors, and ulcers, and blisters' (VII, 83). Similarly, Donne tells his congregation that 'The Lambe is not immured in *Rome*, not coffined up in the ruines, and rubbidge of old wals, nor thrust into a corner in *Conventicles*' (V, 105). In another context, the eyes of 'discretion and religious wisdome' in God's ministers allow them to 'see that they harken neither to a superstitious sense from Rome, nor to a seditious sense of Scriptures from the Separation' (VIII, 50). And in his first sermon as vicar of St Dunstan's, Donne uses this rhetoric once more to position the minister as dwelling in the house of God: '*Idolaters* must not, *Separatists* must not be admitted to these marriages, to these widow Churches' (VI, 83).[42]

[41] The brilliance of Donne's rhetorical strategy of framing his position between carefully constructed extremes is nowhere better illustrated than in McCullough's essay in this volume. McCullough argues that in Donne's 1626 court Lent sermon, he supports only the doctrinal position defended by Neile and Montagu at the York House debates, but frames his case in the rhetorical garb of a compromise emerging from dialectical opposition between both sides (the Calvinist and the Arminian). I have argued in ' "Speaking Openly" ' that the metaphor of hearing with both ears mediates between strict Calvinist and anti-Calvinist ears, but that Donne's point is that both ears together 'hear' the whole or right doctrine, as Donne invites his hearers 'from one Text [to] receive both Doctrines' (VII, 74).

[42] Because Donne consistently articulates the extremes of the spectrum as separatist, I find it difficult to concur with Achsah Guibbory in her argument that Donne, like Richard Montagu, 'was engaging in much the same rhetorical move as the Arminians did in the

Within these separatist extremes, Donne reiterates his advice not to apply names too hastily, and to use language at the ends of the spectrum to exclude only those who cannot be accommodated into the Church of England's 'mediocrity'. Consistently, Donne stresses that Churches named after mere men (that is, Calvinists, Lutherans, papists) are not 'our' Church, the Church of England. On the issue of ceremonies, for example, Donne positions 'our' Church in relation to these others: 'That Church, which they call Lutheran, hath retained more of these Ceremonies, then ours hath done; And ours more then that which they call Calvinist; But both the Lutheran, and ours, without danger, because, in both places, we are diligent to preach to the people the right use of these indifferent things' (VIII, 331). Donne's concept of the English Church is that it is neither Calvinist, nor Lutheran, nor papist, nor puritan, but Christian. A long passage in a Whitsunday sermon implies these same extremes and excludes them as un-Christian. Donne explains:

> If men who desire a change in Religion, and yet thinke it a great wisdome, to disguise that desire, and to temporise, lest they should be made less able to effect their purposes, if they should manifest themselves [that is, Church-papists, specifically, as the passage makes clear, the Gunpowder plotters], . . . If others, who are also working in the fire, (though not in the fire of envy and of powder, yet in the fire of an indiscreet zeale, and though they pretend not to change the substance of the metall, the body of our Religion, yet they labour to blow away much of the ceremony and circumstances . . . [that is, separatists]) If these men, I say, of either kind, They who call all differing from themselves, Error, and all error damnable [that is, Catholics]; or they . . . which call the abolishing and extermination of all Discipline and Ceremony, purenesse and holinesse [that is, nonconforming puritans, or separatists]; If they thinke they have received their portion of this legacie, their measure of true knowledge in labouring onely to accuse, and reforme, and refine others, . . . The Holy Ghost makes men Christians, and not Alchymists. (IX, 243)

If there are disagreements in religion, Donne makes clear, they are not to be resolved by calling 'any man *Lutheran,* or *Calvinist,* or by any other name, ignominiously, but for such things, as had been condemned in *Luther,* or *Calvin,* and condemned by such, as are competent Judges between them, and us; that is, by the universall, or by our own Church' (II, 111).

Because naming polemically, controversially, is unsuitable in sermons, the work of 'Alchymists' who want to accuse, reform, and refine, rather than the Holy Ghost who wants to transform men into Christians, Donne himself prefers to name by analogy and historical precedent. Consequently, he uses the heretical Cathari of the primitive Church, as well as the Pharisees, to stand in for puritans, and he uses the terms Pelagian, and semi-Pelagian, to stand in for those who attribute too much to human will. In fact, the Synod of Dort

1620s and 30s – extending the category "puritan" to include the Calvinism that had been the orthodox mainstream of the English reformed church' ('Donne's Religion', 420).

had effectively branded the Remonstrants as Pelagians and several books condemning Arminianism as Pelagian were published after that Synod. While the British delegates did not concur in this public act, Milton concludes that 'even moderate Calvinists such as Ward and Davenant ultimately assured themselves that the Dutch Arminians were guilty of the Pelagian heresy'.[43] White adds that comparison of the English delegates' document, *Collegiat Suffrage*, with the official Dort canons justifies the claim of one delegate, Walter Balcanqual, that the British judgment 'was most just and equal, condemning the rigidity of some of the Contra-Remonstrants' opinions, though not by that name, as well as the errors of the Pelagians, Semi-Pelagians, and Remonstrants'.[44] It is notable, then, that in a sermon delivered at the height of the controversy over Richard Montagu's alleged Arminian-ism, Donne resorts to the coded term 'Pelagian' to illustrate the extreme view of universal grace against which a moderate position must be articulated. This is not the first time Donne uses the word 'Pelagian' to describe those who over-compensate for the rigidities of Calvinist predestination by attributing too much to human will. And increasingly, Donne resorts to this name, rather than to the word 'papist', to name that extreme when the issue is the theology of grace. So, in a sermon preached 5 November 1626, Donne rejects the notion that God works upon persons 'Not disposed by nature, without use of grace; that is flat and full Pelagianisme; Not disposed by preventing grace, without use of subsequent grace, . . . that is Semi-pelagianisme. But persons obsequious to his grace, when it comes, and persons industrious and ambitious of more and more grace, and husbanding his grace well all the way, such persons God proposes to himselfe' (VII, 240). In fact, in 1629, Donne articulates a spectrum of those religious positions which have 'white-ness, a colour of good', but which are in reality 'a mischievous leprosie'. This spectrum ranges from papist and Arminian excesses at the one end to puritan excesses at the other: 'It is a *Whole-pelagianisme*, to think nature alone sufficient; *Halfe-pelagianisme*, to think grace once received to be sufficient; *Super-pelagianisme*, to thinke our actions can bring God in debt to us, by merit, and supererogation, and *Catharisme*, imaginary purity, in canonizing our selves, as present Saints, and condemning all, that differ from us, as reprobates . . . . There is no good whiteness, but a reflection from Christ Jesus, in an humble acknowledgement that wee have none of our own, and in a confident assurance, that in our worst estate we may be made partakers of his' (IX, 67). Super-Pelagianism appears to comprehend Catholics, with their doctrines of merit and supererogation. But, that Donne distinguishes *three*

---

[43] Milton, *Catholic and Reformed*, p. 417. R. V. Young suggests that Arminianism took a more radical stand on free will than the pre-Reformation Catholic Church had, and was the Reformation form of Pelagianism: *Doctrine and Devotion in Seventeenth-Century Poetry* (Cambridge: D. S. Brewer, 2000).

[44] White, p. 192. The citation is from John Hales, *The Golden Remains of the Ever-Memorable Mr John Hales of Eton College: Letters from the Synod of Dort*, 2nd edn (London, 1673), p. 117.

forms of Pelagianism is also significant, reflecting his sense that the current 'Pelagian' assault on moderate Reformed theology was widespread, not limited simply to papists, and as much to be resisted as the puritan challenge.[45]

Anthony Milton has documented how some of these terms were used polemically in religious controversy of the 1620s.[46] The connection between Arminians and Pelagians was frequently made, as was the connection between papists and semi-Pelagians. James, for one, equated Arminianism with Pelagianism, so it is conceivable that Donne, whom we have seen elsewhere working within the terms of official Jacobean religious discourse, was doing so too.[47] However, Daniel Featley, George Carleton, and William Prynne made the same connection, suggesting that the association was commonplace and spread across a wide religious spectrum.[48] In fact, there was no consistency with which the term 'Pelagian' was exchanged. But it seems significant to me that Donne's use of the terms increases in the Caroline sermons, and shows him, however sympathetic to Arminian theological positions on God's mercy, the universality of grace, and the conditional nature of his contract with men, avoiding the name Arminian as a term of division, discord, and controversy, and suggesting that all forms of new-style Pelagianism are distinguishable from the 'good whiteness' and 'mediocrity' of the Christianity of the Church of England.

I have paid so much attention to Donne's use of names, particularly those of the ancient Pelagian and Catharist heretics, because recently a new name, 'Arminian', has been added to the Donne catalogue. In concluding, I would like to explain why I think it especially unhelpful, however accurate in an abstractly doctrinal sense, to label Donne's religion as Arminian by looking briefly at one sermon preached in the first half of 1626 for what it reveals about his religion in the early Caroline years.[49] Preached in the context of the York House Conference to debate Arminianism in February 1626 and the Parliamentary debates of that period (debates about the orthodoxy of Montagu's publications), this sermon illuminates the way in which Donne framed his own public religious discourse at a particularly sensitive moment

---

[45] That these observations occur at the end of Donne's April 1629 Court sermon might qualify McCullough's claim that after 1627 Donne's sermons avoid politically charged opinions and frequently parrot Laudian truisms.

[46] Milton, *Catholic and Reformed*, p. 210. 'Where anti-Calvinist divines were directly accused of Pelagianism, the Roman Church was distinguished from them, and seen instead as inclining more towards semi-Pelagianism'.

[47] W. B. Patterson, p. 281: 'James acquiesced in Bishop Carleton's view that the Remonstrants were Pelagians, analogous to the opponents of St Augustine of Hippo'.

[48] White, pp. 230–2.

[49] The following discussion supports McCullough's distinction between doctrinal and political Arminianism, but argues that the 'Arminian' label cannot be so separated. I am saying that Donne cannot be called an Arminian, because an Arminian was more accurately a political rather than a doctrinal category in the 1620s.

in his professional career. In particular, I want to look at the kind of middle way that Donne draws for 'our' Church in this sermon, a middle way, I will argue, that is not a fixed or absolute doctrinal point, but a point still being reformed by a process of mutual consensus, and altering under the pressure of historical circumstances.[50] Donne's sermon for 18 April 1626, was preached on John 14:2 ('In my fathers house are many mansions; if it were not so I would have told you'). In the 'many mansions' sermon, Donne first handles the issue of controversy itself by considering where controversy arises, how controversy leads to distempered extremes or polarities in religion, and how controversy ought to be handled. The interpretative conflict which Donne is trying to mediate is announced early as he notes the distempers 'both theirs, that think, That there are other things to be beleeved, then are in the Scriptures [namely, papists], and theirs that think, That there are some things in the Scriptures, which are not to bee beleeved [namely, rigid predestinarians who do not believe there are 'many mansions' in heaven]' (VII, 119). He says 'I would at last contentious men would leave wrangling, and people to whom those things belonged not, leave blowing of coales' (VII, 121–2). The contentious issue to which he refers is the doctrine of election, but the sermon focuses on how doctrine of any sort is to be established, and that is by God's will as recorded in his testament, 'since he that made the Will, hath made it thus cleare' (VII, 122). In contrast to the Catholic Council of Trent that decided finally in many particulars without general consent, Donne offers the example of the British delegates to the Protestant Synod of Dort where the participants delivered the doctrine of election with 'blessed sobriety' (VII, 127). The sobriety of their statement consisted in its sentence 'That all men are truly, and in earnest called to eternall life, by Gods Minister' (VII, 127). They knew, he said, the doctrine of 'our Church' which had declared 'That we must receive Gods promises so, as they be generally set forth to us in the Scriptures' (VII, 127). The scriptural evidence, appropriated from Article XVII of the *Thirty-Nine Articles*, allowed the English delegates to retain their interpretative independence, and to make any doctrine confirmed by any synod dependent on that interpretative consensus. What the Synod of Dort confirmed for English divines, according to Donne, was the freedom to establish doctrine according to their interpretation of Scriptures. It is this aspect of the Synod, as well as the process by which the formulations were prepared, that Donne most valued. As his own language shows, he wasn't trying to use the Synod to endorse his own views, but to endorse his own

---

[50] For this discussion, I am particularly indebted to Scodel's essay cited above, especially pp. 63–70. Scodel argues that Arminianism, with its apparent mean between Catholic and Protestant, was exposed by Donne in 1627 as a travesty of the mean between Catholic and radical Protestant, which was James's vision of the Church of England. Here he is building on Norbrook's suggestion that the 'middle way' adapted from Augustine was an attitude or process, not a fixed point. Guibbory, 'Donne's Religion', 434–5, sees no evidence of anti-Arminianism in the 1627 sermon they are both discussing.

responsibility to interpret, and the 'sobriety' of the Synod lay as much in ensuring that freedom of interpretation was established in words than in any particular doctrinal formulation. Definitions could be 'over-precise' and Donne's language shows his caution not to be caught in this linguistic trap. The point is that – in the Church of England – the details of the law are left to ministers to interpret, although the fundamentals remain.

Only following that moment of 'blessed sobriety' does Donne paraphrase the Synod's statement on election, 'That conditionall salvation is so far offered to every man, as that no man may preclude himselfe from a possibility of such a performance of those Conditions which God requires at his hands, as God will accept at his hands, if either he doe sincerely endevour the performing, or sincerely repent the not performing of them' (VII, 127–8). That is, while no person can be absolutely sure of his election, neither can he be so sure of his reprobation as to justify his spiritual inertia. This is a statement that expresses the theology of grace (that is, who is saved and how) in conditional rather than absolute terms, and which is a statement similar to that which the more moderate Calvinist majority, and certainly the English delegates at the Synod of Dort, had accepted.[51]

Achsah Guibbory cites this section of the sermon to show how Donne's articulation of the doctrine of election is different from the Synod's and much closer, in fact, to the Arminian position that the Synod rejected. Her main point is that Donne's modifications of Calvinist doctrine and his references to rigid Calvinists as 'over-good husbands of Gods large and bountifull Grace, [who] contract his generall promises' (VII, 126), indicate his Arminian sympathies. It is true that Donne criticises 'contentious' men and does enlarge the interpretation of the number of the elect in this sermon. In her study, however, Guibbory collapses 'contentious' men and those who 'contract' God's promises, to suggest that Donne is referring only to Calvinists as 'contentious', but one could equally infer that he is criticising all contentious men, including Arminians, including Montagu, who had politicised the doctrinal issue of God's grace, making it difficult, if not impossible, to move moderate men towards the 'blessed sobriety' of Dort which Donne favours (and had favoured, long before Montagu's books were published). In fact, we both notice that against the rigid predestinarianism that the Synod of Dort, and particularly the British delegates, had sought to mitigate, Donne's sermon emphasises that, though the elect are numbered, there are *many* mansions in heaven, a promise recorded clearly in Scripture.[52]

---

[51] Further examination of the *Collegiat Suffrage* of the English delegates is required to elaborate this point.

[52] Although Guibbory does not distinguish between the official Dort articles, which the English delegates signed, and the records of their own internal debates on the substance and wording of the articles, examined by Lake and White, such a distinction seems crucial to any study of the kind of consensus achieved by the Synod and the process by which it was accomplished.

[53] This point is discussed by Whalen in Chapter 3 of *The Poetry of Immanence*. McCullough,

So, I agree entirely with Guibbory that Donne was deliberately enlarging the interpretation of the Dort decree on grace, but not, as she concludes, to undermine Calvinism. Her question is how far a person can qualify a position before it becomes a completely different position. And this is precisely the question. Do Donne's temperate modifications of rigid Calvinist theology make him an Arminian? My answer is no.[53] I believe that here, as elsewhere, Donne, like those experimental predestinarians described by Peter Lake,[54] was showing his congregation how to bring their consciences and beliefs into alignment with a Reformed consensus, such as that achieved at Dort, by not taking statements at their most literal and narrow. This was all the more important for Donne because he believed that the position of the Church of England on many of these doctrines had not yet been defined, except in the language of the *Thirty-Nine Articles*, and that 'over-precise' definition risked hardening positions and reducing the liberty and responsibility of interpretation of Scriptures which even the Calvinist Synod of Dort had accorded preachers.

In the April 1626 sermon, the elect are numbered, but there are 'many' mansions. Rigid Calvinists might stress the limits, while Donne stresses the large number. Nor do I agree that Donne's balanced rhetoric and gestures of inclusion were designed to support the views of any faction. Quite the opposite. It is not just a difference in means that separates Donne and Montagu from a similar end (namely, the enlarging of God's grace). Donne's means *are* his end. Each time in that sermon that Donne interprets his text generously while still within the literal bounds of orthodoxy, each time he expresses himself discreetly, he is embodying his religion and his politics. Moderation, inclusivity, compromise are sometimes taken to express politically neutral and therefore unprincipled positions. But I would argue that political neutrality and religious inclusivity were strenuously achieved political commitments in the 1620s.[55] Guibbory concedes that Donne was much more cautious and subtle in his rhetoric than Montagu.[56] But the differences between Donne and Montagu that this sermon illustrates were not simply superficial, differences in rhetorical posture and dress, differences in 'lifestyle'. Such differences in dress expressed differences in being. Donne had been working for years to extend the interpretation of the operation of grace,

---

too, finds that Donne's comments support an Arminian reading, but I am arguing that it is unwise to separate doctrine and politics (or rhetoric) in establishing Donne's profession of faith.

[54] Peter Lake, 'Calvinism and the English Church', *Past and Present* 114 (1987): 56, says that 'the stress of the English delegation was always pastoral and edificational. They played up those aspects of the Calvinist case which left room for an element of human responsibility and effort and which avoided the possibility of fatalism and desperation in the laity.' Lake calls attention to this 'experimental predestinarianism' which 'can be seen operating on and subtly changing the doctrinal core of credal Calvinism' at Dort (p. 58).

[55] See Milton, *Catholic and Reformed*, especially pp. 541–2.

[56] Guibbory, 'Donne's Religion', 426.

quoting Calvin increasingly to show that Calvin could yield the generous interpretations Donne found in him.[57] In trying to shift and expand the middle ground of orthodoxy within the Church of England, Donne was surely obstructed by Montagu's divisive, provocative, and very public rhetoric, and by Montagu's efforts to include all Calvinists in the separatist language used against radical puritans. I believe that Donne was rejecting this Arminian move, excluding in his rhetoric only separatist puritans, and rigid predestinarians, not all Calvinists. I also agree with David Norbrook that while Montagu was using divisive rhetoric to create doctrinal differences with puritans, Donne was still insisting that the differences were disciplinary, and hence not fundamental. Donne's primary targets are Pelagians and Catharists, separatists outside the Christian foundations of the Church of England. And this rhetoric of inclusivity is Donne's politics.

Critics can find in these sermons, then, as in so many others, Donne's care to balance positions, and to reveal them as extremes, or as unnecessarily contentious, in order to illuminate a place of 'mediocrity' which, for him, distinguishes the Church of England, 'our' Church, from other Reformed institutions and from the Church of Rome. 'Our' Church is Christian, not named after mere men, and yet named for that divine name which is most applicable to humans, namely, Christ. I think that it is only by articulating Donne's characteristic habits of thought across all of his sermons that we can discern what he meant by 'mediocrity' and how he represented it rhetorically. Donne's 'mediocrity' was a pulpit space that he hoped to model on the 'blessed sobriety' of the Synod of Dort rather than on the contentious wrangling of the Council of Trent. And it was an inclusive place, rhetorically pointed by Donne's redefinitions of the terms of controversy. One more thing is certain. Donne's public religious identity as constructed in his sermons springs from the same habits of thought that inform his earlier prose writings, and even his poetry, and expresses how intimately and discreetly conscience and public speech were connected in his practice.

---

[57] The significance of one's quoting from Calvin requires careful interpretation. My point that Donne increasingly quotes from Calvin is not to prove that 'Donne remained a Calvinist' (Guibbory, 'Donne's Religion', 427, n. 39), but to show that, unlike Montagu and other Arminians, Donne was not 'anxious to denigrate him' (Milton, *Catholic and Reformed*, p. 427). Milton discusses the use of Calvin as a discursive counter among anti-Calvinists in *Catholic and Reformed*, pp. 427–35, 450–3. Instead, I have argued that Donne uses Calvin, as he uses other expositors, to support his own generous interpretations of the *Thirty-Nine Articles*, which he accepts as the foundational articles of the doctrine of the Church of England. Like many of the terms Donne is renovating in his sermons, 'Calvin' is, in some sense, one of these.

Chapter 8

JOHN DONNE AS A CONVENTIONAL PAUL'S CROSS PREACHER

MARY MORRISSEY

THIS chapter will address the subject of John Donne as a professional preacher, particularly as he practised that vocation at Paul's Cross in London. Although not a professional group as such, Paul's Cross preachers undertook a very particular task in addressing the London community from that pulpit. Millar MacLure has described the Paul's Cross preacher as 'the physician to the body politic; he is the servant of the Church of England whose canons he is bound to defend, and in defending them to justify the Church's existence by this audible and visible demonstration of her care for the body politic'.[1] Many of the sermons preached there emphasised the political role of these preachers, being in commemoration of accession days or the Gunpowder Plot, or particularly notable events like the Armada or the Essex rebellion. It is on these occasions that Paul's Cross was used to deliver not just the 'common message' of 'Moyses or Christ, Law or Gospell' such as was preached '*every Sabbath day*, out of this chaire' as Bishop John King put it,[2] but to set topical events in a religious context. Consequently, the emphasis in this chapter will be on Donne as a political preacher. It will examine the strategies used by Donne in his sermons at Paul's Cross that allowed him make public statements on political subjects without diverging from a strict definition of his role as preacher of the Gospel.

We are well accustomed to the idea that Elizabeth and her early Stuart successors 'tuned' the pulpit for political ends.[3] None the less, we should not

---

[1] Millar MacLure, *The Paul's Cross Sermons, 1534–1642* (Toronto: University of Toronto Press, 1958), pp. 120–1. This study remains the only major published work on this pulpit.

[2] John King, *A sermon at Paules Crosse. on behalfe of Paules church* (1620), p. 31. In all references to early modern publications, the original spelling is retained but u/v and i/j are modernised.

[3] Peter Heylyn, *Cyprianus Anglicus* (1668), p. 161. It is worth noting in this context that Heylyn's comment refers to plans to copy the example of Elizabeth I and 'tune' the pulpits to support the forced loan of 1627. Heylyn notes that 'some of the preachers did their parts' but the examples he gives are Sibthorpe and Manwaring, both of whose sermons caused an outcry (p. 167).

159

assume from this, or from the common occurrence of political themes at Paul's Cross, that this was an unquestioned or uncontroversial practice. In his accession day sermon at Paul's Cross of 1608, Richard Crakanthorp remarks that 'it is not my meaning, nor is it fit, to make a panegericall Oration in this place at large'.[4] As the preacher's primary task when addressing his hearers was to rouse them to godliness and piety, he would be misusing his position if he used this forum for the delivery of political pronouncements: such statements had to be integrated into the doctrines delivered in the sermon.[5] Many of the topics that were considered within the preacher's brief – the duties of obedience and loyalty most notably – pertained to the community and the polity, and so they lent themselves readily to political treatment. In his 1640 accession day sermon, Henry King spends considerable time discussing theories of sovereignty and resistance, but near the end of his sermon he remarks that he had not forgotten '*where* I am' or '*whose errand* I deliver': his aim in praising Charles I, he insists, is to remind the hearers of their duty to thank God for the blessing of a good king.[6] In addressing a sermon on a political topic, the preacher had to be careful not to 'wrest' Scripture by interpreting it in an unusual or heterodox way that obviously served party or factional interests. William Laud's accession day sermon in 1631 opens with the remark that he has chosen a prayer from Scripture because 'the age is so bad, they will not endure a good King to be commended, for danger of flattery: I hope I shall offend none by praying for the King'.[7]

In order to understand the strategies used by Donne and his fellow Paul's Cross preachers in their negotiation between the demands of their public functions as preachers and government spokesmen, we must examine the conventional ways of structuring a public sermon that he and his contemporaries recognised. The most fundamental assumption governing Elizabethan and early Stuart preaching theory was that the preacher's function was to explain a text from Scripture (to *explicate* or expound it) and then apply its teachings to the hearer's lives or the

[4] Richard Crakanthorp, *A sermon at the solemnizing of the happie inauguration of our most gracious and religious soveraigne King James* (1609), sig. B4r. None the less, two accession day sermons of the period refer to their sermons as panegyrics: Thomas Holland, *Panegyris D. Elizabethae . . . A sermon preached at Pauls in London* (1601), and Joseph Hall, *An holy panegyrick. A sermon preached at Pauls Crosse* (1613).

[5] In *The defense of the aunswere to the Admonition*, John Whitgift accuses Cartwright of having 'slandered both the Prince & the whole state of religion, in this Churche' by suggesting that 'princes pleasures' were defended from the pulpit: *The defense of the aunswere to the Admonition* (1574), p. 558.

[6] Henry King, *A sermon preached at St Pauls March 27 1640. Being the Anniversary of his Majesties happy inauguration to his crowne* (1640), p. 57.

[7] William Laud, 'Sermon VII, preached at St Paul's Cross in commemoration of King Charles' Inauguration', in *The Works of the Most Reverend Father in God, William Laud, D. D.*, ed. by W. Scott and J. Bliss, 7 vols (Oxford: John Henry Parker, 1847–60) I, 188.

occasion at which he spoke (the *application*).[8] As preachers at Paul's Cross were allowed to choose the texts on which they preached, it can be assumed that their choice, and the interpretations they put forward, were intended to facilitate the argument they wished to make. When beginning his sermon, the preacher usual '*opened*' the text by describing its context in the Bible and what teaching it delivered. The text was then '*divided*' into smaller sections. The detailed discussion of these *divisions*, and the doctrines they contained, was usually given considerable attention, as it was here that the preacher demonstrates how the argument that he presents arise from his biblical source and could be related to the occasion on which he spoke. Elaborating on the relationship between the text's doctrine and the circumstances of the sermon was the task of *applying* the text to the hearers, and it usually included exhortations to some virtue.

The analysis of how Donne *explicated* and then *applied* the texts on which he preached provides us with an historically sensitive method for investigating his use of Scripture to engage with current affairs. In what follows, I will look at the structure of Donne's three Jacobean Paul's Cross sermons, all preached on political occasions: the 1617 accession day sermon, the 1622 sermon on the *Directions to preachers* (preached on 15 September) and later in the same year, a Gunpowder Plot sermon.[9] On these three occasions, Donne's description of the subject's duties and the monarch's responsibilities are carefully placed within the larger context of Christian doctrine that circumscribed all pulpit pronouncements. We can also see how Donne exercises a stronger sense of rhetorical decorum than many other Paul's Cross preachers, as he takes care to treat his texts in ways that provide advice for those present, James' subjects, without dictating precepts for, or defining, the duties of the king.

David Cressy has shown how the celebration of the accession day became widely established as an annual festival day by the 1580s.[10] To a great extent, the conventions for Jacobean accession day sermons at Paul's Cross followed on from Elizabethan ones, in which the providential reading of Elizabeth's succession took a central place. By this reading, as Cressy says; '17 November represented more than the accession day of a monarch. Rather, it signified the turning point in England's religious history, a providential divide between the

---

[8] English words used as technical terms in preaching are italicised.

[9] *A Sermon preached at Pauls Cross to the Lords of the Council, and other Honourable Persons, 24. Mart. 1616*, in *Sermons* I, no. 3; *A sermon upon the fift of November 1622. being the Anniversary celebration of our Deliverance from the Powder Treason*, IV, no. 9; *A sermon upon the XX. verse of the V Chapter of the Booke of Judges. Wherein occasion was justly taken for the Publication of some Reasons, which his Sacred Majestie had been pleased to give, of those Directions for Preachers, which hee had formerly sent foorth. Preached at the Cross the 15th of September. 1622*, *Sermons* IV, no. 7.

[10] David Cressy, *Bonfires and Bells: National Memory and the Protestant Calendar in Elizabethan and Stuart England* (London: Weidenfeld and Nicolson, 1989), pp. 50–2.

nightmare of popery and the promise of the development of God's true church.'[11] James' accession on 24 March represented a continuation of that promise, in spite of the prognostications of England's Catholic enemies, because God had ordained a legitimate, Protestant, godly and wise king for England. It was not enough, however, for preachers to simply commemorate this providential event or to extol the virtues of their monarch. The sermon had to preach a lesson that could be *applied* to the hearers and teach them a lesson in their Christian duty. Contemporary comments suggest that this was understood by hearer and preacher alike. For example, John Chamberlain complimented the way Donne 'held himself close to the text without flattering the time too much' in the latter's 1617 accession day sermon.[12] Staying 'close to the text' implies that Donne kept his sermon focused on the doctrines contained in his biblical source and did not merely use the text as a pretext for 'flattering the time', and therefore the king whose accession was being celebrated. Paul's Cross preachers usually chose to use the hand of providence visible in James' accession as the context within which praise for the king could be set while exhorting their hearers to thank God for this benefit. So writes Richard Crakanthorp in his 1608 accession sermon. Among the blessings for which England must thank God:

> The first is our long tranquility and happie peace, with all the blessings and blessed fruites of peace. A blessing which God began to bestow on this land, at the joyful entrance of our late Soveraigne QUEENE ELIZABETH, . . . Having enjoyed long and happy peace, under her long and happy raigne, it was expected by the Agents and vassals of Antichrist, that the day which ended her life, should have ended all our comforts, and beene to us a dismall day, a day of murthers and massacres, a day of warres, of tumults, and of utter desolation; . . . Behold, hee that sits in heaven laught them to scorne, the Lord had them in derision. Himselfe placed on his owne Throne, after *David, Salomon; A man of rest and peace, for God hath given him, and in him to us, rest and peace from all his, and our Enemies, round about.*[13]

The Old Testament David (or often Deborah) being succeeded by the peaceful, wise and Temple-building Solomon matched well with the image of peacemaker that James wished to present. Although the kinds of texts chosen by preachers for this occasion varied (some choosing to compare Old Testament events to recent history, others taking New Testament precepts relating to political life), all interpreted their texts to reach similar conclusions: that good government was a blessing for which the hearers should give

---

[11] Cressy, *Bonfires and Bells*, p. 53.

[12] *The Letters of John Chamberlain*, ed. by Norman Egbert McClure, 2 vols (Philadelphia: The American Philosophical Society, 1939) II, 67.

[13] Richard Crakanthorp, *Sermon*, sig. B4r; See also, Joseph Hall, *An holy panegyrick*, pp. 49–59; John White, *A sermon delivered at Pauls Crosse*, in *Two sermons, the former delivered at Pauls Crosse. The latter at the Spittle* (1615), pp. 2–3.

thanks to God. Consequently, the most common themes of accession day sermons were the subject's duty of thanksgiving to God and of obedience to the monarch.

Donne's task in delivering the 1617 accession day sermon was more complicated than most, for it was delivered shortly after James I embarked on his carefully orchestrated, but unpopular, 'long progress' to Scotland.[14] With him, James took many of the best English preachers and many of the upper clergy, including Andrewes, Laud and Hall.[15] The Lords of the Privy Council left in England were present at Donne's sermon, including the new Lord Keeper, Francis Bacon.[16] Their presence may have been encouraged by Bacon, as part of his campaign to have the Council attend sermons in the city, a practice that had fallen into some abeyance in James' reign because of the king's wish that the council attend court sermons with him.[17] It is not impossible that Donne's choice of a text that spoke more of the worthiness of counsellors than the providence of the succession was partly dictated by the presence of the Privy Council at the sermon.

When preaching this sermon, then, Donne had to preach on the blessings of James' succession without turning the sermon into a political panegyric or drawing attention to the king's absence. That the sermon was a success (Chamberlain reports that it was 'exceedingly well liked generally')[18] is testimony to Donne's skill as an astute and discrete political preacher. It also demonstrates Donne's emphasis on decorum in political preaching: preaching to a popular audience, his emphasis is on the subject's duty rather than the merits or obligations of the king.

Donne chose a text from the Book of Proverbs (Proverbs 22:11, 'He that loveth pureness of heart, for the grace of his lips, the king shall be his friend'), an abstract, rather gnomic sentence that does not lend itself to the exemplary treatment by which preachers on political subjects usually connect their text with the occasion of their sermon.[19] The text of the sermon is *divided* into two sections, the first describing the 'picture' of the good subject in terms of his honesty ('pureness of heart') and his ability to do public service ('grace of his

---

[14] John Chamberlain remarked that he 'never knew a journy so generally misliked both here and there': Chamberlain, *Letters* II, 63.

[15] Peter E. McCullough, *Sermons at Court: Politics and Religion in Elizabethan and Jacobean Preaching* (Cambridge: Cambridge University Press, 1998), pp. 115, 128.

[16] Chamberlain, *Letters* II, 67.

[17] McCullough, *Sermons at Court*, p. 131.

[18] John Chamberlain, *Letters* II, 63.

[19] Richard Crakanthorp's 1609 sermon draws extensive analogies between Solomon and James: *A sermon at the solemnizing of the happie inauguration of our most gracious and religious soveraigne King James* (1609), sig. B4r–v; Laud's 1631 sermon (on Psalm 72: 1) dealt with the figures of David and Solomon implied in the text at least as fully as he did the virtues of judgement and righteousness mentioned: 'Sermon VII', in *Works* I, 185; John Rawlinson begins his sermon by disavowing any comparison between Saul, mentioned in the text, and James: *Vivat Rex* (1619), p. 2.

lips'). The matching 'picture' of the good king shows that the good king is 'friendly and gracious' to the good subject. These two sections are then used (in a conventional way) as the two 'parts' of the sermon:

> Here in our Text, we finde the subjects picture first; And his Marks are two; first, *Pureness of Heart*, That he be an *honest* Man; And then *Grace of lips*, that he be good for something; for, by this phrase, *Grace of lips*, is expressed every ability, to do any office of society for the Publike good. The first of these, *Pureness of heart*, he must *love*; The other, that is, *Grace of lips* (that is, other Abilities) he must *have*, but he must not be in love with them, nor over-value them. In the Kings picture, the principal marke is, That he shall be friendly and gracious; but gracious to him that hath this *Grace of lips*, to him that hath endeavored, in some way, to be of use to the Publike; And, not to him neither, for all the grace of his lips, for all his good parts, except he also *love pureness of heart*; but, *He that loveth pureness of heart* (There's the foundation) *for the grace of his lips* (There's the upper-building) *the King shall be his friend* (p. 184).

The first of the two parts of the sermon is given by far the fullest discussion and is subdivided according to the words of the text ('puritas', 'amor', 'gratia labiorum'), but the emphasis is on general, abstract discussion of the first subdivision, the moral quality of purity. Purity is described in terms of what it is, where it is found and how it is got and kept. 'Amor' simply describes the affection with which we should embrace purity, and at least part of the discussion of 'gratia labiorum' is devoted to a contrasting of the love of pureness that is enjoined on us from the mere possession of useful abilities.

The *division* of the sermon points to part two as the section in which the king's duty will be described, but Donne does not present the 'picture' of a good king in the detail with which he discussed the picture of the good subject. Having described the good king as one who gives his friendship to good men, Donne does not pursue the king's duties any further. This can be contrasted with other accession day sermons, where these duties are elaborated on more fully with much slighter cues for the biblical text. Rawlinson's *Vivat Rex* contrasts the subject's duty to the king implicit in the exhortation 'vivat rex' with the king's duty to love his subjects, a love manifested in his keeping them 'in *tranquillity*, in *sufficiency*, in *security*', all of which obligations are described in detail. William Laud's 1631 sermon explicates the words 'judgment' and 'righteousness' in his text in relation to the virtues needed by the king. Similarly, Richard Gardiner's accession day sermon of 1642 discusses the 'mutuall duty' between kings and subjects.[20] Donne confines himself rigidly to the words of his scriptural text in this discussion ('the king shall be his friend'), effectively using the text to inhibit further discussion rather than using it as a starting point for elaborating on this theme.

---

[20] John Rawlinson, *Vivat Rex*, pp. 13–18; Laud, 'Sermon VII', in *Works* I, 190–1, 194–8, 205–8; Richard Gardiner, *A sermon appointed for Saint Pauls Crosse* (1642), pp. 16–17.

Donne begins this 'second general part' by describing how the text awards particular honour to the pure and publicly useful man. The king's friendship promised in the text is a 'superlative friendship . . . He that is thus qualified, all the world shall love him' (p. 210). If any reference is intended in this for the particular members of the Privy Council who attended the sermon, it is not elaborated on by Donne. When he does draw such a conclusion from his discussion, it is in the form of a general exclamation that precludes any doubts that the Privy Councillors possess these attributes:

> And who would not imploy the thoughts of a pure heart, and the praises of graceful lips, in thanksgiving to Almighty God, who hath bless'd us with such times, as that such Subjects have found such a King! (p. 213)

When Donne goes on to compare bad counsellors who have 'insinuated themselves into the friendship of the King, without these two endowments' (p. 215) with those good ones to whom the king's love is promised, he does not *apply* this point to James or his counsellors, even to their advantage. In effect, then, Donne keeps the discussion of this topic at an abstract level so that his text acts as a barrier to the consideration of topics inappropriate for private citizens, such as the king's duties or the reality of his choice of counsellors.

Donne is equally skilful in his use of preaching methods when he comes to deal with the occasion commemorated on that day. He marks the transition from the *explication* of his text to its *application* in the accession day celebrations by very emphatically drawing a line under his discussion of his text and doctrines:

> This is the capacity required (to be religious and useful;) this is the preferment assured, *The King shall be his friend*; and this is the compass of our Text.
>
> Now, Beloved, as we are able to interpret some places of the *Revelation*, better then the *Fathers* could do, because we have seen the fulfilling of some of the *Prophecies* of that Book, which they did but conjecture upon; so we can interpret and apply this Text by way of accommodation the more usefully, because we have seen these things performed by those Princes whom God hath set over us (p. 216).

This emphatic division between the text's doctrines and its *application* to the circumstances of the accession, is, I suggest, in order to make clear that what will now be said of James and Elizabeth is merely illustrative of what the text describes. Any teaching the text has to offer on the king's duty to love good men is definitely not *applied* to an auditory made up of subjects, for whom such advice would be inappropriate: the lesson that they are to take from Donne's sermon is that England has been blessed with good and religious monarchs who can therefore be trusted to befriend good advisors. Much of the next section of the sermon is independent of the scriptural text, and it does not use or rephrase the words of the scriptural text in Donne's characteristic way, a technique that would foreground the text throughout. Instead, he dispatches the conventional themes of the day rather briefly. He recalls his contemporaries' anxiety at Elizabeth's death and their joy at the peaceful succession of James. The citizens were 'like Ants with their eggs bigger then themselves, every man with his bags, to seek where to hide them safely', when the Queen died (p. 217). He reminds his London hearers of their gathering at Paul's Cross when James' accession was proclaimed, and exhorts them to give thanks to God for this blessing (p. 219). In keeping with the tradition of accession day sermons, Donne recounts the events of the reign (most notably the Gunpowder Plot) and the king's achievements. He has brought peace to Europe (p. 218) and supported religion, particularly by his writings (p. 220).

Lastly, Donne deals with the tricky issue of James' absence from England. The peaceable state of the kingdom argues for James' good government, a compliment to the Lords of the Council present that Donne might have referred back to his text explicitly (clearly James is fulfilling the duty to love the pure and serviceable) but does not (p. 221). Donne reassures his hearers that James' absence is not a cause of anxiety by emphasising the union of the crowns and the security of the succession, two advantages brought by James' accession:

> He is not gone from us; for a *Noble* part of this Body, (our Nation) is gone with him, and a *Royal* part of his Body stays with us. Neither is the farthest place that he goes to, any other then *ours*, now, when, as the *Roman* Orator said; *Nunc demum juvat orbem terrarum spectare depictum, cum in illo nihil videmus alienum;* Now it is a comfort to look upon a Map of the World, when we can see nothing in it that is not our own; so we may say, Now it is a pleasant sight to look upon a *Map of this Island*, when it is all *one* (p. 221).

The comparison with the end of Elizabeth's reign, so graphically evoked earlier, is not made explicit. Donne quells anxiety over James' absence by mentioning the security of the succession this time, but he does so without drawing unflattering comparisons with James' predecessor.

It is only in the conclusion that Donne returns to the words of his text, and their previous neglect is made up for by continuous repetition in this final paragraph. Their reference has changed, however, from promising the friendship of the king to that of the 'King of kings'. In this conclusion, Donne connects the duties of the subject directly to his biblical text, giving it all the sanction of scriptural authority. This use of the scriptural text, and its absence from the previous section, is significant. The ability to draw direct links between the text and the *exhortation* was the strongest argument that the preacher could put forward. The text is the preacher's anchor: it authorises and verifies his argument. By ending the sermon with a reference to the promise of the 'King of kings' to his loyal subjects, Donne places the political duties that he described in the context of Christian salvation. By leaving his application of the sermon to the accession day apart from his discussion of the text and its teachings, even to the exclusion of the words of the text from that section of the sermon, Donne brackets off his discussion of England's monarchs from any reference to kings and their duties. In short, Donne uses his *explication* of the text to delimit its political reference to the subject's responsibilities only. This sermon, therefore, exemplifies one general characteristic of Donne's political preaching *ad populum*: if the preacher is to keep decorum, addressing his hearers with lessons that pertain to them, then he should not describe to them the duties of their rulers. Discretion in preaching before such auditories also dictates that the failings of others (be they counsellors or monarchs, living or dead) were not to be dwelt on.[21]

The duty to preach the Gospel while quelling political tensions was even more problematic at Donne's next appearance at Paul's Cross. This, the most studied of Donne's sermons and the one around which much of the debate over 'Donne the absolutist' has gathered,[22] was preached to defend James' promulgation of the 1622 *Directions to Preachers* on 4 August. In the immediate context of their promulgation, the *Directions* appeared to many to be an attempt to muzzle the pulpits from discussing James' unpopular decision to negotiate a 'Spanish match' for Prince Charles. Even more alarming to many in England, these negotiations went on at a time when James appeared to be doing little to recover the patrimony of his daughter's children in the Palatinate.[23] Appearing only two days after the formal suspension of the laws against recusants, the *Directions to Preachers* were seen by those already alarmed by James' foreign policy as the first sign of a plot by the Spanish to manipulate James into fatally weakening the Reformation in England.[24] That public uncertainty over James' willingness to support

---

[21] On the importance of discretion to Donne in his sermons, see Jeanne Shami, 'Donne on Discretion', *ELH* 47:1 (1980): 48–66.

[22] Millar MacLure described this sermon as 'a poor performance' marred by 'embarrassment, preciosity, awkwardness', and he considered Donne's subsequent account of the sermon in a sermon at Paul's, 1 May 1626 (*Sermons* VII), as tying 'the pulpit to diplomacy in a gross and Erastian way' that was 'surely disingenuous': *The Paul's Cross Sermons*, p. 105. R. C. Bald writes that Donne was 'at least in part, in sympathy with the King's directions', which he interprets as effectively stifling opposition to the king's policies: Bald, pp. 433–5. More stridently, John Carey writes that 'Donne, the absolutist, was stirred by the image of numinous majesty, scattering opposition as the sun disperses clouds': *John Donne: Life, Mind and Art* (London: Faber and Faber, 1981, new edn 1990), p. 102. A much fairer account of Donne's attempt to balance the different tasks facing him in this sermon is Jeanne Shami, ' "The Stars in their Order Fought Against Sisera": John Donne and the Pulpit Crisis of 1622', *JDJ* 14 (1995): 1–58. A fuller account of the structure of this sermon than that given here is in my 'Rhetoric, religion and politics in the St Paul's Cross sermons, 1603–1625' (unpublished Ph.D. thesis, University of Cambridge, 1998), chapter 1.

[23] Thomas Cogswell, *The Blessed Revolution* (Cambridge: Cambridge University Press, 1989), pp. 32–4. On popular feeling for the recovery of the Palatinate, see pp. 20–31.

[24] On the suspension of the recusancy laws, see John Rushworth, *Historical Collections of Private Passages of State* (1659), pp. 63–6. Thomas Scott, the author of *Vox populi, or newes from*

Protestants abroad was one of the major concerns to be addressed by Donne in his sermon is evident from the letter he sent to Thomas Roe, ambassador in Constantinople, with a copy of the sermon:

> many men, measuring public actions with private affections, have been scandalised and have admitted suspicions of a tepidness in very high place. Some Civil Acts, in favour of the Papists, have been with some precipitation, over-dangerously misapplied too. It is true there is a major proposition, but the conclusion is too soon made, if there be not a minor too. I know to be sorry for some things that are done (it is sorry that our times are overtaken with necessity to do them) proceeds of true zeal, but to conclude the worst upon the first degree of ill is a distilling with too hot a fire. One of these occurences gave the occasion to this sermon, which by commandment I preached, and which I send your Lordship.[25]

John Chamberlain, however, wrote that the sermon was not a success. Donne, he said, had chosen 'somwhat a straunge text for such a business',[26] Judges 5:20 ('They fought from Heaven; the stars in their courses fought against Sisera'), a text that does not appear to have been used as a 'proof text' on preaching.[27] Chamberlain also remarked, 'how he made yt hold together I know not', which must refer to the extremely complicated structure of this closely-argued sermon.

Examination of this lengthy sermon reveals much about Donne's aims in preaching it: his *division* of his text and his use of it to structure his sermon strongly suggest that he was trying to quell anxiety over the king's pro-Spanish policy while defending the *Directions to Preachers* by careful balancing the scriptural imperative that the Gospel should be preached 'in season, out of season' (2 Timothy 4:2) with the equally scriptural precept that 'all things be done decently and in order' (1 Corinthians 14:40). Donne's *division* states that he will *explicate* it by analogy. He promises to provide the 'historical sense' of the text in his *explication* and then *apply* it to the occasion:

> So the first part of our Text, will bee as that first *Hemisphere*; all which the ancient Expositors found occasion to note out of these words, will be in that: but by the new discoveries of some humors of men, and rumors of men, we shall have occasion to say somewhat of a second part to. The parts are, first, the Literall, the Historicall sense of the words; And then an emergent, a collaterall, an occasionall sense of them. The *explication* of the wordes, and the *Application*,

---

Spayne (1620) presents the silencing of preachers by Star Chamber as part of the plot by Gondomar to overthrow England: repr. in *Somers Collection of Tracts* (1809) II, 508–24, 520–1.

[25] Gosse II, 174.

[26] Chamberlain, *Letters* II, p. 451.

[27] Neither preaching nor order in the Church are referred to in the glosses on this passage in the Geneva Bible or the Julius / Tremellius Latin Bible. Donne's is the only printed sermon preached at Paul's Cross on this text.

Quid tunc, Quid nunc, how the words were spoken then, How they might be applied now, will be our two parts (p. 181).

This is not the way Donne structures his sermon, however. Although the first part certainly provides the historical sense, it also includes an 'occasional' sense in discussing those who helped in the fight against Sisera. Here, Donne protests that he does not wish to 'give fire to them that desire war', and insists that, however willing his hearers are to support their co-religionists, God will fight his own battles (pp. 182–3). This is a clear reference to the Bohemian crisis. Though not mentioning the political situation and yet pointedly *applying* this point (which is embedded in what he initially described as purely explicatory material), Donne preaches a quietist course of action to those concerned about the Spanish Match. By presenting the explicatory material as arising naturally from the text, in need of little exposition to apply it to his hearers, Donne presents it as a duty directly and incontrovertibly assigned to the Christian hearers by Scripture. It stands, unlike the section that follows, as a direct, scriptural precept. By presenting this advice in the context of a religious war, however, and clearly basing his comparison on religious wars, Donne slyly suggests what James I would not then admit: that, however much peace may be wished for, the politics of Europe had become polarised on confessional lines with the outbreak of the Thirty Years War. The cause for which some may desire to fight, and the war which they are ready to support financially, is, for Donne, God's cause and a holy war. Donne's sympathy with the plight of Elizabeth and Frederick and the Protestant cause in Europe is the assumption upon which he bases his exposition.[28]

Having ended the first half of his sermon, Donne should, according to his original *division,* provide a 'collateral, an occasionall' sense of the text. The occasion about which Donne was supposed to be speaking was, of course, the promulgation of James' *Directions to Preachers,* but Donne does not simply *apply* that occasion to the text in the straightforward way that his initial division suggested. Firstly, he redivides his text, a technique I have not come across elsewhere; this provides a new *explication* and *application* of the text that is totally separate from his rather covert discussion of the Bohemian crisis. He rather disingenuously introduces this second division as an innocuous introduction to his second part, as promised in the first division. The structure of the sermon, therefore, completely dissociates the two controversies. This is important, because Donne effectively argues that the

---

[28] Koos Daley has argued that Donne's paraphrase of the Lamentations of Jeremiah can be dated to 1622, and both this work and Donne's 1622 Gunpowder Plot sermon reflect Donne's anti-Spanish politics: '"And Like a Widdow Thus": Donne, Huygens, and the Fall of Heidelberg', *JDJ* 10:1&2 (1991): 57–69. On Donne's role in the 1619 diplomatic mission of Viscount Doncaster, designed to mediate in the Bohemian crisis, see Paul R. Sellin, *So Doth, So Is Religion. John Donne and Diplomatic Contexts in the Reformed Netherlands, 1619–1620* (Columbia: University of Missouri Press, 1988).

Directions have nothing to do with the extraordinary politics of the Spanish Match without needing to state this explicitly. This can be taken as a rather typically Donnean manoeuvre: he uses the structuring principles of sermon composition (the *division, explication* and *application* of the text) as part of his argument.

In the second *division* and the second section of the sermon, Donne provides a metaphoric reading for his text by which God's battle against evil is fought by his preachers (the 'stars') keeping 'their orders and courses' (as the Vulgate reading of his text, which he provides, translates Judges 5:20):

> In which, we owe you by promise made at first, an *Analysis*, a distribution of the steps and branches of this part, now when wee are come to the handling thereof: And this wee shall proceede; first, the *Warre*, which wee are to speake of here, is not as before, a *Worldly warre*, it is a *Spirituall War.* And then the *Munitions*, the provision for this warre, is not as before, temporall assistance of *Princes, Officers, Iudges, Merchants*, all sorts of *People*, but it is the *Gospell of Christ Iesus, and the preaching thereof.* Preaching is *Gods* ordinance, with that *Ordinance* he fights from heaven, and batters downe all errors. And thirdly, to maintain this War, he hath made *Preachers Stars*; and *vae si non, woe be unto them, if they doe not fight, if they doe not preach*; But yet in the last place, they must fight, as the Stars in the heaven doe, *In their order*, in that Order, and according to those directions, which, they, to whom it appertaines, shall give them: for that is *to fight in Order.* And these foure branches, wee shall determine this second part.
> (p. 192)

As he works his way through the branches of this division, Donne argues for James' *Directions* with great care. He does not defend them by showing their harmony with the teachings of Scripture as found in his text, which would be the strongest proof available to a preacher. Instead, he uses his text to argue that Scripture demands that preaching be orderly and applies *that* doctrine to the various problems caused by disorderly preaching. Donne's defence of the particulars of the 1622 *Directions* is based on the much weaker proofs from secular deliberative rhetoric: Donne argues for their laudability (as they are lawful, and moreover, signs of the king's care for the Church) and utility (as they will promote the orderliness the Church needs). His argument, then, is not that the *Directions* themselves are warranted by Scripture, but that they are in accordance with the good order commanded by Scripture. Order, rather than the particular orders promulgated by James, is defended by Donne with all the force of scriptural authority.

The structure of this sermon, therefore, shows how careful Donne was to delimit the political messages that he could, or should, deliver from the pulpit. By following the division of material practised by preachers at Paul's Cross, Donne effectively divides the matter which is directly commanded by Scripture from matters of government or 'order' in the Church. Therefore, Donne cannot be said to have sacrificed his conscience to political expediency. Far from showing autocratic leanings, this sermon is consistent with Donne's sense of rhetorical decorum: he did not pronounce on foreign or domestic politics, nor did he sacrifice his sense of the preacher's duty to James' policy. Instead, he defended the *Directions* while reiterating the 'necessity' to preach the gospel and 'be instant, in season, out of season'.

Donne faced an equally problematic task in preaching the last of his Jacobean Paul's Cross sermons, the Gunpowder Plot of the same year. The close association between these two sermons has been noted by scholars. Also noted has been the ways in which the details of the 1622 *Directions* impinged on what Donne might say in this sermon.[29] What has been studied less is how Donne accommodated the restrictions placed by the *Directions* with the typical form of the Paul's Cross Gunpowder Plot sermon and what such a comparison might add to our understanding of Donne as a political preacher. As Millar MacLure notes, the staple themes of these sermons were firmly established in William Barlow's sermon preached the Sunday after the plot itself.[30] His sermon, on Psalm 18: 50–1 ('Great deliverances giveth he unto his king, and sheweth mercy to his anointed David and his seed for ever') concentrates on the subject of deliverances, and compares the 'deliverances' of David with those of James (to the disadvantage of the former).[31] The comparison of England and Israel, and of their kings, and the use of a text from the Psalms became central to preaching on this subject at the Cross. The plural 'deliverances' in Barlow's text is used as an invitation to dwell on the fact that the plot threatened England's entire political nation – the bishops and Members of Parliament as well as the royal family – and consequently would have destroyed all those on whom the government of the nation relied and (given the King's heirs were present) would rely in future. As well as denouncing the 'inhumane crueltie', indeed 'hyperdiabolicall divelishnes' (sig. C2v), of the plotters, Barlow does not fail to mention that 'this practise of murthering princes, is made an *Axiom* of *Theologie* among the *Romanists*' who 'make *Religion* the *stawking horse* for *Treasons*' (sigs. E3r–v). The threat of destruction to the whole nation, and the origins of this threat in the Catholic doctrine of the pope's deposing power, also became a staple of preaching on the plot. The *application*, or '*use*' that Barlow states his hearers should take from the plot, as interpreted by his sermon, is the duty of giving thanks to God, 'sithens GOD, hath beene good to us' (sig. Ev) and to pray

29 *John Donne's 1622 Gunpowder Plot Sermon: A Parallel-Text Edition*, ed. by Jeanne Shami (Pittsburgh: Duquesne University Press, 1996), pp. 11–12, 27–8; John N. Wall, Jr and Terry Bunce Burgin, '"This sermon . . . upon the Gun-powder day": The Book of Homilies of 1547 and Donne's Sermon in Commemoration of Guy Fawkes' Day, 1622', *South Atlantic Review* 49:2 (1984): 19–30.
30 Millar MacLure, *The Paul's Cross Sermons*, p. 89.
31 William Barlow, *The sermon preached at Paules Crosse the tenth day of November, being the next Sunday after the Discoverie of this late Horrible Treason* (1606), sig. C2v.

'for the continuance of our good King, our State, and our Religion amongst us' (sig. E4r), and this is the *use* invariably drawn by other preachers.

By the time Donne came to preach the plot sermon of 1622, however, the political situation had altered greatly, with the Bohemian crisis, the Spanish match and the *Directions to Preachers,* all of which complicated the delivery of Barlow's themes of 1605. Among the *Directions* was the instruction to avoid 'biter invectives, and undecent rayling speeches against the persons of either Papists or Puritanes', except when invited by the text, and then to simply 'free both the Doctrine and discipline of the Church of *England,* from the aspersion of either Adversarie'.[32] Although this did not preclude the com-memoration of the plot, Donne cannot have wished to appear to contravene the *Directions* in so public an arena, having preached in their defence only two months earlier. At the same time, interest in the plot and its commemoration was revived throughout England by the apparent imminence of Catholic victory in Europe and James' inactivity in the face of these threats.[33] He needed to find a way of preaching about the plot without 'railing' at Roman Catholics or stirring up greater political anxieties over the situation in Europe.

At first, it appears that Donne adopts an approach to his text very common in other plot sermons at Paul's Cross: he chose a text that lent itself to the theme of deliverance and uses his explication to create an analogy between the events described in his text and the event of the Gunpowder Plot. He *divides* the text (Lamentations 4:20, 'The breath of our nostrils, the anointed of the Lord, was taken down in their pits') by arguing that it can be read historically and prophetically with reference to the ancient Israelites and to us. This 'handling' of the text, which he makes distinct from the division, sets up the stages in the sermon's argument:

> These considerations will, I thinke, have the better impression in you, if we proceed in the handling of them thus: First, the main cause of the Lamentation was the Ruine, or the dangerous declination of the Kingdome, of that great and glorious State, *The Kingdome*; But then they did not seditiously sever the King, and the Kingdome, as though the Kingdome could doe well, and the King ill, *That* safe, and *he* in danger, for they see cause to lament, because misery was fallen upon *the Person of the King*; . . . but this lamenting because he *was fallen,* implies a deliverance, a restitution, he was *fallen,* but he did *not ly* there: so the Text, which is as yet but of *Lamentation,* will grow an houre hence to be of *Congratulation.* (pp. 239–40)

This is a rather unusual manoeuvre: preachers tended to *divide* their text in a way that provides the stages of the argument in the subsequent body of the sermon. This was one of the reasons for giving the *division* a prominent place

---

[32] The *Directions* are reprinted in *Documentary Annals of the Reformed Church of England,* ed. Edward Cardwell (1839) II, 146–51.
[33] David Cressy, *Bonfires and Bells,* p. 150.

at the start of the sermon: it could act as an *aide memoire* for the rest. Here, it is the 'handling' of the text that sets out the stages of Donne's argument, as can be seen from the marginal notes of the manuscript version[34] and the printed version. These reveal the following structure:

1. Kingdom	Kingdom in the King	A good king
		A bad king
Breath of our nostrils	Breath is speech	Not a curse
		A blessing
	Life	
	Soul [that is, religion]	
Anointed of the Lord		
Taken		
Pits		
Their		
was taken		
Helps	Let us not sin	
	Honour	
	Aid	
	Religion	

When presented in this way, we see clearly how the first and final sections of Donne's sermon (that the kingdom depends on the king and the 'helps' for preventing future harm to the king) are independent of Donne's scriptural text. Of course, it would have been simple for Donne to explain that the terms 'breath of our nostrils' and the 'anointed of the Lord' refer to the king, and proceed accordingly. Instead, he uses the context of his text in the Bible to facilitate a discussion of kings and their sovereignty. Why then was a text with these words not chosen? Precisely because the words 'king' and 'kingdom' are not found in the text, they carry no associations from the biblical context with them, allowing Donne to discuss kingship at a theoretical level. The choice of a text from the prophetic books is foregrounded in the *division* and is also significant, as it too is freer than most political proof-texts from associations with particular Old Testament kings. Indeed, Donne points out at the beginning that it is not clear which king is referred to in the text. The interpretative freedom that this text gives Donne enables him to give greatest weight to the more abstract of the Plot sermons' themes: that the Plot was a

---

[34] British Library MS Royal 17.B.XX, ed. Shami, *John Donne's 1622 Gunpowder Plot Sermon*. The words 'Rex bonus' (p. 97), 'Non Maledictio' (p. 121), 'Benedictio' (p. 123), 'Vita' (p. 133) are not noted in the margins of the printed edition.

manifestation of the continuing threat posed by the Catholic theory of the pope's deposing power. The war of political theories was one in which James could unambiguously be shown to be on the right side, as the author and defender of the Oath of Allegiance.

Donne's break with convention in his *division* also shows the impact of the 1622 *Directions to Preachers*. By taking the topic of kingship and sovereignty as his first subject, he can dwell on questions of political theory rather than the particulars of the Gunpowder Plot or the character of the plotters. The difference can be seen by comparison with Robert Tynley's 1608 Plot sermon. It takes a long text, Psalm 124:1–8, which cannot be divided phrase by phrase. Yet his choice of topics is tied to the words of the text, in all of which emphasis is placed on the cruelty of the plotters in particular and Roman Catholics in general:

> 1. the subtilite of the adversaries of the Church, in laying snares to entrap it, as fowlers doe to catch birds, out of the 7. verse. 2. Their crueltie, in seeking to teare it in peeces, yea to swallow it up quicke, as some cruell beasts doe their prey; or, as, might inundations, overflow whatsoever commeth in their way, out of the 3.4.5. and 6. verses. 3. The cause producing these effects of subtiltie and crueltie in these adversaries; namely, their wrath; out of the 3. verse. 4. The deliverance of the Church from her enemies, notwithstanding their craft and crueltie; by the omnipotent power of almighty God; out of the 1.2.6. and 7. verses. Last of all, the dutie performed for this deliverance; praise and thanksgiving to the Lord, verse 6.[35]

Where William Barlow, Robert Tynley, John Boys and Martin Fotherby name the gunpowder plotters or denounce them particularly, Donne does not.[36] His explication of his text is quite different.

---

[35] Robert Tynley, *Two learned sermons, the one of the mischievous subtiltie, and barbarous crueltie. . . . of the Romish Synagogue. Preached, the one at Paules Crosse the 5 of November, 1608* (1609), p. 3.

[36] Barlow read out the confessions of the plotters and '*such Papers . . . as concerned the confession which was then known*' in his sermon: *The sermon preached at Paules Crosse the tenth day of November*, sigs. Dv, Er; Martin Fotherby uses his Gunpowder Plot sermon as a warning against complacency in the new peace with Spain. If foreign enemies are lacking, there are enough 'secret Papists' and 'open recusants' whose outward rejoicing in commemorating the plot is 'nothing else but *Ementita frontis serenitas, The false glimpse of a lying countenance*', which must count as 'railing at the persons' of Catholics. He does not name the plotters but describes them as 'pestiferous confederates': *The Third Sermon, at Pauls Cross*, in *Foure sermons lately preached* (1608), pp. 77, 79. Robert Tynley uses Garnet's false names as evidence of Jesuit duplicity, cites and answers Robert Parsons' *The Judgment of a Catholike English-man* (1608) and refers to '*Catesby* that Arch-Traitor': *Two learned sermons*, pp. 6, 7, 12. John Boys, in a sermon that is at least as concerned with defending feast days in the Church of England, mocks the canonisation of Henry Garnet and refers to '*Catesbie, Winter, Rookwood*, and the rest of the Cole-saints and hole-saints' as 'these bellowing Buls of Basan, and Canon-mouthed hell-hounds': *An exposition of the last psalme: in a sermon at Pauls crosse, the fifth of November 1613* (1613), pp. 7–8.

That Jeremiah mourned the loss of the king and made it the cause of the kingdom's downfall is the starting point for a long discussion of the supremacy of monarchy among all forms of government. This discussion is brought to bear on the English: monarch implies sovereignty, and submission to the pope's claim to dispensing power over kings would be to sacrifice the sovereignty given by God. When Donne ties together these points in order to relate them to the plot, his emphasis is on the Catholic teaching that justified the event, rather than the wickedness of the individual plotters:

> Our errand is to day, to apply all these branches to the day; Those men who intended us, this cause of lamentation this day, in the destruction of *our Josiah*, spared him not, because he was so, because he was a *Josiah*, because he was *good*; no, not because he was *good to them*, his benefits to them, had not mollified them, towards him: for that is not their way; . . . . Thus it is Historically in their proceedings past: And Prophetically it can be but thus, since no King is good, in their sense, if he agree not to *all points of Doctrine* with them: And when that is done, not good yet, except he agree in *all points of Jurisdiction too*; and that, no King can doe, that will not be their Farmer of his Kingdome (p. 248).

Later, in the brief section that focuses on the Gunpowder Plot more particularly (pp. 256–7), Donne concentrates on the subsequent justifications of the plot rather than the plotters themselves. Contrary to the libels published abroad, Catholics were not persecuted for their religion, and the plot was not merely the act of a few 'unfortunate gentleman' but an enterprise supported by the church, which subsequently canonised 'the principall person'. Donne is almost at pains not to name names here. Those who spread libels justifying the plot are, he says, subjects of James, and it seems most likely that this is a reference to Robert Parsons' *The Judgment of a Catholike English-man*, published anonymously in 1608 (although the authorship was widely known) in answer to James' *Apology for the Oath of Allegiance*. Parsons insists on the persecution of Catholics for religion, and not political rebellion, and refers to the plotters as 'unfortunate gentlemen'.[37] The 'principall person' involved in the plot who was made a Catholic martyr is Henry Garnet. Only once in Donne's sermon is the name of a Catholic apologist given, and that is only in the margin of the printed edition. The man mentioned is not Parsons, but the obscure figure Leonardus Coquaeus, who joined in the debate on the oath of allegiance. Donne is scrupulous in his

---

[37] [Robert Parsons], *The Judgement of a catholike English-man, living in banishment for his religion . . . concerning a late booke set forth and entituled Triplici nodo, triplex cuneus, or An Apologie for the oath of allegiance* (1608). The plotters are referred to as 'unfortunate Gentlemen' on p. 6; Catholics are said to be persecuted for their religion by James on pp. 26, 42–6, 125. Robert Tynley's 1608 sermon mentions this work as being by 'the very fierie match of this state and kingdome' and also denounces the description of the plotters as 'unfortunate': *Two learned sermons*, p. 7.

citation: he gives folio numbers for the statements by Coquaeus that he denounces, and the quotations are accurate and fair.[38]

The theme of political quietism in this sermon provides another link between this sermon and the earlier sermon on the *Directions*. When Donne discusses the implications for his interpretation of the text's relating to bad king Zedekiah, he argues that a king may sometimes have political reasons for departing from 'the exact rule of his duty' (p. 249), but it is not for the subject to judge their actions. When he comes to elaborate on the phrase 'breath of our nostrils', the quietism he advocates in response to the political tensions of 1622 are again visible. Breath is speech, and therefore the people's speech should be loyal to the king. Even their thoughts and their prayers for him should not be suspicious (pp. 252–3). Donne here inserts an elaborate defence of James' sincerity in religion, the personal tone and direct address of which makes it strikingly more vehement than the rather abstract and theoretical discussion in which it is inserted:

> For, beloved in the bowels of Christ Jesus, before whose face I stand now, and before whose face, I shall not be able to stand amongst the righteous, at the last day, if I lie now, and make this Pulpit my Shop, to vent sophisticate Wares, In the presence of you, a holy part, I hope, of the Militant Church, of which I am, ...I...doe deliver that, which upon the truth of a Morall man, and a Christian man, and a Church man, beleeve to be true, That hee, who is *the Breath of our nostrils*, is in his heart, as farre from submitting us to that Idolatry, and superstition, which did heretofore oppresse us, as his immediate Predecessor, whose memory is justly precious to you, was (p. 254).

The phrase 'the breath of our nostrils' is explored further: breath is life, and so the life of the people should be ready at the king's service. Lastly, breath is soul, and the souls of the people are the kings insofar (and only insofar) as he has responsibility for the outward face of religion. Subjects should submit to his directions for the outward worship of God. James' Roman Catholic subjects have been guilty of breaking all of these precepts: in their libels against him and in their denial of allegiance to him.

In dealing with the plot, therefore, Donne concentrates on comparing the Bible's monarchical theories with the doctrines of the Roman Catholics. The erroneous teachings they hold are presented as the source of the actions of the plotters. This means that he does not need to dwell on the individuals concerned, and their 'hyperdiabolicall wickedness', which might have left him uncomfortably close to contradicting the August *Directions to Preachers*. It

[38] F. Leonardus Coquaeus Aurelius, *Examen Praefationis monitoriae, Jacobi I magnae Britannia et Hibernaie regis praemissae apologiae suae pro iuramento fidelitatis* (Freiburg im Breisgau, 1610), pp. 18, 43, 78, 65. Donne mistakenly describes these as folio rather than page numbers. It may also be worth noting that Coquaeus' name is deleted in BL MS Royal 17 B.XX, the copy presented to James I by Donne with the expectation that the king would authorise its publication: *John Donne's 1622 Gunpowder Plot Sermon*, ed. by Shami, pp. 155, 12.

also allows him to emphasise the continued threat of events like the Plot, and therefore turn his sermon into something of an admonition to his hearers. He ends his discussion of the text with a 'prophetic note'. He has 'reserved at first, . . . for the knot to tie up all' the 'consideration' that 'he that was truely affected in the sad sense of such a danger, and the pious sense of such a deliverance, would use all means in his power, to secure the future, . . . from the like dangers' (p. 260). The king uses peaceful means in Europe to this end. The subject, for his part, should 'put off your sinnes', as well as supporting the king in practical matters. 'No Prince', Donne affirms, 'can have a better guard, then Subjects truly religious' (p. 261), a moral more usually associated with prophetic preaching (the 'Jeremiads').[39] Donne includes a loyal trust in the religious zeal of the king as one of the ways that the subject can avert national disaster, a *use* definitely pertinent to the tense political situation of 1622. Significantly, Donne concludes with this point, by recapitulating his text in the form of an admonition rather than a prayer:

> Cities are built of families, and so are Churches too; Ever man keeps his owne family, and then every Pastor shall keep his flock, and so the Church shall be free from schisme, and the State from sedition, and our *Josiah* preserved, Prophetically for ever, as he was Historically this day, from them, in whose pits, the breath of our nostrils, the anointed of the Lord, was taken. *Amen* (p. 263).

The sermon's rather abrupt conclusion without a prayer might be used by Donne to give a heightened, dramatic tone to the final, admonitory recapitulation of the text. It might also suggest Donne's reluctance to allow his interpretation of the text to draw him any further into any discussion of the reasons for James' policy. Again we see Donne's discretion in preaching politics before a popular auditory: in the face of popular disapproval of James' pro-Spanish policy, a disapproval that was associated with commemoration of the Gunpowder Plot, Donne does not engage in controversies but preaches a lesson pertinent to the hearers (here, the lesson of prophetic sermons): peace is a blessing that comes with godliness.

All three sermons discussed here demonstrate Donne's discretion in preaching about the subject's duties while avoiding any prescriptions to the king in a sermon *ad populum*. The political messages we can expect to find Donne delivering at Paul's Cross will be circumscribed by this assumption. These sermons also demonstrate Donne's particular skill in using all of the resources of the preacher, from the choice of text, the method of *division*, the *explication* and the choice of points for *application*, in the development

---

[39] The same *application* of his text was made by William Goodwyn in the 1614 Plot sermon, on Ezekiel 24:2. The reason for choosing a text dealing with Israel's exile in Babylon is to warn his hearers against bringing the same fate on England: 'A sermon preached at Pauls Cross the 5 of November 1614', Dr Williams' Library, MS 12: 10, f. 12v.

of the argument. In particular, his use of techniques that silently pass over or separate matters of controversy shows the subtlety of his method as a political preacher. We should hardly wonder that the writer of some of the most complex English poems is no less a virtuoso in the pulpit.

Chapter 9

DONNE AS PREACHER AT COURT: PRECARIOUS 'INTHRONIZATION'

PETER E. McCULLOUGH

T HE institutional focus of this volume offers a welcome opportunity to scrutinise the details of when, where, and why Donne preached at the courts of James I and Charles I. Donne might have agreed that being a preacher was a 'profession', but not that being a preacher at court was. No preacher in the period was so exclusively attached to the court to deserve the misleading epithet 'court preacher'. But it is true that for Donne, the court was a preaching venue where, more than any other, he felt 'what an inthronization is the comming up into a Pulpit'.[1] Scrutiny of Donne's court preaching raises questions about the canon of Donne's sermons that we perhaps have wrongly assumed were already answered in George Potter's and Evelyn Simpson's edition. Furthermore, attention to matters of text, place, auditory, and dating of Donne's court sermons demonstrates two more general points: that 'the court' itself is a social space much more complex than usually allowed in literary study, and that Donne's sermons (like all others) are fundamentally, although never simplistically, occasional pieces of writing. Putting these two points together, I want to join in the increasing insistence of many Donne scholars that we absolutely must not wade into Donne's sermons looking for evidence of his theological or other views without much more carefully considering the place, time, and occasion of the individual sermons.[2] After reviewing the surviving evidence of Donne's

---

[1] *Sermons* VII, 134.

[2] See Lori Anne Ferrell, 'Donne and His Master's Voice, 1615–1625', *JDJ* 11:1–2 (1992): 59–70; Ferrell and Peter McCullough, 'Introduction: Revising the Study of the English Sermon', in *The English Sermon Revised: Religion, Literature and History 1600–1750*, ed. by Ferrell and McCullough (Manchester: Manchester University Press, 2000), pp. 2–21; Peter E. McCullough, *Sermons at Court: Politics and Religion in Elizabethan and Jacobean Preaching* (Cambridge: Cambridge University Press, 1998), pp. 178–82; Mary Morrissey, 'Interdisciplinarity and the Study of Early Modern Sermons', *HJ* 42:4 (1999): 11–24; Jeanne Shami, 'Donne's Sermons and the Absolutist Politics of Quotation', in *John Donne's Religious*

appearances as a preacher at court – from his ordination in January 1615, to his last sermon, before Charles I in February 1631 – I use Donne's attendance as preacher at Charles's court as a smaller case study of the way more rigorous bibliographical and historical scholarship can inform our interpretations of Donne's political and literary craftsmanship in the pulpit. This in turn yields valuable new evidence about Donne's always vexed relationship with courts, and about the emergence of Laudianism before the Personal Rule.

First, the question of when Donne made his *debut* as a court preacher after his ordination on 15 January 1615 itself demands some reconsideration. Potter's and Simpson's interpretation of the surviving texts leaves a gap of sixteen months between ordination and first known sermon at court (29 April 1616). This is a highly unlikely hiatus, since Donne was also appointed a Chaplain-in-Ordinary to James, a post with court preaching duties, within a month of his ordination. I here revise some of my own previous scholarship, as well as Potter and Simpson, to argue that the sermon Donne preached at Greenwich on 30 April 1615 (*Sermons* I.1) is not only the earliest surviving sermon by him, but also in fact a court sermon. This sermon is titled 'A *Sermon Preached at Greenwich, Aprill 10. 1615*'. Potter and Simpson disallowed Jessopp's assignment of it to the court of Queen Anne at Greenwich on the grounds that there is no positive evidence that it was delivered at court; they posit instead the parish church at Greenwich.[3] To which, of course, one can counter that there is no evidence for the parochial attribution either. But there is precedent for titling sermons preached at the royal residence simply 'at Greenwich'; indeed there is no sermon printed in the early modern period titled 'at Greenwich' that means anything but at the court. Moreover, I think Jessopp's instincts were good in sensing a possible connexion with Anne: Donne preached before her very intimately at Denmark House in 1617, he had previously sought preferment in her household, and the bishop of London John King, Donne's former colleague at Egerton House who also ordained him, was one of Queen Anne's favourite preacher-prelates.[4] But, we need not have a link with Anne to place this first Donne sermon *at court* at Greenwich. Since James frequently removed from Whitehall to Greenwich for the weeks between Easter and Whitsunday, the sermon could have been preached at Greenwich under the auspices of James', not necessarily Anne's, household on this date. Potter and Simpson, though,

Imagination: Essays in Honor of John T. Shawcross, ed. by Raymond-Jean Frontain and Frances M. Malpezzi (Conway, Arkansas: UCA Press, 1995), pp. 380–412, and 'Introduction: Reading Donne's Sermons', *JDJ* 11:1–2 (1992): 1–20.

3 Augustus Jessopp, *John Donne, Sometime Dean of St Paul's A.D. 1621–1631* (London, 1897), p. 109; *Sermons* I, 115–17. There are no surviving manuscript witnesses of this sermon.

4 *Sermons* I, 5; Peter McCullough, 'Preaching to a Court Papist? Donne's Sermon Before Queen Anne, December 1617', *JDJ* 14 (1995): 59–82; Bald, pp. 160 (for Anne), 97, 282–3, 302 (for King); Izaak Walton, *Lives of John Donne, Sir Henry Wotton, Richard Hooker, George Herbert and Robert Sanderson*, ed. by George Saintsbury (Oxford: Worlds Classics, 1927), p. 46; McCullough, *Sermons at Court*, pp. 171, 172–3, 177n, 182.

build their case on Walton's anecdote that in spite of his connexions with the great, Donne's modesty kept him from accepting invitations to preach in 'any eminent Auditory' for some unspecified time after his ordination; they thus speculate that 10 April 1615 was too soon for the modest Donne to be preaching at court.[5] But James never allowed anything of the sort with any other preacher he fancied: he in fact made chaplains as impulsively as he did knights, and appointment as a royal chaplain was without exception based on his personal evaluation of a probationary sermon, many of which were preached on a special rota arranged at the king's hunting lodges at Newmarket and Royston.[6] Knowing how anxious James had been for Donne to take orders, I find it inconceivable that he could have waited very long at all after Donne's ordination to listen to his newly-minted pulpit prize. James' custom of rewarding a probationary sermon with a royal chaplaincy supports Bald's speculation that Donne was probably appointed Chaplain-in-Ordinary by February; I would add the further likelihood that this followed a probationary sermon before the king at Donne's known January audience at Newmarket. And it is in April, the month of the Greenwich sermon, that we have the first documented rumours of Donne's appointment as a royal chaplain: on 18 April, George Lord Carew, summarising news since January, wrote that 'Mr John Dvn is a Minister, the King's Chaplaine, and a Doctor of Divinitie'. Since, as we shall see, April was for the rest of Donne's life the month he was appointed to attend as chaplain at court, I would speculate that Carew saw, or heard a report of, Donne ministering for the first time as king's chaplain in April, and that the Greenwich sermon of 30 April is a textual survival of that month's first official service at court.[7]

But finally, to shore up this circumstantial evidence with some of a more conclusive bibliographical sort, it must be noted that the Greenwich sermon of 30 April 1615 was first printed in the 1661 folio *XXVI Sermons*.[8] This volume, which actually prints twenty-three sermons incorrectly numbered, is arranged by place of preaching: the first sixteen sermons at court, followed by seven preached in London and Heidelberg, with the whole concluded by the aptly valedictory 'Deaths Duell'.[9] The Greenwich sermon sits squarely in the court group (number eleven). As was typical of seventeenth-century printed sermon titles, in this group the name of a palace ('at Whitehall', 'at Greenwich') stands metonymically for the court seated there, with further

---

[5] *Sermons* I, 116.

[6] McCullough, *Sermons at Court*, pp. 115–16, 125–7.

[7] Bald, pp. 306–7, 305 n. 1.

[8] This paragraph is based on the Potter and Simpson texts in conjunction with the editors' indispensible collation of the folios with their own and Alford's editions (*Sermons* X, 'Appendix B'). For the vagaries of the very poorly printed *XXVI Sermons*, see *Sermons* I, 7–12.

[9] Potter and Simpson seem at first not to have noticed the logic of this arrangement, calling it 'chaotic' (*Sermons* I, 11). Simpson, however, revised her estimate of the folio's arrangement, but not the Greenwich sermon's auditory, in the final volume of the California edition (*Sermons* X, 408).

definition of the auditory used only to note the king's or queen's presence at three of the sermons (*XXVI*.4, 5, 18), and the delivery of one (*XXVI*.8) to the household below stairs. In short, the title '*A Sermon Preached at Greenwich*' is just as clearly a title for a court sermon as the eleven others in the group titled '*A Sermon Preached at White-hall*', and does not call at all for Potter's and Simpson's Waltonesque theory of a sermon humbly preached outside the palace gates in a parochial pulpit. Donne's court sermon *œuvre* needs to be augmented by one from Potter's and Simpson's count of thirty-five, to thirty-six texts.

These thirty-six fit almost without exception into a strict routine pattern of attendance at court that was unbroken over the fifteen years of Donne's ordained ministry (see Appendix): Donne preached two or three sermons each April, the month of his attendance as a royal chaplain, and took the pulpit each year on the first Friday in Lent in the great series of Whitehall sermons on every Sunday, Tuesday and Friday during Lent. This pattern was singled out for notice first by Walton, who observed that by the time of his last sickness in the winter of 1630–1, Donne had not 'for almost twenty years omitted his personal attendance on His Majesty in that month in which he was to attend and preach to him; nor [had] ever been left out of the Roll and number of Lent-Preachers' on 'his old constant day, the first *Friday in Lent*'. The same pattern has since been confirmed by the texts edited by Potter and Simpson, corroborated by Bald, and, for the Lent sermons, given further confirmation by the original court Lent lists.[10] The predictability of this annual pattern of court preaching inevitably influenced Donne's sermon-writing routines, most notably after his appointment to the St Paul's deanery in 1621. Major 'solemn' sermons were demanded of him *ex officio* at the cathedral before the Lord Mayor on Christmas Day and Candlemas (2 February), swiftly followed by the court sermon on the first Friday in Lent, then on Easter Sunday at the cathedral, then at least two more at court during April, followed by Whitsunday again at the cathedral. To this required minimum Donne of course added parochial sermons at St Dunstan's-in-the-West, and sermons preached on special occasions at the command of nobility, gentry, livery companies, and Lincoln's Inn. The particularly heavy crush of study and composition required of Donne from Christmas to Whitsunday meant that he might begin preparing each solemn sermon months in advance of delivery, as he explained about an April 1627 court sermon: 'it was put into that very order, in which I delivered it, more than two moneths since'. And in the years of failing health, Donne would complain that 'sicknesses, had brought me to an inability of Preaching' the required

---

[10] Walton, *Lives*, pp. 73–4; Bald, pp. 312–13. For the court Lent lists see Nicholas W. S. Cranfield, 'Chaplains in Ordinary at the Early Stuart Court: the Purple Road', Appendix 7, in Claire Cross (ed.), *Patronage and Recruitment in the Tudor and Early Stuart Church* (York: University of York, 1996), p. 146; and McCullough, *Sermons at Court*, pp. 68–70, 134–6, 148.

'twelve or fourteen solemn Sermons every year, to great Auditories, at *Paules*, and to the Judges, and at Court; and that therefore I must think of conferring something upon such a man as may supplie my place in these Solemnities'. But of these solemn sermons, Donne considered those appointed for court non-negotiable: in the last months of his life, having arranged a substitute for Christmas Day at the cathedral, he none the less insisted that he still keep 'my Lent Sermon, except my Lord Chamberlaine beleeve me to be dead, and leave me out; for as long as I live, and am not speechlesse, I would not decline that service'.[11] 'That service' produced, of course, Donne's legendary sermonic valediction, 'Death's Duell', preached before Charles I on the first Friday in Lent (25 February), 1631.

Taking note of the finer details of all chaplains' attendance at court can reveal still more about the surviving court sermons of Donne than has been hitherto understood. First, Chaplains-in-Ordinary, since at least the time of Elizabeth, had waited on the court in pairs, sharing the daily services said in the Chapel Royal or Privy Closet, as well as the sermons preached every Sunday and, after 1603, also every Tuesday.[12] By 1621, two pairs of chaplains shared the duties. Donne's partners for April were all rising anti-Calvinists: William Piers (1580–1670) and Francis Dee (*d.* 1638) both became staunch Laudian bishops, and Gabriel Clarke (*d.* 1662), was archdeacon of Durham and chaplain to the Arminian bishop Richard Neile.[13] Tiny glimpses (very easy to miss) of Donne's court service are apparent in his letters. Not surprisingly, Donne seems to have been as keen to hear as to preach court sermons. He anxiously finished a 1615 letter to Sir Henry Goodyer with the comment that 'I had destined all this Tuesday, for the Court, because it is both a Sermon day, and the first day of the Kings being here', noting that if he did not conclude then he would miss the preacher's opening declamation of his text: 'if I stay longer I shall lose the Text, at Court, therefore I kisse your hand, and rest'. Under less sanguine circumstances in April 1627, after determining that the King was not so angry over an offending sermon as to make his further presence in chapel an offence, Donne resolved to come to court 'for that purpose, to say prayers' – that is, to officiate at the daily offices as the appointed Chaplain-in-Ordinary.[14]

---

[11] Donne to Sir Robert Ker, April 1627; to Mrs Cokayne, ?1625–8; to Mr George Gerrard, ?December 1630; in Evelyn Simpson (ed.), *John Donne: Selected Prose* (Oxford: Clarendon Press, 1967), pp. 160, 165, 170.

[12] For chaplains' routine duties under Elizabeth and James, see McCullough, *Sermons at Court*, pp. 73–6, 115–16; Cranfield, 'Chaplains in Ordinary', offers further detail on advancement related to royal chaplaincies, and on the Caroline period. For Tuesday sermons, see McCullough, *Sermons at Court*, pp. 116–18.

[13] Corpus Christi College, Oxford, MS E 297, fol. 188r, transcribed in Cranfield, 'Chaplains in Ordinary', p. 142. For Piers and Dee, see *DNB*; for Clarke see A. G. Matthews, *Walker Revised* (Oxford: Clarendon Press, 1948), p. 140.

[14] *Letters*, pp. 217–21; Simpson (ed.), *Selected Prose*, p. 162.

But there was yet another complication in the monthly duties of a royal chaplain, and that was his service to the two parts of the court itself, the king's household 'above-stairs' (the royal family and its office holders), and the huge service staff, also called a household, 'below stairs'. Social decorum and practical considerations required that these two departments had separate Sunday services. The household below came to service and sermon early in the morning, while the courtier household heard its own service and sermon at about 11 a.m. If the load of preaching and presiding at service was divided evenly, then each of the two royal chaplains would, as the cleric organising the rota in 1612 explained to one royal chaplain, 'preach at the least Two sermons to the King, and 2. or 3. to the howshould'.[15] But by 1621, when four chaplains shared these duties, each may have preached only twice in the month, which would explain why no more than two sermons by Donne survive from April in any given year after 1618.[16]

The bureaucratic detail of a chaplain preaching up to two different sermons to two different auditories while at court makes some sense of a small range of cruxes in the Potter and Simpson edition. The system naturally lent itself to the two-part sermon, or a pair of sermons on the same text, as can be seen in several printed Elizabethan and Jacobean court sermons by Chaplains-in-Ordinary.[17] Donne, too, preached several paired sermons at court, but his California editors are thrown into unnecessary worries over how to account for them. Donne's two sermons preached on I Timothy 1:15 are a good case in point (*Sermons* I.8 & 9; Appendix nos. 7 & 8). The copy text of the 1661 folio exists in two variant states; one dates both sermons 19 April 1618, the other dates the second sermon 2 April 1621. Confronted with the admitted improbability of a two-part sermon preached over a three-year interval, but without a fuller knowledge of court preaching rotas, the California editors could imagine as the only alternative two sermons preached by the same preacher on one day to the same auditory – an arrangement for which there is no documented precedent whatsoever at the early modern English court.[18] 19 April 1618 was in fact a Sunday, and therefore likely a correct date. The logical occasion for Donne to have preached the second part would have been either the Tuesday or the Sunday immediately following, that is, 21 or 26 April – either of which dates in manuscript (but especially the first) could have

---

[15] For the household structures of the court, see David Loades, *The Tudor Court*, revised edn (Bangor: Headstart History, 1992), chapter 2; for the division of preaching, see McCullough, *Sermons at Court*, pp. 115–16, 150–1; Richard Neile to Richard Clayton regarding Valentine Carey, St John's College Cambridge MS D105.337, quoted in McCullough, *Sermons at Court*, p. 112.

[16] See Appendix, and *Sermons* X, 15, n. 35.

[17] Cf. Richard Eedes, 'The dutie of a King, preached before the Kings Maiestie in two Sermons: the former at Hampton Court the 9. of August; the later, at Wilton, neere Salisburie, the 30. of August, in his ordinarie attendance for that moneth', in *Six Learned and Godly Sermons* (1604), fols. 1r–35r.

[18] *Sermons* I, 142–3; McCullough, 'Calendar of Sermons'.

supplied the variant date of 2 April 1621 typeset for the second part in some copies.[19]

Potter and Simpson evidently were also not alert to the ways the Lent rota and the monthly chaplains' rota could intersect, rather like the complicated overlay of the church's moveable and unmoveable feasts and fasts. Donne's sermon on Ecclesiastes 5:13–14, preached on 2 April 1620, looks at first glance as if it must be part of the Sunday–Tuesday–Friday Lent series, preached as it was on the fifth Sunday in Lent (*Sermons*, III.1, Appendix no. 12). But since Elizabeth's time, Sunday preachers before the king in the Lent series were without exception bishops.[20] Rather than having Donne unusually promoted to a bishop's place in the separate Lent series, this is in fact a sermon preached in the course of his routine April duties in chapel, a point furthered by the fact that the sermon is divided in two by the sub-title '*The Second Sermon Preached at White-hall upon Eccles. 5.12&13*'. Again the California editors suggest a number of explanations for this – editor's or printer's emendation, Donne's revision after preaching – none of which attend to institutional matters of how and when the sermon was likely preached: that is, as a two-part sermon on the same text on two different days, as his preaching stint for April.[21]

It must also be stressed that the two auditories that were the potential recipients of Donne's court sermons were potentially quite different, something that should complicate our notions about what it might mean to read a sermon preached 'at Whitehall' or 'at court'. In the 250-odd sermon texts known to have been preached at the Elizabethan and Jacobean courts, not a single one advertises itself as preached for the humbler auditory below stairs. Institutional evidence proves that they existed, and that keen sermon-goers at court attended both, as shown by Richard Neile's quip to King James that by attending only the late-morning sermon for the royal entourage, the king 'had lost an excellent sermon . . . which, though prepared for household fare, yet would have served a royal palate'. As this shows, the early modern appetite for sermons meant that members of the court elite could and did attend both sermons – so a preacher could never pitch a sermon for the household very low. It seems likely that some sermons printed with generic titles like 'preached at court' were in fact preached to the household below stairs. But the Donne canon from the Caroline years gives us what I think is our only certain taste of 'household fare' by a royal chaplain in the sermon preached on Matthew 9:13 '*to the Houshold at White-hall*' on 30 April 1626.[22] The title is the only example I know of a sermon unambiguously assigned to 'the household', and the sermon is preached in a slightly different register from

---

[19] This qualifies my 'Calendar of Sermons', where I followed Potter and Simpson in placing both sermons on 19 April.

[20] McCullough, *Sermons at Court*, p. 69.

[21] *Sermons* III, 3, 391–2.

[22] *Sermons* VII.5; Appendix no. 23.

those other court sermons that we know were prepared for the ears of the king and courtiers. The exordium, or opening summary of the Scriptural text, is descriptive, narrative and hortatory, quite unlike the verbal conceits and doctrinal erudition usually offered a more elite audience. Moreover, there is a marked contrast in the preacher's attitude to his audience in his direct addresses. Two weeks before this sermon Donne had preached before Charles and his entourage, and digressed at some rhetorically elevated length on the honour not only of being a minister, but a minister to the court above stairs. In a passage meant to register humility that in actual fact elevates Donne in a peculiarly obsequious way, he applied metaphorically to himself the temporal titles of the very court grandees he addressed: 'This is that which ministerially and instrumentally he [God] hath committed to me . . . Not as his Almoner to drop his consolation upon one soule, nor as his Treasurer to issue his consolation to a whole Congregation, but as his Ophir, as his Indies, to derive his gold, his precious consolation upon the King himselfe' (*Sermons* VII, 134–5). Here we certainly have an example of what Debora Shuger has called Donne's 'theology of absolutism' – for Donne, the quintessence of his priesthood is to preach to the king in an act that simultaneously asserts both his submission to royal power and his status as privileged conduit of divine power to the king.[23] Although there is a fascinating complex of humility and arrogance in this passage, there is also, in a simpler sense, a frank acknowledgment of the king's and courtiers' worldly dignity. This contrasts sharply with the near condescension of Donne's division of his text in the sermon he preached two weeks later 'to the household' – 'In which, though the pieces may seem many, yet they do so naturally flow out of one another, that they may easily enter into your understanding; and so naturally depend upon one another, that they may easily lay upon your memory' – or his schoolmasterly reassurance later in the sermon that 'He that cannot define Repentance, he that cannot spell it, may have it' (*Sermons* VII, 144, 162).

Sensitivity to different tone and diction for different court auditories encountered in a royal chaplain's monthly waiting might begin to inform other readings of Donne's court sermons. Furthermore, it may assist in dating two last court sermons left in limbo by Potter and Simpson, the pair on Ezekiel 34:19 simply titled '*Preached at White-Hall.*' (*Sermons* X.6 and 7). The California editors suggest a date from Charles' reign based on one internal allusion to James I, to which I will return. But first, noting the pairing of two sermons on one text, Donne's routine month of waiting, April, must be the only likely time of year. And it is noticeable that April sermons survive for every year of Donne's waiting as an ordinary chaplain (1615–31) except 1622, 1623 and 1624, strongly suggesting that these are from one of those years.[24]

---

[23] Debora Shuger, *Habits of Thought in the English Renaissance: Religion, Politics and the Dominant Culture* (Berkeley and Los Angeles: University of California Press, 1990), chapter 5, especially pp. 206–9.

[24] There seems to be no biographical reason why Donne could not have served his routine April

But what of Potter's and Simpson's reasons for a date after Charles' accession, years in which, as the Appendix shows, April sermons are already so well represented? They call attention to Donne's allusion in the second of these sermons to 'the learnedst King, that any age hath produc'd, our incomparable King *James*', suggesting that this 'would probably have been worded differently if the monarch had still been on the throne' (*Sermons* X, 161, 15). It may have been worded more fulsomely and in direct address had James been in the room, but if this was a sermon preached not to the king, but to the household, or even to the court in James' absence, the allusion is perfectly appropriate.[25]

Knowing the routine of Donne's attendance at court should also help in our attempts to gauge the degree of favour Donne was or was not shown by James I and Charles I. The cold facts of the dominant routine into which Donne's court service falls show that the preacher who has in one critical tradition been viewed as the epitome of an absolutist symbiosis between James I and client authors, was but one of many chaplains and prelates who served at their appointed times without very much notice taken.[26] I do not want to suggest that Donne's unbroken years of service as a preacher at court were routine to the point of passing without any notice by his kings. Of course Donne considered James I in some sense the architect of his clerical career. Perhaps following Walton's Jacobean focus, the work of critics as varied in their approaches as Jonathan Goldberg, Annabel Patterson, and Lori Anne Ferrell, have discussed Donne and kings in almost wholly Jacobean terms.[27] But the bibliographical and biographical evidence of Donne's court sermons suggests that he gained a degree of royal favour under Charles that he did not

duty in these years: he preached elsewhere in London during the springs of 1622, 1623, and 1624. Only in 1619, when departing for Germany with Doncaster, did he rearrange his time of court service. Bald, pp. 341–2, 540–2. The likelihood of 1622–5 is further increased by Anthony Milton's observation to me that the controversy over private communion mentioned by Donne in this sermon (p. 175) was at its height at this time, particularly in Presbyterian attacks on the so-called Five Articles of Perth.

[25] Further research, like that of Jeanne Shami (in progress) into the anti-Catholic and anti-puritan controversies to which Donne alludes in these sermons, may provide much firmer dating for them.

[26] See John Carey, *John Donne: Life, Mind, and Art* (London: Faber and Faber, 1981, new edn, 1990); Jonathan Goldberg, *James I and the Politics of Literature: Jonson, Shakespeare, Donne and Their Contemporaries* (Baltimore: Johns Hopkins University Press, 1983); and Shuger, *Habits of Thought*.

[27] Goldberg, *James I and the Politics of Literature*; Annabel Patterson, 'John Donne, Kingsman?', in Linda Levy Peck (ed.), *The Mental World of the Jacobean Court* (Cambridge: Cambridge University Press, 1991), pp. 251–72; Ferrell, 'Donne and his Master's Voice'. An exception is Shuger, *Habits of Thought*, who uses a wide range of sermon evidence from the reigns of both James and Charles, but makes no distinctions between Donne's political or theological engagement with each. Donne's Jacobean preaching career will receive its definitive treatment in Shami's forthcoming book. For changes in James's sermon attendance late in his reign, see McCullough, *Sermons at Court*, pp. 139–41.

enjoy from the king who played some part in chasing him into the pulpit. Although it is most properly an index of the different service-going habits of James and Charles, not Donne's popularity with either, it is at least striking to notice how Charles was present for an overwhelming majority of Donne's Caroline court sermons, while we can be sure that James attended only a tiny minority of Donne's sermons for his court. In fact, we can only prove that James was present for two of the eighteen surviving sermons Donne preached at his court, and the royal presence was also a quite literally dead one for the last of these, '*Preached at Denmark house, some few days before the body of King James, was removed from thence, to his buriall, Apr. 26. 1625.*'[28] No reader can mistake Donne's genuine devotion and grief in that sermon before James' corpse, least of all in its haunting final petition 'to see that face againe, and to see those eyes open there, which we have seen closed here. Amen' (*Sermons*, VI, 291). But in the midst of the fraught transition from one regime to the next, Donne was given the first of several remarkable endorsements by Charles.

James had died on Sunday, 27 March, and the new King Charles determined that his first public appearance would be at the sermon on the following Sunday, 3 April, which was also the fifth Sunday in Lent. But rather than indecorously rushing into his deceased father's palace so soon after his death, Charles also chose to make that appearance at St James's, where both he and his brother, Prince Henry, had presided over their own households as successive Princes of Wales. Donne was then about to begin his traditional month's service in James' household (which would, according to custom, not be disbanded until the monarch's interment). But instead, Donne received a peremptory summons to preach not at the old court, but the new, and that for Charles' first official appearance in only two days' time. Whatever sermon Donne might have prepared in advance for James' funerary court at Denmark House would have been rendered largely useless for this new appointment, and the sermon he delivered before Charles was clearly written (or rewritten) specifically for his ears. The suddenness and the significance of this sermon for Donne prompted a well-known exchange of letters with Sir Robert Ker in which Donne begged the use of his rooms at St James's before and after the sermon, declining Ker's offer of a meal beforehand. Bald and Potter and Simpson chalk this up to a rather quaint nervous habit of Donne's not to fill his stomach before preaching and to Donne's unfamiliarity with the surroundings at St James's.[29] But for Donne there was much more at stake than preaching the first public sermon before the new king in a new place.

It is well known that immediately upon his accession, Charles I inaugurated

---

[28] *Sermons* VI.14; James' only known living attendance was on the first Friday in Lent, 1621 (*Sermons* III.9).

[29] Donne, *Letters*, pp. 313–14; Bald, pp. 467–8; *Sermons* VI, 22–3; Jeanne Shami, 'Anti-Catholicism in the Sermons of John Donne', in *The English Sermon Revised*, ed. by Ferrell and McCullough, pp. 155–8, best captures the importance of this occasion for Donne.

a reformation of court ceremonies and manners that put a renewed emphasis on decorum, and that this reformation consciously imitated Elizabethan practice. The Venetian ambassador reported within days of James' death that Charles 'observes a rule of great decorum . . . and he has declared that he desires the rules and maxims of the late Queen Elizabeth.'[30] As I have shown elsewhere, one of the Elizabethan rituals increasingly neglected by James throughout his reign was his predecessor's regular ceremonial display of her royal person attending public sermons at court during Lent. Camden, in his Jacobean *History of Queen Elizabeth*, had lodged an oblique criticism of James' cavalier neglect of the court Lent series by praising Elizabeth's sober attendance of the same 'dress'd in Mourning, as the gravest and most primitive Habit'. Charles's own careful stage-managing of his first public appearance after his father's death at a Lent sermon, and, of course, in mourning, is therefore perhaps of greater significance than a simple expression of piety. Charles 'dined abroad . . . being in a plain black cloth cloak to the ancle; and so went after dinner into the chapel, Dr. Donne preaching . . . his majesty looking very pale, his visage being the true glass of his inward, as well as his accoutrements of external mourning'.[31] If Charles's funereal appearance at this Lent sermon hearkened back to Elizabethan ceremonial dignity and protestant sobriety, so too did his equally noticeable choice of Donne as preacher for the occasion. The Lord Chamberlain's instructions not only notified Donne that the King wished to hear a sermon at St James's instead of Whitehall, but that he wished Donne to preach not in the morning, which would be the Chaplain-in-Ordinary's routine time after morning prayer, but in the afternoon – which was the time appointed for the solemn sermon in the Lent series. As we have already seen, the Sunday sermon had, since at least the 1560s, been preached by a bishop. In hierarchical terms then, Donne's appointment to the afternoon Lent sermon replaced a bishop with a dean.[32] And the supplanted bishop was not just any bishop, but the bishop of Durham, Richard Neile, who, before Laud's ascendancy, was the leader of the Arminian faction in England which would come to bear his name as the Durham House Group.[33] Donne was the

---

[30] *Calendar of State Papers Venetian* XIX (1625–6), p. 21, quoted in Kevin Sharpe, 'The Image of Virtue: The Court and Household of Charles I, 1625–1642', in David Starkey et al., *The English Court from the War of the Roses to the Civil War* (London: Longman, 1987), p. 228.

[31] McCullough, *Sermons at Court*, pp. 131–5, 48; Sir William Le Neve, in *The Court and Times of Charles the First*, quoted in Bald, p. 468.

[32] In other words, seeing this sermon as a Lent series sermon, and not part of Donne's routine April service corrects Bald's view that 'In 1625 he had been assigned as usual the duty of being in attendance at Whitehall during the month of April, and it fell to his lot to preach the first sermon to the new King on the 3rd of the month' (p. 467).

[33] The Lord Chamberlain's copy of the Lent list for 1624/5 shows for 3 April 'L. Bp of Durham', with 'D. of Paules' added in the margin, clear evidence of a deliberate change. Donne had also already preached his regularly-appointed sermon in the series on the first Friday in Lent, 4 March. PRO MS LC5/183 fol. 1; *Sermons* VI.11.

perfect choice of first preacher to a king who had, like Prince Henry, patronised in that very same chapel at St James's a cadre of chaplains committed to zealous anti-Catholicism, unapologetic affirmation of the Synod of Dort, and the primacy of preaching as a means of grace. Just as Charles' decision to have the sermon at St James's distanced him geographically and ecclesiastically from his father's court at Whitehall, so too his rejection of Neile – the bishop who, according to Nicholas Tyacke, 'more than any other . . . had the ear of King James' – must have been seen as at least a cautious distancing from the increasingly anti-Calvinist trends in his father's ecclesiastical patronage.[34]

Donne seems to have delivered the right message on the day, for the sermon swiftly appeared in print with a dedication to the king, both of which facts imply royal approval. That the sermon was composed or revised specifically for this last-minute appointment is clear first in its status not as a routine Sunday sermon, but as a solemn Lent sermon, declared (as Donne always did in his other court Lent sermons) in its opening exordium: 'Wee are still in the season of *Mortification*; in *Lent* . . .' (*Sermons* VI, 241). Secondly, the sermon directly addresses the possible changes in church and state after his accession. Elaborating the architectural conceit of his text – 'If the foundations be destroyed, what can the righteous doe?' (Psalm 11:3) – Donne was unambiguous in his application of it to Charles: 'governe this first *House, Thy selfe*, well; and as *Christ* sayde . . . Hee shall enlarge thee in the next House, Thy *Family*, and the next, The *State*, and the other, The *Church*, till hee say to thee . . . *Now I have brought thee up to a Kingdome*' (*Sermons* VI, 261).

Most striking about this sermon from a religio-political point of view is how differently Donne treated the matters of Charles' family, church and state from the way that bishop Richard Neile might have done on this auspicious occasion.[35] Donne preached to Charles with a vocabulary and tone well-rehearsed by godly conformists (many of the most prominent of them Charles's own chaplains as Prince of Wales) who opposed the liberal theology and pro-Spanish foreign policy pointedly defended in James' Whitehall pulpit by Neile and his protegés Lancelot Andrewes, John Buckeridge, and William Laud. By 1618 these latter churchmen studiously avoided anti-Catholic polemic in the pulpit, defended the mixed Protestant–Catholic royal marriage, and used praise of Christian pacifism as a not-so-indirect way to condemn calls for English involvement in a Continental religious war.[36] The

---

[34] For the godly 'college of St James's', see McCullough, *Sermons at Court*, pp. 183–209; for Neile, Nicholas Tyacke, *Anti-Calvinists: the rise of English Arminianism c.1590–1640* (Oxford: Clarendon Press, 1987), p. 123, and chapter 5, *passim*.

[35] Neile expected to preach on his appointed day at least as late as 21 March; see *The Correspondence of John Cosin*, 2 vols, ed. G. Ornsby (Surtees Society nos. 52, 55, 1868–72) I, 67.

[36] See Peter Lake, 'Lancelot Andrewes, John Buckeridge, and Avant-Garde Conformity at the

former group, however, articulated their opposing views in a rhetoric of moderation that has been brilliantly analysed by Peter Lake in the works of Donne's contemporary Joseph Hall.[37] In his works from precisely this period (1620–6), Hall deployed the language of Protestant solidarity and irenicism to suppress internecine bloodletting over predestination, and, paradoxically, to urge a bellicose engagement with Roman heresy. And Donne's inaugural sermon before Charles I was a textbook exercise in precisely these strategies. First Donne lamented the failure of the English church to take St Paul's advice – '*Studie to bee quiet*' (1 Thess. 4:11) – when factional dispute over matters not fundamental to the faith threatened: 'onely because wee are sub-divided in divers *Names*, there should bee such Exasperations, such Exacerbations, such Vociferations, such Ejulations, such Defamations of one another, as if all *Foundations* were destroyed'. And in a sure allusion to the print war then raging over the publication in the previous year of Richard Montagu's *A Gagg for the New Gospel*, he lamented, 'And yet every *Mart*, wee see more Bookes written by these men against one another, then by them both, for *Christ*.' But, as Lake has observed of Hall, Donne's appeal here to doctrinal peace at home is in turn a battle cry for at least a spiritual war with Rome. As Jeanne Shami has pointed out, Donne is quite careful in this sermon, as elsewhere, not to equate the Pope with anti-Christ or to deny Rome's status as a true church. But Lake's view of the same concessions by Hall also applies to Donne: 'seeming irenicism was not calculated to argue in practice for closer links with Rome or more moderate treatment of Catholics but instead to render the papists without excuse for their continued adherence to the errors of popery'. And precisely what Donne offers here is a five-page anatomy of heretical Roman abuses, engagement with which is forced upon the peaceful lovers of protestant truth by 'the uncharitableness of the *Church of Rome*'.[38]

Donne even manages, with just such a dexterous slight of hand in controversy, to make lingering national worries about tying a marriage knot with a Catholic (albeit French) princess, into a Catholic, not a Protestant, problem. In the sermon's treatment of family 'foundations', Donne speculates, 'if there bee a window opened in the house, to let in a *Iesuiticall firebrand*, that shall whisper . . . that in case of *Heresie*, Civill and Naturall, and Matrimoniall duties cease, no Civill, no Naturall, no Matri-moniall Tribute due to an *Heretique*', the blame for factious, unnecessary

---

Court of James I', in Peck (ed.), *Mental World*, pp. 113–33; McCullough, *Sermons at Court*, pp. 139–41.

[37] Peter Lake, 'The moderate and irenic case for religious war: Joseph Hall's *Via Media* in context', in *Political Culture and Cultural Politics in early modern England*, ed. by S. Amussen and M. Kishlansky (Manchester: Manchester University Press, 1995); Lake, 'Joseph Hall, Robert Skinner and the rhetoric of moderation at the early Stuart court', in *English Sermon Revised*, ed. by Ferrell and McCullough, pp. 167–85. Donne's connexions with Hall, both of whom counted Sir Robert Drury a patron, deserve further consideration.

[38] *Sermons* VI, 245–50; Lake, 'Moderation at the Early Stuart Court', p. 175; Shami, 'Anti-Catholicism', pp. 140, 155–8; Bald, p. 468.

branding of the non-Roman Catholic spouse (most obviously in this context, Charles) a heretic, falls on the Jesuits. Quite deftly Donne takes the higher moral ground here by charitably not calling the Catholic party of such a marriage (Henrietta Maria) the heretic, but simultaneously scores his polemical points against the nation's favourite papist whipping boys (*Sermons* VI, 255). Donne's condemnation of Roman heresy in this sermon may show, in Shami's terms, 'discretion', or even Bald's 'tact', but at a time when preachers like those replaced by Donne on this day were increasingly accused of 'negative popery' for their refusal to openly condemn Rome at all, Donne's sermon can be most properly appreciated as the 'manifesto to the new reign' that Shami calls it if we read it as offering a polemical view of religious controversy even while it professes irenicism.[39]

I here offer a view of Donne's churchmanship that underwrites Shami's – that Donne should be identified 'with Abbot and Hall rather than Laud or Andrewes, with the conforming Calvinist consensus of the English Church, rather than with the promoters of a more *avant-garde*, Arminian-leaning theology – but for personal and political rather than doctrinal reasons.' Of course, claims have been made to place Donne anywhere on the spectrum from Calvinist to *avant-garde* Arminian, hence Shami's well-judged caveat, 'for personal and political rather than doctrinal reasons'. Certainly included in that caveat is, first, an acknowledgement that Donne's universalist doctrine of grace is unambiguously anti-Calvinist, and secondly, that by personal instinct (and, I would venture, as part of a convert's zeal) he held the Calvinist-conformists' high view of preaching. Lake concludes his study of polemical 'moderation' at the Stuart court with the salutary reminder that 'there were very different sorts of royalists, Anglicans and conformists around in Stuart England', and I would want to insist with him that my own contrast between Donne and Richard Neile is not intended to suggest a crudely bipolar split in English religious culture at the accession of Charles I.[40] Charles could have made Neile's displacement even more dramatic by appointing Abbot or even Hall himself to preach the first sermon before him. The appointment of Donne was much more subtle, and gives us a valuable hint about not only Donne's churchmanship, but Charles' at this crucial juncture. I think Charles saw in Donne a churchman almost *sui generis* – one so complicated in his confessional past and present opinions as to be the almost perfect herald for religious compromise and consensus in the new reign. Here was a preacher whose commitment to the crown was unimpeachable. Furthermore, he was a dedicated preacher whose anti-Catholicism, formed in rigorous self- as well as doctrinal examination, could encourage an

---

[39] Shami, 'Anti-Catholicism', p. 157; Jeanne Shami, 'Donne on Discretion', *ELH* 47 (1980): 48–66; Bald, p. 468; for 'negative popery', see Anthony Milton, *Catholic and Reformed: the Roman and Protestant Churches in English Protestant Thought, 1600–1640* (Cambridge: Cambridge University Press, 1995), pp. 68–72.

[40] Shami, 'Anti-Catholicism', p. 138; Lake, 'Moderation at the early Stuart Court', p. 181.

increasingly defensive Calvinist old guard. Yet his theology of grace and acceptance of the church's right to enforce ceremonial conformity could satisfy Durham House. Charles' accession was a moment of tense religious *equipoise*; the 'war party' still held Commons, king, and favourite in bellicose anti-Catholic pose; radical Arminians like Richard Montagu held their breath wondering whether Charles would support them as much as James had recently begun to do, and although the balance would famously tip within a year as Laud consolidated his influence, Charles' few clerical appointments in these very early months as king suggest a strategy – in which Donne seems to have been used – of avoiding churchmen with clear factional allegiances.[41]

I suggest that because Donne offered Charles an exquisitely rare combination of both the churchmanship in which he had been raised at St James's and the more liberal theology he was increasingly willing to endorse, Donne enjoyed a degree of public favour from Charles that he did not have from James. Donne's first sermon before his new king appeared in print with signs of royal approval, and upon Donne's return to the court pulpit the following year for the first Friday in Lent, he was given royal endorsement for the sermon to be 'by his Maiesties commandement Published'. Whereas James never commissioned the printing of any of Donne's court sermons, Charles countenanced or demanded the printing and dedication to himself of the first two sermons he heard Donne preach after his accession. But in the rapidly changing political and religious climate brought about by the collapse of the 'war party', debates over Arminianism, attacks on Buckingham, and the ascent of William Laud, this special favour was as brief as it was pronounced. Donne's court sermons of 1626 and 1627 show a preacher confidently expounding to Charles' court an almost unique *via media* in theology and churchmanship, a confidence as a political preacher that would come to an abrupt end in April 1627.

The court sermons of 1626 and 1627 are most remarkable for their direct engagement with deeply contentious matters of current political and doctrinal debate, something not found in either Donne's Jacobean or his later Caroline court sermons. There is evidence that Donne's confidence to address such matters came from a sense of common purpose with the king himself. In the dedicatory epistle to his 1626 court Lent sermon, Donne offered no routine acknowledgement of the king's command to print. Rather, he cast that command in an elaborate conceit that figured reciprocity and cooperation between king and preacher: 'your *Majesty* is pleasd . . . not only to *receive* into your selfe, but to *returne*, unto others, my poore *Meditations*, and

---

[41] To Donne as first public preacher before him we should add Charles' otherwise baffling selection of his former chaplain Richard Senhouse – little known outside Cambridge, newly appointed to the distant and lowly see of Carlisle, but a firm anti-Catholic Calvinist – to preach his coronation sermon. By custom this should have fallen to the Lord Almoner or the Bishop of Winchester, high-profile Arminians George Montaigne or Lancelot Andrewes, respectively.

so by your gracious commandement of *publishing* them, to make your selfe as a *Glasse* . . . to reflect, and cast them upon your *Subjects*'. The king is here cast not only as an endorser, but as a promulgator of Donne's text, and this is closer than any early modern court sermon printed by royal command comes to equating a preacher's opinions with the monarch's. The opinions offered in the sermon openly address the most contentious issues of the day, nothing less than war both international and doctrinal. Donne preached on 24 February; parliament had assembled on the sixth and was preoccupied with impending war with France, as Donne acknowledged in the epistle: 'Wee are in Times when the way to *Peace* is *Warre*.' But, as Donne continued, 'my Profession leades not me to *those Warres*'. His 'profession' of ordained ministry did, however, confront him squarely with 'Times when the *Peace* of the *Church*, may seeme to implore a kinde of *Warre*, of *Debatements* and *Conferences* in some points' – a sure allusion to the fact that only one fortnight before he preached this sermon, on 11 and 17 February, Buckingham had convened a conference at his London seat, York House, to debate the Arminian theology promulgated by Richard Montagu. Leading the Calvinist case against Montagu at York House was Donne's long-time confessor and confidante, bishop Thomas Morton; among the moderate Calvinist peers in attendance were Donne's friends and patrons the earls of Carlisle and Pembroke. In his dedicatory epistle, Donne frankly acknowledged that his Lent sermon was to be taken as a direct response to the York House Conference. In a rare statement of such authorial intentions in a sermon, he explained to Charles that 'in this *Sermon*, my onely purpose was, that no *Bystander*, should bee hurt, whilest the *Fray* lasted, with either Opinion'. Even more remarkably, Donne went on to assert, in a graceful return to the mirror conceit, that his irenic 'purpose' after York House was also the king's: 'your *Majestie* accepts it so your selfe, and so reflects it upon others'. Since Charles' views on the matter of York House have been notoriously difficult to ascertain, it is worth looking in Donne's 'mirror' for them.[42]

Upon ascending the pulpit, Donne wasted no time in taking up predestination, one of the points hotly controverted at York House. The very declamation of his text to a court that most likely included observers at the Conference could not have failed to cause a stir: '*Thus sayth the Lord: Where is the bill of your mothers divorcement whom I have put away? . . . Behold, for your iniquities have you sold your selves, and for your transgressions, is your mother put away*' (Isaiah 50:1). The auditory need not have waited for the preacher's summary gloss to apply the prophet's metaphors of divorce and self-condemnation to the debates over the roles of human and divine agency in the 'divorcing' of souls from God's saving mercy. Donne's brilliance in handling the chosen text comes from his exploitation of both metaphors and structures of mediation between extremes to argue a case that is anything but

---

[42] *Sermons* VII, 72–3; Tyacke, *Anti-Calvinists*, chapter 7.

a *via media* in the present religio-political context. In his printed epistle, Donne protested that he feared harm to any bystander from 'either Opinion' in the York House '*Fray*'. One would expect the sermon then to be a painstaking mediation between the 'opinions' on predestination of the prosecutors, Thomas Morton and John Preston (unconditional election), and the defendants, Francis White and Richard Montagu (conditional election).[43] But on the contrary, Donne's choice and application of his text in fact supports only the latter case – but that case is presented in the rhetorical garb of a compromise emerging from dialectic opposition. As interpreted by Donne, his text first offers a moderately liberal affirmation that Christ does not 'put away' souls: 'God is no cause of our perishing'. But the text goes on to affirm (for Donne) the even more radical position that a believer can fall from grace through acts of his own will ('for your iniquities have you sold your selves'), from which follows a revocation by Donne of the strictly Calvinist position of atonement only for the elect: 'There is no necessitie that any Man, any this or that Man should perish.' Like Hall, Donne has simply taken the argumentative form of reconciling opposites (here, unconditional vs. conditional election), but filled it with opposites from *within* his own position in the larger debate (conditional election). And therefore, he can conclude the summary of the points of his own sermon in precisely the fashion he concluded his dedicatory epistle, by way of appeal to a compromise endorsed by higher authority (here God, there the king) – 'And therefore, as *God* hath opened himselfe to us, both wayes, let us open both eares to him, and from one Text receive both Doctrines.' But he simultaneously elides the fact that he is actually propounding only one of the disputed 'doctrines' while tacitly rejecting the other (*Sermons* VII, 74).

As much as the Lent 1626 sermon might have pleased the Arminian disputants at York House, it would be a gross oversimplification to conclude that Donne was a promoter of the Durham House group, much less a defender of Richard Montagu.[44] Donne's sermons at court in the ensuing

---

[43] Tyacke, *Anti-Calvinists*, p. 178.

[44] Tyacke's quite accurate pinpointing of Donne's doctrinal Arminianism should not be used by others to lump Donne with the political cabal of Andrewes, Laud, Neile, *et al.* that emerge as the eponymous protagonists of his seminal *Anti-Calvinists*; see pp. 182, 261. This essay was prepared for publication before the appearance of Achsah Guibbory, 'Donne's Religion: Montagu, Arminianism, and Donne's Sermons, 1624–30', *ELR* 31:3 (2001): 412–39, and my arguments that follow here should be closely compared with her treatment of the same issues and texts. Briefly, I concur with Guibbory's conclusions that on matters of grace Donne is clearly anti-Calvinist, and that after the mid-1620s he takes a 'Laudian' line on church authority and ceremonies. But I attach far more importance to Donne's remaining differences with Laud before 1627, especially his views on preaching, and I find far more to incense Laud in the court sermon of 1 April 1627 than a simple insult to Henrietta Maria's Catholicism (see below). Finding liberal views on grace in Donne is not nearly enough to brand him an 'Arminian' in the inflammatory political sense of that term as used in the 1620s.

twelve months make it very clear that a liberal view on matters of grace and the atonement was not enough to make Donne a card-carrying Arminian in the contemporary *political*, rather than strictly *doctrinal* sense of the term. For example, perhaps even more distressing to conformist Calvinists than Montagu's stance on conditional election was his alarming reduction of the number of differences separating Rome and the Church of England. Following suit, defenders of Montagu were open to godly charges of avoiding or subduing their condemnations of Roman error. But Donne's anti-Catholicism continued to be broad-based and unapologetic. A majority of his next sermon at court in 1626, preached 'to the King in my ordinary wayting' on 18 April, was given over to a satiric anatomy of Roman abuses, including a parodic treatment of the invocation of saints, precisely one of the Roman practices that Montagu had infamously removed from the list of things necessarily heretical.[45]

The same sermon, however, contains yet more unambiguous insistences that election and grace are not limited by God, but these insistences are hedged about by prefatory protestations that Donne is in fact avoiding, rather than engaging in controversy: '*I dispute not, but* . . . That as all were dead, so one dyed for all'; '*I am not exercised, nor would I exercise these Auditories with curiosities, but* I heare the Apostle say . . . though they might perish, yet Christ dyed for them'; or, in a disarmingly personal rhetorical question reminiscent of the holy sonnets, 'for if any man had been left out, how should I have come in?' (*Sermons* VII, 126, italics mine). Anthony Milton has shown how several leading moderate Calvinists (Hall among them) also articulated such liberally-inclined views of 'hypothetical universalism'. But what set them apart from anti-Calvinists, those I have called 'political' Arminians, was their refusal to attack the totems of the Calvinist consensus. One of those – anti-Catholicism – I have already shown Donne upholding. But also high among these totems was the Synod of Dort (1619), which, though it roundly condemned the teachings of Arminius, allowed hypothetical universalism. Milton even points to how universalists defended themselves from charges of Arminianism by in turn affirming Dort, as did the quintessentially godly Ezekiel Culverwell in a tract also published in 1626: 'I renounce all *Arminius* his errors: and giue my full consent to the *Synod of Dort*.'[46] And this is precisely the argument used by Donne to conclude his defense of universalism in his 1626 court sermon: 'In the last forraine Synod, which our Divines assisted, with what a blessed sobriety, they delivered their sentence, That all men are truly and in earnest called to eternal life, by Gods Minister.' At a time when Dort was the butt of sarcastic derision in court sermons by the likes of

---

[45] *Sermons* VII, 120–6, 130–33. For Montagu's reduction of the points of necessary dispute with Rome, see Milton, *Catholic and Reformed*, chapter 4, *passim*; for Montagu on the invocation of saints, Milton, *Catholic and Reformed*, pp. 66–8, 206–8.

[46] Milton, *Catholic and Reformed*, pp. 420, 423–4, 428; Ezekiel Culverwell, *A briefe answere . . . Clearing him from the errors of Arminius, vniustly layd to his charge* (1626), sig. A10r.

Andrewes, when even moderate Calvinists like Pembroke and Carlisle balked at the idea (mooted at York House) of making the Dort articles canonical in England, Donne still boldly appealed to its doctrinal authority in the king's presence.[47]

One further point of contact between Donne and the churchmanship of 'Dortists' like Hall and Culverwell will return me to the matter of 'professional' Donne, and throw into some bolder relief what I believe were the reasons for the abrupt end to Donne's confident but brief 'inthronization' in Charles I's court pulpit. As Shami has argued, Donne's care taken to avoid overt controversy in the pulpit was borne not of an instinct to trim or to curry favour with the great, but of a sincere and heartfelt grief at open schism in the church. Similarly, I believe that his endorsements of universalism were not craven attempts to jump on an arriving Laudian bandwagon, but an independent doctrinal conviction. But in addition, the promise of the availability of salvation to all, especially as that promise was described by the Synod of Dort, spoke to Donne's deepest convictions about the profession of being an ordained minister, which for Donne (though not for the Laudians gathering strength around him), was synonymous with being a preacher. Taken to its most extreme logical end, the notion of unconditional election and predestination of some few to salvation calls into question evangelism and the need for evangelical preaching. Conversely, taken to its most extreme logical end, the notion of universalism affords evangelism and evangelical preaching its greatest possible scope and urgency. Hence, even for those for whom universalism might be only hypothetical, the preacher who brings the good news is a 'professor', indeed a 'professional', of the highest order. Even the canonical prose of the Dort articles strains to contain hyperbole on this matter: 'whosoeuer beleeueth in Christ crucified, should not perish, but haue life everlasting: which promise . . . ought promiscuously and without distinction to be declared'. Hence the comfortable union of universalism and evangelism in a puritan like Culverwell: 'this is manifest, that GOD in his Word hath made a generall offer of salvation in *Christ,* and inviteth all (to whom he sendeth his servants, the Preachers of the Gospel) to come to Christ . . . that is, . . . every man and woman'. With similar urgency, but greater rhetorical power and art, the evangelical and pastoral demands to preach the Gospel to all wholly animate Donne's profession as minister, and nowhere more intensely than at court. For here Donne could feel not only the exhilaration of being God's mouthpiece ('whatsoever is promised or offered out of the Gospel by the Minister, is to the same men, and in the same manner promised and offered by the Author of the Gospel, by God himselfe'), but be presented with a confirmation both humbling and thrilling that the message he was privileged to offer was a message he was bound to declare to the fullest

---

[47] *Sermons* VII, 127; Tyacke, *Anti-Calvinists,* pp. 103, 176–7. Donne, of course, was given, on his visit to Germany in 1621, a gold medal commemorating the Synod. See Bald, pp. 364, 563.

possible spectrum of humanity – from 'ignobler creatures, and of brutall natures and affections' to 'the King himselfe'. And at court, in 1625–7, Donne, as we have seen, felt some confidence that just as he was a mirror of and for God, he was the same of and for the king.[48] It should be no surprise, then, to find some of Donne's most exalted royalism in the same sermon with some of his most exalted praise of preaching, knitted together by his doctrinal conviction that the preacher preached, in the words of Dort, most 'promiscuously' before his king.

But promiscuous preaching, and the broader churchmanship it so typified, would nearly unseat John Donne from his beloved 'inthronization' in the court pulpit. Concerns about preaching-centred (vs. liturgical, or sacramentally-centred) piety had been voiced publicly since at least the late 1590s, and, shown the way by Andrewes' late Jacobean court sermons, the emerging Laudian bloc was making the adjustment of emphasis from preaching to liturgy a fetishised totem of what Peter Lake calls 'avant-garde conformity'. A full-scale 'suppression' of preaching would be statutorily promulgated nationwide by Charles in 1629–30, but Laud began to get his way on the matter at court late in 1626 – and it was into precisely this first gathering of the Laudian net that Donne was trapped.[49]

The case can be made most clearly by contrasting Donne's further remarks in the court sermons for April 1626 already under discussion, with the sermon he preached exactly one year later before the King (1 April 1627), and Laud's reaction to it. Andrewes and his acolytes had by the late 1620s ranked the administration of the two sacraments, baptism and the eucharist, as superior conduits of divine grace to preaching – an almost complete reversal of Elizabethan Calvinism's insistence that the Word preached was primary for the initiation and sanctification of the believer. Conformists looked on with horror as their avant-garde brethren moved to subordinate preaching to the liturgy and sacraments, seeing in it a backsliding into supine papist ceremonial religion. So in his sermon before the household on 30 April 1626, Donne's decision to broach not only the topic of preaching, but the negative effects of a state's failure to sponsor preaching, was to take a clear position on an increasingly devisive matter of churchmanship: 'so how long soever Christ have dwelt in any State, or any Church, if he grow speechless, he is departing; if there be a discontinuing, or slackning of preaching, there is a danger of loosing Christ' (*Sermons* VII, 157). A 'slackning' of preaching was precisely what the spiritual sons of Andrewes – the preacher who gave Laudian satire one of its stock phrases,

---

[48] The translation from the fifth article of Dort is from Culverwell, *Briefe Answere*, A5r; Ezekiel Culverwell, *A Treatise of Faith* (1623), pp. 24–5; *Sermons* VII, 134–5, 73.

[49] Peter Lake, 'Lancelot Andrewes, John Buckeridge and Avant-Garde Conformity at the Court of James I', in Peck (ed.), *Mental World*, pp. 123–6; Peter McCullough, 'Making Dead Men Speak: Laudianism, Print, and the Works of Lancelot Andrewes, 1626–42', *HJ* 41:2 (1998): 401–24; 410–11.

that 'All our *holinesse*, is in hearing: All our *Service* eare-service' – devoutly wished for the Church of England.[50]

It was Andrewes' death that let William Laud subordinate preaching to prayer at court several years before he could began to do so nationally. Charles – showing himself very much the son of his father and a product of the godly household at St James's – had persisted in his father's custom of allowing sermons to take precedence over liturgical service in the chapel royal: sung service was to proceed only until the monarch was comfortably settled in the royal closet, whereupon service was suspended so sermon could commence. Charles inherited his father's Dean of the Chapel Royal, none other than Andrewes, who, from at least early 1625 was in such poor health as to take very little evident role in Chapel matters under Charles before his death in September 1626. But as his successor, named within a week of Andrewes' death, Laud wasted no time reforming this, to him the most objectionable chapel royal custom, by securing Charles' promise that 'at whatsoever part of the Prayers he came, the Priest who Ministred should proceed to the end of the Service' before the preacher took the pulpit.[51]

So between Donne's routine April waiting at court in 1626 and 1627 there stood Laud's appointment as Dean of the Chapel, a crucial institutional change. And given this change, Donne's sermon '*to the King, at White-Hall, the first of April, 1627*' was either a deliberate attack on Laud's priorities, or a deeply naive failure to account for a changed political and ceremonial climate in the Chapel Royal. In either case, it was a near disaster for Donne as a preacher there, as he was commanded by Laud to produce a copy of the sermon for the king's scrutiny, and to justify himself in an interview with him. Previous comment on this sermon has failed to offer a convincing explanation of what in it might have offended Laud and Charles; Bald, like Potter and Simpson and even Gosse before them, assumes that Donne's 'High Churchmanship' should have made him an ally of Laud, and are surprised to find Donne accused by him of sympathy for the discredited Calvinist Archbishop Abbot. A richer understanding of the complexities of early Caroline churchmanship than was available to those scholars now allows us to see that liberal views on grace and a high view of regal power were not enough to make one a protegé of Laud or an enemy to Abbot. Donne's sermon in fact reads like a shopping-list of things most noxious to Laud's sensibilities – and Donne waved them under Laud's nose in the only arena (the chapel royal) where Laud had enough authority to prosecute him for it before the king.

Donne was clearly emboldened by the king's ringing endorsements over the past two years of his sermons that directly engaged public controversies. The sense of shock and disappointment at the king's disapprobation, as well as his

[50] Lancelot Andrewes, *XCVI Sermons*, ed. William Laud and John Buckeridge (1629), p. 992.
[51] Peter Heylyn, *Cyprianus Anglicus*, p. 158; McCullough, *Sermons at Court*, p. 155.

naive overconfidence, is palpable in his first letter to Sir Robert Ker after Laud's demand for a copy: 'I hoped for the Kings approbation heretofore in many of my sermons; and I have had it. But yesterday I came very near looking for thanks; for, in my life, I was never in any one peece, so studious of his service.'[52] At a time when governing elites, both secular and ecclesiastical, were in a frenzy of debate over the Forced Loan, war with France, and Abbot's refusal to licence both Montagu's Arminian defense *Appello Caesarem* and the absolutist sermons of Sibthorpe and Manwaring, Donne waded into the fray with a sermon on a text that itself whispered of dark intrigue – 'Take heed what you heare' (Mark 4:24).

He thought the sermon preached obedience and condemned sedition, but he crucially failed to adjust his vocabulary for those ideals to fit Laudian definitions of them. First Donne included one of his by now trademark effusions on the power of evangelical preaching. We know that Laud accused Donne of sympathising in his sermon with one offensive to him and the king delivered by Archbishop Abbot – although we do not have Abbot's sermon, it is almost without doubt the sermon he would have preached *ex officio* as Archbishop of Canterbury in the court Lent series on Palm Sunday, exactly two weeks before. Even if Donne did not, as he protested, know anything of Abbot's sermon, his evocation of mighty prophetic preachers proclaiming orthodoxy to assembled thousands is close enough to a description of a court Lent sermon in the huge concourse of the Whitehall Preaching Place to at least bring back bad memories of Abbot on Palm Sunday: 'His Ministers are an *Earth-quake* . . . They are as the fall of waters, and carry with them whole Congregations; 3000 at a Sermon, 5000 at a Sermon . . . that is, Orthodoxall and fundamentall truths, are established against clamorous and vociferant innovation'. (*Sermons* VII, 396). Having hyperbolically praised the pulpit's power, Donne went even further by declaring what sorts of things a preacher should preach about in the courts of princes. His recipe is taken straight from the book of unabashed advice to princes written by Edwardine and Elizabethan protestants like Edward Dering and Edmund Grindal, and now associated with no churchman more than Abbot: 'So the Apostles proceeded; when they came . . . to a new State, to a new Court, to Rome it selfe, they did not enquire, how stands the Emperour affected to Christ, and to the preaching of his Gospel.' Any consideration of political and religious contingencies must bow to the overpowering obligation to proclaim the gospel, Donne proclaimed, 'Never tell us of displeasure, or disgrace, or detriment, or death for preaching of Christ. For, *woe be unto us*, if we preach him not' (*Sermons* VII, 397–8). And then, in an almost unbelievable piece of temerity, Donne cited as his example of morally compromised preaching the preaching of those tainted by Roman doctrines, a shot

---

[52] The episode is recounted in three letters by Donne to Ker, reprinted in *Sermons* VII, 39–42 (quoted here).

undoubtedly aimed at those Durham House divines like Montagu thought to be edging ever closer to defending intercommunion with Rome, or at the maverick Godfrey Goodman, who had recently preached a court sermon that came scandalously close to affirming transubstantiation.[53] 'All these' theologians, Donne dared, 'have a brackish taste; as a River hath that comes near the Sea, so have they, in comming so neare the Sea of Rome' (*Sermons* VII, 398).

And Donne's praise of 'orthodoxall' preaching continued; he probably offended yet one more article of the new Laudian creed, clerical monopoly on interpretation of the Scriptures. Significantly this occurs in an extended satire on the Romish abuse of locking the Scriptures up from the laity in Latin with the key held only by canonists. In 1607 this would have been unremarkable evangelical anti-Catholicism. But by 1627, the critique of excessive preaching, coupled with increasing attempts to restrict the rights of Scriptural interpretation to the clerisy made it possible to hear in a satire against Rome a satire against emerging Carolo-Laudianism. Donne does not recommend lay preaching, or even hearing sermons on controverted doctrinal fine points, and in that sense no doubt thought that he was toeing a good establishment line. Yet still, what Donne offered as every protestant's picture of the perfect alternative to Romish lay ignorance could have been scenes from Andrewes' or Laud's worst nightmare of an interpretively empowered laity, including sermon orgies ('if a man could heare six Sermons a day, all the days of his life, he might die without having heard all the Scriptures explicated in Sermons'), and unsupervised lay Bible reading ('men have a Christian liberty afforded to them to read the Scriptures at home') (*Sermons* VII, 401).

Donne persisted in his belief that he had written nothing in this sermon to deserve being called on the royal carpet. Confirmation of this can be found in the fact that he preached nothing in April 1627 that he had not preached before Charles (and been rewarded for) since 1625. The difference must be William Laud's new influence at court as Dean of the Chapel Royal, which makes Donne's career as a preacher at court a small but significant piece of evidence in debates now raging over the relative responsibility of Charles and Laud for the ecclesiastical reforms of the1630s. It is important to remember that Donne did not win this little contest; at best he was able to convince the king to accept his apologies. The entry in Laud's diary makes clear who the victor was: '*Apr. 4. Wednesday,* When his Majesty King *Charles* forgave to Doctor *Donne* certain slips in a Sermon'. The gloating winner continues, 'what he [Charles] then most graciously said unto me, I have wrote in my Heart with indelible Characters, and great thankfulness to God and the King'.[54] This not only suggests that Donne was viewed as in the wrong by

---

[53] For Goodman see Milton, *Catholic and Reformed*, p. 199.
[54] Quoted in Bald, p. 494.

Laud and Charles, but that Laud was relieved to have secured a pivotal symbolic victory in winning the king over to his views.[55]

Charles did not spring from his mother's womb a Laudian. On the contrary, he was raised in precisely the tradition rejected by Laudianism, and the early years of his reign saw the confused, sometimes contradictory reconciliation of himself to that new agenda. John Donne seems to have had his unwitting part to play in that process, and he never preached the same at court again. The nine surviving sermons that Donne preached at court after 1627 are striking as a group for their complete avoidance of the politically charged opinions that Donne expounded so confidently in the first two years of the new reign.[56] Often lyrical, and including some of his best literary prose, these are, however, no longer sermons in what had become by 1627 the oppositional voice of prophetic, evangelical protestant preaching. When a politicised topic is touched by Donne after 1627 it is in fact to parrot Laudian truisms, like the primacy of prayer over preaching, that actually contradict his early Caroline positions.[57] But even more frequently, and especially in his remaining Lent sermons (including of course his last, *Deaths Duell*) when the season gave encouragement to do so, Donne preached at court with an introspective eloquence on themes of universal import that confirmed his reputation, at least for future generations, not as a political preacher, but something perhaps much greater.

---

[55] Laud's securing a reprimand of Donne in 1627 can be seen, then, as an anticipation of Laud's wider control over ecclesiastical patronage from 1628, demonstrated by Ken Fincham, 'William Laud and the Exercise of Caroline Ecclesiastical Patronage', *Journal of Ecclesiastical History* 51 (2000): 69–93.

[56] It is also notable that Donne received no further royal commands for printing his court sermons.

[57] Cf. *Sermons* VIII, 339; IX, 176, 218–19.

Appendix: Donne's Sermons at Court

Occasion	Date	Place	Auditory	Scriptural Text	1st Printed	Potter & Simpson
1. Sun. Easter 3	30 April 1615	Greenwich		Isaiah 52:3	XXVI.11	I.1
2. Sun. Easter 3	21 April 1616	Whitehall		Eccles. 8:11	XXVI.6	I.2
3. Sun. Trinity 20 (also All-Hallowstide / Gunpowder Revels)	2 Nov. 1617	Whitehall		Psalm 55:19	XXVI.7	I.4
4. Sun. Advent 3	14 Dec. 1617	Denmark Hs.	Queen Anne	Prov. 8:17	XXVI.18	I.5
5. 1st Fri. in Lent	20 Feb. 1618	Whitehall		Luke 23:40	XXVI.1	I.6
6. Low Sunday	12 April 1618	Whitehall		Gen. 32:10	XXVI.12	I.7
7. Sun. Easter 2	19 April 1618	Whitehall		I Tim. 1:15	XXVI.13	I.8
8. Sun. Easter 2?	19 April 1618 [?]	Whitehall		I Tim. 1:15	XXVI.14	I.9
9. 1st Fri. in Lent	12 Feb. 1619	Whitehall		Ezek. 33:32	XXVI.2	II.7
10. Easter Day	28 March 1619	Whitehall		Psalm 89:48	LXXX.27	II.9
11. 1st Fri. in Lent	3 March 1620	Whitehall		Amos 5:18	LXXX.14	II.18
12. Sun. Lent 5	2 April 1620	Whitehall	(Household?)	Eccles.5:13–14	XXVI.[9], 10	III.1
13. Sun. Easter 2	30 April 1620	Whitehall		Psalm 144:15	LXXX.74	III.2
14. 1st Fri. in Lent	16 Feb. 1621	Whitehall	King James	I Tim. 3:16	XXVI.4	III.9
15. Low Sunday	8 April 1621	Whitehall		Prov. 25:16	LXXX.70	III.10
16. 1st Fri. in Lent	8 March 1622	Whitehall		I Cor. 15:26	LXXX.15	IV.1
17. 1st Fri. in Lent	28 Feb. 1623	Whitehall		John 11:35	LXXX.16	IV.13
18. 1st Fri. in Lent	4 March 1624	Whitehall		Matt. 19:17	LXXX.17	VI.11
19. Sun. Lent 5	3 April 1625	St James's	King Charles	Psalm 11:3	Q,1625	VI.12
20. Tues. Easter 1	26 April 1625	Denmark Hs	'before the body of King James'	Cant. 3:11	Fifty.33	VI.14
21. 1st Fri. in Lent	24 Feb. 1626	Whitehall	King Charles	Isaiah 50:1	Q,1626	VII.2
22. Tues. Easter 1	18 April 1626	Whitehall	King Charles	John 14:2	LXXX.73	VII.4
23. Sun., Easter 3	30 April 1626	Whitehall	the Household	Matt. 9:13	XXVI.8	VII.5
24. Sun (?) Lent 1	11(?) Feb. 1627	Whitehall	King Charles	Isaiah 65:20	Fifty.26	VII.14
25. Low Sunday	1 April 1627	Whitehall	King Charles	Mark 4:24	Fifty.27	VII.16
26. 1st Fri. in Lent	29 Feb. 1628	Whitehall		Acts 7:60	XXVI.15	VII.7
27. Public Fast	5 April 1628		King Charles	Psalm 6:6–7	LXXX.54	VIII.8
28. Easter Tues.	15 April 1628		King Charles	Isaiah 32:8	LXXX.75	VIII.10

Peter E. McCullough

Appendix (cont.)

Occasion	Date	Place	Auditory	Scriptural Text	1st Printed	Potter & Simpson
29. 1st Fri. in Lent	**20 Feb. 1629**	Whitehall	King Charles	James 2:12	XXVI.3&17	VIII.15
30.	April 1629		King Charles	Gen. 1:26	Q 1635	IX.1
31.	April 1629		King Charles	Gen. 1:26	Q 1635	IX.2
32. 1st Fri. in Lent	12 Feb. 1630		King Charles	Matt. 6:21	XXVI.5&16	IX.7
33. 'in Lent', but *vere* Tues. Easter 3?	20 April 1630		King Charles	Job 16:17–19	LXXX.13	IX.9
34. 1st Fri. in Lent	25 Feb. 1631	Whitehall	King Charles	Psalm 68:20	Q,1632	X.11
35. (April?)	(*temp. Jacob.?*)	Whitehall	(Household?)	Ezek. 34:19	*Fifty*.24	X.6
36. (April?)	(*temp. Jacob.?*)	Whitehall	(Household?)	Ezek. 34:19	*Fifty*.25	X.7

Key:

Dates in **bold** indicate sermons in Parliament-time.

LXXX = LXXX Sermons Preached by . . John Donne (1640)
Fifty = Fifty Sermons, Preached by . . John Donne (1649)
XXVI = XXVI Sermons Preached By . . John Donne (1661)

III

Professing the Body:
Anatomy and Resurrection

Chapter 10

REVERENT DONNE: THE DOUBLE
QUICKENING OF LINCOLN'S INN CHAPEL

JAMES CANNON

TO his Jacobean contemporaries Donne's 1623 Encaenia sermon would
have been one of his most well-known pieces of oratory. Notoriously, its
original performance, at the consecration of Lincoln's Inn Chapel, was
attended by such a huge crowd that lives were threatened by the crush: as
Chamberlain reported after the event, 'there was great concourse of noblemen
and gentlemen wherof two or three were endaungered and taken up dead for
the time with the extreme presse and thronging'.[1] The sermon was soon
available to a wider audience in print, and its popularity is attested to by its
being reprinted thrice in the next three years.

The sermon's preface gives a clear reason why the often print-shy Donne
was willing to see his preaching reach a wider audience. Donne had been
urged to have the sermon printed by the Society of Lincoln's Inn, and, in his
own words:

> to this latter service I was more inclinable, because, though in it I had no
> occasion to handle any matter of Controversie between us, and those of the
> Romane Perswasion, yet the whole body and frame of the Sermon, is opposed
> against one pestilent calumny of theirs, that wee have cast off all distinction of
> places, and of dayes, and all outward meanes of assisting the devotion of the
> Congregation. For this use, I am not sorry that it is made publique, for I shall
> never bee sorry to appeare plainely, and openly, and directly, without disguise
> or modification, in the vindicating of our Church from the amputations and
> calumnies of that Adversary.[2]

The conception of Donne as an anti-Catholic polemicist is hardly new or
surprising; but nevertheless, as with most sermon prefaces, such arguments
should be treated with a pinch of salt. Anthony Milton has shown that, in the

---

[1] *Sermons* IV, 40.
[2] *Sermons* IV, 362–3.

1620s, a new breed of anti-Catholic polemic was emerging, which aimed not such much to create 'clear blue water' between the Church of England and Rome, but to distance the former as much from puritan ideas and practices. Indeed the best example of this, Montagu's *A New Gagg for an Old Goose*, was printed only a year after Donne's Encaenia sermon.[3] Donne's aim in this sermon, I would argue, was not so much to rout Catholic superstition, but to address issues that were contentious within the Church of England.

Donne's sermon text was an unusual though appropriate choice for the consecration of a place of worship, John 10:22: 'And it was in Jerusalem, the Feast of the Dedication; and it was Winter; and Jesus walked in the Temple in Salomon's Porch.' In his 1622 sermon on the *Directions to Preachers*, Donne had been constrained by the need to keep to his text to deal with the controversial material he wished to discuss in his Application at the end of the sermon; but the text of his Encaenia sermon allowed him to broach controversial matters more directly. By concentrating on the phrase 'the feast of the dedication' Donne was able to devote the majority of the hour to discussing two topical matters: first, the validity of church-ordained festivals, and secondly, more particularly, the ceremony of Dedication. Before the hour was out, Donne had also touched on the importance of common prayer in worship, and the need for both mental and bodily reverence in God's house. All of these were topics over which the Church of England in the 1620s was becoming increasingly polarised, debate inflamed by the new ideas and vehement rhetoric of the rapidly cohering Laudian movement.

The controversy given most extended consideration in the Encaenia sermon is that over the extent and origins of church sacrality. In his sermon introduction, Donne unambiguously stated his belief that churches were sacred buildings, made so by the ceremony of consecration as well as the presence of believers.

> These walles are holy, because the *Saints of God* meet here within these walls to glorifie him. But yet these places are not onely consecrated & sanctified by your comming; but to bee sanctified also for your comming, that so, as the Congregation sanctifies the place, the place may sanctifie the Congregation too.[4]

When he returned to this theme in the body of the sermon, Donne asserted first that God was indeed present in churches, and that this belief in no way undermined the doctrine of Divine Omnipresence.

> It diminishes not, prejudices not Gods Ubiquity and Omnipresence, that wee give him his Ubi, certaine places for Invocation. Thats not the lesse true, that the most High dwells not in Temples made with handes, though God accept at

---

[3] Anthony Milton, *Catholic and Reformed: The Roman and Protestant Churches in English Protestant Thought 1600–1640* (Cambridge: Cambridge University Press, 1995), pp. 63–72.

[4] *Sermons* IV, 364.

our hands our dedication of certaine places to his service, & manifest his working more effectually, more energetically, in those places . . . God is in Heaven, but yet hee is here, within these walls.[5]

Donne then went on to discuss how it was that Lincoln's Inn Chapel had become a holy building. It was, he said, a two-fold process, which he described as a *Lay Dedication,* and an *Ecclesiasticall Dedication.* The first stage was 'the voluntary surrendring of this piece of ground thus built, to God'. The second stage, the 'Ecclesiasticall Dedication', Donne explained with a typically metaphysical conceit, by comparing the building to a child, and its consecration to baptism.

Here is a House, a Child conceiv'd (we may say borne) of Christian parents, of persons religiously disposed to God's glory; but yet, that was to receive another influence, an inanimation, a quickening, by another Consecration. Oportet denuo nasci, holds even in the children of Christian parents; when they are borne, they must be borne again by Baptisme: when this place is given for you, for God, oportet denuo dari, it must be given againe to God, by him, who receives it of you.[6]

These assertions were not, as Donne's preface would have us believe, doctrines universally accepted by the Church of England. On the contrary, ever since Richard Hooker had rehabilitated the theology of consecration in 1597, debate over whether a church was a sacred place, and to what its holiness could be ascribed, was becoming increasingly widespread in sermons and theological treatises.

In the years after the Elizabethan settlement, when the church was struggling to overcome a superstitious belief in the holiness of churches, shrines and relics, separatists such as Barrow and more mainstream puritans such as Perkins had accepted that churches were not sacred places, because God's chosen dwelling place under the new covenant was the human heart.[7] The homilies argued more moderately that churches were hallowed 'because God's people resorting thereunto, are holy, and exercise themselves in holy and heavenly things', but affirmed that churches were not 'meet dwelling places' for God, who could not 'be enclosed in *temples* or houses *made with* man's *hand*'; His real temples were 'the bodies and minds of true Christians'.[8]

In Book V of *The Laws of Ecclesiastical Polity,* first printed in 1597, Hooker decisively changed the boundaries of debate by recovering the theology of consecration. Defending the consecration of churches in chapter twelve, he

---

[5] *Sermons* IV, 372.
[6] *Sermons* IV, 372.
[7] Henry Barrow, *A Brief Discoverie of the False Church* (1590), p. 132; William Perkins, *Works,* 2nd edn, enlarged (1603), p. 418.
[8] *The Two Books of Homilies Appointed to be Read in Churches,* ed. by John Griffiths (Oxford: Oxford University Press, 1859), pp. 275, 153–4.

claimed that a church was indeed 'the dwelling-place of God', and that churches were made special places of God's presence by its consecration, in which 'we invest God himself within them'. A model for the nature and origins of the sacrality of Christian Churches could be found in the holy places of the Old Testament:

> the solemn dedication of churches . . . [serves] to surrender up that right which otherwise their founders might have in them, and to make God himself their owner. For which cause at the erection and consecration as well of the tabernacle as of the temple, it pleased the almighty to give a manifest sign that he took possession of both.[9]

When Hooker wrote his opinions, it was very much a theoretical discussion; the rate of church building and reconstruction in the Elizabethan church was minimal. Even so, Hooker's ideas did have an immediate impact, as a small surge in consecrations followed.[10] Within ten years, however, the restitution of church funds under James I led to a gradual increase in new building, which was becoming particularly visible by the late 1610s. As a result the debate became a practical one, and resolution on the issue more urgent: when one built a new church, should one consecrate it, and in doing so, what was one doing?

By the time of Donne's Encaenia sermon, opinion on the nature and origins of church sacrality had shifted and diversified. Hooker's belief that churches were sacralised by their consecration was taken up by others in the early part of the seventeenth century. Lancelot Andrewes became a firm believer in God's special presence in churches; in his Gunpowder sermon of 1617, he reproved his audience for their slovenly behaviour in church, 'when we come before the presence of the LORD'.[11] Andrewes explained this perception of church sacrality at the beginning of his consecration liturgy for the Jesus Chapel in Southampton in 1620, which was to become the most popular liturgical model for the consecration of churches in the 1620s and 1630s.[12] As Donne was to do six years later, Andrewes qualified the sentiments of God's omnipresence in I Kings 8:27 by arguing that God's delight 'hath been ever with the sons of men', and that 'in such places as are set apart and sanctified to Thy name, and to the memory of it, there Thou hast said Thou

[9] Richard Hooker, *Works*, ed. by W. Speed Hill, 6 vols (Cambridge, Mass.: Belknap Press and Binghampton, NY: Medieval & Renaissance Texts & Studies, 1977–93) II, 47–8.

[10] J. W. Legg, *English Orders for Consecrating Churches in the Seventeenth Century* (London: Henry Bradshaw Society, 1911), appendix IV (pp. 318–25).

[11] Lancelot Andrewes, *Works*, ed. by J. P. Wilson and James Bliss, 11 vols (Oxford: J. H. Parker, 1841–54) IV, 374.

[12] Andrewes' liturgy was used, either verbatim or in a close adaptation, for the consecration of Peterhouse chapel in Cambridge, Lincoln College chapel in Oxford, Abbey Dore in Herefordshire, the chapel in Mersham Hatch, Kent, the chapels in Stanmore and Hammersmith, the chapel at St Bartholemew's chapel in Chichester, and Ightham parish church in Kent.

wilt vouchsafe Thy gracious presence after a more special manner, and come to us and bless us'.[13]

Although Horton Davies has cast attitudes to church sacrality as polarised and static in the early seventeenth century, many conformist preachers and writers had clearly shifted from positions of absolute denial.[14] By the 1620s such views found expression most typically from extremists or reactionaries such as William Prynne and Peter Smart; the high commission punished both for their views.[15] Most seventeenth-century conformists were ultimately willing to accept that God was in some way present in churches. Even William Whately, the 'roaring boy' of Banbury, taught in his catechism on the ten commandments that divine service should be performed 'reverently, with a speciall apprehension of Gods presence.'[16] But instead of explaining church sacrality by Hooker's view of consecration, it was argued that God manifested himself in churches through the presence of believers, and in the worship performed by them. This model of sacrality was derived from Matthew 18:20, 'where two or three are gathered together in my name, there am I in the midst of them'. Thomas Adams, in his St Paul's sermon on 2 Corinthians 6:16, preached at Paul's Cross and printed as *The Temple* in 1624, explained that in addition to his dwelling in heaven and in the hearts of men, God dwells in 'a house of Stone, so this materiall one is his Temple', and that 'the testification of his presence' in Matthew 18:20, presented a vision of God's presence as worship-dependent: 'every materiall Temple, wherein the Saints are assembled, the truth of the Gospell is preached and professed, the holy Sacraments duely administred, and the Lords Name is invocated and worshipped, is the *Temple of God*'.[17]

This view was attractive even among those who performed or preached at consecrations, but did not necessarily support Hooker's idea of what a consecration was. Since consecration liturgies fused as many rites as possible, the sacralisation of the church could be attributed to the worship performed within, rather than a more supernatural inspiration. In December 1623, John Hall preaching at the 'reconcilement', as he termed it, of the 'happily restored and reedified chapel of the right honourable the Earl of Exeter', took an almost identical position to Adams, arguing that God has 'an house of stone' as well as one of flesh, and that his dwelling on earth is twofold, 'in the hearts and assembly of his children'.[18] Hall chose not to attribute God's presence to

[13] Andrewes, *Works* XI, 312.

[14] Horton Davies, *Worship and Theology in England: From Cranmer to Baxter and Fox, 1534–1690* (Princeton: Princeton University Press, 1970 and 1975, repr. 1996), pp. 19–20.

[15] William Prynne, *A Quench-Coale* (1637), fol. B3r; Peter Smart, *A Sermon Preached in the Cathedrall Church of Durham July 7 1628* (1628), p. 18.

[16] William Whately, *A Pithie, Short and Methodicall Opening of the Ten Commandments* (1622), pp. 60, 50.

[17] Thomas Adams, *The Temple* (1624), pp. 7–8.

[18] Joseph Hall, *The Glory of the Latter House* in *Works*, ed. by Philip Wynter, revised edn, 10 vols (Oxford, 1863) V, 187.

the ceremony of consecration, but 'by testification of presence' in Matthew 18:20. In his sermon at the consecration of the Freeschool chapel in Shrewsbury in 1617, Samuel Price stated his belief that a church is 'a place of *Angels*, the Court of *Heaven*, and Heaven it selfe. . . . It is Gods *house*', believing that, although God is omnipresent, 'he *especially* affordeth his *presence* in those places, which he calleth his *houses*'; but, although he defended the lawfulness of consecrating churches, he had little perception that such rites summoned God to manifest Himself in the church as He had done in the Jewish temple.[19] In his dedicatory sermon for the new chapel in Epping in 1623, Jeremiah Dyke came closer to Hooker's formulation of God's presence, not only explaining the divine presence in terms of Matthew 18:20, but also by using another standard archetype for consecration, the tabernacle of Moses: 'So soone as the Tabernacle was raysed, the Altar and the rest of Gods Ordinances were erected; and *Moses had finished the worke: Then a cloud covered the Congregation, and the glory of the Lord filled the Tabernacle.* No sooner his house up, but then God came and tooke possession.'[20] However, although it presents a view of God's more tangible entrance into places of worship, Dyke's consecration lacks any sense of the church being set apart with any ceremony.

These other consecration sermons shed light on Donne's own practice: far from being an attack wholeheartedly directed at Roman Catholic doctrine, Donne's Encaenia sermon instead intervenes in a dispute that was developing within the Church of England. The theory Donne lays out is not just a repetition of current ideas and expression, but is more interesting and original. On the one hand, in his unambiguous assertion that 'the Congregation sanctifies the place', Donne finds a place for the moderate opinion that a church is made holy by the presence of Christ among the faithful in worship, as testified in Matthew 18:20. However, by pointing out that 'these places are not onely consecrated & sanctified by your comming; but to bee sanctified also for your coming' Donne vigorously asserts the importance of consecration to church sacrality. His conceit of the chapel as like a child born doubly, first bodily and then in the spirit through baptism, bridges the two positions with grace and skill: while it upholds Hooker's theology of consecration, it is more accommodating of alternative positions than Laudian 'beauty of holiness' writers of the 1630s were to be.

Although Donne's theology of consecration is accommodating of the Laudian position, it is crucial to recognise that the Encaenia sermon does not display the remarkable similarities in expression that one finds in the Laudian 'beauty of holiness' sermons and pamphlets of the 1630s. One common technique was to use the legal language of property transfer.

---

[19] Sampson Price, *The Beauty of Holines: or, the Consecration of a House of Prayer, by the Example of our Saviour* (1618), p. 22.

[20] Jeremiah Dyke, *A Sermon Dedicatory. Preached at the Consecration of the Chappell of Epping in Essex. October 28 1622* (1623), p. 14.

Foulke Robarts is typical, explaining consecration with the technical terms of 'alienation', the taking of anything from its owner, and 'assignation', the action of legally transferring a right or property. According to Robarts, all these processes occurred during a consecration service: by *alienation* the building was ritually surrendered from human ownership and use into the hands of God's agent the bishop, and by assignation God was invested 'in the right and possession of the building ... whereupon it becommeth now the house and ground of God, and God himself is thereof specially possessed'. Solemnities, baptism, confirmation, holy communion, marriage and church-ing accompanied the transfer of property.[21] Donne's original conceit of baptismal 'quickening' avoids such formulas. Similarly, Donne's tone is more accommodating and less bellicose than it might otherwise be, and he does not, like much Laudian literature, try to cover as many aspects of their ceremonial programme as possible. For instance, we know from a Paul's Cross sermon of 1627 that Donne's stance on images bore many similarities to the Laudian approach, yet there is no mention of the matter in his Encaenia sermon – a surprising omission, given that the most potentially contentious feature of the chapel's design was its scheme of Van Linge painted glass, which surrounded the congregation to whom Donne spoke.[22] Consecrating a similarly adorned chapel at Lincoln College in 1630, Richard Corbett was to incorporate a defence of the stained glass into the consecration liturgy, attacking those who might condemn the 'seemly glazing' as 'nothing but a little brittle superfluity'.[23] If Donne had been a card-carrying Laudian 'beauty of holiness' writer in the 1630s, similar sentiments could easily have been worked into the argument of his sermon.

Donne's ability to create bridges between the moderate and Laudian camps on this issue is testified to by the enthusiastic reaction of Donne's original audience, the distinctly unlaudian Society of Lincoln's Inn. Not only did members of the Inn throng to hear Donne's opinions, but they were enthusiastic enough about what Donne had said to encourage him to print his sermon. Historians should perhaps be wary of exaggerating the attested puritanism of Lincoln's Inn when it comes to ceremonial matters; as Wilfred Prest has observed, close scrutiny of the worship in the Inns of Court 'indicates that the influence of puritanism in the inns was less marked that might at first appear'.[24] The chapel contains several features, particularly its

---

[21] Foulke Robarts, *God's Holy House and Service, according to the Primitive and Most Christian Forme* thereof (1639), pp. 9–10.

[22] *Sermons* VII, 432.

[23] Andrew Clark (ed.), 'The Consecration of Lincoln College Chapel', in *Collectanea IV*, Oxford Historical Society, 47 (1905), pp. 136–55; p. 148.

[24] Wilfred R. Prest, *The Inns of Court under Elizabeth I and the Early Stuarts 1590–1640* (London: Longman, 1972), p. 190. Prest's evidence is drawn from the appointment of lecturers in the Inns; the decoration and ceremonial of their chapels also seem to lend some support to his opinions.

stained glass, which could have caused consternation among particularly zealous puritans. It is also notable that in 1623 the Masters of the Bench were keen to protect the dignity of their new communion table, forbidding those who sat near it during divine service to 'sit, leane or rest their hattes or arms upon or any other part of their bodies upon or against the Communion Table, or lay their hats or books upon the same'.[25] The design of Lincoln's Inn's new chapel suggests that like many moderates in the Jacobean church the Society was eager to recover some dignity in worship, and was tempering its attitudes on some theological and ceremonial matters away from the hard-line anti-ceremonialism of sixteenth-century Puritanism, while at the same time avoiding what they would have seen as the excesses of Laudian worship. Donne's inclusion of the more moderate opinion in his formulation of church sacrality, and tempering of the Laudian position, is therefore likely to have met with their approval.

The question of Donne's allegiances in the increasingly polarised politics of the English church in the 1620s has re-emerged in recent years as a topic for academic discussion. Daniel Doerksen and Paul Sellin have positioned Donne among the ranks of conformist Calvinists, while Achsah Guibbory has presented him as closer to Laudian throught.[26] It would be foolish to determine Donne's entire religious stance on the basis of one issue alone. Having said that, the Encaenia sermon does give us some indication of how Donne involved himself in one aspect of the growing debate over church ceremony that was being stimulated in the 1620s by the rapidly cohering Laudian movement. Throughout the course of the sermon Donne dealt with three more topics that were important facets of Laudian ceremonialism: on these issues, he shows some sympathy with Laudian thinking, but also attempts a fusion with the more moderate position, not only in his theology, but particularly in his choice of language and image. In the Encaenia sermon we see a Donne who is keen to involve himself in the growing debates over public worship and is obviously stimulated by Laudian thought, but who, true to the sentiments of *Satire III*, does not follow absolutely the ideology, and particularly the rhetoric of one particular faction, instead using his insight to reach firmly held, yet more accommodating formulations.

---

[25] *The Records of the Honourable Society of Lincoln's Inn: The Black Books*, ed. by W. P. Baildon and James Douglas Walker, 5 vols (London: Lincoln's Inn, 1897–1968) II, 243.

[26] Daniel Doerksen, *Conforming to the Word: Herbert, Donne, and the English Church before Laud* (Lewisburg: Bucknell University Press, 1997); Paul R. Sellin, *John Donne and 'Calvinist' Views of Grace* (Amsterdam: VU Boekhandel/Uitgeverij, 1983), Paul R. Sellin, *So Doth, So is Religion: John Donne and Diplomatic Contexts in the Reformed Netherlands, 1619–1620* (Columbia: University of Missouri Press, 1988); Achsah Guibbory, 'Donne's Religion: Montagu, Arminianism, and Donne's Sermons, 1624–30', *ELR* 31:3 (2001): 412–39.

Chapter 11

ESSAYING THE BODY: DONNE, AFFLICTION, AND MEDICINE

STEPHEN PENDER

I N late November 1623, God was busy writing on John Donne's body. Between the seventh and twelfth days, 'critical days,' of a severe illness,[1] maculae appeared on Donne's abdomen. The '*spotts*' occasioned in Donne both a fear of malignity and a hope that, by their manifestation, his physicians will 'see more clearly what to doe.'[2] Already, his doctors had administered cordials and applied doves to his feet; he had been assured by their consultations and prescriptions that 'there are *remedies* for the present case.' Yet Donne's confidence in his physicians, and in accurate diagnosis and effective therapy, is frangible. Although the appearance of spots might 'declare' the nature of his infection, 'the malignitie may be so great, as that all [his physicians] can doe, shall doe *nothing*' (47, 67). Signs are suspect, disease is mercurial – it murmurs, mutates, and achieves its ends in secret (52). Unsure if the maculae result from the maturation of his illness or from his physicians' remedies, Donne compares his symptoms to a forced, public confession. Symptoms made apparent by physic are akin to confessions 'upon the *Rack*' and thus cannot be trusted to indicate cause or cure.[3] Until a sinner freely confesses, until 'we shew our *spotts*,' Donne argues, God 'appliest no *medicine*' (68–9). For Donne, the appearance of spots invites a taxonomy of

---

[1] Bedridden for over three weeks, recuperating for months, Donne was seriously ill; leaving his bed only once, on 3 December 1623, for his daughter's marriage to Edward Alleyn, actor and founder of Dulwich College, he was out of serious danger by 6 December. He did not preach until 28 March 1624 (Bald, pp. 448–55).

[2] *Devotions*, p. 67. See also Sister Elizabeth Savage's edition, *John Donne's Devotions upon Emergent Occasions*, 2 vols (Salzburg: Institut für Englische Sprache und Literatur, 1975).

[3] While both forced and voluntary confession meet with 'gracious Interpretation' from God, Donne clearly prefers a 'humble manifestation' of sin by means of '*corrections*' or affliction; when he confesses, Donne 'present[s]' to God 'that which is His' (pp. 69–70; cf. p. 108). Confession is medicinal; it 'works as a vomit' and as an 'ease to the patient' (*Sermons* IX, 304; cf. I, 114–31). On Donne and confession, see Jeffrey Johnson, *The Theology of John Donne* (Cambridge: D. S. Brewer, 1999), pp. 92–8.

sin; physical signs urge spiritual diagnosis. Thus the 'heates' that prick his body become God's '*seale*,' his variform signs avatars of spiritual crisis, and the maculae divine '*letters*' inscribed on his fragile, febrile body.

For Donne, as for his physicians, reading these signs and '*markes*' is 'intricate work' (46). 'I am surpriz'd with a sodaine change, & alteration to the worse,' Donne writes, 'and can impute it to no cause, nor call it by any name.' Imputing causes is fraught with uncertainty; it proceeds by conjecture, hypothesis, and abduction: 'we are not sure we are ill; one hand askes the other by the pulse, and our eye askes our own urine, how we do' (7). Although Donne is sure that every bone, every muscle 'hath some *infirmitie*' (116), the heats and sweats of his sickness (12, 34, 121), his melancholy (8, 34, 61, 78), and his loss of appetite (12) conspire to conceal the causes of his illness both from him and from his 'beholders' (15). Donne attempts to circumvent potential misprision by thickly describing his illness as affliction. '[A]ffliction,' he declares in 1625, 'is my Physick.'[4] Naming his maculae divine inscription does not obviate problems of spiritual or medical hermeneutics, for, like the sick king Hezekiah, Donne must test his faith in signs and, like Scripture, God's somatic writing is copious and metaphorical; God writes in figures and allegories (70, 99–100). If, in the days of prophets, God's activity in the world was confirmed by signs, shall we, like skeptical Pharisees, deny God's activity 'for all those evident *Indications* . . . which are afforded us [now]?' (74). 'But what is my *assurance* now? What is my *seale*?' Donne asks. 'It is but a *cloud*; that which my *Physitians* call a *cloud*, is *that*, which gives them their *Indications*' and they proceed to purge. His physicians have trusted his cloudy urine to indicate a remedy; however, noting that the Jews credited signs and that God has forsaken them, Donne refuses to trust these '*signes* of *restitution*'. Action taken on the evidence of uncertain signs, Donne argues, is imprudent. Similarly, to take physic '*not according to the right method, is dangerous*'. His physicians' counsel, like all counsel, is determined in action; evidence is tried by '*doing*'. 'Why then, O my *God*,' Donne asks, 'in the waies of my *spirituall strength*, come I so slow to *action*?' (107–8).

This deliberate intrication of sickness, self-scrutiny, scriptural wrangling, and semiotics typifies the *Devotions*, a text that documents Donne's 'Humiliation' by the 'furtherance of a vehement fever' (3, 83). Scores of early modern texts engage questions of spiritual anatomy, of sickness and spirit, of medicine and faith, but relatively few do so by mooring these inquiries to the suffering of their authors. Partly because of Donne's focus on his own purulent body, the *Devotions* fits awkwardly into the devotional tradition. Although, like most devotional writers', Donne's purpose is broadly ethical, the *Devotions* is intimate rather than merely didactic, 'experiential' rather than proscriptive.[5] The *Devotions* is a spiritual autobiography, a

---

[4] *Sermons* VI, 237.
[5] See, for example, Thomas Van Laan, 'John Donne's *Devotions* and the Jesuit Spiritual

'*Mortification* by *Example*' (82); it shares with the *Anniversaries* an attention to the passions, to reason, and to probable inference. The *Devotions'* structure, typology, numerology, and place in English and European meditative traditions have been interrogated thoroughly, and although it has been mined for Donne's views of sickness,[6] rarely has the *Devotions* been examined for Donne's attitudes toward medical thought.

While Donne's concern with sickness drew on metaphorical traditions present in scripture, the church fathers, and early modern homiletics, his knowledge of medicine was profound. Although he did not undertake formal medical education,[7] Donne cited and borrowed medical ideas from

Exercises', *SP* 60 (1963): 191–202; Joan Webber, *Contrary Music: the Prose Style of John Donne* (Madison: University of Wisconsin Press, 1963), pp. 183–201; N. J. C. Andreason, 'Donne's *Devotions* and the Psychology of Assent', *Modern Philology* 62 (1965): 207–16; Janel Mueller, 'The Exegesis of Experience: Dean Donne's *Devotions upon Emergent Occasions*', *JEGP* 67 (1968): 1–19; Reinhard H. Friederich, 'Strategies of Persuasion in Donne's *Devotions*', *Ariel* 9 (1978): 51–70; David Sullivan, 'The Structure of Self-Revelation in Donne's *Devotions*', *Prose Studies* 11 (1988): 49–59; Mary Arshagouni Papazian, 'Donne, Election and the *Devotions upon Emergent Occasions*', *HLQ* 55 (1992): 603–19; P. G. Stanwood, ' "In Cypher Writ": The Design of Donne's *Devotions*', *JDJ* 13 (1994): 181–5, and Kate Frost, *Holy Delight: Typology, Numerology, and Autobiography in Donne's* Devotions Upon Emergent Occasions (Princeton: Princeton University Press, 1990). Frost argues convincingly that the *Devotions* is a spiritual autobiography.

[6] The exact nature of Donne's illness remains an open question. While Kate Frost and Clara Lander have taken retrospective diagnosis to new heights and argued that Donne had typhus, it seems that Donne suffered from a combination of ailments, including relapsing fever, rather than from typhus alone. On sickness in the *Devotions*, see Gosse II, 181–96, 208; I. A. Shapiro, 'Walton and the Occasion of Donne's *Devotions*', *RES* n.s. 9 (1958): 18–22; Jonathan Goldberg, 'The Understanding of Sickness in Donne's *Devotions*', *Renaissance Quarterly* 24 (1971): 507–17; Clara Lander, 'A Dangerous Sickness which Turned to a Spotted Fever', *Studies in English Literature 1500–1900* 9 (1971): 89–108; Kate Frost, 'John Donne's *Devotions*: an Early Record of Epidemic Typhus', *Journal of the History of Medicine* 31 (1976): 421–30; *eadem*, 'Prescription and Devotion: the Reverend Doctor Donne and the Learned Doctor Mayherne – Two Seventeenth-Century Records of Epidemic Typhus Fever,' *Medical History* 22 (1978): 408–16, and Sharon Cadman Seelig, 'In Sickness and in Health: Donne's *Devotions upon Emergent Occasions*', *JDJ* 8 (1989): 103–13. In his introduction to his edition of the *Devotions*, Raspa offers a cogent account of the scholarship about Donne's illness (xiii–xix) as does Frost, *Holy Delight*, preface. The diagnosis of typhus rests mainly on the appearance of maculae, but various malignant fevers could occasion similar symptoms (see, for example, John Johnston, *The Idea of Practical Physick in Twelve Books*, trans. Nicholas Culpeper (London, 1657) VII, 36). Perhaps Donne suffered from a one of the 'combined fevers' (the *febres confusae*), which, like typhus, were amorphous in contemporary nosology; see Saul Jarcho, 'A History of Semitertian Fever', *Bulletin of the History of Medicine* 61 (1987): 411–30. For my purposes, and indeed for Donne's *devotional* purposes, the actual nature of his disease is less important than its spiritual significance. We should heed David Harley's warning that retrospective diagnosis is 'deeply misleading not only because it relies on naive acts of translation but also because it privileges supposedly stable modern categories' ('Rhetoric and the Social Construction of Sickness and Healing', *Social History of Medicine* 12 (1999): 419).

[7] Without evidence, John Carey insists that Donne's 'objective view of bodily organs was plainly stimulated by his medical education' (*John Donne: Life, Mind and Art*, 2nd ed. (London: Faber

Hippocrates, Aristotle, Galen, and Paracelsus; he used specific, sometimes obscure medical terms; he ruminated about the uncertainty of medical reasoning and medical practice; and he was profoundly aware of both continuity and change in the history of medicine and natural philosophy. Medicine provided Donne with the means and the metaphors to speculate about ecclesiastical history[8] and controversy,[9] to imagine the putrefaction and disintegration of the body, to discover striations in his heart during an imagined autopsy, and to offer his readers excursions on vapours, the perforated septum, purgations, and cordials. For Donne in the *Devotions*, as we shall see, medical thought encompassed clinical practice, therapeutics, anatomy, surgery, and hygiene. He had an acute sense of the work necessary to the maintenance of the human body, the 'true and proper use of physick'. Physical health, like salvation, is 'long & regular work'.[10]

With the exception of Winfried Schleiner's glassy dismissal ('Donne rarely appealed to any specialised knowledge'), three generations of scholars have recognised Donne's debt to medicine.[11] The 'intrinsic agonies' of his viscera,[12] his indebtedness to various medical writers for some of his most splendid metaphors, and his use of anatomical terms and concepts have received

and Faber, 1990), p. 144). Thomas Willard, 'Donne's Anatomy Lesson: Vesalian or Paracelsian?' *JDJ* 3 (1984): 35–61, relying on Allen's meagre evidence, claims that Donne studied Vesalius (37). Donne's medical 'education' might have been gleaned from his stepfather, the successful physician John Syminges, and his proximity to St Bartholomew's Hospital (Bald, pp. 37–8); it is also possible that Donne received some informal medical instruction while at Oxford, which was common in the second half of the sixteenth and early years of the seventeenth century (see Gillian Lewis, 'The Faculty of Medicine', in T. H. Aston, gen. ed., *The History of the University of Oxford*, 8 vols (Oxford: Clarendon Press, 1984–) vol. 3: 'The Collegiate University,' ed. by James McConica (1986), 213–56, esp. 238–41).

8   See *Letters*, pp. 13–16, where Donne uses 'Physick' as a model for the role of controversy in the development of the church.

9   *Essays*, pp. 50–1, 10–11.

10   According to the 'Physicians Rule', no man possesses 'true and exquisite health'. The 'best state of Mans body is but a *Neutrality*, neither well nor ill' (*Sermons* II, 80, 76). Sickness destroys health 'in an instant' (*Devotions*, p. 7).

11   *Imagery of John Donne's Sermons* (Providence: Brown University Press, 1970), p. 83. Compare Horton Davies, who insists that 'Donne far excels the rest [of the 'metaphysical preachers'] in the wide range of knowledge, varied experiences, in the esoteric reading disclosed in his images' (*Like Angels from a Cloud: the English Metaphysical Preachers 1588–1645* (San Marino: Huntington Library, 1986), p. 448).

12   See, for example, Mary Paton Ramsay, *Les Doctrines Médiévales chez Donne, le Poète Métaphysicien de l'Angleterre (1573–1631)* (Oxford: Oxford University Press, 1917), pp. 268–80; Charles M. Coffin, *Donne and the New Philosophy* (New York: Columbia University Press, 1937); Don Cameron Allen, 'John Donne's Knowledge of Renaissance Medicine', *JEGP* 42 (1943): 322–42; W. A. Murray, 'Donne and Paracelsus: an Essay in Interpretation', *RES* 25 (1949): 115–23; F. N. L. Poynter, 'John Donne and William Harvey', *Journal of the History of Medicine and Allied Sciences* 25 (1960): 233–46; and David M. Woollam, 'Donne, Disease and Doctors: Medical Allusions in the Works of the Seventeenth-Century Poet and Divine', *Medical History* 5 (1961): 144–53. The phrase 'intrinsic agonies' is Allen's (322).

thoughtful scrutiny.[13] If we accept Izaak Walton's assessment – and I shall argue that we should – Donne knew both the 'grounds and use of *Physicke*'.[14]

To substantiate Walton's view, here I focus on Donne's use of medical semiotics. First, I place the *Devotions* in the context of the early modern discourse of affliction; like other devotional writers and theologians, Donne conceived sickness as an emblem of sin. Imagining sin as the cause of sickness spurs the sufferer to probe and evaluate his or her sick body for evidence of the soul. In the *Devotions*, affliction inspires a rough materialism, motivating Donne to open and anatomise his body. He roots about in his viscera and discovers that there are 'no *sinews*, no *ligaments*, that do not tie, & chain sin and sin together' (48). However, once anatomised, his sick body must be '*read*' (46). In the second part of this essay, I examine the ways in which Donne enlists medicine in general and medical semiotics in particular, in the *Devotions* and elsewhere, as means to explore the relationship between rhetoric and reason, knowledge and inference, reading and rectitude. Either through the lens of affliction, through medical semiotics, or through a combination of the two, sickness is made visible. For Donne, mapping the contours of the soul as they are manifest in the body depends upon the ability to reason prudently from symptoms to syndromes, from signs to intentions, from bodies to souls.

My point is that recent critical attention paid to Donne's fascination with anatomy (that is, with *dead* bodies) has led to a relative neglect of the role of the living body, and thus medical semiotics, in Donne's thought. Although metaphors and methods drawn from real and theoretical anatomy served Donne and his contemporaries well, in the *Devotions*, suffering from an erratic fever, anatomy failed him. If his anatomical animadversions signify a desire to adduce what he calls 'God's method' (54), in his tractable semiotics I see a tempered attention attuned to probability, to the rhetoric of exemplarity, and to the living body as a manifold, perplexed thing. Medical semiotics offers Donne models of discretion, prudence, and sign-inference suitable for a diverse array of uncertain matters. Furthermore, Donne's experience of illness motivates an inquiry into the problematics of knowledge, which is central to his diagnostics of sin. For Donne, knowledge, reason, and judgement are embodied. 'All that the soul does,' Donne writes at Easter 1623, 'it does in, and with, and by the body.'[15] Even the '*Naturall faculties* . . . might preserve us from *some sinne*' (109). Thus, against claims that he is

---

[13] Willard, 'Donne's Anatomy Lesson'; Constance Elderhorst, 'John Donne's *First Anniversary* as an Anatomical Anamorphosis', in *Explorations in the Field of Nonsense*, ed. by William Tigges (Amsterdam: Rodopi, 1987), pp. 97–102; and David A. Hedrich Hirsh, 'Donne's Atomies and Anatomies: Deconstructed Bodies and the Resurrection of Atomic Theory', *Studies in English Language and Literature* 31 (1991): 69–94.

[14] 'An Elegie upon Dr. Donne,' line 46; *Poetical Works*, ed. by Sir Herbert Grierson (London: Oxford University Press, 1966), p. 345. All further references are to this edition.

[15] *Sermons* IV, 358.

'committed to an intellectuality that obviates emphasis on the senses',[16] I argue that Donne enlists the 'natural faculties' in order to confirm embodied experience as one key to knowledge of the soul.[17] In late November 1623, turning his attention to God's somatic writing, to symptoms and signs, Donne locates the coordinates of his soul in his living, sick body.

AFFLICTION IS MY PHYSICK

'How *ruinous* a *farme* hath *man* taken, in taking *himselfe?*' Donne writes in meditation twenty-two, 'how ready is the *house* every day to fall downe, and how is all the *ground* overspread with *weeds*, all the *body* with *diseases?*' The world is a 'diseasefull world.' Ruin and misery define nature, in which '*precipitation*' is the body's pace and measure (116, 57, 51, 11). Adrift in a sea of decay and sickness, confronted with the variability of his condition and the difficulty of discovering its natural causes,[18] Donne envisioned his sickness as a divine visitation that censured and chastised him for sin.[19] 'I fall sick of *Sin*,' he writes, 'and am bedded and bedrid, buried and putrified in the practise of *Sin*, and all this while have no presage, no pulse, no sense of my *sicknesse.*' Sin 'is the *root*, and the *fuell* of *all sicknesse*' (9, 118). Imagining sin as the cause of physical distemper enfolds the sufferer in an occasionalist, providential mode of thought: divine purpose is inscribed on the surfaces and in the recesses of the sick body. Although there was some variation, nonconformists, Anglicans, and Roman Catholics treated sickness in similar ways: it was an occasion to sift through one's spiritual inventory, to test one's faith, to engage and to exemplify tolerance, patience, and humility. All agreed that disease was purposively sent by God; sins were wounds, diseases corrections. Call this sickness 'correction', Donne writes early in the *Devotions*. 'Let me think no degree of this thy correction, *casuall*, or without *signification*' (14, 40; cf. 18, 34, 115). The experience of sickness argues God's presence in the world; many agreed with Calvin, for example, who argued in his sermons on Hezekiah that 'God faileth not to se[n]d down certein beames hither . . . he stretcheth fourth his hand hether by lowe to have care of us.' God sends his punishment to reward and to 'mark' the

[16] Frost, *Holy Delight*, p. 8.
[17] Terry G. Sherwood, 'Reason in Donne's Sermons', *ELH* 39 (1972): 353–74, and Noralyn Masselink, 'Donne's Epistemology and the Appeal to Memory', *JDJ* 8 (1989): 57–88, argue that Donne's epistemology is essentially Aristotelian–Thomist in its focus on the sensory apprehension of God.
[18] On the infinite number of sicknesses, see *Sermons* II, 62–3, 82 (Donne has 'a universall debility upon [him], that all sicknesses are in [him], and have all lost their names, . . . [he is] sick of *sicknesse*, and not of a *Fever*, or any *particular distemper*'). Although Donne assures readers of the *Devotions* that the exact nature of the illness is obscure, even trivial, elsewhere, he worries about the natural causes of fevers (*Sermons* I, 173).
[19] Schleiner, *Imagery of Donne's Sermons*, uncovers many of the antecedents to the vision of sin as sickness (pp. 68–85).

sufferer.[20] By way of *'dissolution,'* Donne writes, the sinner is 'married *indissolubly'* to God (80).[21] As one divine argued, God's power is more 'magnified and declared in adversitie' than in prosperity; Donne agreed.[22] Sufferers were enjoined to open the wounds and maladies of their souls, to confess their sins, and to seek forgiveness. Affliction, perseverance, and recovery were seen as benefactions; relapse, or 'after-affliction', signified obduracy.[23] '[A]ffliction is not evil; it is rather evil to have none.'[24]

Physical, spiritual, and material affliction manifests God's glory and indignation: it chastens human error; exercises grace as a 'tryall of . . . vertue'; prevents future sin; testifies to the resurrection ('the godly are . . . in this life so evill intreated,' so they may be assured of a 'blessed change and alteration' in the life to come); intensifies the recollection of Christ's suffering; and, if it is borne with dignity, suffering offers an example to the godly.[25] Through affliction, a sinner is tried[26] and granted the 'understanding' which makes '[God's] Image more discernible, and more durable in us'. Affliction is the 'seale of the living God'.[27] There is 'no greater cause of discomfort, then when wee are altogether free from afflictions'; to live without affliction is 'signe of weakenesse'.[28] As one late-seventeenth-century

---

[20] *Sermons of John Calvin, upon the Songe that Ezechias Made after He had been Sick, and Afflicted by the Hand of God*, trans. A[nne] L[ocke] (London, 1560), pp. 16, 53.

[21] Compare Charles Richardson, *The Benefite of Affliction* (London, 1616), pp. 33–4. As Donne insists, even though he is 'ground even to an *attenuation,'* because God's hand is upon him in his sickness, 'thou wilt never let me fall out of thy hand' (pp. 106, 33).

[22] Richardson, *Benefite*, p. 28.

[23] *Sermons* VIII, 215. David Harley, 'The Theology of Affliction and the Experience of Sickness in the Godly Family, 1650–1714: the Henrys and the Newcomes', in *Religio Medici: Medicine and Religion in Seventeenth-Century England*, ed. by Ole Peter Grell and Andrew Cunningham (Aldershot: Scolar, 1996), comments that 'afflictions, whether of mind, body or estate, were sent by God as a correction for sin, for the good of the sinner' (p. 277). Compare Donne: 'Even *casual things* come from *thee*; and that which we call *Fortune* here, hath another *name* above' (44).

[24] *Sermons* III, 67.

[25] Richardson, *Benefite*, pp. 29–39. In the most popular devotional manual of the early seventeenth century, Lewis Bayly provides a similar list of the benefits of affliction: it corrects past sins, cultivates a deep loathing of human corruption, weans 'our hearts, from *too much* loving *this World'*, exercises grace and seals divine adoption, demonstrates the veracity of divine love and the importance of service to God, furthers true conversion, instils pity and compassion towards others, exemplifies faith and virtue, refines humility and strengthens an individual's conformity to Christ, who was '*made perfect through sufferings'*. Most of all, affliction is a '*signe* . . . an assured *pledge* and token of [God's] favour and loving kindness' (*The Practise of Piety*, 3rd ed. (London, 1613), pp. 822–42, 799). There were at least twenty-two editions of Bayly's text between 1613 and 1640.

[26] The collocation of the law and sickness cannot be explored fully here, though it does figure largely in the *Devotions* (pp. 105, 121, for example). For the intersection of law and sickness in the *Sermons*, see I, 225; III, 203; V, 284–85, 334–5.

[27] *Sermons* II, 67, 354, III, 193; John Mabb, *The Afflicted Mans Vow: with His Meditations and Prayers* (London, 1609), p. 19. Mabb personifies affliction as a goddess (pp. 6–7).

[28] Richardson, *Benefite*, p. 45; John Hall, *Meditations and Vowes Divine and Morall* (London,

theologian insists, it is 'a most certaine *signe* of everlasting damnation, where a life is led without affliction'.[29] Affliction is not 'a punishment of sinne, but a tryall of our vertue'. The greater the affliction, the greater the glory.[30] 'I know,' Donne writes in the fourth expostulation, 'that . . . my sicknes [is] an occasion of thy sending health' (22).

Remedies for physical affliction were diverse: while prudently seeking the help of physicians, the sick searched scripture for types and examples of rectified suffering and implored the assistance of divine medicine. When his friend, the physican Simeon Foxe, is sent for, Donne asks 'how soone wouldest thou [God] have me goe to the *Phisician*, & how far wouldest thou have me go with the *Phisician*' (21). Donne's answer, that God has made the man, the matter, and the art, legitimises 'professional' medical assistance.[31] While sufferers were not supposed to refuse terrene medicine, divine physic provided the only certain cure.[32] In the eleventh meditation, Donne's physicians use cordials to keep his fever from affecting his heart. However, as long as he remains in 'this great *Hospitall*,' Donne writes, 'this Heart . . . will still be subject to the invasion of maligne and pestilent vapours'. Human medicine cannot provide unassailable prophylaxis against infirmity; every 'pestilentiall disease directs it selfe to the heart' (57). Even the ethical 'cordials' that maintain and strengthen the seat of the passions – contrition,

1605, 1609), book 1, p. 40, in *The Seventeenth-Century Resolve*, ed. by John L. Livesay (Lexington: University Press of Kentucky, 1980), p. 13. 'This is the proper work of sickness,' writes Jeremy Taylor, 'faith is then brought into the theatre, and so exercised, that if it abides but to the end of the contention, we may see that work of faith which God will hugely crown' (*The Rule and Exercises of Holy Dying* [1651], in *Holy Living and Holy Dying*, ed. by P. G. Stanwood, 2 vols (Oxford: Clarendon Press, 1989) II, 91). For contemporary conceptions of illness as providential, see Keith Thomas, *Religion and the Decline of Magic: Studies in Popular Beliefs in Sixteenth- and Seventeenth-Century England* (Harmondsworth: Penguin, 1971), pp. 90–132; Lucinda McCray Beier, *Sufferers and Healers: the Experience of Illness in Seventeenth-Century England* (London: Routledge and Kegan Paul, 1987), and Andrew Wear, 'Puritan Perceptions of Illness in Seventeenth-Century England', in *Patients and Practitioners: Lay Perceptions of Medicine in Pre-Industrial Society*, ed. by Roy Porter (Cambridge: Cambridge University Press, 1985), pp. 55–99.

[29] John Harris, *The Divine Physician* (London, 1676), pp. 9–10.

[30] Richardson, *Benefite*, pp. 31, 52.

[31] Ecclesiasticus 38:4. As Donne writes, citing Jer. 8:22, 'it is thine owne voyce, *Is there no Phisician*? That inclines us, disposes us to accept thine *Ordinance*' (21). Compare *Biathanatos* (London, 1648), pp. 216–17. In 'The Theology of Affliction', David Harley notes that even Calvinist nonconformists 'preferred learned medicine, both because they were expected to employ the best available means and because of the analogy with learned preachers' (280). Humphrey Everinden is typical: 'Seeke for the lawfull assistance of Physick in the time of sicknesse; it is as lawfull, as to seeke for meate and drinke in the time of hunger and thirst' (*A Brothers Gift: Containing An Hundred Precepts* (London, 1623), precept 82).

[32] 'Keep me back *O Lord*,' Donne writes, 'from them who misprofesse artes of healing the *Soule*, or of the *Body*, by meanes not imprinted by thee in the *Church*, for the *soule*, or not in *nature* for the *body*: There is no *spiritual health* to be had by *superstition*, nor *bodily* by *witchcraft*; thou *Lord*, and onely thou art *Lord* of both. Thou in thy selfe art *Lord* of both, and thou in thy *Son* art the *Phisician*, the *applyer* of both' (23).

patience, humility, obedience – are made redundant by the fear that accompanies a tenacious affliction. As a consequence, laid out in his bed of afflictions and affections, Donne implores God's presence in his sickness (for example, 60–1). To cure the '*sharpe accidents* of *diseases*, is a great worke,' Donne writes, and to cure disease itself, greater; both might be accomplished by human medicine. But 'to cure the *body*, the *root*, the *occasion* of *diseases*, is a worke reserved for the great *Physitian*' (116–17). God the punisher is God the healer: Donne is frequently confident in his physicians' remedies (for example, 49), but the profound infirmity, the deeply-seated 'venom' in the body, can only be cured by God.[33] 'Gods physick, and Gods Physician [are] welcome unto you,' Donne writes in a sermon preached at Lincoln's Inn, 'if you come to a remorsefull sense, and to an humble, and penitent acknowledgement, that you are sick.'[34] Divine '*purpose terminates* every action', including sickness (102).

God's purpose is epitomised by the exemplary suffering of Job, David, Paul, and Christ.[35] In the crucible of sickness, Donne has the 'desire' of Job to reason with God. Can Donne, like Job, lift up his maculate face to God and not fear? (21, 30, 69). God 'admits, even expostulation from his servants,' Donne writes, alluding to Jacob.[36] Fearing relapse, Donne takes comfort in Paul's example in 2 Corinthians 11: Paul was shipwrecked three times and still saved.[37] David, of course, is an exemplary sufferer, whose bed was sickness and tribulation, and whose lamentations balance afflatus with decorum, rectitude with fear (16, 18, 22, 53–4, 113, 125). David's example 'is so comprehensive, so generall, that . . . it concerne[s] and embrace[s] all'. In the psalms of affliction, '*David* was the *Patient*, and there, his *Example* is our *physick*.'[38] These examples help Donne manage and shape his own suffering (32–3). Unlike his use of scripture in the sermons, in the *Devotions* biblical passages, scriptural echoes, and citations are subordinated to his 'personal cogitations', legitimising rather than defining his intellection.[39] For Donne in 1623, perhaps the most powerful type is Hezekiah.

---

[33] On God as a physician and *Christus Medicus*, see, for example, *Sermons* I, 197, 303, 312–13; II, 179; III, 179–80; VI, 41, 72, 206.

[34] *Sermons* II, 94.

[35] Preaching on Psalm 38:2, a favourite text, Donne is inspired by 'the infirmities of these great, and good Men, *Moses, Job, Elias, Jeremy*, and *Jonah*' (*Sermons* II, 54). Frost, *Holy Delight*, deftly examines Donne's typology in the *Devotions* (pp. 39–77, *passim*). The *imitatio Christi* is a frequent concern; see *Sermons* II, 300; III, 332; X, 245–8, and Goldberg, 'The Understanding of Sickness in Donne's *Devotions*'.

[36] *Sermons* III, 145.

[37] *Devotions*, p. 127. Compare Richardson, *Benefite*, p. 17.

[38] *Sermons* V, 299; II, 74–5. Donne focuses on David's *experience* of sickness as an example to sufferers. '*Medicorum theoria experientia est, Practice is a Physicians study*; and he concludes out of events: . . . Therefore, in this spirituall physick of the soul, we will deal upon *Experience* too' (*Sermons* II, 76–7, citing Paracelsus).

[39] See Savage, *John Donne's Devotions*, pp. xviii–xix and Mueller, 'Exegesis of Experience', who

When Hezekiah was sick, Isaiah came to him and repeated God's words: 'Put thine house in order, for thou shalt die, and not live.' Hezekiah turned his face to the wall, prayed that God remember his perfect heart and wept bitterly. Unsure of his recovery, Hezekiah asks for a 'signe, that [he] shall goe up into the house of the Lord'. God made the sun rise ten degrees over the horizon after it had set.[40] During his sickness, with exemplary forbearance Hezekiah embraced medical remedies (38:21), the office of confession (18–19), and the knowledge of the true cause of his illness, sin (12). The 'life of my spirit *shall be kno[w]en*,' he says, using his affliction as an occasion to search the meanings of sickness and sin.

Often called to mind by David's suffering, Hezekiah's example exerted a significant influence on the discourse of affliction in the sixteenth and seventeenth centuries; it focussed Donne's and his contemporaries' attention on the spiritual and physical complexities of signs and sickness, sin and signification, recovery and representation. In 1616, for example, Charles Richardson argues typically that affliction 'is very necessary and profitable, because it causeth a ma[n] to know himselfe'. '[B]eing as corrupted and distempered as wee are,' he continues, 'wee stand neede to bee purged and let bloud by affliction.' As skilful physicians prescribe medicine to safeguard us from sickness, so 'the Lord use affliction to preserve his children from sinne'. He ends his sermon with the example of Hezekiah, who, 'religiously and devoutly affected in the time of sicknesse', made 'a holy Song of thanksgiving' upon his recovery. Richardson concludes that, by serving as an example of rectification, Hezekiah sows the 'fruit of affliction' by trumpeting his experience of sickness to the children of God.[41]

For Donne, too, Hezekiah is an exemplary sufferer.[42] In the *Devotions*,

argues that in the *Devotions* Scripture does not function as a 'recourse to authority', but as a tool to 'understand his crisis of body and soul' (pp. 3, 6, 17). As Mueller insists, in his sermons on Psalm 6, Donne's use of patristic writings allows him to draw 'figurative equivalents . . . of the physical symptoms and psychological states of David in his illness' (p. 12). The same hermeneutic applies to the *Devotions*.

40 Isaiah, 38:1, 7, 22; compare 2 Kings 20, 2 Chron. 32: *The Bible, that is, the Holy Scriptures* [Geneva Bible] (London, 1599). Though it is clear that Donne used the Authorized Version in the *Devotions*, the commentary and cadences of the Geneva echo throughout his work (see Savage, *John Donne's Devotions*, I, xviii, and *Sermons* X, 328).

41 *Benefite*, pp. 23, 67, 35, 34, 94. In 1622, Elias Petley travelled to London to preach on Hezekiah at Paul's, dedicating his sermon to Donne. In *The Royall Receipt: or, Hezekiahs Physicke. A Sermon Delivered at Pauls-Crosse, on Michaelmas Day, 1622* (London, 1623), Petley examines the 'admirable and royall patterne of *Hezekiahs* godly behaviour' (p. 1). Bald suggests that Petley, 'a rector of a Lincolnshire parish', would have been known to Donne through Peter Petley, brother or father to Elias (pp. 394–5).

42 Donne's interpretation of Isaiah 38 is common. See, for example, references to Hezekiah in Mabb, *The Afflicted Mans Vow*, p. 8; M.M., *An Ease for a Diseased Man. Published for the Instruction of Those which are Visited with Sicknesse of the Body* (London, 1625), pp. 10, 12. The author of the latter offers Hezekiah as an 'example' of a sick man 'exercising' himself in spiritual things (citing 2 Kings 20:2). In Nehemiah Wallington's collection of puritan letters

Donne takes Hezekiah, the king of Judah who '*writt the* Meditations *of his* Sicknesse, *after his* Sicknesse,' as one of his 'Examples' (3, 120).[43] 'I remembred that *Hezekiah* in his sicknesse,' Donne writes, 'turn'd himself . . . to pray *towards that wall*, that look'd to *Jerusalem*.'[44] Donne's use of Hezekiah's example establishes sin, divine medicine, and prayer as the central concerns of an afflicted Christian; he also focusses on Hezekiah's sagacity. Hezekiah's skill at reading the signs of his sickness, recovery, and salvation, his desire to know and make known the life of the spirit, resurfaces in the early seventeenth century as an attention to medical semiotics as one key to unlocking the meanings of sickness and sin.[45] Affliction spurred Donne and his contemporaries to search for a rudimentary knowledge of the soul via the sick, living body. Reasoning in this way required diligent, circumstanced sign-inference; an elaborate, specialised vocabulary was developed in order to describe the effects of illness on the body and the soul. Using these tools, and following the examples of Hezekiah and Job, Donne explores the ethics, rhetoric, and hermeneutics of affliction in order to '*reason with God*' (21). Donne's method in the *Devotions* is preparative, purgative, and restorative (108).

The rhetoric of exemplarity carries with it ethical and discursive strategies that emphasise accommodation and proportion: one's practice must conform to the example.[46] Sickness brings exemplarity into focus for

(British Library Sloane MS 922), Wallington recalls that in 1624 he was suffering from a fever and that he had 'little hope of life and then . . . turned [his] face to the wall (like Hezekiah) and prayed' (fol. 118v, quoted by Wear, 'Puritan Perceptions of Illness', p. 73).

[43] Frost, *Holy Delight*, gives the most thorough treatment of Hezekiah. According to Frost, Hezekiah functions as both an exemplary sufferer and an exemplary ruler for Donne and many of his contemporaries (see, for example, *Sermons* VIII, 238–9); he is also connected to traditions of temperance and, through number symbolism, eschatology (28–39, 44–52, 55–77, 124–5). Frost does not, however, discuss Hezekiah's sagacity or his exemplary prudence. One of the benefits of affliction, argues Robert Hill, is that it allows the sinner to set his 'soule in order.' By doing so, the sinner shall 'give example to such as come visit you, to doe the like' (*The Path-Way to Pietie*, 8th ed. (London, 1619), p. 449).

[44] *Sermons* II, 112. Other references to Hezekiah in the sermons include I, 233; II, 68, 70, 112, 157, 216, 357; III, 83, 206, 327; V, 191, 240 (which also refers to his prayer), 290, 349 (which refers to his medicine), 384, 387; VI, 47, 260, 311; VII, 58 (again referring to his prayer), 93; VIII, 238–45 (where Hezekiah is the figure of a just ruler), 279; IX, 185, 208, 387.

[45] As David Harley has argued persuasively, medical sign-inference offered divines ample material for diagnosing spiritual signs; see 'Medical Metaphors in English Moral Theology, 1560–1660', *Journal of the History of Medicine and Allied Sciences* 48 (1993): 396–415, esp. 411ff.

[46] On early modern examples and the rhetoric of exemplarity, see John D. Lyons, *Exemplum: The Rhetoric of Example in Early Modern France and Italy* (Princeton: Princeton University Press, 1989) and *Unruly Examples: On the Rhetoric of Exemplarity*, ed. by Alexander Gelley (Stanford: Stanford University Press, 1995). On Donne's use of examples, see Jeanne Shami, 'Donne's Protestant Casuistry: Cases of Conscience in the *Sermons*', *SP* 80 (1983): 53–66, and Noralyn Masselink, 'A Matter of Interpretation: Example and Donne's Role as Preacher and Poet', *JDJ* 11 (1992): 85–98. Masselink concludes that Donne is concerned to 'establish the

Donne.[47] Indeed, the sickbed is a school of adversity.[48] In such a school, teaching consists of rules and examples. As Donne argues in the sermons, 'the Rule itself is made of Examples'. Using a physiological term, Donne suggests that examples 'concoct' rules and make assimilation easy.[49] The knowledge of God is propagated by 'good example'; even 'God himselfe works by Patterns, by Examples.'[50] Writing about his insomnia, and mentioning several biblical figures who sleep and '*doe well*', 'Shall I have no use, no benefit, no application of those great *Examples?*' Donne asks (79). Examples must be used and applied: Donne's purpose in the *Devotions* is to edify and instruct rather than 'affright' his readers (15, 24, 90, 105). It might be enough, Donne allows in his dedicatory letter to Prince Charles, that 'God *hath seene my* Devotions,' but, like Hezekiah and like Peter in his second epistle, he has published these meditations as instruction to the community of the faithful. 'Thou has not opened my lips, that my mouth might shew *thee* thy praise,' Donne writes, 'but that my mouth might shew *foorth* thy praise.' Adrift in a sea of sickness, he owes to God the '*glory of speaking*' of affliction and to the community the duty of its application (17, 101). The '*exemplar* miseries of others' must be applied 'to our selves'; in another man's, Donne considers his own condition (88–9). Disease implies a community of feeling (25, 36–7, 121). Just as Donne takes cold comfort in the bells that ring out another's death, so too does he present his own trials as an example to his readers. Afflictions, as Henry Vaughan notes, 'turn our *Blood* to *Ink*'.[51]

validating power of precedent examples' but that this tendency is ultimately circumscribed by the necessity of multiplying examples (87, 93).

[47] In the *Devotions*, Donne applies his hierarchy of proof and the rhetoric of exemplarity to his own, sick body for a distinctly pedagogical purpose: as he writes in 1625, after his recovery, 'all example is powerfull upon us, so our own example most of all' (*Sermons* VI, 227).

[48] 'No Study is so necessary as to know our selves; no Schoole-master is so diligent, so vigilant, so assiduous, as Adversity' (*Sermons* IX, 256–7). Bishop John King writes of the adversity of the sickbed: 'The bed of a sicke man is as a schoole, a doctorall chaire of learning and discipline; then are his words written with an adamant claw, and go deepe into the minds of them that heare them; then is his tongue, the tongue of the learned, as touched with a coal from the altar; and his mouth the veine and fountaine of life, when the soule is weaned from the world; . . . he seeth and heareth those things which he never saw nor heard aforetime' (*A Sermon of Publicke Thanks-Giving for the Happie Recoverie of his Majestie from his Late Dangerous Sicknesse* (London, 1619), pp. 42–3). Jeremy Taylor thought the 'sick bed . . . a school of severe exercise, in which the spirit of man is tried, and his graces are rehearsed' ('Epistle Dedicatory', in *Holy Living and Holy Dying* II, 7). For Donne's meditations on the sickbed in the *Devotions*, see step three.

[49] *Sermons* IX, 274; cf. I, 292; III, 142; V, 50; VIII, 95; Donne cites Hippocrates when he uses the word 'concocted' in *P-M*, p. 20; cf. p. 27.

[50] *Sermons* V, 343; II, 153; IV, 93; *Devotions*, pp. 122–3.

[51] 'On Sir Thomas Bodley's Library; the Author being then in Oxford', line 21, in *The Works of Henry Vaughan*, ed. by L. C. Martin, 2nd ed. (Oxford: Clarendon Press, 1957), p. 633; as Vaughan writes in his translation of Henry Nollius' *Hermetical Physick*, 'every disease is an expiatory penance, and by this divine affliction, correction and rod of judgement is the

Tutored by fever in a 'good *University*', with his own ink Donne draws an 'Image *of* [his] Humiliation' (83, 3; cf. 48). The *Devotions* is a 'piece of art, & cunning', a 'shew of *humilitie,* and *thankfulnesse*' in which, Donne worries, he might have magnified himself without justification (43). Humility and humiliation are key words in Donne's lexicon; they imply patience, temperance, and decorum. Where there is humility, Donne writes on the first page of the *Essays in Divinity*, '*ibi Sapientia*'. Not a 'grovelling, frozen, and stupid Humility, as should quench the activity of our understanding', he continues, but a humility joined with studiousness, both of which are 'limbes and members of one vertue, *Temperance*'. In controversies about church ceremony and sacrament, 'humility . . . may, in the sight of God, excuse and recompence many errours, and mistakings'. Humility and temperance relate to prudence, decorum, judgement, and *mediocritas*; they also, of course, relate to the body.[52] As Donne confirms, 'intemperance, and licentiousness, deforme' both human bodies and the body of Christ.[53] Humility is Donne's shorthand for the qualities that define a 'constant' or 'neutral' man.[54] As he writes in the preface to *Pseudo-Martyr*, seeking to slough off the influence of his Jesuit education, he 'proceeded therein with humility, and diffidence in [his] selfe' by means of frequent prayer and 'equall and indifferent affections'.[55]

Throughout the *Devotions*, Donne is concerned with ethical and emotional constancy. Not only are sufferers subject to the violent symptoms of illness, but also their suffering is compounded by the passions and humours, by fear, melancholy, and 'vain imaginings'; '*fear* may disorder the effect, and working of [his physician's] practice' (29).[56] Donne contrasts the 'variable, and therefore miserable condition of Man,' his 'slipperie condition,' with the 'constant assurance' of God (8–11, 46–7, 105). Its causes hidden from view, sickness disorders the passions and faculties; the passions, in turn, disorder

---

patient called upon, and required to amend his life' (ibid., 587). Nollius' work was published in Frankfurt, 1613.

[52] Donne, *Essays*, p. 5; *Sermons* VII, 97, 104.

[53] *Sermons* VI, 268–71.

[54] 'Bee not over faire,' Donne writes, 'over witty, over sociable, over rich, over glorious; but let the measure be *Sufficientia tua, So much as is sufficient for thee*' (*Sermons* III, 235). Although the affections and passions were enlisted in Donne's ethical and theological inquiries, 'God delights in the constant and valiant man, and therefore a various, a timorous man frustrates, disappoints God' (VI, 108; cf. VI, 242). Health, for Donne, was a question of 'neutralitie' or humoral balance, which had both doctrinal and ethical meanings (*Devotions*, p. 74); on neutrality, see Theodore J. Tracy, *Physiological Theory and the Doctrine of the Mean in Plato and Aristotle* (The Hague: Mouton, 1969), and Timo Joutsivuo, *Scholastic Tradition and Humanist Innovation: the Concept of Neutrum in Renaissance Medicine* (Helsinki: Academia Scientiarum Fennica, 1999).

[55] *P-M*, p. 13.

[56] Fear has physical effects. John Johnston's description is typical: '*Fear*, dissolves the strength of the Body, by reason of the sudden recourse of Heat, Blood, and spirits, into the outward parts' (*The Idea of Practical Physick* I, 20).

human perception and action. Fear 'insinuates' itself into 'every *action*, or *passion* of the *mind*' (29). Although it can provide a certain 'ballast,' fear confounds Donne's 'tender, and supple, and conformable affections' (32, 34). It is the busiest and '*irksomest affection*'. On his sickbed of affections, Donne has melancholy and excessive passion in mind when he writes that there 'are too many *Examples* of men, that have bin their own *executioners*' (63, 68, 114, 122). Unfettered affections contribute to self-destruction, particularly when an individual is weakened by illness. The 'vapours' of pride, will, and invention must be subdued in order for the rhetoric of exemplarity, for the application of biblical types, to function (65–6). Yet, just as humiliations also taste of consolation, the passions and the natural faculties also aid the sufferer and mollify the experience of sickness (39). As one passion might drive out another, 'wee may correct in our selves one disease by another.'[57] Thus Donne seeks a 'middle heart' (and the heart is of course the seat of the passions), one that is broken and wounded with contrition, so that he is not betrayed a confidence in his own 'morall Constancie' (59). Ethical and emotional constancy mitigates the 'variable' condition of man.

For Donne, affliction indicates spiritual, ethical, and epistemological crisis (73, 115). As his physicians are not deterred from their practice by fear, so too Donne is undeterred from 'receiving from *God*, and *Man*, and *my selfe*, *spirituall*, and *civill*, and *morall* assistances, and consolations' (30). Temperance, for example, is not merely an admixture of humility, studiousness, and moderation. It is also the *use* and *application* of all three in the diligent searching of the scriptures, which had a practical, prudential corollary. Christians were enjoined to '*Scrutari Scripturas, to search the Scriptures*, not as thou wouldest make a *concordance*, but an *application*; as thou wouldest search a *wardrobe*, not to make an *Inventory* of it, but to finde in it something fit for thy wearing.'[58] A discernible path from biblical hermeneutics, from the judicious ways in which words and actions are interpreted as a reflection or series of effects of the divine Word, to normative human practice in the world is evident throughout Donne's work. Although the discourse of affliction partakes abundantly of paradox, practice in the sickbed should exemplify practice in the world. In human affairs, including sickness, we are referred to action and works as evidence. In 'the most eminent, and obvious, and conspicuous place, stands *doing*' (107). Fevers 'enrage us, and we are mad,' Donne writes in 1620; sickness recedes and erupts, recalling the perplexity and variation of human affairs.[59] Affliction implies its own careful ethics, characterised by humility, discretion, and application. Otherwise, we are '*active*, in our owne ruin' (62–3, 122).

In Donne and his contemporaries, then, affliction engenders meditations

---

[57] *Biathanatos*, p. 171, margin, citing Hippocrates' *Aphorisms*; on this citation, see Allen, 'Donne's Knowledge': 324.
[58] *Sermons* III, 367.
[59] *Sermons* III, 53.

on godly practice, community, physical health, and spiritual rectitude. Imagining sickness as affliction opens up several metaphorical and theological vistas – there are 'maladies' of the soul as well as the body, sin is a wound, God is a surgeon, sermons and devotional manuals disclose symptoms, causes, and remedies[60] – while it limits, to a degree, the necessity of establishing the exact nature of his illness or its specific, physical cause.[61] 'My *God*,' Donne writes in expostulation twenty-two, 'what am I put to, when I am put to *consider* . . . the *root*, the *fuell*, the *occasion* of my *sicknesse*? What *Hypocrates*, what *Galen*, could shew me that in my *body*?' The cause lies in actual and original sin, which stains both the body and the soul. Yet Donne is able to envision a body, 'before *inanimation*', and a soul, before it was 'infected' with flesh, free from sin. Although sin is the fuel and occasion of illness, 'that which destroies *body & soule*, is in *neither*, but in *both together*; It is in the *union* of the *body* and *soule*; and O my *God*, could I *prevent* that, or can I *dissolve* that?' (118). Sickness is about seeing ('mans infirmity requires *spectacles*, and affliction does that office') and what is seen in part are the ligatures with which the soul is joined to the body.[62] His soul is spotted; it has pulses, pulsions, and passions. The heats and sweats of his fever thaw Donne's spiritual coldness and 'indevotions'. Affliction is 'a fomentation to supple and open his Body for the issuing of his Soule'.[63] The symptomatology Donne enlists throughout the *Devotions* becomes a mechanism for probing the relationship between the body and the soul. '[W]hy is not my *soule*, as sensible as my *body*?' Donne asks, 'why is there not alwayes a *pulse* in my *Soule*, to beat at the approch of a tentation to sinne?' (8). Freed of the necessity of determining the physical causes of his sickness, Donne nevertheless employs medical thought as a way of establishing the relationship between his sick body and the state of his soul.

[60] Imagining, in Thomas Taylor's words, 'sinne as a gash or wound in the soule', conversion as 'the cutting of a sicke and wounded soule', the sickness of the body as 'the soundnesse and health of the soule' allowed for an application of medical metaphors to the process of repentance and salvation. Affliction was relieved by a 'vomit' (*Davids Learning, or the Way to True Happinesse* (London, 1617), pp. 135, 112, 81); see also, Richardson, *Benefite*, pp. 89–90. In his sermon on covetousness, William Wheatlie insists that he has demonstrated 'what covetousnes is, the causes, effects, signes, & remedies' (*A Caveat for the Covetous* (London, 1609), p. 127). On these metaphorical registers, see Harley, 'Medical Metaphors.'

[61] The 1559 Elizabethan prayer-book is unequivocal: 'Derely beloved know this . . . whatsoever your syckenesse is, know you certainlye, that it is Goddes visitacion' ('The Order for the Visitacion of the Sicke', *The Prayer-Book of Elizabeth, 1559*, ed. by William Benham (Edinburgh: John Grant, 1911), p. 130). M. M., in *An Ease for a Diseased Man*, agrees. Look 'not too much on the mea[n]es whereby, or the manner who thou are afflicted,' he writes, 'but looke especially to thy sinne, as the principall cause of it' (p. 4). The phrase 'earthly eye' is Mabb's: *The Afflicted Mans Vow*, pp. 16, 19.

[62] *Sermons* IV, 171.

[63] *Devotions*, p. 34; *Sermons* VIII, 190; compare Richardson, *Benefite*, p. 81. 'Fomenation' is a specifically medical term meaning the application of warmth (through cloth or medicated liquids) to the surface of the body. The term also meant cherishing with heat and instigating (see *OED*, 2nd ed.).

As the Anglican Daniel Featley put it in 1633, 'he that would learn *Theologie*, must first study *Autologie*. The way to God is by our selves: It is a blinde and dirty way; it hath many windings, and is easie to be lost.'[64] Donne's 'autologie' is characterised by a rough materialism that relies upon sense perception, example, sign-inference, and the stuff of the sick body. Thus our sick days, Donne writes, 'must be *criticall* to us' so that 'we may make a *Judgment* of our *spiritual health*'. In order to judge his spiritual health, Donne turns to his body. 'I know,' Donne writes, addressing God in expostulation twenty-two, 'that in the state of my *body*, which is more *discernible*, than that of my soule, thou dost *effigiate* my *Soule* to me' (119).[65]

INDICATIONS

In 1586, the physician Timothy Bright claimed that he had 'layd open how the bodie, and corporall things affect the soule, & how the body is affected of it againe'.[66] Writing about the passions in 1604, the Jesuit Thomas Wright thought that the contours of body–soul interaction might be mapped using probable inference. Wright is optimistic that he and his contemporaries might 'trace out passions and inclinations by some effects and eternal operations' as 'Philosophers by effects find out causes' by 'conjecture'. However, by the end of the book he displays a trenchant skepticism: 'I will infer our extreme Ignorance, that few or none of these difficulties, which concern us so near as our souls and bodies, are thoroughly as yet, in my judgement, declared even of the profoundest wits.'[67] Edward, Lord Herbert of Cherbury, a close friend of Donne's, claims that mind and body are so 'ingeniously united that the ways in which they interact elude our grasp'.[68] As we have seen, Donne's experience of sickness motivates a possible (and tangible) solution to this intractable problem: he argues that God has 'effigiated' his soul in his ailing body. Like an early modern physician, Donne presses the body into epistemological service: to anatomise and read effects is to begin to discern causes, to know the sick body is to begin to know

---

[64] Phineas Fletcher, *The Purple Island, or The Isle of Man* (Cambridge, 1633), sig. ¶4r.

[65] To 'effigiate' is to represent, to fashion into a likeness; it came into popular usage in the early seventeenth century. The *OED* cites its use by John King (1605), George Hakewill (1627) and John Wall (1628).

[66] *A Treatise of Melancholy* (London, 1586), sig. *iiv. Although he extols the virtues of a just, proportionate balance of the humours, which 'breedeth an indifferencie to all passions' (pp. 94–5), Bright writes explicitly against a strain of Galenism which claimed that the soul is nothing other than the proper proportion and 'temperature' of the body (cf. *Devotions*, p. 91).

[67] Thomas Wright, *The Passions of the Minde in Generall* (London, 1604; other editions 1601, 1620–1, 1630), pp. 165, 309.

[68] Edward, Lord Herbert of Cherbury, *De Veritate* [1633], trans. Meyrick H. Carré (Bristol: Arrowsmith for the University of Bristol, 1937), p. 151. On Donne's relationship with Cherbury, see See Bald, pp. 119, 184–5, 304–6 and Arthur F. Marotti, *John Donne, Coterie Poet* (Madison: University of Wisconsin Press, 1986), p. 196ff.

the sick soul. Both processes are difficult; even the signs of his sick body have 'sworn' to say nothing (7, 29, 52, 92). At stake in Donne's inquiry are the ways in which the visible traces of the soul, its 'pulse', are represented and examined. He does not seek to 'materialise' the soul; rather, with considerable felicity, he piles conjecture upon conjecture, metaphor upon metaphor, in order to test the limits of human knowledge and reveal reliance on probable reasoning. The intrication of sickness with forms of knowing is central to the *Devotions*. That his faculties and his senses on their own seem to fail him, then, is unsurprising: 'they see, that invisibly, & I feele, that insensibly the *disease* prevails' (52). Yet 'seeing invisibly' and 'feeling insensibly' epitomise the method by which Donne attempts to understand the union of souls and bodies in order to discern the ways in which 'the bodie, and corporall things affect the soule' and vice versa. Like contemporaries who employ affliction to devotional purposes, Donne probes wounds, sifts symptoms, and proposes various forms of piety as remedies; however, unlike his contemporaries, he nuances and interrogates the discourse of affliction. Sickness, for Donne, is a theological and epistemological problem. Donne draws his heuristic and metaphorical tools for this inquiry from a register with which his audience would be familiar: medical thought.

Knowledge of the soul, like all knowledge, depends upon the senses. '*Nihil in intellectu, quod non prius in sensu*,' Donne writes, following Aristotle, 'till some *sense* apprehend a thing, the *Judgment* cannot debate it; It may well be said in *Divinity* too.'[69] Faith is predicated on knowledge and reason; reason, knowledge, and moral virtue are neither redundant nor jejune.[70] Indeed, Donne's occasional mistrust of human knowledge is mitigated by the urgency of knowing the world, the self, and God. Donne's skepticism is based on his assessment of useless human learning, which often takes opinion for knowledge and probability for certainty. That scholars and philosophers engage in empty controversy is risible; arguing about opinion and perception, Donne insists, is futile. Its futility derives from the absence of demonstration in human affairs.[71] Nevertheless, to be 'a good Divine,' Donne writes, 'requires

---

[69] *Sermons* V, 176; cf. IV, 225. On Donne's conceptions of reason and knowledge, see Webber, *Contrary Music*, pp. 4–31, Sherwood, 'Reason in Donne's Sermons', and Masselink, 'Donne's Epistemology'.

[70] 'Mysteries of Religion,' Donne writes, 'are presented, and induc'd, and apprehended by Reason' (*Sermons* I, 169). '*Knowledge* cannot save us,' he avers in 1621, 'but we cannot be saved without Knowledge; Faith is not on this side of knowledge, but beyond it; we must necessarily come to knowledge first, though we must not stay at it, when we are come thither. For, a regenerate Christian . . . hath also a *new facultie of Reason*: and so believeth the Mysteries of Religion, out of another Reason, then as a meere naturall Man, he believed naturall and morall things' (*Sermons* III, 359). Reason and virtue are two elements in a 'close box of druggs' (*Biathanatos*, p. 41).

[71] 'Demonstration is the powerfullest proofe'; it is a spur to action (*Sermons* VI, 226–7). Compare divine with human logic: while 'the actions of men are so ambiguous, as that we cannot conclude upon them' and there 'hath alwaies beene ambiguity and equivocation in

human knowledge'. Thus his suspicion of reason is balanced against his view that necessary but insufficient probabilities are the stuff of knowledge: from 'ratiocination and discourse, and probabilities, and very similitudes, at last will arise evident and necessary conclusions'. In this world, 'we see nothing but outsides.'[72]

For Donne, to know is to make visible. It was commonplace to assert that '[r]eason draweth out and concludeth invisible things of visible, of corporall things it concludeth things without bodies, and secret things of plaine and evident matters, and generalles of particulars.'[73] Physical evidence – stars, comets, earthquakes, even human bodies – indexes the metaphysical. God uses natural elements and events to make visible the 'emblemes and instruments of his Jugdements.' Donne's Christmas sermon, 1624, proposes the birth of Christ as a 'sign' and he unfolds before his auditory 'what this sign is in general'.[74] 'Signes, externall things, assist' both natural and regenerate men in apprehending 'the visible means of knowing God'. Indeed, 'Man hath a natural way to come to God, by the eie, by the creature; So *Visible things*, shew the *Invisible God.*'[75] Things nearer to men are discerned more clearly because they are visible; 'we could not assure our selves of the mercies of God, if we had not outward and sensible signs and seals of those mercie'.[76] Yet there is a 'right way' to proceed from signs to things signified for Donne. This way is 'to go . . . from things which we *see*, to things which we *see not*'. Just as excessive curiosity about divine purposes is condemnable, to refuse the assistance of signs is obdurate.[77] God is perceived through '*reflexion*, & by *instruments*'. His 'blessed *spirit* instructs mee,' Donne writes, 'to make a difference of [his] blessings in this

words, but now in actions, and almost every action will admit a diverse sense, . . . Gods ordinary working is by Nature, these causes must produce these effects; and that is his common Law' (*Sermons* III, 226–9).

[72] *Sermons* II, 308; IX, 128, 254, 255; II, 151. Although reason is to an extent dependent on opinion, God enjoins man to embrace the lower strata of his hierarchy of proof, which Donne calls 'likelyhood' and 'faire probability' (*Sermons* V, 380; VI, 317). We are 'to exercise our owne devotions, we are content with similitudinary and comparative reasons' (III, 144).

[73] Pierre de La Primaudaye, *The Second Part of the French Academie*, trans. T[homas] B[owes] (London, 1594), p. 162.

[74] *Sermons* VI, 173, 169, 179.

[75] *Sermons* VI, 175; II, 253; VI, 217, citing Romans 1:20. Engaging Aquinas' meditations on Romans 1:20, Donne confirms the sensible apprehension of God's incorporeality; see IV, 167–8 and Masselink, 'Donne's Epistemology and the Appeal to Memory', 69.

[76] *Sermons* II, 254–5. On the seal as a form of proof, see Schleiner, *Imagery of John Donne's Sermons*, pp. 120–1.

[77] *Sermons* I, 222; III, 111; VI, 133. About Ahaz's refusal of God's signs (Isaiah 7:13), Donne writes that if 'God, of his abundant goodnesse, doe give me a signe, for my clearer directions, and I resist that signe, I dispute against that signe, I turn it another way, upon nature, upon fortune, upon mistaking, that so I may goe mine own way, and not be bound, by beleeving that signe to be from God, to goe that way, to which God by that signe calls me' (VI, 176). Hezekiah did not turn from God's signs, but demanded clear signification.

world' (44). Because it does not 'easily *lie in proof*, nor is [it] easily demonstrable by any *evidence* taken from my *heart*', even faith is made visible in works, actions, in 'the hand'. 'I know, my *God*,' Donne declares, 'that thou considerest the *heart*; but thou takest not off thine *eie*, till thou come to the *hand*' (106–7). How does one know if he has a soul, Donne asks at the beginning of *An Anatomie of the World*, 'unlesse / It see, and judge, and follow worthinesse, / and by Deedes praise it?'

What then might function as visible evidence of the human soul? When the bells ring out a neighbour's death in steps sixteen to eighteen, they spur Donne to speculate about the dead man's soul. His soul is gone; where, Donne asks? 'Who saw it *come in*, or who saw it *goe out*? *No body*; yet every body is sure, he *had one*, and *hath none*' (91). Inflecting his own rough materialism, Donne then takes issue with 'meere *Philosophers*' who understand the soul as nothing but the '*just and equall composition of the Elements in the body*'. The impious arguments of physicians and philosophers, who think the soul mortal and material,[78] and the idle disputes of philosophical divines, who contest the soul's '*immediate infusion from God*', lead Donne to draw an Aristotelian distinction between the tripartite soul as the principle of life and the lifeless '*clay*' to which the body is reduced when the soul takes 'but one step from thence to *Heaven*'.[79] Like a river that dries up over the course of a single day, when the soul departs the body loses its name and dissolves to putrefaction. At stake here is a form of representation adequate to the body's dissolution: 'wee cannot expresse it *so fast*, as it growes *worse* and *worse*'; even the image of a dry river is a lame picture, a faint representation, of its precipitation. If limning the body is challenging, what of the soul?

Philosophers distinguish sensitive, vegetative, and intellective (immortal) souls. 'The *immortall soule* did not forbid other *soules*, to be in us before, but when this *soule* departs, it carries all with it; no more *vegetation*, no more *sense*'; after the separation of the soul, the body is 'so much *bone*' (91–3). Yet all that the soul does, 'it does in, and with, and by the body'. The 'perfect

---

[78] John Woolton is typical: 'For whereas all men almoste consent therein, even by the authority of Aristotle, that the soule is of a differinge substance from the bodye, and cannot by any meanes be confounded or mingled with the same: Yet he is so affixed and coupled with the bodye, that they two make one person or lyvyng creature indued with many powers and faculties. And therefore Galen is well liked of manye, in that hee writeth, the soule so followe the complexion of the body, that it may seeme after a sorte to be a temperature of the same' (*A Treatise of the Immortalitie of the Soule* (London, 1576), sigs. E6v–7).

[79] If Donne asked not a few men, but whole Churches, about the souls of the righteous, the answers would be equally conflicting. Donne resolves these disputes by recourse to Augustine: 'It is the *going out*, more than the *coming in*, that concernes us' (p. 92; cf. *Sermons*, V, 354–5 on the unity of the tripartite soul and 'spirit'). This extended passage is largely a résumé of Renaissance debates about Aristotle's *De Anima*; see Emily Michael, 'Renaissance Theories of Body, Soul, and Mind', in *Pysche and Soma: Physicians and Metaphysicians on the Mind–Body Problem from Antiquity to Enlightenment*, ed. by John P. Wright and Paul Potter (Oxford: Clarendon Press, 2000), pp. 147–72.

naturall state of the soul is to be united to the body', both in life and at the resurrection.[80] We naturally love and desire the health of the body; God would not 'have us marre his work' and deform it with 'incontinency, and licentiousnesse'. In Donne's *vita activa*, the 'body must testifie and expresse our love, not onely in a reverentiall humiliation thereof, in the dispositions, and postures, and motions, and actions of the body, but in the discharge of our bodily duties, and the sociable offices of our callings, towards one another'. Deforming the body, the senses, and the faculties deforms the soul: the soul 'must have a body to worke in, and an Organ to praise God upon, both in a devout humiliation of his body, . . . and in a bodily performance of the duties of some calling'.[81] Knowledge of the soul is accumulated by a judicious reverence of the body and by the transaction of bodily duties (charity, for example) in a community. For evidence of the soul, God directs us to the hand, to action, and to works; this collocation is especially poignant in times of affliction.

As it renders mercurial signs meaningful and offers to reveal aspects of the relationship between the soul and the body, affliction brings to Donne's mind both the clinic and the anatomical theatre: in one, a cadaver is opened, its viscera exposed to view; in the other, a living body is probed and observed. Although close attention to the living body, to the 'constitution, and bodily inclination to *diseases*,' might sustain physical and spiritual health (119), Donne turns first to anatomy. Sickness, he suggests, is revealed by means of well-placed cuts. In a sermon preached in 1624–5, Donne uses his own anatomical knife and draws a parallel between the spiritual and physical searching of wounds.[82] Donne also dissects himself in the *Devotions*, offering his 'ruinous Anatomie' to his physicians' scrutiny.[83] 'I offer not to counsell them, who meet in *consultation* for my *body* now,' Donne writes, 'but I open my infirmities, I anatomise my *body* to them' (48). Although no anatomist can reveal the seat of sickness or sin, anatomy lays open the sinews, ligaments, and bones of sin that undergird affliction.[84] In these assertions, Donne is

---

[80] *Sermons* IV, 358.

[81] *Bianthanatos*, pp. 164–5; *Sermons* VI, 269–70; VII, 104, 107.

[82] *Sermons* IX, 256. Potter and Simpson suggest that the sermons on the penitential psalms in volume 9 date 'most likely' from the winter of 1624–5 (IX, 35–7). 'No wound is cured,' John Mabb writes, 'except it be searched, and that is painful to the patient' (*Afflicted Mans Vow*, p. 7, citing Hosea, 5:13–14, which Donne cites in the *Devotions*, pp. 23, 55). The notion of searching wounds is commonplace; see Barbara Lewalski, *Donne's* Anniversaries *and the Poetry of Praise: the Creation of a Symbolic Mode* (Princeton: Princeton University Press, 1973), p. 233.

[83] On self-dissecting figures, see Jonathan Sawday, *The Body Emblazoned: Dissection and the Human Body in Renaissance Culture* (London: Routledge, 1995), pp. 110–29, which treats Donne extensively. The phrase 'ruinous Anatomie' is from 'A Valediction: Of My Name in the Window', line 24; *Poetical Works*, p. 24.

[84] In the dialectic between the soul and the body, structural aspects of the body – its sinews, ligaments and bones – are transferred to the soul (see, for example, *Sermons* II, 84, 159, 288–9; V, 353; VI, 101; IX, 300–1). Sin even imprints 'deformity' on the soul (II, 56).

conventional; numerous early modern texts propose anatomy as the shortest and surest way to knowledge of the human body and to the disclosure of sin. What distinguishes Donne's use of anatomical metaphors is his sense that, while the 'body emblazoned' is a useful heuristic tool, the knowledge it produces is normative and static. Anatomical knowledge seems to lack the particularity (and the particularity of application) necessary for a living Christian; it merely exposes sin. If one accepts that anatomy in the early modern period is essentially about the soul, it is a very blunt instrument indeed.[85]

In contrast to the ways in which anatomy underwrites the 'provocative indeterminacy of the spirit–matter relationship' in Donne's other work,[86] in the *Devotions* the fluctuations of the soul are mapped onto the living body. From the opening of the text, even as he questions the possibilities of accurate somatic knowledge, Donne enlists forms of inference which attest to a dialectic between the soul and the body revealed by affliction. Adjusting his readers' focus from his 'open infirmities' to his symptoms, Donne writes that his physicans have 'seen me, and heard mee, and arraign'd mee in these fetters, and receiv'd the *evidence*; I have cut up mine own *Anatomy*, dissected myselfe, and they are gon to *read* upon me' (45–6). In this imaginative anatomical scene, metaphorical anatomy exposes hidden pathologies, but these, too, must be read and interpreted. His physicians read signs and indications; in his 'examination' of the traces of his soul in his body, so must Donne. The sufferer and the physician, then, have a similar, conjectural task: reading mute, probable, somatic signs.

'I am surpriz'd with a sodaine change,' Donne announces on the first page of the *Devotions*, 'and can impute it to no cause, nor call it by any name.' Nor could his physicians.[87] How 'intricate a worke then have they,' he declares, 'who are gone to *consult*, which of these *sicknesses* mine is, and then which of these *fevers*, and then what it would do, and then how it may be countermind'

---

[85] '[A]natomy in the western tradition was essentially about the soul' (Andrew Cunningham, *The Anatomical Renaissance: the Resurrection of the Anatomical Projects of the Ancients* (Aldershot: Scolar Press, 1997), p. 196).

[86] Harold Love, 'The Argument of Donne's *First Anniversary*', *Modern Philology* 64 (1966): 131.

[87] Two doctors attended Donne. Dr Simeon Foxe, son of the martyrologist John Foxe, was Donne's primary physician. During Donne's illness, Foxe, elected to the College of Physicians in 1630 and president from 1634 until 1641, probably consulted with Sir Theodore Turquet de Mayerne, first physician to both James I and Charles I. As Donne wrote, '*The King sends his owne Phisician*'; he calls Foxe his '*Physician*, who is [his] faithfull *friend*' (*Devotions*, pp. 40, 28). Mayerne was considerably influential both at court and in the College. Neither published in his lifetime. On both Foxe and Mayerne, see Harold J. Cooke, *The Decline of the Old Medical Regime in Stuart London* (Ithaca and London: Cornell University Press, 1986), pp. 81, 95–9, 103, 116, 266, 269, 281–2 and Bald, pp. 452, 454, 478, 510–33. On Mayerne's extensive casebooks and his theory of temperaments, see Brian K. Nance, 'Determining the Patient's Temperament: an Excursion into Seventeenth-Century Medical Semiology', *Bulletin of the History of Medicine* 67 (1993): 417–38 and *idem*, *Turquet de Mayerne as Baroque Physician: the Art of Medical Portraiture* (Amsterdam: Editions Rodopi, 2002).

(46). Donne describes sickness as 'manifold, and entangled'; any one disease may be 'made up of many several ones' (20; cf. 35–6). Earlier in his life, Donne claimed that assiduous medical practice afforded physicians a certain knowledge of disease. In 1623, his illness muted this view: fever had established its *arcana imperii* in his body.[88] His physicians employ their '*examiners*' against his disease, inferring causes from effects, but like the passions, illnesses 'complicate, and mingle themselves with every infirmitie of the body'; '*wind* in the body will counterfet any disease' (29). Donne's 'discomposition' is 'perplex'd' precisely because he and his physicians 'can scarce express the number, scarce sound the names of the diseases of mans body.'[89] In early modern nosology, fevers such as Donne's were labelled *febres confusae* (combined fevers). A combined fever is difficult to classify. All its 'symptoms and signs' are 'mixed together, and it is scarcely possible to tell them apart.'[90] Donne's contemporary, the physician Philip Barrough, classi-fies these fevers as '*Synochus*' because 'their nature is not all one'. They are called '*Erraticae*' since 'they keepe no certaine and just time, nor any order of fits, nor the intermission between them'. Some have 'manifest signes and tokens of rottennesse,' some none at all.[91] In a living, febrile body, sifting the signs of distemper, naming the sickness, and imputing its causes is the 'intricate work' of medical semiotics.

But how, Montaigne asks, 'shall [a doctor] find the proper symptom of the disease, each disease being capable of an infinite number of symptoms?'[92] In his treatment of 'symptoms, or signes' of melancholy in the body, Robert Burton echoes this commonplace sentiment: 'as the causes are diverse, so must the signes be, almost infinite'.[93] The complexities of diagnosis and prognosis preclude knowing if a patient is recovered by 'art or accident'.[94] As Hobbes put it in 1637, 'in *Physicke* Fallacies are pernicious'.[95] The negotiation of cause and effect, of the 'infinite kindes, manners and natures' of cause and the 'varietie of accidents' is an arduous task. The possibility of diagnostic or inferential error was grave: some symptoms 'bring certaine knowledge, some

[88] 'Of our bodies infirmities,' Donne wrote to Sir Henry Goodyer in March 1608, 'though our knowledge be partly *ab extrinseco*, from the opinion of the Physitian, and that the subject and matter be flexible, and various; yet their rules are certain and if the matter be ritely applyed to the rule, our knowledge thereof is also certain' (*Letters*, pp. 70–1).
[89] *Sermons* II, 62.
[90] The terms are Daniel Sennert's, from his *De Febribus, Opera Omnia*, 5 vols in 3 (Paris, 1641) II, pp. 657–63, quoted in Jarcho, 'A History of Semitertian Fever' p. 416.
[91] Philip Barrough, *The Method of Physick, containing the Causes, Signes, and Cures of Inward Diseases*, 4th ed. (London, 1610), sigs. p3v–p4v. He produces a 'tabula febrium' at 5r. Barrough's book went through several editions from 1583 to 1639.
[92] *Essays*, pp. 585, 587.
[93] *The Anatomy of Melancholy*, ed. Thomas C. Faulkner, Nicolas K. Kiessling and Rhonda L. Blair, 3 vols (Oxford: Clarendon Press, 1989–90) II, 381ff.
[94] Bacon, *Works* III, 371; IV, 63, 381.
[95] *A Briefe of the Art of Rhetorique*, in *The Rhetorics of Thomas Hobbes and Bernard Lamy*, ed. John T. Harwood (Carbondale: Southern Illinois University Press, 1986), p. 65.

artificiall conjecture, some matter of presumption and probability'; some symptoms are manifest and clear, some ambiguous, some significant alone, some ciphers. The symptoms that accompany fevers, for example, perplex even the most perceptive.[96] Diseases 'ofttimes . . . mocke one the other, that a good eye may easily deceive it selfe.' Illness does not only afflict the sufferer, it poses problems of inference since, as John Cotta insisted in his fervent attack on empirics in 1612, 'one circumstance alone co[m]monly altereth the whole co[n]dition.' Cotta's résumé of the problems associated with medical inference reads like a rhetorical treatise. Indeed, in order to interpret the probable signs of a sick body, physicians drew upon their training in logic, rhetoric, and grammar and cleaved to an 'idea of prudent deliberation' in order to 'judge rightly of the causes and differences of . . . diseases'.[97] As Bernard Lamy insisted in 1683, 'What can the physician do but conjecture?'[98]

In the early stages of his illness, before the appearance of spots, Donne's symptoms 'say *nothing*, . . . of any dangerous *sicknesse*' (52). After Donne experiences insomnia, sweats, and melancholy, his physicians observe that his illness falls on 'critical' days, and they offer him purgatives after seeing '*good signes of the concoction of the disease*' (97). In the constellation of the probable, what are these 'good signs'? They are '*Indications*, and *critical Iudicatures*'[99] which evidence an implicit hierarchy of signs in his physicians' scrutiny of Donne's sickness. In meditation thirteen, 'the *Phisicians* see more clearly what to doe' by indications (74, 67). Indications are 'outward declarations', 'witnesses' to the disease. Shortly after the appearance of his maculae, Donne's illness entered its '*Indicatory dayes*'. When, in steps nineteen and twenty, his physicians examine his urine and see a 'cloud', they are once again aided in their conjectures, in their schematisation of his illness, and in 'sensibly joining' effects with causes, by indications.

'The exquisite method of healing,' Helkiah Crooke wrote in 1615, 'cannot bee performed but by indications, and indications are not onely derived from the disease, but also from the part affected, and the remedies must bee changed and altered, according to the divers and severall nature, temperature, scituation, connexion and sence of the part.'[100] 'Indication' (*endeixis*) is an

---

[96] John Cotta, *A Short Discoverie of the Unobserved Dangers of Severall Sorts of Ignorant and Unconsiderate Practitioners of Physicke in England* (London, 1612), pp. 2–3, 17.

[97] Cotta, *A Short Discoverie*, pp. 2–3, 17, 118, 121–2; [Duncan, Eleazar], *The Copy of a Letter written by E. D. Doctour of Physicke to a Gentleman, by Whom it was Published* (London, 1606), pp. 22–5, 33.

[98] Quoted in Douglas Patey, *Probability and Literary Form: Philosophic Theory and Literary Practice in the Augustan Age* (Cambridge: Cambridge University Press, 1984), p. 64.

[99] A word meaning 'mental judgement; formation of authoritative expression or opinion' (*OED*). The *OED* cites Donne as the first usage, presumably from a sermon (the text is *Selections from the Works of Donne* [1840], citation at p. 205).

[100] *Microcosmographia: a Description of the Body of Man* (London, 1615), pp. 16–17 (page 16 is mispaginated as 14). Crooke is building a case for the supremacy of anatomy in medical practice.

ancient, complex medical-semiotic term; it could mean simply 'sign', but, drawing on classical medical semiotics, early modern physicians understood the term to mean a sign of sufficient magnitude or importance that pointed, often by analogy, to a cause. Indications suggest and define medical intervention. Not that indications are easily interpreted; they enlist a physician's 'mental sight'.[101] For example, Galen distinguishes between mere signs and *semeia endeiktika* or indicative signs which, by pointing to the cause of a disease, suggest a therapeutic path.[102] Discovery by *endeixis* is a 'method of inferring to some conclusion which involves reference to the essential nature of things'.[103] However, the term's cognates include *significatio* and *demonstratio*, suggesting that *endeixis* occupies a middle ground between the demonstrable, repeatable proofs required for science and rhetorical proofs that obtain in medicine.[104] But, as Crooke insists, indications are the primary starting points for any therapy since they point the way to causes and thus to effective therapy; indications are decisive. The accretion of several indications will clear a way, by 'long argument' and 'logical method', to the causes of disease.[105] With an adequate knowledge of anatomy and physiology, taking into account the whole course of the disease, a physician transforms conjectural signs into evident signs, thus making the basic structures of diagnosis possible.[106] Still, conjecture is central to this process. Indeed, probable reasoning 'is inference by way of *endeixis*'.[107] This conception of indication, and the rhetoric of observation that accompanies it, persists

[101] For example, in *The Science of Medicine*, Hippocrates, whom Donne certainly knew well, insists that what 'escapes our vision we must grasp by mental sight, and the physician, being unable to see the nature of the disease nor to be told of it, must have recourse to reasoning from the symptoms with which he is presented. . . . By weighing up the significance of various signs it is possible to deduce of what disease they are the result, what has happened in the past and to prognosticate the future course of the malady' (in *Medical Works*, trans. by John C. Chadwick and W. N. Mann (Oxford: Blackwell, 1950), pp. 87–9). Oswei Temkin puts the issue succinctly: 'The speculative element cannot be eliminated from medicine. It is both possible and necessary to penetrate beyond the visible, because what is visible does not account for the elements of which things are composed' (*Galenism: Rise and Decline of a Medical Philosophy* (Ithaca: Cornell University Press, 1973), p. 16).

[102] Fridolf Kudlein argues that 'one has to keep in mind that in all these cases, "indication" does not mean a mere "sign" but rather an action (for instance, "indicatio symptomatica" is not to be understood as "what the symptoms show"; actually, it points to the treatment of certain symptoms of the disease in question)' ('Endeixis as a Scientific Term: A) Galen's Usage of the Word (in Medicine and Logic)', in *Galen's Method of Healing*, ed. by Kudlein and Richard J. Durling (Leiden: Brill, 1991), p. 103; see also 105–6). The term could also be used in a legal context, as Donne does in his *Devotions* (p. 111).

[103] *Inst. Log.* 11.1, quoted in Galen, *On the Therapeutic Method*, trans. by R. J. Hankinson (Oxford: Clarendon Press, 1991), p. 204.

[104] See Richard J. Durling, ' "Endeixis" as a Scientific Term: B) "Endeixis" in Authors other than Galen and its Medieval Latin Equivalents', in *Galen's Method of Healing*, 112–13.

[105] Jonathan Barnes, 'Galen on Logic and Therapy', in ibid., 99–100.

[106] Garcia-Ballester, 'Galen as Medical Practitioner', in ibid., 34–5.

[107] Hankinson, 'Introduction', in Galen, *On the Therapeutic Method*, p. xxviii.

through Celsus, Quintilian, even Augustine until the early modern period.[108] It is prominent in Sextus Empiricus' criticism of the Stoic theory of language, later important for Montaigne.[109]

Largely through the scholarship of Thomas Linacre and Thomas Gale, the Galenic notion of *endeixis* was available to and utilised by sixteenth- and seventeenth-century English physicians and other writers.[110] A physician employing '*Semiotica*', according to Gale's Englishing of Galen, 'doth judge by signes, and toke[n]s' the nature and causes of disease. A surgeon ignorant of this aspect of the art, Gale continues, errs 'by mistaking of the *Symptomata* and accidents' of an illness. Chief among symptoms are indications which disclose the vehemency, magnitude, and potential for cure of a disease.[111] While its earliest use in England is in a Galenic medical text from 1541, the term seems to have a particular currency in the seventeenth century.[112] The 1657 *Physical Dictionary* explains:

> *Indication*, is some kind of signes or symptoms appearing in the sick patient whereby the Physitian is hinted, or as it were pointed with the finger to such and such a course of Physick or particular remedy, as abundance of blood.[113]

---

[108] See Heinrich von Staden, 'Anatomy as Rhetoric: Galen on Dissection and Persuasion', *Journal of the History of Medicine and Allied Sciences* 50 (1995): 63–4. Staden cites Quintilian, *Institutio Oratoria*, 5.9.1 and Aristotle, *Rhetoric*, 1393a19–1401a. Galen's Renaissance commentators focused on method and Galen's conception of medicine as a discipline of 'reasoning and experience'. See Neil W. Gilbert, *Renaissance Concepts of Method* (New York: Columbia University Press, 1963), p. 19 *et passim* and Oswei Temkin, *Galenism*.

[109] Sextus Empiricus argues that indicative signs are those which Stoics understand to be 'not clearly associated with the thing signified' (*Outlines of Pyrrhonism*, 2.101, in *Sextus Empiricus*, trans. by R. G. Bury, 3 vols (London: Heinemann, 1933) I, 215). Indicative signs, he continues, do not exist because they signify (if they signify at all) non-evident things about the existence of which there is much controversy (see also I, 227; II, 12). Inference by signs, he claims, will lead to regress *ad infinitum*, since neither the sign nor its signified is stable or evident (II, 124; I, 231). On indications in this context, see Giovanni Manetti, *Theories of the Sign in Classical Antiquity*, trans. Christine Richardson (Bloomington: Indiana University Press, 1993), pp. 100–3 and on the influence of Sextus, see Victoria Kahn, *Rhetoric, Prudence and Skepticism in the Renaissance* (Ithaca: Cornell University Press, 1985), esp. p. 119ff.

[110] On this diffusion of early modern Galenism, see Temkin, *Galenism*, Andrew Wear, 'Galen in the Renaissance', in *Galen: Problems and Prospects*, ed. by Vivian Nutton (n.p.: Wellcome Institute for the History of Medicine, 1981), pp. 229–67. C. D. O'Malley, *English Medical Humanists: Thomas Linacre and John Caius* (Lawrence: University of Kansas Press, 1965) treats Galenism in sixteenth-century England (pp. 3–25).

[111] Thomas Gale, *Certaine Works of Chiurgerie* (London, 1563), fols. 29r–v, 77r–v, 79r, 80r.

[112] The *OED* records its derivation from Paré. See, for example, *Galens Art of Physic*, trans. Nicholas Culpeper (London, 1652), pp. 45–6, 83–4, and so on.

[113] *A Physical Dictionary* (London, 1657). 'Indication' was used in its technical sense in the following works: Walter Bailey, *A Treatise of the Medicine called Mithridatium* (London, 1585), sig. E2r and William Clever, *The Flower of Physicke* (London, 1590), pp. 83, 101 (the first use of 'indicate'), 111 (using 'indicable' for 'evident'). See the entries under *indication* in R. W. McConchie, *Lexicography and Physicke: the Record of Sixteenth-Century English*

Marshalling the 'Sign before the Causes, that [he] might assist the natural method of humane Conception, in the finding out of things', the Polish physician John Johnston proposes a complex schema of indications as part of his method of healing or '*Art of Inventing*'. Drawing together semiotics, logic, and medicine, Johnston argues that the 'Indicant' is related to the 'Indicatum, as of a signe to the thing signified, or an Antecedent to its Consequent'.[114] The concept of the indication seems to ground the largely aleatory process of diagnosis: not only does *endeixis* stem the potentially infinite regress in which every sign might be an important symptom, but also it organises the disease temporally. Indeed, the relationship between antecedents and consequents and the sequence of events in time of sickness are crucial to interpreting the meaning of indications, which appear at critical times during an illness. Thus, following his physicians' lead, in steps nineteen and twenty Donne writes of indications and 'indicatory' days.

Disease has, as it were, two temporal registers: the first is the course of the disease itself (71, 97–8) and its critical, judicial, and mortal days; the second is its relationship to an individual's '*Climactericall yeares*' (73).[115] Diseases have crises, or 'swift and suddain change[s], . . . whereby the sick is either brought to recovery or death'; critical days are 'dayes wherein a man may discern a disease, or give Judgement upon it, be it good or bad' and judicial days are the number of days between crises in a specific illness. Calculated by the position of the moon in the zodiac, critical days are usually the '7, 14, 20, or 21, 27, 28 or 29. dayes of a sicknes'.[116] In order to calculate a critical, judicial, or mortal day, the 'day and hour [must be] knowne in which the sicke person tooke his Bed'.[117] When his physicians observe that his spots fall upon critical days,

---

Medical Terminology (Oxford: Clarendon Press, 1997). As McConchie insists, to 'scant the medical terminology of the sixteenth century . . . distorts the understanding of many commonplace modern words which began their lexical career in this specialist area, for example, deflation and *indication*' (p. 9; my emphasis).

[114] *The Idea of Practical Physick* IV, 1 and ff.

[115] The latter, in the 'virile', were ages 40, 60, 80, 100, and 120, or ages 9, 18, 27, 36, 45, 54, 63, and so on, or 7, 14, 21, 28, 35, 42, and so on, in those of weaker constitutions. Since the numbers varied, depending on the source, climacterical years were difficult to calculate; see Thomas Wright, 'A Succinct Philosophicall Declaration of the Nature of *Clymactericall Yeeres*,' an appendix to *The Passions of the Minde in Generall*, pp. 2–3, *passim*. Acute diseases, Wright argues, have odd 'decretory' days (p. 13).

[116] Nicholas Culpeper, *Semeiotica Uranica. Or an Astrological Judgment of Diseases from the Decumbiture of the Sick* (London, 1651) II, 17, 37; I, 5. Donne was clearly aware of some of the important aspect of astrological medicine. As he comments in the preface to *Pseudo-Martyr*, 'as *Physitians*, when to judge of a disease, they must observe the *Decubitum*, that is, the time of the Patients lying downe, and yeelding himselfe to his bedde; because it is not alike in all sicke men, but that some walke longer before they yeelde, then others doe; therefore they remoove that marke, and reckon *ab Actionibus lesis*: that is, when their appetite, and digestion, and other faculties fail'd in doing their functions and offices' (p. 26). Raspa briefly treats Donne's engagement with astrological medicine in the *Devotions* (for example, p. 164).

[117] John Fage, *Speculum Aegrotorum. The Sicke Mens Glasse* (London, 1606), sig. E1r.

Donne draws on astrological medicine in order to propose his physical crisis as a spiritual trial. Sifting through the varied use of 'days' in scripture, Donne declares that 'our daies must be *criticall* to us, as that by consideration of them, we may make a *Judgment* of our *spiritual health*; for that is the *crisis* of our *bodily health*' (73). He then envisions his illness conforming to an hexameral week, concluding that his final day, the day of judgement, 'is truely, and most literally, the *Critical*, the *Decretory day*' (76).[118] Yet attempting to divine the temporal progress of a disease is akin to interpreting '*Comets* and *blazing starres*, whose effects or significations, no man can' interrupt, frustrate, or foresee (51–2).

Basing their assessment of his illness on the appearance of indications (spots and cloudy urine in this case), Foxe and Mayerne administer purgatives. That his physicians act on these indications occasions in Donne rumination about the relationship between evidence and ethics, counsel and action, that questions his and his physicians' reliance on signs. Donne's skepticism marks the difference between probable sign inference and God's singular, secretive purpose. Although he admires the execution of his physicians' counsel (105), he remains unconvinced of its efficacy; instead, he shifts the coordinates of his physicians' action onto a spiritual register, arguing, with Galen, that physic that 'does no good' nevertheless might do no harm (108). Purging is a '*further weakening*' but such weakening is better than inaction (106). However, it is worrisome to Donne that Foxe and Mayerne, conforming to contemporary professional medical practice, ground their action on indications. For all '*evident Indications*,' for two reasons Donne refuses to trust in these various '*signes* of *restitution*'. First, it was not properly his but his physicians' intricate work to reason from indications. 'What it may indicate or signifie,' Donne writes, 'concerning the state of my *body*, let them consider to whom that consideration belongs' (80–1). Attempting to apprehend the state of the body based on symptoms alone is like drawing conclusions from 'single Instances'. Neither the course of sickness nor the course of nature can be prevailed upon (98). As Donne writes on the cusp of relapse, arguing that even the relative certainty of *endeixis* is questionable, 'wee must stand at the same *barre*, expect the *Physitians* from their *consultations*, and not be sure of the same *verdict*, in any good *Indications*' (121–2). The witnesses had been brought into court and interrogated, as it were, but refused to confess: his symptoms have 'all . . . sworn to say *nothing*, to give no *Indication* of any dangerous *sicknesse*' (52; cf. 35–6). Second, if he takes 'comfort . . . in the *indication* of the *concoction* and *maturity*' of his disease, his affliction might lose its spiritual lustre (100). A solely physical interpretation of his illness ignores the nature of affliction and imports too

---

[118] For Donne's awareness of time in the *Devotions* and the importance of the hexameral week to the text's structures, see Frost, *Holy Delight*, pp. 106ff. Donne's use of astrological medicine requires further study.

much of the probable into God's certain, demonstrable action. Care must be taken to avoid the fallacies of philosophers and physicians, who treat the soul as nothing but the '*just and equall composition of the Elements of the body*', and to avoid the temptation of thinking affliction itself as merely a '*Naturall accident*'. The indications by which his physicians prescribe, in which Donne might take some assurance, are 'but a *cloud*' (102–4); if Donne confides too much in these signs of restitution, God's significatory work is redundant. There is a serious and significant transformation here: Donne trusts his physicians, he employs the specific terminology and method of medical semiotics, but stops short of trusting solely in physical symptoms and indications as evidence of God's writing on his body.[119] Instead, he joins the implicit hierarchy of signs, at the top of which are indications, with strictures about proper textual interpretation.

Recall that God's somatic writing is, to human perception, copious and ambiguous. God communicates in '*Curtaines of Allegories*', commanding persuasions, and harmonious locutions; the Holy Ghost is 'amourous in his Metaphors'.[120] Scripture is at once the most eloquent and the most simple of texts; its very simplicity is an argument for its truth. Broadening the literal sense of scripture to include '*peregrinations* to fetch remote and precious metaphors', Donne folds several senses into one (100–1). The meaning of scripture, particularly the psalms, is reflected perfectly in its mode in order that men might better comprehend the intention of the Holy Ghost. 'Neither art thou thus a *figurative*, a *Metaphoricall God*, in thy *word* only,' Donne writes, 'but in thy *workes* too.' By this figurative language, the fathers of the church were encouraged to 'proceede the same way in their *expositions* of the *Scriptures*,' he continues,

> to make their accesses to thee in such a kind of *language*, as thou wast please to speake to them, in a *figurative*, in a *Metaphoricall language*; in which manner I am bold to call the comfort which I receive now in this sicknesse, in the *indication* of the *concoction* and *maturity* thereof, in certain *clouds*, and *residences*, which the *Physitians* observe, a discovering of *land* from *Sea*, after a long, and tempestuous *voyage*. (100)

Donne's use of 'bold' recognises at once the presumption of reasoning from probable signs to a certain conclusion (therapy and recovery) and the necessity of doing just that, given the limitations of human perception. God has, after all, afforded us visible signs; the question is, how are those

---

[119] In some cases, using methods similar to Donne's, symptoms were used to differentiate between affliction and a merely physical distemper, such as melancholy; see Bright, *Treatise of Melancholy*, pp. 182–7.

[120] *Sermons* VII, 87; for other examples, see Barbara Kiefer Lewalski, *Protestant Poetics and the Seventeenth-Century Religious Lyric* (Princeton: Princeton University Press, 1979), pp. 39–53. Donne's comments about the figurative nature of Scripture are well known; see Schleiner, *Imagery of John Donne's Sermons*, pp. 185–200.

signs, symptoms, and indications read? Donne's views about scriptural composition and interpretation echo his statements about the mingling of signs, symptoms, and indications in the book of the body.

For Donne, reading the symptoms of his body is a textual, rhetorical process. Expostulating on the consultations of his physicians, Donne images the universe as a gathering of texts (86). Although God appears 'subobscurely, and in shadowes' in nature, he otherwise proceeds '*openly, intelligibly, manifestly, by the book*' (48–9). To the books of life, nature, scripture, and laws, God has added 'the *Manualls*, the *pocket*, the *bosome books* of our own *Consciences*.'

> And if thou refer me to these *Bookes*, to a new reading, a new triall by these *bookes*, this *fever* may be but a burning in the hand, and I may be saved, thogh not by my book, mine own *conscience*, nor by thy other *books*, yet by thy *first*, the book of *life*, thy *decree for my election*, and by thy *last*, the book of the *Lamb*, and the shedding of his blood upon me; If I be stil under *consultation*, I am not condemned yet; if I be sent to these books I shall not be condem'd at all: for, though there be somthing written in some of those *books* (particularly in the *Scriptures*) which some men turne to *poyson*, yet upon these *consultations* (these *confessions*, these takings of our particular cases, into thy consideration) thou intendest all for *phisick*, & even from the *Sentences*, from which a too-late *Repenter* will sucke *desperation*, he that seeks thee early, shall receive thy *morning dew*, thy seasonable *mercy*, thy forward *consolation*. (49)

Interpreting illness is a question of diligent searching and judicious reading in the books of the body, scripture, and individual conscience. It is an explicitly ethical pursuit, in which Donne exhibits not hollow moralism, but an ethics refined by practice. From the evidence of, say, *Satyre II*, the sermons, and *Biathanatos*, it is clear that Donne excoriates textual and contextual 'detortion' as unethical ('turne[ing] to *poyson*'). In the *Essays in Divinity*, he sees the perplexities and complications in 'Textual Divinity'as the fruit of insincere translation, 'rasure and mis-interpretation', and the 'beggarly wresting of Scriptures' from their contexts. Misapprehension results from human 'transposition', from interpreters who indulge their caprice; with respect to *interpretatio scripti* at least, it has a history.[121] Those who illustrate the meaning of the Trinity by 'weak and low comparisons' are suspect, and those overcurious in their interpretations are guilty of 'ill Grammar'.[122] As an antidote, Donne seeks 'Meane waies' to sift the sometimes contradictory meanings of human interpretation. On the one hand, 'mean ways' exercise charity and, on the other, prudence and decorum.[123] During his sickness,

---

[121] See *Satyre II*, lines 100–2, *Essays*, p. 27, *passim*, *Sermons* IV, 142–3; VI, 56, 150, 179, 182; IX, 71, 150; *Biathanatos*, p. 20 and *P-M*, pp. 81–2.

[122] *Sermons* VI, 134; III, 166.

[123] 'The Litanie', lines 109–17; *Poetical Works*, pp. 312–13. On decorum, see Gosse I, 222 and on Donne's notion of charity, see, for example, *Sermons* IX, 94–5.

Donne applies the tools of medical semiotics and scriptural hermeneutics to 'particular cases', in this instance to the indications of his condition. Donne's model for medical semiotics is reading; in turn, the probable inference involved in medical semiotics is a paradigm of textual interpretation, of reading signs.[124] In interpretation's expansive workshop, the tools he uses, as we have seen, are humility, discretion, and prudence.

Even though his negotiation of the meaning of his sick body relies on adducing intention, purpose, and meaning from indications, immediately following the nineteenth prayer, Donne questions the ability to suture probable effects to causes. 'Wee cannot alwaies say, *this was concluded*', since for men '*actions* are alwaies determined in *effects*': once again, we stand at the threshold of action.[125] Yet in the natural world, of which the human body is part, the analysis of effects does not always confirm human assumptions about causes, thus muddying the waters of practice. His physicians' counsels are legitimised by their determination to act on their conclusions; while most arts and sciences are referred to intellection ('to the *head*'), the arts of logic and rhetoric, and by implication medicine, are referred to the hand, to practice (105; cf. 47). Practice requires prudence, 'constancy', and reason, but also the open fist of rhetoric. Indeed, the sick are distracted in their use of reason[126] and thus susceptible to suasion. Working on 'weak men,' rhetoric 'trouble[s] the understanding' and disorders judgement; but it also 'stamp[s] and imprint[s] new formes, new images, new opinions in it'.[127] Rhetoric could be perfidious, of course, but on the whole Donne draws an important distinction between rhetoric as empty persuasion and rhetoric as an instrument that enables and fortifies the work of reason and knowledge.[128] The basis of this distinction is the prudence and humility he identifies as the necessary constituents of both inquiry and action.

Donne writes in 1622 that, while the human intellect alone is incapable of fully expressing God, 'Rhetorique will make absent and remote things present to your understanding.'[129] Rhetoric is 'seeing invisibly', reasoning from effects to causes, from parts to wholes, from examples to rules; it is akin to a physician's 'mental sight' and one of the means through which knowledge is

---

[124] 'He that desires to *Print* a book,' Donne writes, 'should much more desire, *to be* a book; to do some such exemplar things, as men might read, and relate, and profit by' (*Sermons* VII, 410). Affliction itself is figured as a book (II, 354).

[125] Yet whether of sickness or sin, Donne prefers action and remediation over 'long *consultations*' (pp. 106–7).

[126] Donne thought his own understanding was affected by his sickness: everything that '*disorders* a faculty, & and the function of that is a sicknesse' (*Devotions*, pp. 81, 46; see also Taylor, *Holy Dying* II, 136–46). Like the sick, the 'habituall, and manifold sinner, sees nothing aright; Hee sees a *judgement*, and cals it an *accident*' (*Sermons* II, 114).

[127] *Sermons* III, 174; II, 282.

[128] Donne, *Essays*, pp. 16, 20, 56; for 'rectified reason', see, for example, *Sermons* III, 120, 258, 359; VII, 251.

[129] *Sermons* II, 87.

made visible. Like dialectic, rhetorical reasoning treats examples, which are gleaned from scanning 'the trueth of every case that shall happen in the affaires of man'. Rhetorical reasoning, making absent things present, depends upon practical, interpretive techniques, the most important of which is '*Analogie* or a convenient proportion . . . between the sence and the sensible' aligned with discretion.[130] This species of analogy is akin to *estimatio* and Galen's *analogismos*.[131]

In his last sermon, while experiencing his final sickness, Donne explicitly moors the concept of indications to prudent, rhetorical reasoning. 'Those *indications* which the *Physitians* receive, and those *presagitions* which they give for *death* or *recovery* in the *patient*, they receive and they give out of the grounds and the *rules of their art*.'[132] 'Presagition' means presaging, divining by signs; its cognate terms include sagacity and prudence, '*that* whereby the heart of the wise *fore*-knowest the time, and judgement.' In John Hall's words, a prudent man works '*according to fore-knowledge; yet not too strictly, and fearefully*'.[133] Foreknowledge requires imagining and deliberating about outcomes and counterfactuals, a process that seems not to apply to the dying.[134] But in charting the signs and indications of his living, sick body, in seeing invisibly and feeling insensibly, Donne offers a map of his soul's affliction. This process is aided by rhetorical inquiry in which 'absent remote things [are] present to [the] understanding'. Seeing invisibly is ultimately the work of a faith that embraces these probabilities as indications of the presence of God.

In the nineteenth and twenty-second steps in his sickness, Donne's thoughts about signs and indications, and about the intimate connection between medical semiotics, hermeneutics, and rhetorical reasoning, become clear. In expostulation nineteen, Donne returns to the question of whether or not it is sanctioned to use earthly medicine. At this point in his illness, his symptoms are acute and he seeks solace in the 'means', in his physicians,

---

[130] George Puttenham, *The Arte of English Poesie*, ed. by Gladys Doidge Willcock and Alice Walker (Cambridge: Cambridge University Press, 1936), p. 262. According to Aristotle, the example (*paradeigma*) is 'a variety of induction which brings out the meaning of a thing by comparing it with one or more other things which are like it *but clearer or better known*' (Gerald F. Else, *Aristotle's Poetics: the Argument* (Cambridge, Mass.: Harvard University Press, 1957), p. 19).

[131] 'Estimatio' was the apprehension of the inwardness of a thing together with its external appearance.' It might be defined, writes David Summers, 'as the activity of the first faculty by means of which the spiritual or inward could be intuited in particular things' (*The Judgment of Sense: Renaissance Naturalism and the Rise of Aesthetics* (Cambridge: Cambridge University Press, 1987), pp. 206–10, at p. 208; see also his chapter on prudence). For Galen's notion of *analogismos* (analogy), see Michael Frede, 'On Galen's Epistemology', in *Galen: Problems and Prospects*, p. 80.

[132] *Sermons* X, 241.

[133] *Salomons Divine Arts. of 1. Ethics, 2. Politickes, 3. Oeconomics* (London, 1609), pp. 28–9.

[134] We 'have no such rule or art to give a *presagition* of *spirituall death* and damnation upon any such *indication* wee see in any *dying man*' (*Sermons* X, 241).

granted him for his recovery. Yet if he focuses too much on means, even if they are legitimate, he is 'opened to great danger'. 'Except they who are our *ships*, the *Physitians*,' Donne writes, 'abide in that which is theirs, and our *ship*, the *truth*, and the *sincere* and *religious worship of thee*, and thy *Gospell*, we cannot promise our selves, so good *safety*.' The efficacy of the means – physic and physicians – is causally dependent on faith: 'meanes are not meanes, but in their *concatenation*, as they *depend*, and are *chained* together' (102). Once this concatenation is established, with occasional hesitancy Donne is able to reconcile purpose, means, and remediation and see, for example, that his cloudy indications also symbolise rainbows (recovery), pillars of the church (community), even God, who *'appeared in a cloud'* (103). Making absent things present depends on divine analogy, on a God of figures and metaphors. Buoyed by the ways in which a diligent searching of scripture, a comparing of place with place, yields consistent meaning, Donne applies the same hermeneutic to his sickness. Is that which gives his physicians their indication, Donne asks, but a cloud? His answer is that, metaphorically, God has declared himself in his cloudy urine. In the longest expostulation in the *Devotions*, Donne weaves together medical learning, scriptural exegesis, and an extended, traditional metaphor of sickness as a sea of sin in order to conclude that none of God's *'Indications* are *frivolous.'* God makes *'signes, seales'* and *'Seales, effects'*. His signs are the accidents of a sick body; his effects are consolation and restitution (103). The uncertainty of Donne's interpretation of indications is resolved in the certainty of God's method. As Donne writes, punning, God's 'purpose' establishes identity, links visible with invisible means, in the mutable and miserable life of men; divine purpose *'terminates* every action, and what was *done* before, is *undone* yet' (102).

'WHAT IT MAY INDICATE OR SIGNIFIE'

In 1626, Donne excoriates the state of medical learning. His contemporaries still looked 'upon the body of man, but with *Galens'* spectacles, he writes, lamenting that the progress, the 'emproving', of knowledge is neglected for the lure of the new. Much earlier, in 1609, Donne had insisted that 'the world at last longed for some certain Canons and Rules, how . . . cures might be accomplished'. He explains that, after '*Galens* time', humoral theory had become jejune because 'men perceiv[ed] that all effects in Physick could not be derived [from] these beggarly and impotent properties of the Elements'. More recently, he avers, Paracelsus' medical theory has been lauded, 'but (indeed) too much to his honour'.[135] Is Donne here as elsewhere exhibiting an 'esoteric knowledge' or is he merely rehearsing

---

[135] *Sermons* VII, 260; *Letters*, pp. 13–15. Donne's lifelong skepticism about the development of medical knowledge culminates in the *Devotions*, 'that treatise on the futility of medicine' (Allen, 'Donne's Knowledge', 336).

notions that could have been understood by most literate men and women in the period? The latter, I think, because of course Donne's point, whether in letters, in sermons, or in the *Devotions*, is to be understood. Even though recent scholarship has made much of his anatomical learning, for example, the metaphors he draws from the anatomical theatre purposely fail to rise above the commonplace.

What is uncommon is Donne's sure command of the terms and concepts, and of the metaphorical fecundity, of medical semiotics. Although the first scholar to evaluate seriously Donne's medical learning concludes that 'we hear little or nothing of cures or symptoms' in his work,[136] as we have seen Donne clearly indulges his knowledge of the promises and perils of symptomatology and medical reasoning in the *Devotions*.[137] Through his use of medical thought, not only does Donne offer an extended meditation on the 'poetics of corporal experience' that has garnered much attention in recent scholarship,[138] but also his '*Mortification* by *Example*' engages what Charles Coffin argued, over sixty years ago, are the two cardinal issues in Donne's work: his 'conception of the problematical nature of human learning' and the 'relation of the body and soul.'[139] These two central concerns – filtered, as it were, through affliction – are present on every page of the *Devotions*. As we have seen, both medical semiotics and affliction are discourses of cause and effect; in each, the state of the body is made subject, up to a point, to rational apprehension. But if, in the gradations of knowledge from probability to demonstration, the human intellect is confined to the lower strata, to 'crums and fragments of appearances and verisimilitudes',[140] how does one apprehend the state of the soul or God's intention in visiting men with affliction? How is individual experience enfolded in providential history? For Donne, these questions are answered by using available intellectual means (signs and sign-inference, for example) to discern God's purpose and method: building proofs using analogy and exemplarity, typology and scriptural hermeneutics, Donne establishes mediated inference from parts (of the body) to other parts (the soul) to, potentially, the whole (God) as the legitimate work of affliction. He uses medical semiotics, mixed

---

[136] Allen, 'Donne's Knowledge', 336.

[137] Donne's use of medical semiotics might be seen as one element in the construction of a 'grammatology' of the encounters between literature and medicine in the early modern period. As G. S. Rousseau suggested twenty years ago, 'The signs of Literature and Medicine need to be codified into a grammatology. . . . The record of suffering constitutes a gold mine waiting to be quarried, if we will only learn to decode its signs and languages' ('Literature and Medicine: Towards a Simultaneity of Theory and Practice', *Literature and Medicine* 5 (1986): 171).

[138] The phrase is Michael C. Schoenfeldt's, *Bodies and Selves in Early Modern England: Physiology and Inwardness in Spenser, Shakespeare, Herbert, and Milton* (Cambridge: Cambridge University Press, 1999), p. 171.

[139] *John Donne and the New Philosophy*, pp. 253, 277.

[140] *Essays*, p. 21.

with rhetorical reasoning and hermeneutics in affliction's alembic, to see invisibly and feel insensibly the presence of God in his maculate flesh.[141] In doing so, he recognises and mimics the practices of his physicians, whom he so diligently 'observe[s]' (29), and who attempt to discover the causes of his fever from its various effects. Like his physicians, Donne reasons with due temper and prudence, making absent things present; rhetoric and medicine are practical, interventionist arts and both are underwritten by examples and experience. Indeed, medicine is an 'art of inventing' and signs, examples, and indications are its 'grounds'. Like a rhetor, who 'does not create probabilities, but instead perceives them; . . . a doctor does not create healthful things, but instead perceives them'. The means of that perception are rhetorical: Donne uses analogy, sign inference, and the physiology of the passions to suture his afflicted body to his soul, presenting the 'image' of his humiliation as instruction to his audience. While it cannot lead to demonstrable knowledge of the soul, by revealing the limits of community and consent, deliberation and action, essaying the probable signs of a sick body cultivates discretion, humility, and constancy. Perhaps that is why John Rainolds, in his lectures on Aristotle's *Rhetoric* delivered at Oxford in the 1570s, thought 'medical practice itself will become a part of rhetoric'.[142]

---

[141] In the process, Donne realises that affliction itself has its signs and indications: it is a 'symptom of the working of the grace of God' by 'holy insinuations' (*Sermons* V, 347; VI, 230). As Donne writes in a late sermon, insisting that sickness prepares us for God, 'I shall thank my fever' (IX, 88).

[142] *John Rainolds's Oxford Lectures on Aristotle's* Rhetoric, ed. and trans. by Lawrence D. Green (Newark: University of Delaware Press, 1986), p. 161 ('Inno haec ipsa medicina rhetoricae pars erit'). For other references to rhetoric and medicine in the text, see pp. 159, 279–81, 331. On the relationship of rhetoric to medicine, see Patey, *Probability and Literary Form*, Nancy Struever, 'Rhetoric and Medicine in Descartes' *Passions de l'Âme*', *Renaissance-Rhetorik/ Renaissance Rhetoric*, ed. by Heinrich F. Plett (Berlin: Walter de Gruyter, 1993), pp. 196–212, and David Harley, who argues, in 'Rhetoric and the Social Construction of Sickness and Healing', *Social History of Medicine* 12 (1999): 407–35, that rhetoric structures and constitutes the experience of sickness and healing (420–1). I would like to thank David Colclough, Jeffrey Johnson, David Harley, and especially Tamara Kowalska for their patient reading of early drafts of this essay.

Chapter 12

IZAAK WALTON AND THE 'RE-INANIMATION' OF DR DONNE

JESSICA MARTIN

WHO was the author of Donne's *Life*? Izaak Walton himself, while ready to accept a formal responsibility for the *Life of Donne*, tended to reascribe the source of its claim to be read. He described himself as responsive mediator for a kind of creative partnership between the Holy Spirit and Donne himself: the divine '*hand of truth*', he explains in his Introduction, guided his own halting, provisional and contingent '*pensil*' sketch.[1] In this Walton uses the commonplaces of portraiture analogy and a modesty *topos* of particularly urgent utility to a lay writer embarking – most unusually – on clerical commemoration. He continues:

> But wonder indeed the Reader may, that I who profess myself artless should presume with my faint light to shew forth his Life whose very name makes it illustrious! But be this to the disadvantage of the person represented: Certain I am, it is to the advantage of the beholder, who shall here see the Authors Picture in a natural dress, which ought to beget faith in what is spoken: for he that wants skill to deceive, may safely be trusted. (p. 21)

A great deal has been written about Walton's use of portraiture analogies, and indeed about the professionalised nature of Walton's supposed artlessness.[2] Here it is perhaps only necessary to say that Walton posed his author textually via a method not dissimilar from that used to foreground professional aspects of Donne in this volume: that is, to divine clues of language from (usually) Donne-authored texts to a *persona* of public function; as (for

---

[1] Izaak Walton, *Lives of John Donne, Sir Henry Wotton, Richard Hooker, George Herbert and Robert Sanderson*, ed. by George Saintsbury (Oxford: Worlds Classics, 1927), p. 21. Unless otherwise indicated, all further references to the *Lives* will be to this edition: page numbers are given in the text.

[2] See, for example, Judith Anderson, *Biographical Truth* (New Haven: Yale University Press, 1984); Richard Wendorf, *The Elements of Life: Biography and Portrait Painting in Stuart and Georgian England* (Oxford: Clarendon Press, 1990).

example) Donne the lawyer. Walton attempted something comparable in 1640, mediating his 'reading' of Donne through Donne's words and self-consciously Donneian language to a remarkable degree. His declared concentration on clerical function has not, however, made him universally popular with the enlightened critic.

Perhaps the point may be illustrated incidentally by way of another posthumous – and overtly professional – treatment of the priestly Donne. In the *Life of Thomas Morton, Late Bishop of Duresme* (written by at least two men in Morton's service, Richard Baddeley and Joseph Naylor, during Morton's lifetime and published in 1669) we find this passage on Donne himself in an early section written by Baddeley:

> For doubtless the holy Spirit had the greatest stroak and power to incline, and draw him to that sacred profession: for my selfe have long since seen his Picture in a dear friends Chamber of his in *Lincolnes Inne*, all envelloped with a darkish shadow, his face & features hardly discernable, with this ejaculation and wish written thereon; *Domine illumina tenebras meas*; which long after was really accomplished, when . . . he took Holy Orders.[3]

When Morton died in 1659, he was ninety-five and had already had two commemorators working under his eye. The manuscript history of the Baddeley/Naylor account has a few dating clues: Baddeley makes it clear in his opening epistle that his knowledge of Morton extended only to the Civil War, and Naylor's section must have been written about 1650, since he says that Morton is a healthy eighty-six. When Naylor, who was an opportunistic snapper up of unconsidered trifles,[4] takes up the story, he tells us that his 'rude . . . Pencill' will 'darken and obscure' Morton's 'heavenly ornament'.[5] This is suspiciously Waltonian and written a secure decade after the 1640 *Life*. But was Baddeley's declared use of the *chiaroscuro* portrait as Augustinian conversion image of Donne's calling, seen and refined by Walton, or did it make explicit what Walton had only hinted? Or was the common source, for both Baddeley and Walton, Donne's own self-conscious stance?

It is not easy to distentangle the exemplary account from exemplary (thus, and also, histrionic) practice. Walton declares Donne's priestly intentions mainly through a peculiar and inventive combination of narrated preaching and dying, within a format – the commemorative preface – which privileges the exemplary particularly as it pertains to preaching and dying. On the other hand, preaching and dying combine in Donne's own writing in some curious and intimate ways. If the last third of the *Life of Donne* is an *ars moriendi* text,

---

[3] R[ichard] B[addeley], *The Life of Dr Thomas Morton, Late Bishop of Duresme. Begun by R. B. Secretary to his Lordship. And Finished by J.N., D.D. his Lordship's Chaplain* (York, 1669), pp. 101–2.

[4] For instance, in his adaptation of the opening words of Hooker's Preface to the *Lawes of Ecclesiastical Polity* to begin his section of his account of Morton: ibid., pp. 113–15.

[5] Ibid., p. 115.

it is, perhaps, collaboratively shaped; but the nature of the collaboration is as shadowed as Donne's portraits. The most common critical charge brought against Walton's *Life of Donne* (leaving aside questions of Walton's accuracy) is that the passionate and secular Donne was made subservient to the Dean of St Paul's. But whose was this intention, and how far in any case can it be said to be a true charge?

The conventions of the clerical biographical preface (the 1640 *Donne* was such a preface)[6] require exactly the subservience of secular portrayal to clerical exemplarity which Walton follows in the *Life of Donne*. This certainly complicates the question of Walton's faithfulness to Donne's intentions of self-presentation. Since the genre was also one which privileged consistency and piety especially in its account of deathbed decorum,[7] the latter question can at any rate be contextualised by looking at the extent to which Walton allows a profane or uncertain Donne to speak within such a context.

Walton begins the deathbed section by making a formal distinction between the shifting particularity of Donne's life and the perfected imitability of his dying: 'Thus *variable*, thus *vertuous* was the Life; thus *excellent*, thus *exemplary* was the Death of this memorable man' (p. 82). In doing so he borrowed Donne's own frequent uses of 'inconstancy' to characterise the mutable nature Walton would choose as a universalised point of contrast with his 'constancy' both of deathbed decorum and of 'modest assurance' (p. 81).

Donne, in the octave of *Holy Sonnet* XIX, writes:

> Oh, to vex me, contraryes meet in one:
> Inconstancy unnaturally hath begott
> A constant habit; that when I would not
> I change in vowes, and in devotion.
> As humorous is my contritione
> As my prophane Love, and as soone forgott:
> As ridlingly distemper'd, cold and hott,
> As praying, as mute; as infinite, as none.

Donne's joining of mutable penitence with 'prophane Love' to open his series of febrile paradoxes is picked up chronologically by Walton throughout the life in two ways. First, he flattens it into the simple sense that his profane years are deemed to be those of his youth, his 'penitential years' (p. 61) those of his age, and he divides the *Life* accordingly. The point of division is one of spiritual struggle and conversion, and Augustine's *Confessions* are made a hook upon which to hang Donne's own transformation of life: 'Such strifes as these St. *Austine* had, when St. *Ambrose* indeavoured his conversion to Christianity; with which he confesseth, he acquainted his friend *Alipius*.

---

[6] To John Donne the younger's edition of Donne's *LXXX Sermons* (London, 1640).
[7] See Jessica Martin, *Walton's Lives: Conformist Commemoration and the Rise of Biography* (Oxford: Oxford University Press, 2001), chapters 1–3, *passim*.

Our learned Author (a man fit to write after no mean Copy) did the like' (p. 47).

Donne's writing after the Augustinian copy is allowed to be textual and experiential: textual, in that Donne too is a 'learned Author' comparable to Augustine in his theological acuity; but equally clearly the shape of Augustine's life is being called upon to model Donne's transformatory change (he 'did the like'). Experience and authorship meet in the phrase Walton uses to describe Donne's decision for ordination: to 'put his hand to that holy plough' (p. 46), which he culls from the opening couplet of Donne's poem 'To Mr Tilman after he had taken Orders'.[8] Throughout Walton's description of Donne's conversion he eschews the word 'constancy' and skilfully employs the word 'change' only to mean a single and irreversible transformation, after which his Donne 'accounted the former part of his life to be lost' (p. 80).

But Walton does also make an attempt to deal with the clear signs, in *Holy Sonnet XIX*, that Donne will upset the shape of Walton's chronology by using the 'former part of his life' as an apt simile for the mutability of his devotional practice in his 'penitential years'. A possible allusion to the sonnet, somewhat buried, appears as part of Walton's set-piece preparation, via a comparison of two portraits, for Donne's final deathbed performance. 'Dr *Donne*' he writes

> would often in his private discourses, and often publickly in his Sermons, mention the many changes of both his body and mind: especially his mind from a vertiginous giddiness; and would as often say, *His greatest and most blessed change was from a temporal, to a spiritual imployment* (p. 80).

Although the reported speech underlines again the use of 'change' to mean single transformation, the 'many changes' of the previous phrases nevertheless stand outside the chronology, for the reader to place on both sides of Donne's conversion if so minded.

Indeed, the opening of the final deathbed section takes the word 'change' and applies it deftly and simultaneously to the mutability of a dying '*vile . . . changeable body*' (p. 80) (both Donne's, and, by exemplary extension, that of the thoughtful reader) and to the earnest expectation, over the fifteen days of his last sickness, of an 'hourly change . . . as his body melted away and vapoured into spirit' (p. 81):[9] that is, the final and most definitive transformation from dying life to immutable immortality. Donne's conversion, by this model, is only an imperfect anticipation of this most certain change to a state beyond changeability. Walton takes the formal comparison of two portraits of the young and the dying Donne, to introduce an astonishing

---

[8] John Donne, 'To Mr Tilman', in *Complete Poetry and Selected Prose*, ed. by John Hayward (London: Nonesuch Press, 1932), p. 304: 'Thou, whose diviner soule hath caus'd thee now / To put thy hand unto the holy Plough'. All other references to Donne's poetry are to this edition.

[9] See 'A Valediction: Forbidding Mourning', stanza 2: 'So let us melt . . .', p. 36.

deathbed, permeated with images of an unswerving will for death at the same time as it traces 'hourly decay' (p. 80):

> having brought him through the many labyrinths and perplexities of a various life: even to the gates of death and the grave; my desire is, he may rest until I have told the Reader, that I have seen many Pictures of him, in several habits, and at several ages, and in several postures: And I now mention this, because I have seen one Picture of him, drawn by a curious hand at his age of eighteen . . . and his Motto then was,
>> *How much shall I be chang'd*
>> *Before I am chang'd.*
>
> And if that young, and his now dying Picture, were at this time set together, every beholder might say, *Lord! How much is Dr.* Donne *already chang'd, before he is chang'd?* (pp. 79–80)

Walton may assert 'this is not written to much for my Readers *Memento*'; but that this is indeed part of its function is sufficiently clear: with Donne we regard the image of the shrouded body for which he has spent his last histrionic energies posing on an urn, against the 'giddy gayeties' (p. 79) of his youthful regard. The 'Motto' itself is altered in focus: the original Spanish *'ante muerdo que mudado'* ('sooner dead than changed')[10] becomes a statement which anticipates death's final change via the proleptic change of conversion, which stands both for mutability and yet for a decision towards, or plea for constancy. Walton gestures towards the declarations of the 1624 *Devotions Upon Emergent Occasions* for evidence of the aptness and longevity of Donne's study in *ars moriendi*:

> In a former sickness he called God to witness *he was that minute ready to deliver his soul into his hands, if that minute God would determine his dissolution.* In that sickness he beg'd of God the constancy to be preserved in that state for ever; and his patient expectation to have his immortal soul disrob'd from her garment of mortality, makes me confident he now had a modest assurance that his Prayers were then heard, and his Petition granted (p. 81).

The ephemeral nature of 'that minute' becomes a fixed state of mind which (or so Walton implies) lasts from the fever of 1623 to the final sickness of 1631: 'that minute' is placed in a textualised past frozen by the publication of the 1624 *Devotions*, and reiterated with a conditional prefix '*if that minute God would determine his dissolution*'. We know that he did not die in 1623, therefore God did not so determine; but Walton extends the possibilities of the crucial moment of preparedness by granting, retrospectively, a prayer for 'the constancy to be preserved in that state for ever' which holds Donne in readiness ('for he had studied it long') for him to die possessed of the

---

[10] See David Novarr, *The Making of Walton's Lives* (Ithaca: Cornell University Press, 1958), pp. 118–19.

certainty of an eight-year 'now' reaching its culmination 'in the last hour of his last day' (p. 81).

His 'constant infirmity' (p. 60) had been prepared for in Walton's section on the illness of 1623, allowed to mix almost indistinguishably into that of 1630–1 in the words 'God that then [that is, in 1623] restored his health continued it to him, till the fifty-ninth year of his life'. Thus from 1623 to 1631 we, 'his beholders' might indeed 'say, as St *Paul* of himself, *He dyes daily*': that is, Donne participates physically in a constant show of mutability through 'frequent Fevers' (p. 73) – fevers which also recall the images of *Sonnet XIX*'s octave.

The tableau of perfect decay is finally closed for us in Donne's last physical act, described as simultaneous with the departure of his spirit and exhalation of his dying breath, but seeming to follow both in Walton's syntax: 'As his soul ascended, and his last breath departed from him, he closed his own eyes; and then disposed his hands and body into such a posture as required not the least alteration by those that came to shroud him'. It looks as if Donne died first 'and then' arranged himself ready for burial: for a second time, he has twitched the folds of his shroud into a becoming 'posture as required not the least alteration'; but Walton, this time, is the painter who makes immortality out of changeableness. Perhaps the homiletic usefulness of his portrayal was what made him able to dare to replace Donne's assertion, made in *Deaths Dvell*, that 'it is *not . . .* the last *word* nor *gaspe* that *qualifies* the *soule*' with a description which so strongly implies that it did.

We see another, rather different instance of Walton's use of a Donneian image in the theological wit of the peroration to his concluding Character. Here he recasts a joint authorship for the *Life* of the Almighty and Donne himself by transforming Donne's words into God's acts. Donne had written of the Holy Ghost this in 'The Litanie':

> O Holy Ghost, whose temple I
> Am, but of mudde walls, and condensed dust,
>   And being sacrilegiously
> Halfe wasted with youths fires, of pride and lust,
>   Must with new stormes be weatherbeat;
>   Double in my heart thy flame
> Which let devout sad teares intend; and let
> (Though this glasse lanthorne, flesh, do suffer maime)
> Fire, Sacrifice, Priest, Altar be the same.[11]

Walton takes Donne's Pauline image of the brittle temple of 'condensed dust' and submerges 'youths fires' into a finished past by using his favourite word (or act) of oblivion: 'now'. At the same time the 'glasse lanthorne' which is

---

[11] John Donne, 'The Litanie', stanza 3, lines 19–27, in *Donne's Poetical Works*, ed. by H. J. C. Grierson, 2 vols (Oxford: Clarendon Press, 1912) I, pp. 338–9.

Donne's transparent living body is collapsed into a heap of 'Christian dust'; the 'mudde walls' of this temple become desiccated rubble: 'those bodies that were the *temples of the holy Ghost*, come to this *dilapidation*, to ruine, to rubbidge, to dust' – as Donne puts it in *Deaths Dvell*.[12] The passion of 'devout sad teares' which attend simultaneously on carnal and heavenly fire in 'The Litanie' (dowsing the first while fuelling the second in paradox) are transmuted into a description of longing satisfied:

> He was earnest and unwearied in the search for knowledge; with which, his vigorous soul is now satisfied, and employed in a continual praise of that God that once breathed it into his active body; that body, which once was a Temple of the Holy Ghost, and is now become a small quantity of Christian dust.
>   But I shall see it re-animated (p. 84).

Where Donne's verse looks forward out of imperfection to the perfected moment of a completed heart: 'Fire, Sacrifice, Priest, Altar be the same', Walton uses it retrospectively to celebrate the union his subject desires. He moves from a narrative-led past tense '*He was earnest and unwearied*' to an effectively continuous present transparently intended to signify eternity: '*his vigorous soul is now satisfied, and employed in a continual praise of . . . God*'. The deft insertion of the indefinite article before '*continual*' (making the eternal Now pointedly one action *in process*) is a remarkable balance to the repeated (and thus inconclusive) narrative actions of the living Donne's search for knowledge, and to the perfect single action of God's first animation of the dust that became Donne.

So far so elegantly orthodox. The last line, though, is startling: '*But I shall see it re-animated*'. Even on the terms it retains here, in Walton's last and best known revision of 1675, concluding what is acknowledged to be biography pure and simple (Dryden had even invented the word by then),[13] the first-person pronoun stands out. '*I shall see*', where '*I*' is viewed in conjunction with a future tense offered with no hint of the provisional and yet governing a verb '*see*' apparently chosen to minimise any suggestion of agency on the part of the speaker, Walton seems here to beg a question or two. What shall he do to see? *Shall* he do to see, or is the passivity of seeing his only acknowledging marker of divine grace? In what context shall he see? The sentence expresses a notably firm conviction of the speaker's salvation (especially for its first manifestation of 1640), view it how you will; but it is worth observing that this is a stance adopted to allow Walton to act in his preferred role of authentic witness to the immortality of his subject.

If we look at Walton's original version of 1640 other vital dimensions emerge. The 1640 *Life of Donne* appeared in a clerical context where it was a commonplace not only that the printed words of deceased subjects operated

---

[12] 'Deaths Dvell', p. 748.
[13] See *OED*, 'biography', which gives its first usage as 1666.

as an effective metaphor for immortality, but that their acts in life (which were, after all, rather frequently sermons) should be perceived conversely as 'walking texts', or 'words translated into works'.[14] These awaited only a commemorator – biographer, editor or both – to live posthumously in print, and thus to obtain experiential longevity in the imitative acts of readers. 'He being dead yet speaketh' a quotation taken more or less wilfully out of context from Hebrews 11:4, was one of the most frequently reiterated seventeenth-century commonplaces of the clerical funeral sermon and thus of the commemorative preface, running from the 1620s comfortably into the next century.[15] Walton, though, never quotes it. A literal minded man, he went one better: he did it. While Donne speaks throughout the *Life*, in eminently traceable paraphrase or straight quotation (though the context might sometimes have given him pause), I want here to consider Walton's mediation as it appears in this affirmation of the resurrection of the body; both corpse and *corpus*.

In 1640 Walton rendered the *Life*'s last sentence: '*But I shall see it re-inanimated*'.[16] The *OED* gives us only one user of this remarkable word, and it is Donne. Apparently its earliest printed example dates as late as the *XXVI Sermons* of 1660, where it appears as 're-inanimating' in *Deaths Dvell*. Certainly earlier editions of *Deaths Dvell* do not use it: in 1632 one finds 'reanimating' and in the second edition of 1633, the edition we know Walton owned, the rather disappointing word 'remaining' is inserted.[17] Yet if one was narrating Donne's death in Donne's words, one would surely go straight to *Deaths Dvell*? Certainly Walton uses it heavily in the rest of his narrative of Donne's long-drawn-out dying process; and the antitheses of its subtitle 'a Consolation to the Soule, Against the Dying Life, and Living Death of the Body' permeate his deathbed narrative, where decay always signifies immortality and life always harbours incipient dissolution. And where, if not there, did Walton get 're-inanimated' from in 1640?

The answer is that Donne used it in his evening sermon in St Paul's for Easter Day 1626, preaching on 1 Corinthians 15:20: 'Else what shall they do that are baptized for dead? If the dead rise not at all, why are they then baptized for dead?'[18] The text for *Deaths Dvell* from Psalm 68 was to answer Paul's question: 'to God the Lord belong the issues from death'. But the later sermon uses the certainty of the psalmist's promise as a licence to

[14] Samuel Clarke, *The Life of Samuel Crook*, in *Lives of Thirty-Two Eminent Divines, in a General Martyrologie, Containing a Collection of all the Greatest Persecutions . . .*, 3rd edition (London, 1677), second pagination, p. 204.

[15] See Martin, *Walton's Lives*, chapter 3.

[16] Walton, *Life of Donne*, in John Donne, *LXXX Sermons*, ed. by John Donne the younger (London, 1640), sig. C1.

[17] John Donne, 'Deaths Dvell, or, a Consolation to the Soule, Against the Dying Life, and Living Death of the Body . . .' in *XXVI Sermons* (London, 1660), p. 405; *Deaths Dvell* (London, 1632), p. 17; *Deaths Dvell*, 2nd edition (London, 1633), p. 17.

[18] *Sermons* VII, 112–17.

meditate upon the particularities of corruption: the *exitus a morte*, God's deliverance from the death-in-life which encompasses us from womb to grave, is notably an

> *introitus in mortem;* though it bee an *issue from* the manifold *deaths* of this *world*, yet it is an *entrance* into the *death of corruption* and *putrefaction* and *vermiculation* and *incineration,* and dispersion in and from the *grave*, in which every dead man dies over again.[19]

Yet the former sermon, the text of which offers no such assurance, affirms resurrection with as little ambivalence as Donne is ever able to manage. Both sermons, in their sister passages on 're-inanimation' use the same textual frame; Paul and the psalmist each give way to Ezekiel in the valley of dry bones – the text Walton also recalls as he describes Donne preaching *Deaths Dvell.*

> And, when to the amazement of some beholders he appeared in the Pulpit, many of them thought he presented himself not to preach mortification by a living voice: but, mortality by a decayed body and dying face. And, doubtless, many did secretly ask that question in *Ezekiel; Do these bones live?* Or, *can that soul organize that tongue, to speak so long a time as the sand in that glass will move towards its centre, and measure out an hour of this dying man's unspent life?*
> (p. 75)

Only the first italicised question 'Do these bones live?' is from Ezekiel 37:3 (the marginal reference Walton gives); the meditations which follow are again variations which recall the Walton's games with time, as the measuring hourglass (recalling not only Donne's 'glass lanthorne' but Herbert's fleshly 'glasse, which holds the dust/that measures all our time' in 'Church-Monuments') becomes a kind of synecdoche for the 'living voice' which balances itself against the exemplary message of a 'decayed body and dying face'. What Ezekiel sees in the valley of dry bones is not a message of dissolution but one of resurrection: '*God* seemes to haue caried the declaration of his *power* to a great height, when hee sets the *Prophet Ezechiel* in the *valley of drye bones*, and says, *Sonne of man can these bones liue?* as though it had been impossible, and yet they did', comments Donne in *Deaths Dvell.*[20] And while Walton uses the Ezekiel passage to set up a visual *memento mori* which is also an homiletic text doubly preached (in words and in sight), the original of that text promises resurrection in a frame of corruption:

> This death of *incineration* and dispersion, is, to naturall *reason*, the most *irrecouerable death* of all, & yet . . . *vnto God the Lord belong the issues of death,* and by *recompacting* this *dust* into *the same body,* and *reanimating* the *same body* with the *same soule*, hee shall in a blessed and glorious *resurrection* giue

[19] 'Deaths Dvell', p. 745.
[20] 'Deaths Dvell', pp. 749–50.

mee such an *issue from* this *death*, as shal neuer passe into any other *death*, but establish me into a life that shall last as long as the *Lord of life* himself (p. 750).

Its sister passage of 1626 is more comfortably distant, less dark, less urgent. The fear of death absolute, of lifelessness, is much more immediate in the 'I' of the 1632 text than in the cool reference to 'that man' of 1626: 'God that knows in which Boxe of his Cabinet all this seed Pearle lies, in what corner of the world every atome, every grain of every mans dust sleeps, shall recollect that dust, and then recompact that body, and then re-inanimate that man, and that is the accomplishment of all.'[21]

Why did Walton pick the earlier passage of 1626 for the 1640 *Life*? There are signs that the 1632 version influences Walton's mediation in its own right – in the citation of the Ezekiel passage, for example. There is also, perhaps, something to be said for the way the defiant assurance of 'hee shall in a blessed and glorious *resurrection* . . . establish me' is translated into Walton's self-consciously biographical testimony: 'I shall see it re-inanimated.' Walton was always better at being audacious by proxy. But granted a presence from the *Deaths Dvell* passage, why retain a word unique to Donne which drew attention to the earlier sermon?

It is perfectly possible that Walton just liked the word, and found it characteristic of a loved man. It vanishes at the edition of 1658, never to reappear; so whatever value he accorded it in 1640 it had lost over the intervening eighteen years. But I want to suggest that he had a reason both for retaining, and for losing the word, which was more than personal. It was homiletic, and so (for Donne) professional.

Walton knew that the biographical preface must be exemplary in the specific context of being an introduction to the living words of the book's real author: in this case Donne, author of the *LXXX Sermons*. A primary aspect of the clerical biographer's task was to facilitate the translation of words into works by mediating his subject's exemplary virtues via the book into the acts of the reader. The task was double: the preface writer on the one hand eased the reader into the sermon texts, and on the other demonstrated the rectitude of the author through an homiletically conceived narrative. Add to this a literalist approach to the Hebrews text, and Walton's imperative is clear. He must demonstrate an exemplary and absolute assurance on the part of his clerical subject in order that Dean Donne might continue posthumously to affirm the body's resurrection at the point of death. Perhaps this imperative might be somewhat eased when the *Life* ceased to be a preface to Donne's own sermons, and became instead a vehicle which, as it were, preached only from Donne's lived acts (as happened from 1658, after which the *Life of Donne* appeared either singly or bound in with other *Lives* by Walton).

Deaths Dvell – the sermon Walton picked as *exemplum* of Donne's dying

---

[21] *Sermons* VII, 116.

life – is a good many things; it is, for instance, virtuoso about worms and it is virtuous about hope; but it is not in itself hopeful. Its dominant images are of dissolution, and the passage I have quoted is one of the few places in which that obsession is overcome by any re-vivifying image, and even then it seems to owe a good deal to the 1626 Easter sermon. I think we see here a typical Waltonian manoeuvre, as with the way he seems to have fudged the dating of *Hymn to God my God in my Sickness* to make it look like a deathbed composition of 1630 when 1623 is so much more likely.[22]

Walton in his final passage declares, with a clear homiletic intention ventriloquised through Donne's pastoral function, the blazing hope of the earlier sermon edged with the urgency of what was once called the '*reall experiment of mortality*'.[23] While *Death's Dvell* permeates Walton's description of Donne's final preaching to us of mortality by a 'decayed body and dying face', for the last words on Donne's '*clear knowing soul*', on the expectation of a recollected dust breathing, not with the translated breath of reader or listener, but with the original vitality of the words' first speaker, he deliberately reverts to Donne's earlier declaration of the 'accomplishment of all'. He being dead, yet speaketh.

---

[22] Novarr, *Making of Walton's Lives*, p. 101.
[23] θρενοικος, *The House of Mourning. Furnished with Directions for, Preparations to, Consolations at the Houre of Death* (London, 1640), preface to the reader, sig. A3v.

INDEX

Index

DONNE, JOHN
  and Church Fathers 32
  and diplomacy 15
  and female patrons 15
  and Inns of Court 13, 15
  and Sir Edward Hoby 15
  and Sir Thomas Egerton 15, 21
  and the court 4–5
  as 'Jack Donne' and 'Dr Donne' 3
  as judge 22
  biography 1–16, 38–71
  critics on 2–3
  Lothian portrait of 122, 123 (ill.), 129
  manuscripts of 70, 105
  marriage to Ann More 8
  miniature painted by Hilliard 41
  motto of ownership in books owned by 56
  MP for Brackley 8, 55–6
  MP for Taunton 11, 66
  priest 11
  Reader in Divinity at Lincoln's Inn 13, 22
  seal of 11
  secretary to Thomas Egerton 8
  vicar of St Dunstan's in the West 13
  Poems 70, 76
    planned publication of 74
    Anniversaries 11, 81, 87, 106, 117, 233
    Divine Poems
      'Holy Sonnets' 2, 8, 13, 24, 251, 252, 254
      Holy Sonnet XII 24–36
      La Corona 24
      'Hymn to God my God in my Sickness' 259
      'The Litanie' 24, 30, 243, 254
    Elegies 99
      Elegy I ('Jealosie') 104–5, 106
      Elegy VII ('Natures lay ideot' / 'Tutelage') 105, 115
      Elegy IX ('The Autumnall') 56
    Epithalamions
      'Ecclogue at the mariage of the Earle of Sommerset' 66–7, 81
    Metempsychosis 57
    Satires 5, 8, 21, 53, 99, 110, 111, 112, 214, 243
      Satire V 23–4
    Songs and Sonets 2, 8, 21, 24, 62
      'The Curse' 58
      'The Sunne Rising' 81, 86
      'Twicknam Garden' 3
    Verse letters 3, 5, 53

  'To Mr Tilman after he had taken Holy Orders' 252
  'To the Countesse of Bedford at New-yeares Tide' ('This twilight of two yeares') 115
  'To the Countesse of Bedford' ('Madame, you have refin'd mee') 100, 112
  'To the Countesse of Bedford' (T'have written then') 111, 112
  'To the Countesse of Huntingdon' ('Man to Gods image') 101, 102, 113, 115, 116
  'To the Countesse of Huntingdon' ('That unripe side of earth) 97, 98, 99–100, 104, 105, 115–16
  'To the Countesse of Salisbury' ('Faire, great, and good') 98, 118
  Prose works
    Biathanatos 9, 78, 79, 83, 84, 85, 88, 89
    The Courtier's Library 52, 55, 62–3, 124
    Devotions upon Emergent Occasions 14, 89, 253, chapter 11 passim
    Essays in Divinity 8, 11, 12, 22, 24, 57, 89, 227, 243
    Ignatius his Conclave 8, 10, 21, 75, 76, 121, 129
    Letters 4, 57, 59, 60, 62, 64, 74, 84, 100, 102, 106, 107, 108, 109, 113, 115, 117, 142, 183, 247
    to Ann More 54
    Paradoxes and Problems 9, 43–4, 52, 56, 63, 70
    Pseudo-Martyr 2, 3, 8, 9–10, 12, 15, 21, 28, 42, 57, 64–5, chapter 4 passim
    dedication copy for Lord Keeper Egerton 64, 65
    Sermons 2, 70, 75, 105–6, 112, 113, 216, 223, 231, 232, 234, 242, 243, 245, 246, chapter 7 passim, chapter 8 passim, chapter 9 passim, chapter 10 passim
    Deaths Duell 14, 181, 183, 245, 255, 256–7, 259
    printing of by royal command 193
Donne, Revd. John, D.C.L. (D's son) 11, 22, 62
Donne, Katherine (D's sister) 39
Donne, Mary (D's sister) 39
Dort, Synod of 142, 144, 145, 146, 151–2, 154–6, 157, 190, 196–7, 198
Dove, John 49, 51
Downame, George 50

264

Index